Freedom of Services in the European Union

Labour and Social Security Law: The Bolkestein Initiative

Editor: Roger Blanpain

Contributors
Roger Blanpain
Niklas Bruun
Michele Colucci
Arnout De Koster
Chris Engels
Wouter Gekiere
Ronnie Graham
Frank Hendrickx
Mijke Houwerzijl
Alan C. Neal
Catelene Passchier
Frans Pennings
Jacques Rojot
Andrzej Swiatkowski
Willy van Eeckhoutte
Anne Van Lancker
Manfred Weiss

KLUWER LAW
INTERNATIONAL

A C.I.P Catalogue record for this book is available from the Library of Congress.

ISBN 90-411-2453-5

Published by:
Kluwer Law International
P.O. Box 85889
2508 CN The Hague
The Netherlands
E-mail: sales@kluwerlaw.com
Website: http://www.kluwerlaw.com

Sold and distributed in North, Central and South America by:
Aspen Publishers, Inc.
7201 McKinney Circle
Frederick, MD 21704
USA

Sold and distributed in all other countries by:
Turpin Distribution Services Ltd.
Stratton Business Park
Pegasus Drive
Biggleswade
Bedfordshire SG18 8TQ
United Kingdom

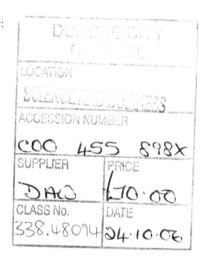
Printed on acid-free paper

© Kluwer Law International 2006

Printed in The Netherlands

CONTENTS

10. The Point of View of the Federation of Belgian Enterprises on the Services Directive 127
Arnout De Koster

11. The Point of View of the ETUC 141
Catelene Passchier

15. Towards a More Effective Posting Directive   179
Mijke Houwerzijl

16. Implementation of the Posting Directive in Belgium   199
Roger Blanpain

17. The Implementation of the Posting Directive in Italy   219
Michele Colucci

18. Implementation of the Posting Directive in the
Netherlands   225
Mijke Houwerzijl

NOTES ON CONTRIBUTORS

Roger Blanpain, Universities of Leuven and Limburg, Belgium and Tilburg, the Netherlands

Niklas Bruun, Hanken School of Economics, Helsinki, Finland and National Institute for Working Life, Stockholm, Sweden

Michele Colucci, Agent of the Legal Service of the European Commission and Researcher at the University of Salerno, Italy

Arnout De Koster, Director of the Federation of Belgian Enterprises, Belgium

Chris Engels, Professor KU Leuven, Belgium and Lawyer, Partner Claeys & Engels

Wouter Gekiere, Legal Adviser to the European Parliament

Ronnie Graham, Legal Secretary to the European Court of Justice

Frank Hendrickx, Universities of Leuven, Belgium and Tilburg, the Netherlands

Mijke Houwerzijl, Researcher at the Department of Labour Law and Social Security Law at Tilburg University, the Netherlands

Alan C. Neal, Professor of Law and Director of the Employment Law Research Unit at the University of Warwick, United Kingdom; Convenor of the European Association of Labour Court Judges; previously founding editor of the International Journal of Comparative Labour Law and Industrial Relations

Catelene Passchier, Confederal Secretary of the European Trade Union Confederation

Frans Pennings, Professor of International Social Security Law at Tilburg University and Utrecht University, the Netherlands

Jacques Rojot, University of Paris, France

Andrzej Swiatkowski, Professor of Labour Law, Jagiellonian University of Krakow, Poland; Vice President of the European Committee of Social Rights, Council of Europe, Strasbourg

Willy van Eeckhoutte, University of Ghent, Belgium; Member of the Bar of the Supreme Court of Belgium

Anne Van Lancker, Member of the European Parliament, Rapporteur for the Committee on Employment and Social Affairs

Manfred Weiss, University of Frankfurt, Germany

FOREWORD

This bulletin contains the papers which were presented at the European Forum on Freedom of Services and Labour and Social Security, which was held under the auspices of the Society for International and Social Cooperation and the Royal Flemish Academy for Sciences in Brussels, Belgium on 16-17 June 2005. The programme was as follows:

The Proposed Directive on Services. An Overview
  Drs. Wouter Gekiere, KU Leuven, Belgium

The Proposed Directive on Services and Labour Law
  Prof. Niklas Bruun, University of Stockholm, Sweden

The Rome Convention on the Law Applicable to Contractual Obligations and Labour Law (1980)
  Prof. Willy van Eeckhoutte, University of Ghent, Belgium

The Posting Directive, 96/71, Content and Implementation
  Dr. Mijke Houwerzijl, University of Tilburg, the Netherlands

Posting of Workers and Social Security
  Prof. Frans Pennings, University of Tilburg, the Netherlands

Free Movement of Workers and Equal Treatment
  Prof. Chris Engels, KU Leuven, Belgium

The Country of Origin Principle and Labour Law, including the *Acquis Communautaire*
  Prof. Manfred Weiss, University of Frankfurt, Germany
  Prof. Alan C. Neal, University of Warwick, United Kingdom

Problems of Surveillance and Control of Labour Standards
  Prof. Andrzej Swiatkowski, University of Krakow, Poland
  Prof. Michele Colucci, University of Salerno, Italy

Recognition, Prior Declarations, Employment Documents and Representatives
  Prof. Frank Hendrickx, KU Leuven, Belgium
  Prof. Jacques Rojot, University of Paris, France

FORUM – PANEL DISCUSSION

Mr. Ronnie Graham, European Court of Justice
Mrs. Anne Van Lancker, European Parliament
Mr. Arnout De Koster, VBO
Mrs. Catelene Passchier, ETUC
Mr. Jan Denys, Randstad
Mr. Jan Wouters, University of Leuven

A CRUCIAL MOMENT

The forum came at a very topical and interesting moment, namely after the two referenda which were held on the European Constitution, which amounted to two times a resounding NO, in France as well as in the Netherlands. After these referenda, Europeans have to ask themselves whether we have to reconsider the European project again:
–   What Europe we should stand for;
–   What the Member States should do and
–   What about the role of the social partners?

One has to reflect, it was said, on the "social Europe" we want. The overall framework is open again for discussion. Where to go and what to do?

FREEDOM OF SERVICES

Due to the Bolkestein initiative, aimed at speeding up the market for services, that specific fundamental freedom is itself the subject of a very heated debate.

No one really discusses that we have to foster the market of services in order to increase economic growth and the number of jobs: services already account for 70% of EU jobs! A more open market promises more employment. No doubt.

Freedom of services, however, is nothing new. It is one of the four fundamental freedoms, which are enshrined in the Treaty on the European Community since 1957: freedom without discrimination and restrictions is provided for in Article 49 TEC. There is abundant case law of the European Court of Justice accepting that Member States can impose their own labour law system and generally binding collective agreements, provided these requirements are proportional and necessary.

So where is the problem?

POINTS TO BE DISCUSSED

The fact is that the sweeping approach of Commissioner Bolkestein, especially at the exact moment of the widening of the EU with ten new Member States and increased globalisation, forced us to look again at the balance between fair competition in the market on the one hand and adequate social protection of workers on the other hand. Points of discussion include:

– The notion of service, including the meaning of the so-called "definite period";
– The sectors, which should be included or excluded. Does it really matter if the temporary work agency sector would be excluded from the Services Directive, since it still falls under the scope of Article 49 EC?
– The applicable labour law and social security standards;
– Acceptable administrative conditions;
– Required documents and languages;
– Control: by the country of origin or the country of work?
– Collaboration between Member States and social partners;
– How to deal with Directive 96/71, leave it or amend it? Exclude it from the scope of the Services Directive?
– Do national systems have to adapt in order to provide, e.g., the possibility of extension of collective agreements in countries where this is not the case?
– How to effectively control and eliminate the black market, illegal work, at home and from abroad?
– What about the self-employed, coming from low wage countries?

The purpose of the European Forum was to discuss these questions in an open and academic way.

This happened in an unprecedented manner.

AN OPEN ACADEMIC DISCUSSION

Numerous questions ware tackled:
– The legal basis for the Services Directive was questioned;
– What are services of public interest? Should they be excluded from the scope of the Services Directive?
– What is the difference between the principles of mutual recognition and country of origin?
– Is there a European concept of labour law?
– The role of the Court of Justice;
– Rome I[1] and Directive 96/71;

---

1   Applicable law in case of contracts.

- Choice of applicable law? At which moment?
- European labour inspectors, their freedom to move;
- The lack of cooperation between Member States;
- The problem of the 21 languages;
- How to define sectors?

Did the Bolkestein initiative come at a bad moment? For France this seemed to be the case, given globalisation, the widening of the EU and the deterioration of the French model at that particular moment. The definitions of the Services Directive were too wide: thus, the notion of services, of sectors (social, education, health to be excluded), the notion of authorisation; the country of origin principle was too general, the uncertainties of the laws of other Member States a real problem.

The notion of public order was too extensive. There would be a concurrent application of various legal systems. What about the role of the organisers of providers of services? The complexity of the control was underlined, as well as the absence of cooperation between Member States; why should one not harmonise more before proceeding with a service initiative?

Other proposals, emanating from an EP reporter, favoured a sectoral approach, concerning social policies; these should be excluded from the Services Directive and the Directive be limited to purely commercial sectors. The country of origin principle should be shelved. More harmonisation was an explicit goal in order to create a level playing field. Labour law and collective agreements, including rules on industrial warfare of the work-land, should be the rule. Movement of people in the framework of services should be covered by Rome I and Rome II.[2] Temporary work should be excluded and subject to a proper legal European instrument, the same for services of general interest.

An employers' representative was of the opinion that the Bolkestein initiative was too much, too late and would lead to abuses. Problems arise with the country of origin principle, the scope and the authorisations (they should remain in case of temporary work, security agents and construction).

Also a trade union representative was of the opinion that Bolkestein was too big a step. The proposal came at the wrong moment, was presented in the wrong way, just before enlargement. Social aspects were ignored. There was simply no reply to social questions, raised by the unions. A more careful approach was pleaded for, more mutual help. The country of origin principle should be dropped in favour of the principle of mutual recognition. The country of destination should come first: labour law and collective agreements, including industrial action, should be fully respected. Directive 96/71 was considered to be too narrow and too limited. Rome I and Rome II were considered to be too complicated. More European labour law was necessary. Temporary work agencies should be dealt with separately.

---

2   Applicable law in case of non-contractual obligations.

A spokesman for the temporary work sector pleaded for a grand step forward regarding freedom of services, thus avoiding a standstill for decades. Free movement should be bolstered. Temporary work creates jobs: seven million workers are engaged in temporary work in the EU on a yearly basis. Obstacles to free movement of services should be lifted. The bigger temporary work agencies, situated in the various Member States, were willing to work together to see the appropriate laws and conditions applied in case of transnational temporary work. Control by the country in which the work is done should be effective. The temporary sector does not want to be excluded from the Services Directive, but included as a normal sector of activity. A generalised system of licences was pleaded for, as well as a more positive attitude.

Finally, a global picture was presented, including the WTO and GATT, explaining the 4 ways of supplying services, especially mode 4, concerning the individual providers of services and the restrictions imposed on their movement (requirement of nationality, residence, maximum number and the like).

In short, an excellent forum. Again, my repeated thanks to the Royal Flemish Academy, the participants and the colleagues, whose papers illustrate the importance of the subject and the depth of the discussion.

A special word of thanks for Ronnie Graham, who helped by rewriting some of the papers.

Roger Blanpain

*Honorary President of the International Society
for Labour and Social Security Law,*

*Professor at the Universities of Leuven and Limburg (Belgium)
and Tilburg (The Netherlands)*

POST SCRIPTUM

European Parliament: Report Anne Van Lancker

On 13 July 2005, the Employment Committee of the European Parliament voted with a large majority (23 votes in favour, 6 against and 9 abstentions), in favour of nearly all the amendments of Ms Van Lancker, Belgian Member of the Committee.

A large majority deleted the provisions limiting the possibilities for Member States to monitor and enforce regulations with regard to cross-border posting of workers, reversed the country of origin principle so that it would not apply unless a minimum level of harmonisation was achieved, and decided that the Directive should not apply to a range of sectors with universal or public service obligations.

Most importantly, labour law and collective agreements were excluded from the scope of the Directive. The Directive on posting of workers of 1996 retains complete preference over the Services Directive. Labour and working conditions of the country in which the work is done need to be respected; it is also the country in which the work is done, which will control whether labour and working conditions of posted workers are respected.

Under the EP's procedure, the Employment Committee has the lead on employment related aspects of the Services Directive: worker protection, employment law, collective agreements and social security.

The report of Ms Van Lancker will be discussed by the Plenary of the European Parliament, at the end of October 2005.

R.B.

31 August 2005

PART I. THE SERVICES DIRECTIVE

1. THE PROPOSAL OF THE EUROPEAN COMMISSION FOR A DIRECTIVE ON SERVICES IN THE INTERNAL MARKET: AN OVERVIEW OF ITS MAIN FEATURES AND CRITICAL REFLECTIONS[3]

Wouter Gekiere

1. INTRODUCTION

In January 2004, the European Commission presented a proposal for a Directive on Services in the Internal Market,[4] which sets out a general legal framework to reduce barriers to cross-border provision of services within the European Union. Trade in services is often estimated to generate 70% of GDP in the European Union and the establishment of a genuine internal market in services is considered to be a key step in the process launched by the Lisbon European Council to make the EU the most competitive and dynamic knowledge-based economy in the world, capable of sustainable economic growth with more and better jobs and greater social cohesion. Considering the broad scope of the proposal, its content has direct repercussions for existing national and regional regulations governing the access to and the exercise of many service activities.

The proposal distinguishes two different situations of cross-border provision of services, which are both safeguarded by fundamental freedoms enshrined in the EC Treaty. On the one hand, the proposal aims at reducing restrictions to the freedom of establishment as referred to in Article 43 EC, which means facilitating a service provider to set up a fixed establishment for an indefinite period in a Member State from where the economic activity is actually pursued. On the other hand, it intends to stimulate the freedom to provide services as referred to in Article 49 EC, which

---

3   This contribution draws extensively from W. Gekiere, *Towards a European Directive on Services in the Internal Market: Analysing the Legal Repercussions of the Draft Services Directive and its Impact on National Services Regulations*, research report commissioned by Anne Van Lancker, Rapporteur, Commission Employment and Social Affairs, Institute for European Law, KU Leuven, September 2004, 60 pp.

4   Proposal for a Directive of the European Parliament and of the Council on services in the internal market, COM(2004) 0002 def (hereafter "proposal").

means that a service provider established in one Member State could provide services on a temporary basis in another Member State more easily.

The presentation of the proposal follows the adoption of a report on the State of the Internal Market in Services,[5] in which the European Commission identified a wide variety of legal and administrative barriers to the cross-border service provision. It was concluded that these barriers, which occur at any stage of the business process, affect the entire European economy and cause legal uncertainty, in particular for small and medium enterprises (SMEs) as well as consumers.

In this contribution, we will explain the main features of the proposal. Afterwards, some critical reflections will be formulated, hereby focusing on the principles that provoke most controversy, such as the broad scope, the introduction of the country of origin principle as the basic regulatory principle governing the temporary cross-border provision of services, the relationship with other Community principles and instruments as well as the impact on labour law issues.[6]

2. MAIN FEATURES OF THE PROPOSAL

2.1. Scope

The proposal applies to services supplied by providers established in a Member State of the European Union.[7] The notion of service is described as "any self-employed activity", as referred to in Article 50 EC, consisting of the provision of a service for consideration.'[8] The essential criterion of this notion lies in the presence of a consideration. It implies that service activities fall within the scope of the proposal, provided that they are supplied for a remuneration, i.e. an economic counterpart. As the Commission has clarified,[9] the service should not necessarily be paid by those for whom the service is performed.[10]

The proposal covers all economic activities involving services, except services provided by the state for no remuneration, in fulfilment of its social, cultural,

---

5   European Commission, *Report from the Commission to the Council and the European Parliament on the State of the Internal Market for Services*, 30 July 2002, COM(2002) 441 final.
6   These issues all have been addressed in *Public Hearing on the Proposal for a Directive on Services in the Internal Market*, Committee on the Internal Market and Consumer Protection in Association with the Committee on Employment and Social Affairs, European Parliament, Brussels, 11 November 2004.
7   Proposal, Article 2, para. 1.
8   Proposal, Article 4 (1).
9   Proposal, Recital 15. See also Explanatory Note from the Commission Services on the Activities Covered by the Proposal (10865/04), 25 June 2004, 2.
10   See also case law of the Court of Justice: C-352/85, *Bond van Adverteerders and Others*, [1988] ECR 2085, para. 16; C-51/96 and C-191/97, *Deliège*, [2000] ECR I-2549, para. 56; C-157/99, *Smits and Peerbooms*, [2001] ECR I-05473, para. 57.

educational and legal obligations.[11] So, the notion of service includes a wide range of activities: It consists of activities such as management consultancy, advertising, construction, real estate services, travel agencies, but also health and healthcare services and household support services, such as help for the elderly.[12] Only some services provided for remuneration which are already subject to specific Community instruments, namely in the field of finance, telecommunications and transport, are expressly excluded from the proposal.[13] Furthermore, the field of taxation as such is excluded from the proposal.[14]

2.2. Freedom of Establishment

In order to eliminate restrictions to the freedom of establishment, the proposal contains administrative simplification measures,[15] as well as specific measures on the conditions and procedures of national authorisation schemes governing the access to and the exercise of a service activity.[16]

In order to reduce the complexity and length of administrative procedures, the Commission imposes upon Member States a general obligation to simplify administrative procedures.[17] With regard to the formal requirement to supply certificates, Member States may no longer require from a provider or recipient of services – with some exceptions – that a document proving that a requirement has been satisfied be produced in its original form, or as a certified copy or certified translation.[18] In order to facilitate access to and exercise of a service activity, Member States have to establish single points of contact through which all formalities can be completed and make sure that all procedures can be completed at a distance and by electronic means.[19]

Member States may not make access to or the exercise of a service activity subject to an authorisations scheme unless the scheme is non-discriminatory, objectively justified by an overriding reason relating to the public interest and proportionate.[20] They have to set up a major screening operation, in which they have to prove that their schemes are compatible with the said conditions. The report which results from this operation will be subject to so-called "mutual evaluation"

---

11   Proposal, Recital 16.
12   Proposal, Recital 14.
13   Proposal, Article 2, para. 2.
14   Proposal, Article 2, para. 3. The exclusion does not apply to prohibitions of discrimination provided in Article 14 and 20 of the proposal.
15   Proposal, Articles 5-8.
16   Proposal, Articles 9-15.
17   Proposal, Article 5, para. 1.
18   Proposal, Article 5, para. 2.
19   Proposal, Articles 6-8.
20   Proposal, Article 9.

by other Member States and the Commission and could, where appropriate, lead to other Community initiatives.[21]

The criteria of authorisation schemes should not only comply with the said conditions, but also be precise and unambiguous, objective and made public in advance. Furthermore, the conditions for granting an authorisation should not duplicate requirements that are equivalent and essentially comparable to those which the service provider is subject in another Member State.[22] Other important innovative measures include the fact that an authorisation scheme should enable the provider to have access to the service activity, or the exercise of that activity, throughout the national territory, the introduction of the principle of the unlimited duration of an authorisation and the principle of tacit authorisation by the competent authorities after a certain time has elapsed. Specific exceptions to these measures apply where they are justified by overriding reasons relating to the public interest.[23]

The proposal also prohibits national authorities from maintaining specific restrictive legal requirements in their authorisations schemes, such as:

– Discriminatory requirements;
– The case-by-case application of an economic test making the granting of an authorisation subject to proof of the existence of an economic need or market demand;
– The direct or indirect involvement of competing operators in the granting of authorisations;
– The obligation to provide or participate in a financial guarantee, or to take out insurance;
– ...[24]

Furthermore, the proposal obliges Member States to verify whether certain other legal requirements in their national authorisation schemes are non-discriminatory, necessary and proportionate. These legal requirements include:

– Quantitative and territorial restrictions;
– An obligation for a provider to take a specific legal form;
– Requirements relating to the shareholding of a company;
– Requirements establishing minimum number of employees;
– The prescription of compulsory minimum or maximum tariffs;
– ...[25]

---

21   Proposal, Article 9.
22   Proposal, Article 10, paras 2 and 3.
23   Proposal, Article 10, para. 4, Article 11, para. 1 and Article 13, para. 4.
24   Proposal, Article 14.
25   Proposal, Article 15, para. 2. For both the prohibited requirements (Article 14) and the require-
      ments to be evaluated (Article 15), the Commission orally indicated to have drawn its inspiration
      from case law of the Court of Justice: see e.g. C-439/99, *Commission v. Italy*, ECR I-00305, in
      which the Court of Justice decided that certain requirements included in Italian legislation on

The results of the national screening operation will be subject to the same "mutual evaluation" process, as indicated before. If these requirements do not comply with the conditions of non-discrimination, necessity and proportionality, they will have to be modified or abolished. At the same time, Member States can neither introduce any new legal requirement of this kind, unless it is justified and the need for it arises from new circumstances. They are obliged to notify any new laws containing these requirements to the Commission, after which the Commission examines their compatibility with Community law.[26]

2.3. Freedom to Provide Services

The proposal intends to stimulate the free movement of services on a temporary basis by applying the country of origin principle. This means that a service provider established in one Member State who wishes to provide services on a temporary basis in another Member State, is only subject to the law of the country in which he/she is established. The so-called coordinated field to which the scope of the country of origin principle is linked is very broad: it covers any requirement applicable to access to and exercise of a service activity, in particular requirements governing the behaviour of the provider, the quality of services or content of the service, advertising and the provider's liability.[27] The principle also applies to the responsibility to supervise the provider and the services provided by him/her in another Member State.

Member States may neither restrict the provision of services by providers in another Member State any longer by imposing on the service provider specific requirements, such as to make a declaration or notification to the competent authorities, to have an address or representative in their territory, to apply specific contractual arrangements between the provider and the recipient, or to possess an identity document issued by its competent authorities specific to the exercise of a service activity.[28]

The proposal provides three categories of derogations to the country of origin principle: general derogations, transitional derogations and case-by-case derogations.[29]

The general derogations target a wide variety of matters covered by other Community instruments, specific services, principles and requirements. Firstly, it refers to a series of Community instruments applying the rules of the country in which the service is provided, such as Directive 96/71/EC on the posting of workers, the new

---

trade fairs constituted unjustified restrictions to the freedom to provide services and the freedom of establishment.

26   Proposal, Article 15, paras 3-6.
27   Proposal, Article 16(1).
28   Proposal, Article 16(3).
29   Proposal, Articles 17 to 19.

Directive on recognition of professional qualifications and the provisions of EEC Regulation 1408/71 determining the applicable legislation.[30] Specific services that are already subject to Community instruments, such as postal services, electricity and gas, as well as specific requirements, such as those linked to the particular characteristics of the place where the service is provided and with which compliance is indispensable for reasons of public policy. Public security or for the protection of public health or the environment are also excluded from the principle.[31] Finally, the country of origin principle does not intend to affect certain established rules on conflict of laws by excluding principles such as the freedom of parties to choose the law applicable to their contract and matters such as the non-contractual liability of a provider in case of an accident involving a person and arising from activities in the Member State to which the provider has temporarily moved.[32]

Because of the lack of minimum harmonised rules at EU level, three types of activities are excluded from this proposal for a transitional period: gambling activities, cash-in-transit services and the judicial recovery of debts. The country of origin principle will only apply provided that harmonised measures will apply. In any event, this principle will apply after 1 January 2010, as regards the two latter types of services.[33]

On the basis of the case-by-case derogations, the country in which the service is provided can apply restrictive measures towards a provider established in another Member State on an individual basis. However, these measures can only apply in exceptional circumstances and after a "mutual assistance" procedure during which a Member State has to justify on the basis of one of the following grounds: the safety of services including public health, the exercise of a health profession or the protection of public policy, including the protection of minors.[34]

As regards protection of recipients, the proposal intends to safeguard the right of recipients to use services from other Member States by prohibiting discriminatory measures on the basis of nationality or place of residence and by obliging Member States to provide a mechanism of assistance to recipients.[35] The proposal also aims at protecting the rights of patients as to the assumption of healthcare costs, by clarifying the circumstances in which a Member State can make reimbursement of the costs of healthcare provided in another Member State subject to an authorisation, in accordance with the European Court's rulings.[36]

Finally, as regards the posting of workers, Article 24 of the proposal confirms the responsibility of the host state in the field of checks, inspections and investigations for matters covered by Directive 96/71/EC. At the same time, it stipulates

---

30   Proposal, Articles 17(5)(8) and (9).
31   Proposal, Articles 17(1)(2)(3) and (17).
32   Proposal, Articles 17(20) and (23).
33   Proposal, Articles 18 and 40.
34   Proposal, Articles 19 and 37.
35   Proposal, Articles 21-2.
36   Proposal, Article 23.

that the host state cannot make the service subject anymore to requirements, such as to obtain authorisation from the competent authorities, to make a declaration relating to the service activity, to have a representative in its territory or to hold employment documents in its territory.[37] Instead, it imposes upon the country of origin the responsibility to communicate relevant information to the host Member State and to provide assistance to ensure compliance with the conditions under Directive 96/71/EC.

2.4. Measures Enhancing Mutual Confidence

The proposal complements the measures relating to the two fundamental freedoms enshrined in the EC Treaty with measures which aim at enhancing mutual confidence between Member States.

First of all, it schedules additional harmonisation on very specific issues, such as information on service providers and their services, professional insurance and guarantees, information on after-sales guarantees and settlement of disputes.[38] In order to ensure an effective system of supervision, it also complements the supervisory responsibility of the country of origin with general guidelines on how to enhance mutual assistance between the different Member States involved.[39]

Furthermore, the proposal stresses that Member States are obliged to eliminate all total prohibitions on commercial communications by the regulated professions and make sure that these communications comply with professional rules such as independence, dignity and integrity of the profession as well as professional secrecy. As regards other professions and activities, the proposal prohibits Member States from requiring service providers to supply services exclusively or from restricting the joint exercise of different activities.[40]

Finally, the proposal encourages the drawing up of codes of conduct particularly regarding commercial communications by regulated professions and promotes the elaboration of action on a voluntary basis on behalf of service providers in order to ensure the quality of service provision.[41]

---

37 See also Proposal, Article 25, para. 1 (on posting of third country nationals), according to which the Member State in which the service is provided may no longer require the provider or the posted worker who is national of a third country to hold an entry, exit, residence or work permit or satisfy any equivalent condition.

38 Proposal, Articles 26-8 and 32.

39 Proposal, Articles 34-8.

40 Proposal, Articles 29-30.

41 Proposal, Article 39 and 31.

3. CRITICAL REFLECTIONS

3.1. Scope and Legal Basis

The proposal of the Commission is based on a horizontal approach: it establishes a general legal framework applicable to all economic service activities. This approach is revolutionary in the sense that it breaks with the tradition of sector-specific internal market instruments that have been applied to a number of services in the past.[42] Many have pointed out, though, that, by making purely commercial services as well as healthcare and social services such as social housing and household support services, subject to the same provisions, the proposal does not take into account the substantial differences between service activities.[43] Contrary to purely commercial services, services in the field of healthcare and social welfare are characterised by the presence of a three party model (patient/social beneficiary, service provider and payer of services), by the information asymmetry between patient/consumer and service provider and by the fact that they are (partly or mainly) financed from public funding and confined by social and public health considerations. Given the absence of an impact assessment study of the proposed internal market rules on these specific sensitive services, it indeed remains uncertain what the exact legal implications for the organisation of these services will be.[44]

Together with network industry services, these sensitive services could be said to fall under the notion of services of general economic interest, as referred to in Articles 16 and 86(2) EC. Many have suggested that services of general economic interest should be excluded entirely from this proposal.[45] This notion is not clearly defined at EU level; the discussion about the role of the EU in defining these services and the way they should be organised or financed is the object of a separate reflection process launched by a green paper and followed up by the Commission with a white paper on services of general interest, in which the Commission has

---

42   See e.g. Directive 89/552/EEC on the coordination of certain provisions laid down by law, regulation or administrative action in Member States concerning the pursuit of television broadcasting activities, as modified by Directive 97/36/EC ("Television without Frontiers Directive").

43   See e.g. C. Roumet, on behalf of the European Social Platform and R. Baeten, on behalf of the Observatoire Social Européen, "Health Services", *Public Hearing on the Proposal for a Directive on Services in the Internal Market*, Committee on the Internal Market and Consumer Protection in Association with the Committee on Employment and Social Affairs, European Parliament, Brussels, 11 November 2004.

44   This issue has not been dealt with by: European Commission, *Extended Impact Assessment of Proposal for a Directive on Services in the Internal Market* (Commission Staff Working Paper), 13 January 2004, SEC (2004) 21.

45   See e.g. Draft Report on the Proposal for Directive of the European Parliament and of the Council on Services in the Internal Market, European Parliament, Committee on the Internal Market and Consumer Protection, Rapporteur, Evelyne Gebhardt, 11 April 2005, amendments 53-55 and Draft Opinion on the Proposal for a Directive of the European Parliament and of the Council on Services in the Internal Market, European Parliament, Committee on Employment and Social Affairs, Rapporteur, Anne Van Lancker, amendments 49-50.

scheduled a specific approach to identify and recognise the typical features of social and health services of general interest.[46]

Furthermore, the proposal is legally based on Article 47(2) and 55 EC, which entitles the Council to adopt Directives for the coordination of provisions on the taking-up and pursuit of activities as self-employed persons. The question whether or not this legal basis covers the current proposal should be assessed in the light of the broad explanations of notions of services and barriers to trade in services.[47]

As we explained before, the definition of "service" included in the proposal refers to the notion of service in the sense of Article 50 EC, as it was developed in the case law of the European Court of Justice. However, the proposal's definition seems to go further than the European Court's interpretation. Even though activities concerning goods and the distribution of goods have not been recognised by the Court as a separate service activity, they fall within the notion of service and consequently within the scope of the proposal. Furthermore, another question is whether it is feasible to rely upon the open notion of service that has been developed by the Court of Justice on a case-by-case basis to delimit the scope of a regulatory Community instrument, such as a horizontal framework Directive.

The proposal relies upon a very broad notion of barriers to trade in services. Consistent with the Court's reasoning, it does not only cover legal barriers. But here again, the Commission goes further than the interpretation given by the European Court: to qualify a national restrictive measure as a barrier, it takes into account its indirect effect on other market participants. In its report, the Commission refers to this as "the economic chain". Imposing a national restrictive measure on one service provider is a barrier to the entire economic chain in the sense that it affects the whole chain of market participants.[48]

3.2. Relationship with Fundamental Community Principles

Given the horizontal approach of the proposal and its important measures to eliminate obstacles to cross-border service activities, the proposal is likely to have repercussions on specific policy areas such as public health, culture and social security, for which Community action is only complementary to national regulatory powers and for which the EC Treaty provides a specific legal bases for Community initiatives. According to Article 5, paragraph 2 EC, subsidiarity is a guiding principle of all Community action in areas that do not fall within its exclusive competence.

---

46 Communication from the Commission to the European Parliament, the Council, the European Economic and Social Committee and the Committee of the Regions – White Paper on Services of General Interest, COM 2004 (374), 16-7.

47 B.J. Drijber, "De Bezems van Bolkestein", *NTER* 2004, 114.

48 Report from the Commission on "The State of the Internal Market for Services", COM(2002) 441 final, 55.

An interesting point of debate is whether the inclusion of services of general economic interest in this internal market proposal is consistent with the engagements by the Commission in its white paper on services of general interest, in which it stressed the importance of respecting the principle of subsidiarity and the role of Member States regarding the services of general interest. On the basis of this principle and the absence of a clear definition of services of general economic interest at EU level, many argue that these services should be excluded from the proposal, in order not to affect the freedom of Member States to define what they consider to be services of general economic interest.[49]

Furthermore, according to Article 5, paragraph 3 EC, Community action will not go beyond what is necessary to achieve the objectives of the EC Treaty. As indicated before, the measures included in the proposal will definitely have important effects on national/regional regulations governing establishment and temporary service provision. The far-reaching nature of the proposal raises the question as to whether it respects the fundamental principle of proportionality. This is the case for administrative simplification measures on access to and exercise of a service activity as well as for the incorporation of the country of origin principle. As regards the case-by-case exceptions to the country of origin principle for instance, the list of grounds of exceptions included in the draft is far more restrictive than the "rule of reason" grounds recognised by the European Court on the basis of which a Member State can take measures relating to a provider established in another Member State. So far, the European Court has indeed recognised a wide range of grounds, including protection of workers, social protection of workers, preservation of the financial balance of the social security system, maintaining a balanced medical and hospital service open to all and patient safety.[50]

Finally, the proposal provides important alternative methods to ensure the transposition of many of its requirements, which substantially differs from the traditional European infringement procedure, according to which the European Commission brings action against Member States when it has reason to believe that they are in breach of Community law.[51] As regards the freedom of establishment, Member States will have to submit all their own national authorisation schemes to a major evaluation operation before any allegation of an infringement of Community law. This evaluation intends to lead to the elimination of unjustified requirements

---

49 Specific reference is made to the principle of subsidiarity in *Draft Report on the Proposal for Directive of the European Parliament and of the Council on Services in the Internal Market*, European Parliament, Committee on the Internal Market and Consumer Protection, Rapporteur, Evelyne Gebhardt, p. 92 and Draft Opinion on the Proposal for a Directive of the European Parliament and of the Council on Services in the Internal Market, European Parliament, Committee on Employment and Social Affairs, Rapporteur, Anne Van Lancker, p. 3.

50 W. Gekiere, *Towards a European Directive on Services in the Internal Market: Analysing the Legal Repercussions of the Draft Services Directive and its Impact on National Services Regulations*, research report commissioned by Anne Van Lancker, Rapporteur, Commission Employment and Social Affairs, Institute for European Law, KU Leuven, September 2004, p. 14.

51 EC, Article 226.

and will be subject to mutual evaluation that could, where appropriate, lead to other Community initiatives.[52] This method applies for the national authorisation schemes under Article 9(2), for the requirements to be evaluated under Article 15(4) and for multidisciplinary activities under Article 30(4). Member States will have to make a similar justification and proportionality test within the framework of the mutual assistance procedure in the event of case-by-case derogations from the country of origin principle (Article 37). The Commission has the final responsibility on the compatibility with Community law and on the conclusion whether a Member State's measure is justified and proportional.

3.3. Country of Origin Principle and Minimum Harmonisation

The application of the country of origin principle implies that a service provider will be no longer subject to the host state's regulations governing access to and exercise of service and its supervisory measures. In general, this principle can only work if there is a minimum level of harmonisation at EU level or, at least, if there are comparable rules within the different Member States, which establish a sufficient level of mutual confidence between them. The fields that are actually harmonised by this proposal relate to very specific issues, such as information on service providers and their services, professional insurance and guarantees, information on after-sales guarantees and the settlement of disputes.[53]

In order to ensure that the country of origin principle works, further harmonisation measures at EU level are needed in the field of minimum quality norms, protection of public order, minimum vocational training and professional qualification requirements and supervisory mechanisms.

Further harmonisation also plays an important role in the light of the derogations to the country of origin principle. Regarding case-by-case derogations for instance, we have already pointed out that the proposal substantially limits the grounds on the basis of which a Member State can take measures relating to a provider established in another Member State and introduces a mutual assistance procedure for exceptional circumstances. Under Community law, a Community measure governing a specific matter becomes the only framework of judicial review provided that it deals with the matter exhaustively. In this case, the "harmonising" measure replaces the Treaty as the framework of judicial review.[54] However the proposal does not seem to contain a sufficient level of harmonisation in order to replace the EC treaty provisions: it incorporates the fundamental principle of free movement of services but, at the same time, it reduces the scope of the grounds of "rule of reason" exceptions. Without any further harmonisation at EU level, there

---

52   Proposal, explanatory memorandum, 11.
53   Proposal, Articles 26-28 and 32.
54   C-37/92, *Vanacker and Lesage*, [1993] ECR I-4947, para. 9; C-324/99, *DaimlerChrysler*, [2001] ECR I-9897, para. 32; C-322/01, *Doc Morris*, [2003], para. 64.

is a legal tension between the proposal and the EC treaty provisions on the free movement of services.

The lack of sufficiently harmonised mechanisms could also entail the risk that national inspection services of the host Member State are seriously sidelined by the country of origin principle. This is the case for the provisions included in Article 24 of the draft Services Directive on posting of workers.[55] Article 24 recognises the responsibility of the host state to ensure compliance with employment and working conditions under Directive 96/71/EC, but it prohibits the host state from making service providers subject to certain obligations, such as making a declaration before the posting of workers and holding employment documents on its territory. At the same time, it refers in very broad terms to a general system of communication of information by, and with assistance from, the country of origin to the host state.[56] However, the text of this provision does not clarify how and when exactly the country of origin has to communicate information. Neither does it specify how to ensure that the information of the country of origin will correspond to the employment and working conditions of the host state.

3.4. Recognition of Regional Competences

In its report on the state of the internal market on services, the Commission came to the conclusion that regions play an important role in maintaining barriers to cross-border traffic in services.[57] The proposal presented by the Commission seems to simply ignore the regional policy level, by stating for instance that an authorisation for a new establishment should give the service provider access to the service activity "throughout the national territory".[58] However, in many Member States, such as Germany, Spain, Austria, United Kingdom and Belgium, regional authorities have constitutional rights to enact measures regulating access to, and exercise of, specific service activities in their regions.

Regarding the single points of contact, the Commission seems to have taken into account the internal configuration of Member States. It points out that the number of single points of contact can vary according to regional or local competences, or according to the activities concerned. It clarifies that the measure does not interfere with the allocation of functions among competent authorities within each national system.[59] However, the wordings of Article 6 on single points of contact should be

---

55   Nationale Arbeidsraad (Belgian National Labour Council), Advies No. 1463, 11-2; SERV (Flanders Social and Economic Council), *Aanbeveling over het voorstel van een richtlijn van het Europees Parlement en de Raad betreffende diensten op de interne markt* (14/07/2004), 18, 25.

56   Proposal, Article 24, para. 2.

57   European Commission, *Report from the Commission to the Council and the European Parliament on the State of the Internal Market for Services*, 30 July 2002, COM(2002) 441 final, 47-8.

58   Proposal, Article 10(4).

59   Proposal, recital 25.

adapted in order to clarify the possibility of organising the single point of contact in accordance with each Member State's form of government (i.e. federal state).

3.5. Relationship with Other Secondary Community Initiatives

The proposal overlaps with a number of other Community initiatives. It is true that Article 3 of the proposal states that the provisions of this Directive will not prevent the application of other Community instruments as regards the services governed by those provisions, but it does not take away the legal uncertainty relating to its relationship with other Community rules.

The proposal partly interferes with matters covered by other secondary Community instruments, such as Directive 96/71/EC on the posting of workers and EEC Regulation 1408/71 on the application of social security schemes. At the same time, it anticipates the outcome of certain pending Community initiatives, such as the Commission's White Paper on services of general interest (and maybe eventually a framework Directive), the high-level reflection process on patient mobility and healthcare developments in the European Union and the Green Paper on the conversion of the Rome I Convention,[60] into a Community instrument[61] and the Rome II Draft Regulation[62] establishing rules on conflict of laws as regards contractual and non-contractual obligations respectively.[63]

3.5.1. Posting of Workers

From a labour law perspective, particular concerns have been raised on the possible conflict between the country of origin principle on the one hand, and existing labour law provisions included in the Posting of Workers Directive and Rome I and Rome II instruments, on the other hand.[64]

---

60   1980 Convention on the law applicable to contractual obligations, OJ C 027, 26.01.1998, 34-46.
61   A Green Paper on the Conversion of the Rome Convention of 1980 on the law applicable to contractual obligations into a Community instrument and its modernisation, COM(2002) 654 final, 14 January 2003.
62   Proposal for a Regulation of the European Parliament and the Council on the Law Applicable to Non-Contractual Obligations ("Rome II") COM(2003) 427 final, 22.07.2003.
63   See P. Beaumont, "The Commission's Proposal in the Light of Primary Law; Compatibility with Rome I and II and Private International Law Provisions", *Public Hearing on the Proposal for a Directive on Services in the Internal Market*, Committee on the Internal Market and Consumer Protection in Association with the Committee on Employment and Social Affairs, European Parliament, Brussels, 11 November 2004.
64   See e.g. N Bruun, "Employment Issues, Memorandum" and C. Passchier, on behalf of the ETUC, *Public Hearing on the Proposal for a Directive on Services in the Internal Market*, Committee on the Internal Market and Consumer Protection in Association with the Committee on Employment and Social Affairs, European Parliament, Brussels, 11 November 2004.

As explained before, the Commission excludes matters covered by the Posting of Workers Directive from the scope of the country of origin principle. This Directive provides that the service provider who posts workers to another Member State has to comply with minimum rules laid down by law of the state where the work is carried out, such as maximum work periods, minimum rest periods, minimum rates of pay, conditions of hiring-out of workers, regardless of the law applicable to the employment relationship.[65] At the same time, it allows Member States to apply terms and conditions of employment on other matters than those enlisted before, in case of public policy provisions.[66] Finally, it entitles Member States to apply terms and conditions of employment laid down in collective agreements which are universally applicable.[67] Many Member States have indeed decided to apply these conditions in the case of posting of workers by agencies from other Member States.

It is often argued that the term of "matter covered by Directive 96/71/EC" included in Article 17(5) of the proposal does not provide legal certainty as to the exact reach of the exception to the country of origin principle and it is feared that the Posting of Workers Directive, which establishes the minimum level of employment protection in the country of destination, would turn into a European legislative instrument providing the maximum level of employment protection in the host Member State.[68]

3.5.2. What if the Posting of Workers Directive Does Not Apply?

It is important to remember that the Posting of Workers Directive only deals with the specific situation where a worker carries out work on a temporary basis in another Member State than the Member State in which he habitually works.[69] This Directive does not apply where a worker is not posted to the host country on a temporary basis, but for a longer period or where a worker is posted to another Member State without having been employed by the service provider in the country of origin before the time of posting. Finally, it also does not apply where the worker

---

65   Directive 96/71/EC, Article 3, para. 1. It also mentions conditions of hiring-out of workers; health, safety and hygiene at work; protective measures regarding pregnant women, women who have recently given birth, children, and young people; equality of treatment between men and women and non-discrimination.

66   Directive 96/71/EC, Article 3, para. 10.

67   Directive 96/1/EC, Article 3, para. 10. These terms must apply to activities such as construction, repair, upkeep, alteration or demolition of buildings (Dir 96/71/EC, Article 3, para. 1).

68   N. Bruun, "Employment Issues, Memorandum", *Public Hearing on the Proposal for a Directive on Services in the Internal Market*, Committee on the Internal Market and Consumer Protection in Association with the Committee on Employment and Social Affairs, European Parliament, Brussels, 11 November 2004.

69   Directive 96/71/EC, Article 2, para. 1.

is a citizen from the host country and is employed in the host country by a service provider which is established elsewhere.

In these cases, it follows from the proposal that either the country of origin principle or, at least, the principle of the free choice of law[70] would apply. Here, a conflict seems to arise between the proposal and the rules included in the Rome I Convention. This Convention contains specific rules governing the applicable law for individual employment contracts, which would lead to the application of the law and/or at least the mandatory rule of the host country.[71]

Finally, it is argued that the derogation of the proposal concerning the Posting of Workers Directive does not cover workers' protection that is safeguarded by instruments other than legal and administrative provisions and collective agreements which have been declared universally applicable. In many countries, workers' rights are protected through collective agreements that are not declared universally applicable.[72] On the basis of this argument, several actors within the European Parliament have suggested that the field of labour law, including collective agreements, should be excluded from the scope of the proposal.[73]

4. CONCLUSION

The elimination of obstacles to the cross-border provision of services is beyond doubt essential to achieve the goal set out by the Lisbon European Council to make the European Union the most competitive and dynamic knowledge-based economy in the world capable of sustainable economic growth with more and better jobs and greater social cohesion. The proposal of the Commission for a Directive on Services in the Internal Market aims at bringing legal certainty necessary to facilitate the establishment of providers, particularly SMEs, in other Member States and to encourage them to provide their services in other Member States. However, the reflections mentioned above show that there are still reasons to believe that the proposal may cause legal uncertainty for providers and recipients of services on several important points.

---

70   Proposal, Article 17(20).

71   See e.g. Rome I, Article 6, para. 1 and Article 7.

72   This is the case in the Scandinavian countries. See N. Bruun, "Employment Issues, Memorandum", *Public Hearing on the Proposal for a Directive on Services in the Internal Market*, Committee on the Internal Market and Consumer Protection in Association with the Committee on Employment and Social Affairs, European Parliament, Brussels, 11 November 2004.

73   See Draft Report on the Proposal for Directive of the European Parliament and of the Council on Services in the Internal Market, European Parliament, Committee on the Internal Market and Consumer Protection, Rapporteur Evelyne Gebhardt, amendment 51 and Draft Opinion on the Proposal for a Directive of the European Parliament and of the Council on Services in the Internal Market, European Parliament, Committee on Employment and Social Affairs, Rapporteur Anne Van Lancker, amendments 49, 52 and 53.

In accordance with the co-decision procedure, it is now up to the European Parliament to give its opinion on the proposal in first reading. Parliament is expected to pass amendments in plenary session at the earliest by autumn 2005. In his statement to the European Parliament of 8 March 2005, European Commissioner for Internal Market and Services, Charles McGreevy, confirmed that the Commission would not withdraw its proposal and committed his loyalty to the co-decision procedure.

2. THE PROPOSED DIRECTIVE ON SERVICES AND LABOUR LAW

Niklas Bruun

1. INTRODUCTION

This paper analyses the labour and social law implications of the proposed Services Directive.[74] It consists of two parts. In the first part, I address the compatibility of the proposed Services Directive with EU legislation. This part (chapters 2-4) is taken from my Memorandum on Employment issues which was presented for the European Parliament in a public hearing 11 November 2004. The second part (chapter 5) of this paper takes up the issue of how to regulate the relationship between labour law and services in an amended Directive. In this second part I present and comment on some recent proposals made to the European Parliament.

2. TREATY PROVISIONS

The proposed Directive aims to enhance and guarantee the freedom to provide services in the internal market in accordance with the EC Treaty. Its underlying assumption is that barriers at the national level cannot be removed solely by relying on the direct application of Articles 43 and 49 of the Treaty. Comprehensive secondary legislation is needed.

A central feature of the freedom to provide services in the internal market is that the provision of services, in contrast to free movement of goods, usually involves *employees* of the service provider crossing borders to perform the services. *In practice*, therefore, the free movement of *services* shares many characteristics with the free movement of *workers*. Whatever the parallels in practice, from the *formal legal* viewpoint, as confirmed by the European Court of Justice (ECJ), the freedoms affecting services and workers are analytically quite distinct:[75]

> The Court has held that workers employed by a business established in one Member State who are temporarily sent to another Member State

---

74   COM(2004) 2/3 final.
75   *Finalarte*, Cases C-49-50/98, C-52/98, C-54/98, C-68/98 and C-71/98 p. 22.

to provide services do not, in any way, seek access to the labour market in that second state, if they return to their country of origin or residence after completion of their work.

It is essential, however, whatever the *formal legal* analytical distinction, to take into account the fact that, *in practice*, the movement of *workers* is a feature of cross-border *service* provision in the internal market even if not the central one. A starting point of principle in this respect is Article 50(3) of the EC Treaty (italics added):

> ... the person providing a service may, in order to do so, temporarily pursue his activity in the State where the service is provided, *under the same conditions as are imposed by that State on its own nationals.*

A second point of principle concerns the rules that Member States are *permitted* to apply to restrict cross-border provision of services:[76]

> [The freedom to provide services] ... as one of the fundamental principles of the Treaty, may be restricted only by rules justified by overriding requirements related to the public interest and applicable to all persons and undertakings operating in the territory of the state where the service is provided, in so far as that interest is not safeguarded by the rules to which the provider of such a service is subject in the Member State where he is established.

Justifications for a restriction of the freedom to provide services may include consideration of fundamental rights or freedoms.[77] This is noted in the Preamble to the proposed Services Directive:[78]

> In addition, any restriction of the freedom to provide services should be permitted, by way of exception, only if it is consistent with fundamental rights which, as the Court of Justice has consistently held, form an integral part of the general principles of law enshrined in the Community legal order.

An assessment of the proposed Directive on the free movement of services, in light of the fundamental principles of EC law, is rather complicated. It classifies the subject matter in the formal sense as the free movement of services, not workers. Yet services are mostly provided by workers and this cannot be overlooked when analysing the concrete interpretation of the Treaty as a whole, a Treaty for the Union

---

76   *Arblade*, Case C-369/96, para. 34,
77   Case C-36/02, *Omega*.
78   Recital 40.

that shall "promote economic and social progress and a high level of employment and achieve balanced and sustainable development" through, amongst other things, "the strengthening of economic and social cohesion".[79]

The principles of the proposed Directive on the free movement of services might conflict with the principles governing the free movement of workers. A primary principle governing the free movement of workers is equal treatment and non-discrimination on the grounds of nationality. The principle of equal treatment is extended to nationals of third countries by the EU Charter of Fundamental Rights 2000, Article 15(3).

The proposed Services Directive asserts instead, as a main rule, the "country of origin principle" (Article 16). In practice, this might frequently result in situations similar to discrimination, direct and indirect, based on the nationality of the employees. The country of origin principle is premised on unequal treatment of workers on the grounds of nationality and thereby conflicts with the principles enshrined in Article 39(2 and 3)(c) EC and Article 7 of Regulation 1612/68. The proposal also seems to conflict with other initiatives being considered at the EU level which reflect fundamental principles, including equal treatment. The proposed Services Directive should respect the fundamental principle of equal treatment in the *acquis communautaire*.

Workers moving from one Member State to another encounter different working conditions, laid down in legislation, collective agreements and other legal sources. The fundamental principle of equal treatment regardless of nationality means that workers are entitled to the same terms and conditions regardless of nationality. Workers are entitled to equal treatment under the laws of the host Member State.

The proposed Services Directive seems to prescribe the reverse of equal treatment: employees of service providers moving to another Member State are *not* entitled to equal treatment, but are subject to the principle that they are governed by the rules of their country of origin.

The anomaly is evident when comparing migrant workers with those migrating under the shadow of a service provider. The former are entitled to equal treatment, the latter are not.

The principle of equal treatment – non-discrimination – is rooted in the *acquis* of EU labour law. It is manifest in numerous directives on sex discrimination, on discrimination on other grounds, and in the case of different categories of workers (part-time workers, fixed-term workers and tele-workers).

The proposed Services Directive plans a shift in principle with this established *acquis* by explicitly allowing different conditions to apply to workers doing the same work – on the grounds that they are employed by service providers subject to the law of their country of origin.

---

79   Treaty on the European Union, Article 2.

3. THE PRESENT LEGAL SITUATION

The potential impact of the proposed Services Directive may be appreciated by comparing it with existing principles established in EU law.

Firstly, Directive 96/71/EC applies a specific social policy to workers posted within the framework of free movement of services. Directive 96/71/EC specifies minimum terms and conditions of employment, which must apply to workers posted to the host country. Further, the employer is obliged in general to observe the host country's labour law provisions having a public policy character[80] and that Member State's public law regulations.

The limit to application of the labour law of the host Member State is that it cannot require service providers to pay "double":[81]

> National rules which require a service provider … to pay employers' contributions to the host Member State's fund, in addition to those he has already paid to the fund of the Member State where he is established, constitute a restriction on freedom to provide services.

Secondly, the Rome Convention on the law applicable to contractual obligations (Rome I) provides that the contract of employment is governed:[82]

(a) by the law of the country in which the employee habitually carries out his work in performance of the contract, even if he is temporarily employed in another country; or

(b) if the employee does not habitually carry out his work in any one country, by the law of the country in which the place of business through which he was engaged is situated;

unless it appears from the circumstances as a whole that the contract is more closely connected with another country in which case the contract shall be governed by the law of that country.

Therefore, if the posted worker is temporarily working in the host country and habitually carries out work in that Member State, the rules of that host State apply to regulate the individual employment relationship. Again, if the employee does *not* have any country where he habitually works, the rules of the host country may still apply if he is still closely connected with that country. However, in certain cases, the applicable law may instead be that of the country where the place of business of the employer is situated.

---

80   Article 3(10) gives the Member States an option to apply such provisions.
81   Case C-369/96, *Arblade*. See also, however, Declaration No. 7 attached to the Council minutes when the Directive was adopted 20.9.1996, file No. 00/0346 SYN, ADD 1.
82   Article 6(2).

Finally, as regards social security, there are different rules. The starting principle of the coordination of social security systems is that only the rules of one specific Member State apply.

To summarise: first, in general, the labour law of the *host country* applies, with possible exceptions according to the Rome Convention. Secondly, labour law requirements which restrict the free movement of services may be justified on public policy grounds, but only where they satisfy the "proportionality principle": the labour law rules must be necessary to protect the interests they are intended to guarantee, and only in so far as those objectives cannot be attained by less restrictive measures.

4. THE LABOUR LAW ASPECTS OF THE PROPOSED SERVICES DIRECTIVE

4.1. The Country of Origin Principle and Labour Law

4.1.1. The Proposed Services Directive and Member States' Labour Law

The proposed Directive purports not to "address labour law as such". It asserts that it is only "abolishing certain disproportionate administrative procedures, while also improving the monitoring of compliance with employment and working conditions in accordance with Directive 96/71/EC".[83] However, the very next recital of the Preamble to the proposed Directive states (emphasis added):[84]

> In order to avoid discriminatory or disproportionate administrative formalities, which would be a disincentive to SMEs in particular, it is necessary to preclude the Member State of posting from making postings subject to compliance with requirements such as an obligation to request authorisation from the authorities. The obligation to make a declaration to the authorities of the Member State of posting should also be prohibited. However, it should be possible to maintain such an obligation until 31 December 2008 in the field of building work in accordance with the Annex to Directive 96/71/EC. In that connection, a group of Member State experts on the application of that Directive are studying ways to improve administrative cooperation between Member States in order to facilitate supervision. Furthermore, as regards *employment and working conditions other than those laid down in Directive 96/71/EC, it should not be possible for the Member State of posting to take restrictive measures against a provider established in another Member State.*

83   Preamble, indent 58.
84   Preamble, indent 59.

In this connection it is also worth noting that the proposed Directive contains an Article 19, which states that a Member State can take case-by-case derogatory measures in exceptional circumstances only. The list of grounds included in the proposal are:

– safety of services, including aspects related to public health (a);
– the exercise of a health profession (b); and
– the protection of public policy, notably aspects related to the protection of minors.

This list of grounds included in Article 19 (1) is far more restrictive than the "rule of reason" grounds recognised by the ECJ.[85] In that respect it can even be argued that the Directive transforms the present "proportionality" justification test for a host Member State restriction into a proper rule of conflict of law. It sets aside the regulation in the host Member State also when it is compatible with the Treaty.

4.1.2. The Proposed Services Directive and EU Labour Law

The intention stated in this Preamble text is implemented by Article 17 (General derogations from the country of origin principle) which states that Article 16 (the "country of origin principle") shall not apply to "matters covered by Directive 96/71/EC".

This is a radical change in EU labour law. It seems to be based on a fundamental misapprehension that the country of origin principle is consistent with existing labour law, and that it is sufficient if some limited derogation can be made to this principle to accommodate Directive 96/71/EC.

As a matter of policy, the proposed change is striking in seeking to apply the country of origin principle to labour law. For example, a corresponding clause was recently rejected by the Council as regards consumer protection in relation to the adoption of a common position on the proposal for a Directive concerning unfair business-to-consumer commercial practices in the internal market.[86]

4.1.3. Council Documents on Labour Law

Two explanatory documents prepared by the Commission for the Council highlight the problems created by the application of the country of origin principle to labour law in the proposed Services Directive. The first Council Document concerns the

---

85   See Wouter Gekiere, *Towards a European Directive on Services in the Internal Market: Analysing the Legal Repercussions of the Draft Services Directive and Its Impact on National Services Regulations*. 24.9.2004 (manuscript p. 11).

86   COM(2003) 356 final.

relationship between the proposal and the Rome I and draft Rome II Conventions;[87] the second concerns the relationship between the proposed Directive and the rules on posting of workers.[88]

4.1.4. Member State Labour Law: Conflicts with Rome I

The first explanatory document is explicitly said to be limited to private law issues.[89] It states that the country of origin principle appears to create a choice of law rule, and that this has implications for the existing Rome I and the solutions envisaged by Rome II.[90] It is argued that, in principle, employment relationships are excluded from the scope of the proposed Directive.[91] However, no real analysis is provided of the relationship between the labour law aspects of Rome I and II and the country of origin principle. Yet there appears to be a clear conflict between them in situations where the employee does not habitually work in his country of origin: Rome I allows for host country labour law to apply; the country of origin principle dictates the opposite conclusion.

4.1.5. EU Labour Law (1): Transforming Directive 96/71/EC from a Minimum to a Maximum Standard

The proposal completely alters the underlying general assumption of Directive 96/71/EC. It transforms it, in principle, from a Directive[92] providing a *minimum* of employment protection in the host Member State to one specifying the *maximum* protection available to employees. This is clearly stated in the recital of the proposed Services Directive claiming that "it should not be possible for the Member State of posting to take restrictive measures against a provider established in another Member State".

4.1.6. EU Labour Law (2): Terms of Employment of Posted Workers Safeguarded

The second document stresses that the proposed Services Directive exempts all matters covered by Directive 96/71/EC from the country of origin principle. In

---

87   Council Document 2004/0001 COD, 25.6.2004.
88   Council Document 2004/0001 COD, 5.7.2004.
89   Council Document 2004/0001 COD, 25.6.2004, p. 6.
90   *Ibid.*, p. 13.
91   *Ibid.*, p. 29.
92   The view that Directive 96/71/EC is a minimum Directive is also stated in the Preamble (p. 34) to Directive 2004/18/EC (public procurement).

particular, the country of origin principle is not to affect the application of terms and conditions of employment in matters covered by Directive 96/71/EC and the application of "universally applicable" collective agreements in these areas. The host Member State is to continue being responsible for the necessary controls on all these matters. Specifically, the document stresses that terms and conditions applicable to temporary workers are covered by Directive 96/71/EC and thus exempt from the application of the country of origin principle.

4.1.7. EU Labour Law (3): The Problem of Self-employed Posted Workers

Similarly, the country of origin principle is not to affect the definition of who is a "worker". Self-employment, therefore, appears to be a matter covered indirectly by the Posting Directive. Article 2(2) confirms that the law of the host country defines the notion of "worker". The intention appears to be to combat the posting of "bogus" self-employed workers. However, there is a problem in that, by definition, if there is objectively *no* natural or legal person posting the (bogus) *self*-employed person to work in the host country, such a self-employed person is not covered by the Posting Directive.

4.1.8. EU Labour Law (4): Conditions for Hiring-out of Workers

The Directive covers "the conditions of hiring-out of workers including the conditions regarding the supply of workers by temporary employment agencies".[93] A careful reading of the explanatory document of 5 July 2004 indicates that the aim is not to apply the country of origin principle to conditions for the hiring-out of workers. It states that this could be explained in a recital. However, the conclusions of the explanatory document, where a draft text for new recitals is presented, do not cover this point. Minimum clarity of this crucial issue requires an unambiguous text, at least in a recital. That text should reflect the case law of the European Court of Justice, which has handed down three important decisions on cross-border temporary work.

> In *Webb*, the Court acknowledged the social sensitivity of the issue of temporary agency businesses. It recognised the right of Member States to restrict temporary agency work or even to ban it. But it was necessary to take account of the evidence and guarantees already provided by the business in the Member State of its establishment.[94]

---

93   Council Document 2004/0001 COD, 5.7.2004, p. 5.
94   Case 279/80, paras 17-20.

In 1999, the judgement in *Webb* shaped the substantive content of a unanimous Council Resolution on the transnational hiring-out of workers.[95] Licensing was accepted and it included also a Code of Conduct for administrative cooperation.

> In *Commission v. Germany*, the Court accepted in principle restrictions on the hiring-out of manpower in the construction industry in Germany.[96] However, the Court outlawed the practical application of the restrictions requiring a company to be established in Germany (the host Member State) and to be bound by a collective agreement, either as a member of the employers' organisation or by signing a company level collective agreement in the construction sector, in order to be able send or use temporary workers.

> In *Commission v. Italy*, the Court did not outlaw in principle a requirement to establish a financial guarantee in temporary work; but it outlawed a national scheme that did not take into account the guarantee established in another Member State.[97]

In sum, the conclusion to be drawn from the case law is that the conditions for the hiring-out of manpower do not fall within the country of origin principle.

4.2. The Country of Origin Principle and the *Acquis Communautaire*

The country of origin principle in the proposed Services Directive brings it into direct conflict with some important parts of the *acquis communautaire* of EU labour law and raises difficult problems of interpretation.

4.2.1. *Directive 91/383: Health and Safety*

Directive 91/383/EEC supplementing measures to encourage improvements in the safety and health at work of workers with a fixed-duration employment relationship or a temporary employment relationship imposes duties on the user undertaking, for example, to inform the temporary employment business of the occupational qualifications required and specific features of the job.[98] The Member State in which the user undertaking operates is responsible for fulfilment of this obligation. This

---

95   Officially headed: Fight Against Social Security Fraud And Undeclared Work. See the Resolution of the Social Council of 9 March 1999/ 6491/99 SOC 80,
96   Case C-493/99, judgement of 25 October 2001.
97   Case C- 279/00, judgement of 3 February 2002. Italy at that time required a minimum share capital of 1 bn. ITL for running a temporary work agency.
98   Council Directive 91/383 of 25 June 1991, OJ 1991 L206/19.

conflicts with the application of country of origin rules to service providers who are temporary agency businesses.

The matter is further complicated by the derogation in the proposed Services Directive that the country of origin principle does not apply to "the non-contractual liability of a provider in the case of an accident involving a person and occurring as a consequence of the service provider's activities in the Member State into which he has moved temporarily" (Article 17(23)).

4.2.2. Directive 80/987/EEC: Insolvency Protection

According to Directive 80/987/EEC, the host Member State may become responsible for claims for lost wages in situations of insolvency on the part of the service provider.[99] Article 8a provides that the state where the employees habitually work or worked is responsible for the wage guarantee in the situations of insolvency. When the employees have been hired especially for foreign projects, only the host state can bear that responsibility. Again, this conflicts with the country of origin principle in the proposed Services Directive.

4.2.3. Public Procurement Rules

Within the framework of public procurement the control of matters related to employment conditions is clearly a matter for the contracting authorities:[100]

> If national law contains provisions to this effect, non-compliance …
> with laws, regulations and collective agreements on both national and
> Community level… may be considered to be grave misconduct or an
> offence concerning the professional conduct of the economic operator
> concerned, liable to lead to the exclusion of that economic operator from
> the procedure for the award of a public contract.

Again, the application of "country of origin" rules on public procurement raises questions. The control related to labour law is usually best as near as possible to the work place.

In general, the new EU Directives on public procurement replicate the earlier law. As applied by the European Court of Justice, this arguably allows public authorities to stipulate some labour standards and conditions. These labour standards would bind contractors to the conditions prevailing in the host Member State, or

---

99   Council Directive 80/987/EEC on the approximation of the laws of the Member States relat-
     ing to the protection of employees in the event of the insolvency of their employer; OJ 1980
     L283/23.
100 Directive 2004/18/EC, Recital 34.

region, or laid down in collective agreements. Contractors from other Member States would be bound to observe those standards. It is not clear how this can be reconciled with the proposed Services Directive mandating country of origin rules to apply to service providers from another Member State.

Arguably, there may be no conflict if the labour standards permitted by the public procurement rules are presumed not to be discriminatory (this is a condition of their validity) and are based on a contractual obligation undertaken by the service provider. As such, they do not obstruct the free movement of services, and the proposed Services Directive does not operate to apply the country of origin principle.

4.2.4. Posted Workers: Directive 96/71/EC

What the draft Directive calls a "general derogation" (Article 17(5)) is rather a recognition that its principles conflict with the Posting Directive (Directive 96/71/EC).[101]

The proposed Services Directive creates a separate category of employees of service providers subject to special rules. The Posting Directive provides some protection to temporary posted workers by host country provisions. This protection is extended to full equal treatment when these workers are migrant workers. But the country of origin principle in the proposed Services Directive denies protection when the workers are employees of service providers.

The new legal classification of employees of service providers has in fact the consequence of undermining the principle of equal treatment guaranteed by the *acquis communautaire* on the free movement of workers.

4.2.5. Agency Workers

The draft Directive on agency workers proposes that agency employees in the user enterprise can claim equal treatment with comparators in the user enterprise.[102] This applies also to workers sent by agencies to provide services in other countries: the

---

101 Council Directive 96/71/EEC concerning the posting of workers in the framework of the provision of services was based on the Commission's view that: "National differences as to the material content of working conditions and the criteria inspiring the conflict of law rules may lead to situations where posted workers are applied lower wages and other working conditions than those in force in the place where the work is temporarily carried out. This situation would certainly affect fair competition between undertakings and equality of treatment between foreign and national undertakings; it would, from the social point of view, be completely unacceptable". COM(1991) 230 final, SYN 346, Brussels, 1 August 1991, para. 9 bis.

102 Proposal for a Directive of the European Parliament and the Council on working conditions for temporary workers, 20 March 2002. Amended proposal, 28 November 2002.

applicable provisions will *not* be those in the home country, but those applied to the comparator in the host country.

4.2.6. Recognition of Professional Qualifications

In the area of recognition of professional qualifications, the main principle in EU law is mutual recognition and improved transparency of qualifications. Again, there is no straightforward country of origin principle. The proposal for a Directive on the recognition of professional qualifications instead promotes cross-border services in Europe in a balanced manner.[103]

4.2.7. Collective Agreements

Conditions of work in some Member States are often governed by collective agreements, including those extended by ministerial decree to bind all employers and workers. In the case of provision of cross-border services, some collective agreements may be covered by the Posting Directive and be exempt from the country of origin principle. However, as in the case of the Nordic countries, but also elsewhere, collective agreements may not satisfy the requirements of the Posting Directive ("universally applicable" agreements) and come into conflict with the country of origin principle.

The European Court of Justice has made it clear that collective agreements are protected by EU law. For example, in a case where collective agreements made compulsory the affiliation by employers to pension funds for the workers in the industry, the value attributed to collective agreements by the Treaties and the EU legal order meant that they prevailed in relationship to competing EU principles such as competition law (*Albany*).[104]

The proposed Services Directive does not recognise the protection granted collective agreements by the *acquis*. It is not at all evident that the European Court of Justice would subordinate collective agreements to the country of origin principle based on the free movement of services.

4.2.8. Privatisation and Outsourcing of Services

Service providers may operate in other Member States following privatisation of public services or outsourcing from private enterprises. EU rules in the Transfer

---

103   COM(2002) 119 final, 7.3.2002.
104   *Albany International BV v. Stichting Bedrijfspensioenfonds Textielindustrie*, Case C-67/96; with Joined Cases C-115/97, C-116/97 and C-117/97; [1999] ECR I-5751.

of Undertakings Directive[105] apply to determine conditions of employment for employees transferred from the public service or outsourcing enterprise to the service provider. The Directive guarantees continuity of terms of employment. The terms of employment will therefore be those of the transferor employer, subject to the laws of the host Member State, not those of the transferee service provider (country of origin principle).

The same result may arise where the country of origin of the service provider has incorporated the Transfer of Undertakings Directive, so that the host country conditions of employment apply to workers transferred to the service provider. But again, there appears to be a conflict between host country labour laws and the country of origin principle.

4.2.9. Collective Rights under the EU Charter

The country of origin principle poses a threat for industrial relations regulations in certain Member States (e.g. collective agreements in the Nordic countries), which are not covered by the Posting Directive (because not "universally applicable"). Attempts by trade unions to enforce these agreements, perhaps through industrial action, may be regarded as creating obstacles to the free movement of services, and could be the subject of litigation For this reason and for clarification it is vital that the Directive affirms, like the "Monti" Regulation,[106] that fundamental rights of collective action are protected.

4.2.10. Summary

To sum up: the country of origin principle within social and labour law:

1. Increases legal complexity and reduces transparency by introducing a new principle in a field already regulated by *lex specialis*;
2. Creates ambiguities and consequent confusion concerning the extent to which the proposed Services Directive intervenes in labour regulation;
3. Produces no real advantages, but rather many disadvantages from the social point of view.

---

105 Council Directive 77/187 of 14 February 1977 on the approximation of the laws of the Member States relating to the safeguarding of employees' rights in the event of transfers of undertakings, businesses or parts of businesses, OJ L 61/26, as amended by Directive 98/50/EC of 29 June 1998, OJ L 201/88. Consolidated in Directive 2001/23 of 12 March 2001, OJ L/82/16

106 Council Regulation (EC) No. 2679/98 of 7 December 1998 on the functioning of the internal market in relation to the free movement of goods among the Member States. OJ L337/8 of 12.12.98.

The final recommendation on my part in the Parliament hearing in November was a deletion of Article 17(5) and its replacement by a provision stating that the law applicable to employees of service providers is Directive 96/71/EC, the Rome Convention and relevant Community and national labour law.

5. CURRENT PROPOSALS IN THE EUROPEAN PARLIAMENT

In draft Report I by Gebhardt[107] of 11 April 2005 and the draft Opinion by Van Lancker[108] of the 26 April 2005, several amendments to the proposed Services Directive have been made. Here I only discuss the aspect concerning the relationship between the Services Directive and the labour law. As stated above the problem is that services are often provided by employees and in the context of an encompassing country of origin principle, complemented with "derogations", the problem of how to deal with labour law issues will become important both in theory and in practice. The proposal by Gebhardt reads in this respect:

Article 1(2):

This Directive shall in no way affect labour law, in particular the legislative provisions applicable to employment relationships, including the right to take industrial action and reach collective agreements, or national social security legislation.

Article 16(1a):

The mutual recognition principle shall not apply to legal or contractual provisions of the country of destination in the field of consumer protection, environmental protection or labour law, notably remuneration, working conditions and measures relating to health and safety at work. In addition, the mutual recognition principle shall not apply to law relating to reparation of loss and damage.

The proposal must be read against the background that Gebhardt also proposes that the "country of origin principle" in the Commission proposal in all essential respects should be replaced by a "mutual recognition principle". I will not discuss the content of these principles here.

The proposal by Van Lancker takes the same starting points but is less detailed:

---

107 Draft Report I on the Proposal for a Directive of the European Parliament and of the Council on services in the internal market (COM(2004)0002 – C5-0069/2004-2004/0001(COD)

108 Draft Opinion of the Committee on Employment and Social Affairs 26.4.2005 (COM(2004)0002-C5-0069/2004-2004/0001 (COD).

Article 1 a (1):

This Directive does not affect labour relations between workers and employers.

Article 16 (1a):

The mutual recognition principle shall not apply to legal or contractual provisions of the country of destination in the field of consumer protection, environmental protection or labour law, notably remuneration, working conditions and measures relating to health and safety at work. In addition, the mutual recognition principle shall not apply to law relating to reparation of loss and damage.

The background and rational of these proposals are easy to understand. The proposals have the intention of creating an immunity for labour law towards some kind of intervention by the legal regime regarding the free movement of services. There are many aspects to discuss in relation to these proposals and I will try briefly to take up three of them: first, how to define the legitimate interests to protect in respect to labour law, secondly, how to define labour law, and thirdly, how to protect the national labour law regime in the best way.

5.1. The Starting Point

The legitimate interest for protecting national labour law is not only related to direct social dumping generally, but also related to the interest of defending a transparent and open economy and to fight a growing black economy. Issues like procedures, control and surveillance are an important part of national labour law that can be integrated into tax policy, pension policy and the like. Therefore, the potential intervention in national labour law by the new EU free movement for services regime might have a significant impact on national level.

The case law so far and the debate concerning labour law/free movement of services have concerned the issue of discrimination. The struggle has been to avoid discrimination of foreign (EU) service providers/employers on the internal market. In principle there is a large consensus that discrimination towards service providers who are performing a service in another Member State than the one in which they are established should be abolished. There might be, in particular cases, disputes on how we should draw the line between discrimination and non-discrimination, but in principle all serious parties within the EU agree on the implementation of the non-discrimination principle.

The open, and ideologically highly controversial, question is whether we have situations where the foreign service provider in no way faces discrimination (neither direct nor indirect), but where the national labour law, in spite of this, can be regarded as a market restriction for the service provider in such a way that the national legal regime should be set aside in order to promote free movement of services. My interpretation is that this is the point where opinions at present differ significantly and where the demarcation line goes between those in favour, and those against, the Commission proposal for a Services Directive. The fact that the Directive proposal is badly drafted and very unclear offers several possibilities to give different interpretations on how far the Directive might go in this respect.

5.2. The Concept of Labour Law

The problem with introducing labour law as a legal concept in a Directive is that we must be able to define what we mean by labour law. In various Member States, differing opinions on what it does mean prevail. For instance, in a Nordic environment there is no doubt that when we discuss labour law in general we usually include regulation by collective agreements as an element of labour law, but this, to my knowledge, is probably not the case everywhere. The extension of the concept of labour law is also unclear: Is regulation of trade unions as collective organisations labour law etc? Again the answer will differ in various Member States. Also, international labour law might cause problems – when does a regulation form a part of national law?

Does the proposal indicate that we introduce and apply a general common concept in the European Union or does the application differ (in accordance with the principle of mutual recognition) in different Member States?

The proposed "cited" solutions are not fully consistent in the sense that in Article 1, they exclude "labour law" (shall not apply or affect), but then in Article 16, clearly indicate that the mutual recognition principle might have some impact on parts of labour law.

I do not think it is impossible to find a workable description of labour law that could be used in a possible future Services Directive. It must however be much more specific than in the present proposals.

5.3. A Possible Way Forward

The fundamental task for the Services Directive is to further elaborate on and regulate the already existing principle of free movement of services (Article 49 of the Treaty). If we want to regulate the relationship between national labour law (as further specified) and the principle of free movement of services we should do it in relation to Article 49. There are, in my opinion, valid grounds for an argument according to which Article 49 at present does not affect the application of national labour law in the country of destination for a service provider as long as that labour law does not contain any discriminatory elements or is applied in a discriminatory way. A clear statement in the Services Directive that the application of national labour law of the country of destination to service providers from other Members states falls outside the scope of Article 49 of the Treaty and the Directive therefore does not in any way apply to labour law could give a good starting point for a regulatory solution that is based on the existing Treaty and any emanating case law. Such an approach would make it possible to reach balanced solutions where labour law could prevail, but within the context of international private law and other tools of flexibility.

3. MUTUAL RECOGNITION AND COUNTRY OF ORIGIN IN THE CASE LAW OF THE EUROPEAN COURT OF JUSTICE

Ronnie Graham[109]

1. INTRODUCTION

This paper has a limited objective. It seeks to compare the principle of mutual recognition as developed by the European Court of Justice in the context of the free movement of services and freedom of establishment with the principle of country of origin as proposed by the Commission in the context of the free movement of services under the draft Services Directive.[110] The importance of the mutual recognition principle under the current legal framework which governs the field of services will hopefully become apparent. In addition, changes that could be brought to that legal framework by introducing the country of origin principle will, it is also hoped, become clear.

I will deal first with the evolution of the principle of mutual recognition in the case law of the European Court of Justice, and explain how it came to be applied in the context of the freedom to provide services and of freedom of establishment. The second part of this paper will deal with the country of origin principle and will compare it to the mutual recognition principle. Finally, as an additional point, it might be of interest to outline instances in which certain services are already regulated according to country of origin.

2. THE PRINCIPLE OF MUTUAL RECOGNITION

The classic exposition of the principle of mutual recognition is found in *Cassis de Dijon*. As will be remembered, in that case, the Court declared as contrary to the free movement of goods a national prohibition on the marketing of beverages with an alcohol content lower than the limit set by national rules which prevented

---

109 The author alone is responsible for the views expressed in this paper.
110 Proposal for a Directive of the European Parliament and of the Council on services in the internal market (COM(2004)0002).

beverages legally produced and sold in another Member State from entering the national market. The Court stated:

> There is … no valid reason why, provided that they have been lawfully produced and marketed in one of the Member States, alcoholic beverages should not be introduced into any other Member State; the sale of such products may not be subject to a legal prohibition on the marketing of beverages with an alcohol content lower than the limit set by national rules.[111]

The essence of mutual recognition as expressed here in *Cassis de Dijon* is that the recipient state cannot restrict entry into its market of goods of which the production and the marketing are deemed legal in the originating state.

However, there is an exception to that rule. National provisions which restrict movement:

> may be recognized as being necessary in order to satisfy mandatory requirements relating in particular to the effectiveness of fiscal supervision, the protection of public health, the fairness of commercial transactions and the defence of the consumer.[112]

The Court went on to refer to such mandatory requirements as requirements which serve a purpose which is in the general interest.[113]

Along with the mutual recognition principle, that exception has continued to be applied in the case law of the Court concerning freedom of movement, which often uses the formulation: mandatory requirements may be justified on the basis of an overriding public interest.

In addition, the national provision in question ought not to be discriminatory[114] and must be proportionate to the defence of the relevant public interest.

The possibility that restrictive national rules may not breach freedom of movement rules on the basis that they are mandatory requirements justified on the basis of an overriding public interest, and are proportionate, is a crucial characteristic of the principle of mutual recognition. It places a check on free trade, and recalls Article 2 EC that the Community has other objectives in addition to establishing a common market.

---

111   Case 120/78 *Rewe-Zentral v. Bundesmonopolverwaltung für Branntwein* [1979] ECR 649, at para. 14.

112   *Ibid.* para. 8.

113   *Ibid.* para. 14.

114   However, national rules which do not give rise to equal treatment on grounds of nationality may be found to impede freedom of movement and thereby render it illusory. (See, in the context of the freedom to provide services, Case C-76/90 *Manfred Säger v. Dennemeyer & Co. Ltd* [1991] ECR 4221 and in particular para. 12). Therefore discriminatory treatment is not essential to a finding that such rules are an obstacle to freedom of movement.

In the case law which follows *Cassis de Dijon*, mandatory requirements justified on the basis of an overriding public interest have included provisions relating to public policy, public order, the effectiveness of fiscal supervision, protection of public health, fairness of commercial transactions and the defence of the consumer.

A similar approach to that applied by the Court to free movement of goods in *Cassis de Dijon* was subsequently applied in the context of freedom to provide services and freedom of establishment.

However, before referring to the cases in which the Court made that innovation, it is interesting to note that a parallel formulation in the field of services to that given in *Cassis de Dijon* in 1979 was given previously in *Van Binsbergen* in 1974.[115] In that case, the Court ruled that a national rule which required a link between the place of permanent establishment and the place where services are provided contravenes the objective of Article 49 (ex-Article 59). Such a rule effectively transformed the right to provide services in that state, into the right to be established in that state in order to provide those services. Those statements would appear to have a similar effect on services originating in another Member State to mutual recognition as expressed in *Cassis de Dijon*.

There is also a similarity in the exception allowed by the Court: in *Van Binsbergen* such a national rule could be justified on the basis of the defence of a public interest. In this case the national rule could be:

> objectively justified by the need to ensure observance of professional rules of conduct connected, in particular, with the administration of justice and with respect for professional ethics.[116]

Following the ruling in *Cassis de Dijon*, the principle of mutual recognition, as expressed in that case, came to be applied to the free movement of services under Article 49 EC.

A clear application in that context of mutual recognition as defined in *Cassis de Dijon* is found in *Säger*.[117] The Court held that a patent renewal service provider was entitled to provide its services in Germany without complying with what the Court deemed to be over-rigorous national rules. Those rules, although not discriminatory, had the effect of obstructing the UK provider's access to the German market and thereby protecting German providers from competition. They might be justified by "imperative reasons relating to the public interest" so long as the restriction was no more than necessary to achieve the objective pursued. In *Säger*, Germany put forward the justification that the national rules protected consumers from the harm that might result from inadequately qualified providers. The Court considered that consumer protection could constitute a public interest. But it ruled that the services provided were of a straightforward nature and that

---

115   Case 33/74 *Van Binsbergen v. Bestuur van de Bedrijfsvereniging* [1974] ECR 1299.
116   Para. 14 of the judgement.
117   Case C-76/90 *Manfred Säger v. Dennemeyer & Co. Ltd* [1991] ECR I-4221 (cited above).

the German restriction was disproportionate. The national rules were therefore in breach of Article 49 EC.

Säger appears in most respects to be a loyal application of the *Cassis de Dijon* formula. A restriction on inter-state trade is identified, although there is no obvious discrimination against imports; it is accepted that the restriction may be justified on public interest grounds; the issue of whether such grounds exist is examined alongside whether the restriction is proportionate to achieve the defence of that public interest.

By contrast, *Schindler*,[118] in which the Court found that national rules restricting the freedom to provide services could be justified on grounds of maintenance of order in society, illustrates the Court's willingness to accept a justification for restricting the provision of certain services. Having accepted that national rules prohibiting large-scale lotteries irrespective of their origin revealed a restriction on the freedom to provide services, the Court accepted that the rules could be justified on the basis of several public interests which it went on to specify. They contributed to the prevention of crime and the honest treatment of gamblers; they helped to prevent the encouragement of gambling habits; and they allowed legal lotteries to concentrate on charitable, sporting and cultural purposes.

Schindler indicates that the Court has been willing to consider what might constitute an overriding public interest in broad terms. It recalls that in the context of services as elsewhere, the notion of an overriding public interest is open and may be expanded according to the facts of the case.

More recently, the Court has held that restrictions on the provision of services which are imposed by the Member State of origin are equally able to constitute an infringement of Article 49 EC. Here the mutual recognition principle would appear to amount to an obligation on the home state to recognise the right of a provider established in its territory to provide services in another Member State. In the case concerned, *Gourmet International*,[119] state of origin national rules which prohibited advertising alcoholic drinks in publications were challenged by a provider on the basis that the prohibition prevented the provider from offering the service in other Member States. The Court, applying the traditional *Cassis de Dijon* approach, found that there was a restriction on the free provision of services for the following reasons. The prohibition restricted the right of publishers to offer advertising space to potential advertisers in other Member States. The market in advertising alcoholic products had a particularly strong international dimension which meant that the prohibition had a significant effect on the provision of advertising from one Member State to another. Therefore, since there was a restriction on cross-border service provision, the prohibition had to be justified.

In the field of freedom of establishment, the recognition of Member State of origin rules which is established in the contexts of goods and of services in *Cassis*

---

118   Case C-275/92 *Customs and Excise Commissioners v. Schindler and Schindler* [1994] ECR I-1039.

119   Case C-405/98 *Gourmet International Products* [2001] ECR I-1755.

and in *Säger* respectively is most clearly illustrated in *Gebhard*.[120] There, the Court ruled that any national measure which hindered or made less attractive the exercise of the right of establishment must be justified. Of perhaps particular significance is the fact that the Court expressed the *Cassis* formula not only in relation to the freedom of establishment but rather in general terms:

> national measures liable to hinder or make less attractive the exercise of fundamental freedoms guaranteed by the Treaty must fulfil four conditions: they must be applied in a non-discriminatory manner; they must be justified by imperative requirements in the general public interest; they must be suitable for securing the attainment of the objective which they pursue; and they must not go beyond what is necessary in order to attain it.[121]

This *Gebhard* formulation was applied subsequently in the context of freedom of establishment. *Pfeiffer*[122] is typical in this regard. In that case an Austrian company had applied for a restraining order on the use of a brand name in Austria by subsidiaries of a parent company established in Germany which used the same brand name. The Court, having cited the *Gebhard* formulation, ruled:

> A restraining order of the type sought by the plaintiff in the main proceedings operates to the detriment of undertakings whose seat is in another Member State where they lawfully use a trade name which they would like to use beyond the boundaries of that State. Such an order is liable to constitute an impediment to the realisation by those undertakings of a uniform advertising concept at Community level since it may force them to adjust the presentation of the businesses they operate according to the place of establishment.[123]

Read together with *Gebhard*, that ruling seems to suggest that a subsidiary may use in other Member States an advertising concept used by the parent undertaking in its place of establishment unless there are imperative reasons in the general public interest for not doing so.[124] Furthermore any restriction justified by such reasons must be proportionate.

The case law appears to have arrived at a point at which the mutual recognition principle has been both well-defined and widely applied to the free movement of services and the freedom of establishment in the Community. For present purposes, it

---

120 Case C-55/94 *Reinhard Gebhard v. Consiglio dell'Ordine degli Avvocati e Procuratori di Milano* [1995] ECR I-4165.
121 Para. 37 of the judgement.
122 Case C-255/97 *Pfeiffer Grosshandel GmbH v. Löwa Warenhandel GmbH* [1999] ECR I-2835.
123 *Ibid.*, para. 20.
124 *Pfeiffer* makes clear that a restriction on the use of a uniform advertising concept could be justified.

is significant that it acts as a governing principle in the Community legal framework regulating those fields.

3. THE PRINCIPLE OF COUNTRY OF ORIGIN

The country of origin principle and the related derogations set out in the Commission's proposed Services Directive concerns only the free movement of services and, in contrast to other elements of the proposal, does not apply to the freedom of establishment.

I will consider first the characteristics of the country of origin principle and its derogations as set out in the draft Directive, and compare it to the mutual recognition principle as applied by the Court in the context of Article 49 EC. Secondly, it might be helpful to examine the way in which the Court has in the past approached the applicability of home state rules to the provision of services in another Member State.

The primary distinguishing features of the country of origin principle are that the service provider is in general governed by national provisions of his state of origin which fall within the field coordinated by the Directive (Article 16(1)), and that the state of origin is responsible for supervising the provider and his services, including services provided in another Member State (Article 16(2)). It follows that, as a general rule, it is not for the recipient state to supervise,[125] nor to regulate,[126] the cross-border provision of services.

By contrast, under mutual recognition, the general rule is simply the recipient state must recognise that services legally provided in the home state may be provided in its territory.

In other words, the substantial difference for the regulation of cross-border service provision is that under the draft Directive it is expressly stated that home national rules apply to such provision and there is an express obligation on the home state to supervise those services.[127] That is a fundamental development.

---

125 See Article 16(2).

126 See Article 16(1) and (3).

127 Some commentators contrast the positive obligation laid on the home state under the draft Directive with the far from contradictory emphasis on the passive role of the host state under mutual recognition: "*à la différence du principe de reconnaissance mutuelle, le principe du pays d'origine est intrinsèquement lié à la valorisation de la responsabilité de l'Etat d'établissement sur les obligations qui lui incombent, c'est-à-dire contrôler l'activité des prestataires établis sur son territoire afin que lui-même reconnaisse l'efficacité des contrôles effectués par d'autres Etats membres*", Pellegrino and Jeannin, "Proposition de Directive sur les services" in *Gazette du Palais*, 19 May 2005, p. 15. They continue in a footnote: "*Le principe de reconnaissance mutuelle met plutôt l'accent sur le rôle passif de l'Etat membre de destination puisque ce dernier ne peut interdire à la vente tout produit légalement fabriqué dans un autre Etat membre sauf exception liée à des motifs d'intérêt général, protection de la santé, des consommateurs, ou de l'environnement*".

However, on an initial reading of the draft Directive it seems that the recipient state is able to restrict cross-border service provision in ways that to some extent reflect its ability to do so under the mutual recognition principle. The derogations from the country of origin principle that may be invoked by the host Member State are at least in part somewhat similar to the notion of mandatory requirements on the basis of which the host state may be justified in applying restrictive national rules under mutual recognition.

In particular, in the draft Directive, there are three derogations from the country of origin principle that resonate with the notion of mandatory requirements justified by an overriding public interest. First, there is a general derogation in Article 17, subparagraph 16, that the country of origin principle shall not apply to:

> services which, in the Member State to which the provider moves temporarily in order to provide his service, are covered by a total prohibition which is justified by reasons relating to public policy, public security or public health.

A total prohibition on services is likely to apply to far fewer situations than restrictive rules in general which may be justified under the mutual recognition principle. Nonetheless, the grounds on which a total prohibition may be justified under Article 17, subparagraph 16 – public policy, public security and public health – resemble those which may also justify restrictive rules under the mutual recognition principle.

A second, also general, derogation which partly resembles the possibility of justifying restrictive rules under the mutual recognition principle is found at Article 17, subparagraph 17. It states that the country of origin principle shall not apply to:

> specific requirements of the Member State to which the provider moves, that are directly linked to the particular characteristics of the place where the service is provided and with which compliance is indispensable for reasons of public policy or public security or for the protection of public health or the environment.

Specific requirements relating to service provision which are necessary for reasons of public policy, public security, public health or the environment might also reasonably be expected to cover in part mandatory requirements restricting service provision under the mutual recognition principle. And again the justifications for both – in so far as public policy, public security, and the protection of health and the environment are concerned – seem to overlap.

The third derogation that could also be relevant in this regard is not a general derogation but part of a series of what are termed in the draft Directive case-by-case derogations (Article 19). In exceptional circumstances, a Member State may derogate from the country of origin principle in order to take measures relating to:

i.   "the safety of services, including aspects related to public health" (Article 19(1)(a)), or

ii.   "the protection of public policy, notably aspects related to the protection of minors" (Article 19(1)(c)).

However, reliance on this third derogation is subject to a number of further conditions: the recipient state must have asked in vain the home state to take sufficient measures with regard to the service provider;[128] there must be no Community harmonisation in the field concerned; the measures must provide for a higher level of protection of the recipient than would be the case in the country of origin; and the measures must be proportionate.[129]

The second, third and fourth of those conditions reflect the ability of the recipient state to restrict cross-border service provision under the mutual recognition principle. But the first of those conditions – the following of the mutual assistance procedure – clearly distinguishes this third derogation from the possibility of justifying restrictive host state rules under the mutual recognition principle.

In addition, it should be noted there are several other derogations, either general, transitional or case-by-case in nature, which do not explicitly relate to the justification of restrictive host state rules under mutual recognition.[130]

4.   PREVIOUS APPLICATION OF HOME STATE RULES UNDER ARTICLE 49 EC

Finally, it may be of interest to address situations in which the Court has until now considered the applicability of home state rules in the context of the cross-border provision of services. In view of the importance in the case law of the mutual recognition principle in this area, it hardly needs mentioning that until now the Court has not in general applied the country of origin principle.

Special cases in which the Court has considered the applicability of home state rules to the provision of services in another Member State are of at least two kinds. First, there are cases in which the Court has ruled that home state rules – rather than simply host state rules – which restrict the free provision of services, are contrary to Article 49 EC. Second, the Court has of course applied home state rules to the cross-border provision of services where Community legislation provides that particular types of service provision are to be regulated by the country of origin.

---

128   Article 37(2) and Article 19(2)(c) of the draft Directive. This request is a central component of what is termed "the mutual assistance procedure".

129   Article 19(2).

130   See Articles 17, 18, and 19(c).

In the first category of cases, the Court has held that restrictions on the free provision of services in a host Member State may arise from rules applicable in the provider's home state as well as from host state rules.[131]

The Court's approach in those cases does not appear to coincide with circumstances in which a country of origin principle must be applied. Indeed, they reach the opposite conclusion: country of origin rules restricting service provision in another Member State should not be applied. Those cases, although they signal important developments in the evolution of the case law under Article 49 EC, are therefore not entirely central to the present discussion.

In the second, more significant, instance the Court has simply applied Community legislation which provides that service provision should be governed by home state rules. Before referring to the case law, it may be useful to mention the legislation. Some of the most significant Community instruments in this area have been Council Directive 89/552/EEC, the Television without Frontiers Directive,[132] financial services directives – the First Banking Directive,[133] the Second Banking Coordination Directive,[134] the Investment Services Directive,[135] the Third Generation Insurance Directives[136] – the directive on the protection of personal data[137] and Directive 98/5/EC facilitating the practice of the legal profession on a permanent basis in a Member State other than that in which the qualification was obtained.[138]

In relation to some of those directives, the introduction of home state regulation appears practical for reasons associated with the type of service. In the case of the Television without Frontiers Directive, for example, it would seem obvious to control television broadcasts in the Member State in which they are made. Accordingly, Article 2 of that directive provides that "each Member State shall ensure

---

131 See Cases C-384/93 *Alpine Investments v. Minister van Financiën* [1995] ECR I-1141 at paras 29-31; C-70/95 *Sodemare et al. v. Regione Lombardia* [1997] ECR I-3395 at paras 36-37; C-60/00 *Mary Carpenter v. Secretary of State for the Home Department* [2002] ECR I-6279 at para. 39, although the decision that the home state measure infringed Article 49 EC was disproportionate in that case also took into account breach of Article 8 of the European Convention on Human Rights.

132 Of 3 October 1989 (OJ 1989 L298, p. 23).

133 Directive 77/780/EEC (OJ 1977 L322).

134 Directive 89/646/EEC (OJ 1989 L386).

135 Directive 93/22/EEC (OJ 1993 L141).

136 Directive 92/49/EEC Third Insurance (Life) Directive (OJ 1992 L228); Directive 92/96/EEC Third Insurance (Non-Life) Directive (OJ 1992 L360). Both Directives were amended by Directive 95/26/EC amending Directives 77/780/EEC and 89/646/EEC in the field of credit institutions, Directives 73/239/EEC and 92/49/EEC in the field of non-life insurance, Directives 79/267/EEC and 92/96/EEC in the field of life assurance, Directive 93/22/EEC in the field of investment firms and Directive 85/611/EEC in the field of undertakings for collective investment in transferable securities (Ucits), with a view to reinforcing prudential supervision (OJ 1995 L168, p. 7).

137 This Directive uses a different notion of the country of origin principle; it is the establishment of the "controller" rather than the establishment of the provider that is determinative of country of origin.

138 Directive of the European Parliament and of the Council of 16 February 1998 (OJ 1998 L77, p. 36).

that all television broadcasts transmitted by broadcasters under its jurisdiction, or by broadcasters who, while not being under the jurisdiction of any Member State, make use of a frequency or a satellite capacity granted by, or a satellite link-up situated in, that Member State, comply with the law applicable to broadcasts intended for the public in that Member State". The directive goes on to prohibit receiving Member States from restricting transmission of broadcasts from other Member States (Article 3).

The division between home state and host state regulation in the Second Banking Coordination Directive and the Investment Services Directive similarly seems to adopt a functional approach. For instance, the importance of capital and infrastructure to commercial banks means that they are subject to regulation (more so than investment banks, for example). As a result, capital and infrastructure tend to be a matter preferably regulated by the home state. Additionally, since commercial banking raises less frequently (compared to investment banking) issues of product control, it makes practical sense to regulate this activity in the home state.[139]

The strategy for application of home state control appears to have been developed most fully in the financial services directives. It has been described as follows. The home state authorises and prudentially regulates financial service providers established on their territory. That authorisation is recognised across the Community (clearly there is an overlap here with the mutual recognition approach), resulting in a "single European passport" for the provider. Harmonisation of minimum or "key" national regulatory standards must take place to allow the principle of home state control to work.[140]

But without full harmonisation in national regulatory systems, national regulators operate to some extent under their own and therefore different laws and regulatory powers must be divided between home and host state systems. Consequently, the principle of home state control is partly compromised.[141] And, as discussed below, the distribution of regulatory powers between the two states may not be clear.

Directive 98/5 facilitating the practice of the legal profession on a permanent basis in a Member State other than that in which the qualification was obtained may be of further interest since it relates to the situation in which the provider actually moves to the territory of the receiving Member State to offer services. However, the extent to which a country of origin principle in fact applies to lawyers practising in

---

139 *Dalhuisen on International Commercial, Financial and Trade Law* (2004), pp. 1000-1001.

140 Lomnicka "The Home Country Control Principle in the Financial Services Directive and the Case-Law" in *Services and Free Movement in EU Law* (2002) eds. Andenas and Roth, pp. 297-305.

141 Although, as has been pointed out, the harmonisation that has taken place under the Second Banking Coordination Directive and the Investment Services Directive has "proved decisive progress and allowed the European passport for intermediaries in the financial services industries to emerge largely under their own law and own (home) supervisor (with the regulatory competition connected with it), except for the conduct of consumer business which basically remains under host country supervision" (Dalhuisen, "Financial Liberalisation and Re-regulation" in Andenas and Roth (eds), *Services and Free Movement in EU Law* (2002), at p. 286).

another Member State under that Directive appears to be limited. Article 2 states that any lawyer shall be entitled to pursue on a permanent basis, in any other Member State under his home-country professional title, the legal activities specified in the Directive (at Article 5). Otherwise, the lawyer practising in a Member State other than that in which he is qualified appears to be subject to host state rules, such as registration (Article 3) and rules of professional conduct (Article 6).

Turning to the interpretation by the Court of the country of origin principle under those directives, that principle seems to have been applied with caution.

As regards the Television without Frontiers Directive, the Court appears on the one hand to have applied the country of origin principle in a fairly literal manner.[142] On the other hand, it appears also to have drawn attention to Treaty provisions and previous case law under which the host state may justify imposing restrictions on services originating in another Member State,[143] and it has been relatively generous in interpreting provisions which permit the host state to justify such restrictions.[144]

In the field of the financial services directives, the Court has made clear that the principle of home state control does not take precedence over Treaty provisions or other rules of Community law in the banking sphere.

In *Germany v. Parliament and Council*,[145] a challenge was made to the Directive on deposit-guarantee schemes which partly intended to introduce an element of home state control over consumer protection in the context of such schemes. That Directive was to accompany the introduction of home state control under the Second Banking Coordination Directive. In part, Germany contested a provision of the Directive on deposit-guarantee schemes under which the host state was to ensure that an authorised credit institution established in another Member State and operating in its territory could join a host state scheme in order to supplement a guarantee which was lower than that available to depositors under the host state scheme. Germany argued that such a provision infringed the principle of home state control established under the Second Banking Coordination Directive.

The Court rejected Germany's submission that the principle of home state supervision had been infringed.[146] It ruled:

---

142   See for example Joined Cases C-34/95, C-35/95 and C-36/95 *Konsumentombudsmannen v. De Agostini* and *Konsumentombudsmannen v. TV Shop* [1997] ECR I-3843 at paras 56-62.

143   *Ibid.*, paras 36-37 and 39-54. In relation to the application of home state control conferred by directives, one commentator states the Court "generally starts from first principles, giving priority to the relevant Treaty provisions and its own case law rather than those of the Directives" (Lomnicka "The Home Country Control Principle in the Financial Services Directive and the Case-Law" in *Services and Free Movement in EU Law* (2002) eds. Andenas and Roth, p. 316).

144   See Case C-412/93 *Leclerc-Siplec* [1995] ECR-179, at paras 45-47, where the Court stated that Article 3(1) of the Directive contained no restriction whatever as to which interests could justify the imposition by the host state of stricter rules on broadcasters established in another Member State compared to the rules of the home state.

145   Case 233/94 [1997] ECR I-2405.

146   Reaching a similar conclusion to the Court, in his Opinion in the case Advocate General Léger addressed in detail Germany's submissions on the importance of the principle of home state control (paras 124-131).

it has not been proved that the Community legislature laid down the principle of home State supervision in the sphere of banking law with the intention of systematically subordinating all other rules in that sphere to that principle. Second, since it is not a principle laid down by the Treaty, the Community legislature could depart from it, provided that it did not infringe the legitimate expectations of the persons concerned. Since it had not yet acted in regard to the guarantee of deposits, no such legitimate expectations could exist.[147]

In *Alpine Investments*,[148] the Court did not address the significance of the home country control principle introduced by the Investment Services Directive in a case concerning a national prohibition on cold-calling in other Member States as a marketing practice in commodities futures trading. It seems unlikely that the Directive could have been considered applicable since it does not refer to investment services relating to commodities futures[149] and it had not been adopted at the relevant time. On the other hand, it might have been considered relevant to the case as a legal framework adopted to permit greater free movement of services for investment firms.[150] However, in finding that the home state could justify – by relying on the public interest in the good reputation of the national financial sector – a restriction on cold-calling to other Member States by providers offering services in the field of commodities future trading, the Court referred to Article 59 (now Article 49) EC.

The Advocate General's Opinion in the case points to the difficulty in understanding the division of regulatory powers between home and host state under the home country control principle as expressed in the Investment Services Directive.[151]

That observation, although made in relation to a sector-specific directive, seems particularly relevant in considering the implications of applying the country of origin principle to cross-border service provision as the Commission's draft Directive recommends.[152]

---

147   Para. 64 of the judgement.
148   Cited above in footnote 131.
149   See sections A and B of the Annex to the Investment Services Directive.
150   See para. 14 of the Opinion of Advocate General Jacobs in the case.
151   See paras 15-19.
152   Articles 34-38 of the draft Directive set out detailed provisions for mutual assistance to ensure effective supervision. But elements of the mutual assistance procedure contained in those provisions, such as the establishment in each Member State of single points of contact and electronic exchange of information, indicate that the division of tasks and sharing of information is likely to be complex. Moreover, conferral of jurisdiction under rules of international law (see the Explanatory Memorandum to the draft Directive, at p. 17) may give rise to further difficulties. Were such rules to confer jurisdiction on the courts of the host state in a case concerning cross-border service provision, how would those courts apply the principle (in Article 16(1) of the draft Directive) that the provider is subject exclusively to the national provisions of his home state?

In conclusion, examining previous use of a country of origin principle in the context of the free movement of services demonstrates that there may be practical benefits to its application in particular service sectors. But, because use of the principle has been confined, it does not indicate the effects that its general application to the services market might have. However, as far as derogation from the country of origin principle is concerned, a degree of similarity exists between the possibilities in that regard under the draft Services Directive and the possibility of justifying restrictive national rules on the basis of an overriding public interest under the mutual recognition principle. On that basis, despite a fundamental difference between the two principles, there may nonetheless be an important degree of overlap between them. Perhaps then it is the case law on mutual recognition that deserves our attention as we attempt to envisage the implications of applying a country of origin principle to the freedom to provide services.

4. THE COUNTRY OF ORIGIN PRINCIPLE AND LABOUR LAW IN THE FRAMEWORK OF THE EUROPEAN SOCIAL MODEL

Alan C. Neal

1. INTRODUCTION

Given recent high-profile events within the context of endeavours by the European Commission to promote the proposed Services Directive in the European Union, it appeals to the sense of humour of a United Kingdom observer to note that phenomena such as public misrepresentation of European Union initiatives for the purpose of short-term domestic political advantage, the promotion of ill-informed (even uninformed) public debate, and highly selective media coverage of activity at the European level, are not confined to the shores of "perfidious Albion"!

Even the most sympathetic observer could hardly suggest that this proposed measure has had an easy time of things lately. Hijacked just before Easter 2005 as part of the French domestic debate during President Chirac's unsuccessful referendum campaign, and subsequently attacked on a number of fronts within the European Parliament, the future progress of the draft Directive remains unclear. Indeed, what is arguably one of the most important measures with the potential to extricate the Lisbon Strategy from the sorry plight described by *Kok II* stands facing an uncertain fate as the gathering fall-out from French and Dutch rejection of the 2004 Treaty of Rome begins to be increasingly evident.[153]

In what follows, I have confined myself to a few comments in relation to the particular issues raised by the so-called "country of origin principle" for labour law within the framework of the European Social Model.

---

153 See the Report of the High Level Group on the Lisbon Strategy ("Kok II"), *Facing the Challenge* (presented 3 November 2004). For recent critical receptions for various parts of the proposal within the European Parliament, see, *inter alia*, the first draft opinion (presented on 8 April 2005) from the Rapporteur for the European Parliament Committee on the Internal Market and Consumer Protection (Evelyne Gebhardt), and the draft opinion (presented on 10 May 2005) from the Rapporteur for the European Parliament's Committee on Employment and Social Affairs for the Committee on the Internal Market and Consumer Protection (Anne Van Lancker). The proposal had already shown itself capable of provoking great controversy – see, for example, the events and outcomes of the European Council meeting on 25 & 26 November 2004 in Brussels, set out in Press Release 14687/04 (Presse 323) on the 2624th Council Meeting – Competitiveness (Internal Market, Industry and Research).

2. A DIRECTIVE ON SERVICES IN THE EUROPEAN UNION[154]

The opening up of the services sector at the level of the European Union now forms a significant part of the post-Lisbon version of the European Employment Strategy established in 1997. Initiatives introduced within the context of this process are seen as an element in the completion of the Single Market, with services being regarded as one of the major outstanding areas still in need of attention. In consequence, the underlying motivation for developing an instrument to deal with the provision of services in the European Union remains as set out in the Commission's communication *An Internal Market for Services,* reflecting decisions reached at the Lisbon European Council.[155]

The mantra derived from that 2000 Lisbon Summit – setting an objective for the European Union "… to become the most competitive and dynamic knowledge-based economy in the world capable of sustainable economic growth with more and better jobs and greater social cohesion" has been taken as a quasi-justification for all sorts of "open market" initiatives.[156]

The proposed Directive would apply to providers of services who are established in a Member State.[157] In this context, the definitions provided in Article 4 include "*services*" being defined by reference to provision of a service "for consideration"; "*provider*" including "any legal person" who offers or provides a service; and "*Member State of origin*" being "the Member State in whose territory the provider of the service concerned is established". Meanwhile, "*Member State of posting*" is defined as meaning "the Member State in whose territory a provider posts a worker in order to provide services there".

Chapter II of the proposed Directive addresses the objective of administrative simplification in respect of arrangements regulating the freedom for service providers to establish themselves in a Member State. The primary device for achieving this simplification is the establishment, by 31 December 2008, of so-called "*single points of contact*",[158] which are the conduits through which Member States are obliged to facilitate the provision of information and assistance.[159] Article 8 also requires all "procedures and formalities" relating to access to a service activity or exercise of a service activity to be capable of being completed "at a distance and by electronic means".

---

154 References in this paper to the "Directive" are to the draft of the proposal submitted by the European Commission – see COM(2004) 2 final/3, *Proposal for a Directive of the European Parliament and of the Council on services in the internal market.*

155 COM(2000) 888 final, of 29 December 2000, *Communication from the Commission to the Council and the European Parliament, An Internal Market Strategy for Services.* The roots, however, need to be traced back to the era of the Single European Act – see COM(1985) 310, White Paper from the Commission to the European Council, *Completing the Internal Market.*

156 See *Presidency Conclusions*, Lisbon European Council, 23-24 March 2000, (SN 100/00).

157 Article 1(1).

158 Article 6.

159 Article 7.

Articles 9-13 deal with "authorisations", in situations where "*authorisation schemes*" (defined in Article 4 as "any procedure under which a provider or recipient is in effect required to take steps in order to obtain from a competent authority a formal decision, or an implied decision, concerning access to a service activity or to the exercise thereof") are established by a Member State. As a first step, Article 9 prohibits service provision being subject to any such authorisation scheme unless the scheme is non-discriminatory, is objectively justified by "an overriding reason relating to the public interest", and the objective of the scheme cannot be attained by means of a less restrictive measure. Where, however, such a scheme is introduced, the conditions for a grant of authorisation have to satisfy a list of criteria set out in Article 10(2) – which reiterate the basic Article 9 requirements, and add to these the requirement that the criteria be "precise and unambiguous", that they be "objective", and that they are made public in advance. There is concern that any such conditions should not effectively duplicate requirements already made of the provider either in that or another Member State.[160] Further stipulations provide for any authorisation to be applicable "throughout the national territory", to be granted as soon as it is established that the relevant conditions have been met, and for any refusal of authorisation to be accompanied by full reasons which are susceptible to challenge before the courts. These basic limits upon the operation of authorisation schemes are further amplified in Articles 11-13, which include restrictions upon making authorisation granted only for a limited period, as well as emphasising the need for timely and objective decision-making, such that any procedures and formalities for authorisation "shall not be dissuasive and shall not unduly complicate or delay the provision of the service".[161]

Article 14 sets out a list of potential compliance requirements which are absolutely prohibited. Meanwhile, Article 15 requires Member States to examine whether their systems impose any of a given list of requirements, and, if so, places a duty upon any such Member State to verify that such requirement satisfies the three tests of "non-discrimination", "necessity" and "proportionality".[162] The demand that Article 15(3) be satisfied applies both to existing requirements (which have to be examined and evaluated) and to any new requirement (which may only be introduced provided that it satisfies Article 15(3)). Stringent reporting and notification duties are placed upon the Member States to ensure that matters potentially falling within this part of the Directive are brought to the notice of the Commission.

---

160   See Article 10(3).
161   Article 13(2).
162   Article 15(3).

3. THE COUNTRY OF ORIGIN PRINCIPLE: COMPLETING THE INTERNAL MARKET FOR GOODS AND SERVICES

3.1. The "Principle"

Chapter III of the proposed Directive, which also bears the sub-heading "free movement of services", deals with what is described as the "country of origin principle" and with derogations from that principle.

This "country of origin principle" owes its early development to the case law of the European Court of Justice in the context of the free movement of goods. In particular, since the landmark ruling in the *Cassis de Dijon* case,[163] a number of strands have come together which make clear the prohibition against directly or indirectly discriminatory measures which cannot be justified on narrow "public policy" grounds such as public health and safety. Consequently, at the risk of gross over-simplification, once a product or item has entered the single market in conformity with the regulatory requirements of the Member State into which it has been received, it is anticipated that there should, in general, be no fresh obstacle raised to the free movement of that item.

3.2. The Problem

The outstanding problem for labour law lies in the fact that (whatever certain schools of economic theory on the shores of Lake Michigan might have us believe) workers and the strength or skills which they embody do not lend themselves easily to regulation through mechanisms developed and designed for "goods". To put the point most sharply, in the words of the 1944 Declaration of Philadelphia, which underlies the entire value system of the international labour standards regime overseen by the ILO, "Labour is not a commodity".

Even putting aside the theoretical and moral objection to utilisation of a device such as the so-called "country of origin principle" in the field of labour, a further significant factor comes into play in the form of an acknowledged need to respect collectively bargained arrangements in respect of pay and other terms and conditions of work. This need is justified on the basis of ensuring stability and equity in the labour markets of developed economies, and as a basis for a "floor of rights" to be assured to citizens working within the labour markets of those economies. Put shortly, there is a widely-held view that collectively bargained arrangements

---

163   Case C-120/78, *Rewe-Zentrale AG v. Bundesmonopolverwaltung für Branntwein*, [1979] ECR 649. For comment, see, *inter alia, K.J. Alter, & S. Meuner-Aitsahalia*, "Judicial Politics in the European Community: European Integration and the Pathbreaking *Cassis de Dijon* Decision", (1994) 26 *Comparative Political Studies* 535.

should not be susceptible to interference or undermining through various forms of what is often regarded as "social dumping".

Linked to this objection is the interest in ensuring the susceptibility of employing enterprises to supervision, monitoring and control for the labour standards which they apply, and in respect of national labour law developed, by and large, in order to protect the perceived "weaker party" to the employment relationship.

Here is not the place to debate at any length whether such arguments in favour of separate treatment for labour law subjects is economically justified, objectively justified, or morally desirable. Suffice it to point out that – particularly in the context of a Europe which aspires, in a large number of the EU Member States, to a "European Social Model" along the lines described at Barcelona,[164] – the clash of ideologies, depending upon whether one sets out from a "social" or an "economic" perspective, makes for lively controversy in a context such as the provision of services across the expanded post-2004 European Union.

3.3. The Response of the Proposed Services Directive

So far as the proposed Services Directive is concerned, Article 16 spells out what is encompassed within the "country of origin principle", and proceeds from the basic proposition that "Member States shall ensure that providers are subject only to the national provisions of their Member State of origin which fall within the coordinated field" (where "Member State of origin" is as indicated above, and "the coordinated field" means "any requirement applicable to access to service activities or to the exercise thereof").

It is then provided that responsibility for supervising the provider and the services provided by him (including those provided in another Member State) rests with the Member State of origin. Furthermore, Member States are prohibited, so far as reasons falling within "the coordinated field" are concerned, from restricting the freedom to provide services in the case of a provider established in another Member State.[165]

Having set out the notion of the "country of origin principle", however, the proposed Directive then proceeds to lay down:

(i)   "General derogations";[166]
(ii)   "Transitional derogations";[167] and
(iii)   "Case-by-case derogations".[168]

---

164 *Supra.*
165 Article 16(3), which goes on to set out an indicative list of acts/measures which would be so prohibited.
166 Article 17.
167 Article 18.
168 Article 18.

Among these, Article 17 is of particular significance, since one of the general deroga-tions provided for is in relation to "(5) matters covered by Directive 96/71/EC" – i.e. the instrument well-known to labour lawyers as the "Posted Workers Directive". Other pertinent general derogations include "(11) in the case of the posting of third country nationals, the requirement for a short stay visa imposed by the Member State of posting, subject to the conditions set out in Article 25(2)", and "(20) the freedom of parties to choose the law applicable to their contract".

Where "case-by-case derogations" are concerned, these include the possibility, "in exceptional circumstances only", for a Member State to take measures in relation to a provider established in another Member State which relate to (a) "the safety of services, including aspects related to public health", (b) "the exercise of a health profession", or (c) "the protection of public policy, notably aspects related to the protection of minors".[169] Any such measure taken under this Article's provisions have to satisfy the significant threshold established by Article 19(2) – including an all-embracing requirement that they be "proportionate".

Articles 20–23 then address issues touching the rights of recipients of services, outlawing certain measures,[170] underlining the prohibition against "discriminatory requirements based upon … nationality or place of residence",[171] and setting out the necessity for certain forms of assistance to be provided for recipients of services.[172] As part of this concern for the rights of recipients of services, Article 23 contains specific provisions relating to the assumption of healthcare costs by Member States, and seeking to ensure that timely and "medically acceptable" arrangements are put in place in relation to this matter.

4. "LABOUR IS NOT A COMMODITY"[173] – THE PARTICULAR PROBLEM OF LABOUR LAW AND THE COUNTRY OF ORIGIN PRINCIPLE

4.1. Perceptions of "Abuse"

As has been indicated, the "country of origin principle" has been perceived to pose particular problems and carry special threats in the field of labour law. However, it should be noted that other fields – such as consumer protection and environmental protection – have also been identified as suffering from broadly similar difficulties. However, the particular nature of the threat to labour law and to the floor of rights established at national level and through implementation of the "European Social

---

169   Article 19(1).
170   Article 20.
171   Article 21.
172   Article 22.
173   United Nations, *Declaration of Philadelphia* (1944), I (a).

Model" is sometimes considered to render this a special problem unique to labour law.

One of the reasons for such a view lies in the very fact that the arrangements in different Member States for the setting of pay and other terms and conditions of work, collective bargaining, and, more recently, social dialogue, are so variegated and considered not to be susceptible to harmonisation through classical approaches known to European Union law.[174] In consequence, the arrangements in these respects which are established at national level have come to be carefully framed to take account of the peculiarities of that national context, including not only the institutional relationships to be found within the industrial relations and labour market structures but also the mechanisms for supervision, control, and enforcement of rights. Thus, there is a strong sense of resistance to any suggestion that the nationally established "floor of rights" should be rendered vulnerable to undermining phenomena (often dismissively characterised as variants of "social dumping") which might destabilise or circumvent normative provisions contained in law or collective agreements.

More controversially, it is said, the activity of temporary work placement is seen as a particular area in which "the perils of the free market" may be at odds with "employment protection" values enshrined in the so-called "European Social Model" as it has been identified in recent years.[175] Indeed, this sector of economic activity has for some time been the focus for unsuccessful attempts by the European Commission to launch regulation by way of a Directive – the most recent failure having left the initiative in political "limbo".[176]

In joined cases C-369/96 and C-376/96, *Arblade* and *Leloup*,[177] the European Court of Justice made it clear that Member States are not entitled to impose differential obligations upon enterprises providing temporary work services, in respect of the keeping of records or the payment of special fees in respect of their activities. However, the European Court of Justice did go on to hold that,

---

174 See, for a particularly acute analysis and assessment of this issue, the report prepared for the European Commission by the late Professor Gerard Lyon-Caen, *In Search of the European Collective Bargaining Agreement. Study of Mr. Lyon-Caen*, Doc. V/855/72-E See, too, the report prepared for the European Commission by Friedrich Fürstenberg, Mario Grandi, Alan C. Neal and Jean-Daniel Reynaud, *Les règles du jeu: Industrial Relations in Four Community Countries – Similarities and Uncertainties as Regards the Rules Governing Them,* Doc. V/1433/86.

175 See the formulation adopted at the Barcelona European Council, in March 2002, to the effect that "The European social model is based on good economic performance, a high level of social protection and education and social dialogue."

176 The proposed Directive on temporary work seeks to introduce an additional – and different in kind – model for regulating the field of temporary work placement: the "principle of equal treatment", in common with existing provisions relating to part-time and fixed-term workers. See COM(2002) 701 final – *Amended proposal for a Directive of the European Parliament and the Council on working conditions for temporary workers.*

177 [1999] ECR I-8453.

Articles 59 and 60 of the Treaty do not preclude the imposition by a Member State on an undertaking established in another Member State, and temporarily carrying out work in the first State, of an obligation to pay the workers deployed by it the minimum remuneration fixed by the collective labour agreement applicable in the first Member State, provided that the provisions in question are sufficiently precise and accessible that they do not render it impossible or excessively difficult in practice for such an employer to determine the obligations with which he is required to comply.

In its judgement, the European Court of Justice indicated a number of general basic principles relating to the provision of services at the interface with labour market activity. Thus:

33. It is settled case-law that Article 59 of the Treaty requires not only the elimination of all discrimination on grounds of nationality against providers of services who are established in another Member State but also the abolition of any restriction, even if it applies without distinction to national providers of services and to those of other Member States, which is liable to prohibit, impede or render less advantageous the activities of a provider of services established in another Member State where he lawfully provides similar services...;[178]

34. Even if there is no harmonisation in the field, the freedom to provide services, as one of the fundamental principles of the Treaty, may be restricted only by rules justified by overriding requirements relating to the public interest and applicable to all persons and undertakings operating in the territory of the State where the service is provided, in so far as that interest is not safeguarded by the rules to which the provider of such a service is subject in the Member State where he is established...;[179]

35. The application of national rules to providers of services established in other Member States must be appropriate for securing the attainment of the objective which they pursue and must not go beyond what is necessary in order to attain it...;[180]

---

178 See Case C-76/90 *Säger* [1991] ECR I-4221, para. 12, Case C-43/93 *Vander Elst v. Office des Migrations Internationales* [1994] ECR I-3803, para. 14, Case C-272/94 *Guiot* [1996] ECR I-1905, para. 10, Case C-3/95 *Reisebüro Broede v. Sandker* [1996] ECR I-6511, para. 25, and Case C-222/95 *Parodi v. Banque H. Albert de Bary* [1997] ECR I-3899, para. 18.
179 See, in particular, Case 279/80 *Webb* [1981] ECR 3305, para. 17, Case C-180/89 *Commission v. Italy* [1991] ECR I-709, para. 17, Case C-198/89 *Commission v. Greece* [1991] ECR I-727, para. 18, *Säger*, cited above, para. 15, *Vander Elst*, cited above, para. 16, and *Guiot*, cited above, para. 11.
180 See, in particular, *Säger*, para. 15, Case C-19/92 *Kraus v. Land Baden-Württemberg* [1993] ECR I-1663, para. 32, Case C-55/94 *Gebhard v. Consiglio dell'Ordine degli Avvocati e Procurati di*

36. The overriding reasons relating to the public interest which have been acknowledged by the Court include the protection of workers…;[181]

37. By contrast, considerations of a purely administrative nature cannot justify derogation by a Member State from the rules of Community law, especially where the derogation in question amounts to preventing or restricting the exercise of one of the fundamental freedoms of Community law…;[182]

38. However, overriding reasons relating to the public interest which justify the substantive provisions of a set of rules may also justify the control measures needed to ensure compliance with them…;[183]

The issue of "posting of workers" emerged in the context of litigation before the European Court of Justice in relation to the construction of a new high-speed railway line in France, and resulted in legislative action at the level of the European Union, with a view to addressing some of the perceived threats to the framework of labour law and regulation established throughout the majority of the European industrial relations systems of the time. That litigation concerned the case of *Rush Portuguesa Lda v. Office national d'immigration (National Immigration Office)*[184] and the eventual outcome was the adoption of Directive 96/71/EC, of the European Parliament and of the Council, of 16 December 1996, concerning the posting of workers in the framework of the provision of services.[185]

The regulatory framework established under the 1996 Directive is generally considered to represent a response to the issues highlighted before the Court of Justice in *Rush Portuguesa*, where (under the former numbering of what are now Articles 49 and 50 of the Treaty Establishing the European Community) the Court was asked the following questions:

1.   Does Community law taken as a whole, and in particular Article 5 and Articles 58 to 66 of the Treaty of Rome and Article 2 of the Act of Accession of Portugal to the European Community, authorise a founding Member State of

---

Milano [1995] ECR I-4165, para. 37, and *Guiot*, cited above, paras 11 and 13.

181   See *Webb*, cited above, para. 19, Joined Cases 62/81 and 63/81 *Seco v. EVI* [1982] ECR 223, para. 14, and Case C-113/89 *Rush Portuguesa* [1990] ECR I-1417, para. 18), and in particular the social protection of workers in the construction industry (*Guiot*, para. 16).

182   See, in particular, Case C-18/95 *Terhoeve* [1999] ECR I-345, para. 45.

183   See, to that effect, *Rush Portuguesa*, cited above, para. 18.

184   Case C-113/89, *Rush Portuguesa Lda v. Office national d'immigration (National Immigration Office)*, [1990] ECR I-1417. Reference for a preliminary ruling by the Tribunal administratif de Versailles, France. Judgement of the Court (Sixth Chamber) of 27 March 1990.

185   The legislative initiative was launched in 1991, with COM(1991) 230 final, *Proposal for a Council Directive concerning the posting of workers in the framework of the provision of services*, followed by COM(1993) 225 final, *Amended Proposal for a Council Directive concerning the posting of workers in the framework of the provisions of services*

the Community, such as France, to preclude a Portuguese company whose registered office is in Portugal from providing services in the building and public works sector on the territory of that Member State by going there with its own Portuguese workforce so that the workforce may carry out work there in its name and on its account in connection with those services, on the understanding that the Portuguese workforce is to return, and does in fact return, immediately to Portugal once its task has been carried out and the provision of the services has been completed?

2.   May the right of a Portuguese company to provide services throughout the Community be made subject by the founding Member States of the EEC to conditions, in particular relating to the engagement of labour *in situ*, the obtaining of work permits for its own Portuguese staff or the payment of fees to an official immigration body?

3.   May the workforce, which has been the subject of the disputed special contributions, and whose names and qualifications are mentioned in the list appearing in the annex to the reports drawn up by the labour inspector recording the breaches committed by Rush Portuguesa, be regarded as "specialised staff or employees occupying a post of a confidential nature" within the meaning of the provisions of the annex to Regulation No. 1612/68 of the Council of 15 October 1968?

In response, the Court of Justice held that:

> Articles 59 and 60 of the EEC Treaty and Articles 215 and 216 of the Act of Accession of the Kingdom of Spain and the Portuguese Republic must be interpreted as meaning that an undertaking established in Portugal providing services in the construction and public works sector in another Member State may move with its own work-force which it brings from Portugal for the duration of the works in question. In such a case, the authorities of the Member State in whose territory the works are to be carried out may not impose on the supplier of services conditions relating to the recruitment of manpower *in situ* or the obtaining of work permits for the Portuguese work-force.

4.2. The Posted Workers Directive

The eventually ensuing Directive 96/71/EC was adopted on 16 December 1996 and required transposition by 16 December 1999.[186]

To use the Commission's description of the purpose underlying the Directive, it is said to have been adopted in order:

---

186   Article 7.

to abolish the obstacles and uncertainties that impede implementation of the freedom to supply services, by improving legal certainty and facilitating identification of the employment conditions that apply to workers temporarily employed in a Member State other than the Member State whose legislation governs the employment relationship. It endeavours to strike a balance between the economic freedoms bestowed by the EC Treaty and employees' rights during their period of posting.[187]

By virtue of its Article 1(1) and Article 1(3)(c), the Directive applies to the activities of temporary work agencies established in a Member State when, in the framework of the trans-national provision of services, and being what is described as "a temporary employment undertaking or placement agency", they hire out a worker to a user undertaking established or operating in the territory of a Member State, "provided there is an employment relationship between the temporary employment undertaking or placement agency and the worker during the period of posting".

Article 3 of the Directive, which is entitled "Terms and conditions of employment", provides that:

1. Member States shall ensure that, whatever the law applicable to the employment relationship, the undertakings referred to in Article 1(1) guarantee workers posted to their territory the terms and conditions of employment covering the following matters which, in the Member State where the work is carried out, are laid down:
    – by law, regulation or administrative provision, and/or
    – by collective agreements or arbitration awards which have been declared universally applicable within the meaning of paragraph 8, in so far as they concern the activities referred to in the Annex:
    (a) maximum work periods and minimum rest periods;
    (b) minimum paid annual holidays;
    (c) the minimum rates of pay, including overtime rates; this point does not apply to supplementary occupational retirement pension schemes;
    (d) the conditions of hiring-out of workers, in particular the supply of workers by temporary employment undertakings;
    (e) health, safety and hygiene at work;
    (f) protective measures with regard to the terms and conditions of employment of pregnant women or women who have recently given birth, of children and of young people;
    (g) equality of treatment between men and women and other provisions on non-discrimination.

---

187   See COM(2003) 458 final, Communication from the Commission to the Council, the European Parliament, the Economic and Social Committee and the Committee of the Regions, *The Implementation of Directive 96/71/EC in the Member States*.

> For the purposes of this Directive, the concept of minimum rates of pay referred to in paragraph 1(c) is defined by the national law and/or practice of the Member State to whose territory the worker is posted."

These provisions, which are essentially of a "social model dimension" kind, are complemented by provisions relating to the requirements for, and provision of, relevant information relating to the conditions regulated by Article 3. Thus, Article 4, which is headed "Cooperation on information", makes a variety of administrative arrangements at the level of the Member States, in terms that:

> "1. For the purposes of implementing this Directive, Member States shall, in accordance with national legislation and/or practice, designate one or more liaison offices or one or more competent national bodies.
>
> 2. Member States shall make provision for co-operation between the public authorities which, in accordance with national legislation, are responsible for monitoring the terms and conditions of employment referred to in Article 3. Such cooperation shall in particular consist in replying to reasoned requests from those authorities for information on the trans-national hiring-out of workers, including manifest abuses or possible cases of unlawful trans-national activities. The Commission and the public authorities referred to in the first sub-paragraph shall cooperate closely in order to examine any difficulties which might arise in the application of Article 3(10). Mutual administrative assistance shall be provided free of charge.
>
> 3. Each Member State shall take the appropriate measures to make the information on the terms and conditions of employment referred to in Article 3 generally available.
>
> 4. Each Member State shall notify the other Member States and the Commission of the liaison offices and/or competent bodies referred to in paragraph 1."

It is worthy of note that Article 8 of the Directive on the posting of workers provided for a Commission review of the operation of the Directive by 16 December 2001 at the latest, "with a view to proposing the necessary amendments to the Council where appropriate". That review was completed and presented by the Commission in mid-2003.[188] The group of government experts which carried out the review came to the conclusion that:

– None of the Member States has encountered any particular legal difficulties in transposing the Directive.

---

188   COM(2003) 458 final, presented on 25 July 2003.

–   Implementing the Directive may pose practical difficulties, but most of these should disappear in the course of time thanks to better information and better administrative cooperation between public authorities (Article 4 of the Directive).

–   It seems premature to consider amending the Directive. With regard to Article 4, on which the effective implementation of the Directive primarily depends, it is clear that the information circuits and the cooperation networks will take time to build up.

In consequence, it was declared that:

> These opinions and positions indicate to the Commission that it is not necessary to amend the Directive. The difficulties encountered in implementing it have so far tended to be more of a practical nature than a legal nature. Consequently, as things stand at present the Commission will not be presenting a proposal for a directive amending the arrangements for implementing the posted workers Directive.

4.3. The "Model" Adopted by the Draft Services Directive

The proposal for a Services Directive attempts to address some of the perceived problems relating to work and labour market activity by including specific provisions in relation to the provision of labour in the context of services. Thus, following from the general derogation in Article 16 for "matters covered by Directive 96/71/EC", Article 24 sets out what are described as "specific provisions on the posting of workers", while Article 25 addresses issues in relation to "posting of third country nationals".

Article 24, which is headed "Specific provisions on the posting of workers", provides that:

> "1. Where a provider posts a worker to another Member State in order to provide a service, the Member State of posting shall carry out in its territory the checks, inspections and investigations necessary to ensure compliance with the employment and working conditions applicable under Directive 96/71/EC and shall take, in accordance with Community law, measures in respect of a service provider who fails to comply with those conditions.
>
> However, the Member State of posting may not make the provider or the posted worker subject to any of the following obligations, as regards the matters referred to in point (5) of Article 17:

(a) to obtain authorisation from, or to be registered with, its own competent authorities, or to satisfy any other equivalent requirement;

(b) to make a declaration, other than declarations relating to an activity referred to in the Annex to Directive 96/71/EC which may be maintained until 31 December 2008;

(c) to have a representative in its territory;

(d) to hold and keep employment documents in its territory or in accordance with the conditions applicable in its territory.

2. In the circumstances referred to in paragraph 1, the Member State of origin shall ensure that the provider takes all measures necessary to be able to communicate the following information, both to its competent authorities and to those of the Member State of posting, within two years of the end of the posting:

(a) the identity of the posted worker;

(b) his position and the nature of the tasks attributed to him,

(c) the contact details of the recipient,

(d) the place of posting,

(e) the start and end dates for the posting,

(f) the employment and working conditions applied to the posted worker.

In the circumstances referred to in paragraph 1, the Member State of origin shall assist the Member State of posting to ensure compliance with the employment and working conditions applicable under Directive 96/71/EC and shall, on its own initiative, communicate to the Member State of posting the information specified in the first sub-paragraph where the Member State of origin is aware of specific facts which indicate possible irregularities on the part of the provider in relation to employment and working conditions."

Article 25, which is headed "Posting of third country nationals", sets out limitations upon Member States in respect of the regulatory arrangements established for third country nationals, and declares that:

"1. Subject to the possibility of derogation as referred to in paragraph 2, where a provider posts a worker who is a national of a third country to the territory of another Member State in order to provide a service there, the Member State of posting may not require the provider or the worker posted by the latter to hold an entry, exit, residence or work permit, or to satisfy other equivalent conditions.

2. Paragraph 1 does not prejudice the possibility for Member States to require a short-term visa for third country nationals who are not covered by the mutual recognition regime provided for in Article 21 of the Convention implementing the Schengen Agreement.

3. In the circumstances referred to in paragraph 1, the Member State of origin shall ensure that a provider posts only a worker who is resident in its territory in accordance with its own national rules and who is lawfully employed in its territory.

   The Member State of origin shall not regard a posting made in order to provide service in another Member State as interrupting the residence or activity of the posted worker and shall not refuse to readmit the posted worker to its territory on the basis of its national rules.

   The Member State of origin shall communicate to the Member State of posting, upon its request and in the shortest possible time, information and guarantees regarding compliance with the first sub-paragraph and shall impose the appropriate penalties in cases of non-compliance."

This approach, which reflects in large measure the regime established under the 1996 Posted Workers Directive, therefore seeks to facilitate the administrative simplification and advantages for enterprises to carry out their service activities in the single market (the "internal market dimension"). At the same time, however, it endeavours to ensure that the "social policy dimension" is effectively infused, in order to ensure a measure of "employment protection" in the form of guaranteeing the terms and conditions (and, in particular, the pay levels) governing the relevant labour market in the country of posting. In this way, the framework established also seeks to avoid any undermining of the stability of national industrial relations and/or collective bargaining arrangements, and to counter any temptation to indulge in "social dumping".

It can also be seen that both the Article 24 and Article 25 provisions include express concern for the lifting of administrative obstacles to the provision of services in this area, in line with the general motivation underlying the proposed Directive – including the shifting of responsibility for various administrative checks onto the Member State of posting.

4.4. Another Agenda: Where the "Economic Dimension" Takes Priority over the "Social Dimension"?

At the same time as being held out as the basis upon which to deliver improvements for both enterprises and their workers in a globalised economy, in the eyes of many, the so-called "Lisbon Strategy" has also been used as a "smoke-screen" for diluting significant parts of the Union's "social dimension" developed following the 1989 Madrid declaration to the effect that "in the course of the construction of the single European market, social aspects should be given the same importance as the economic aspects and should accordingly be developed in a balanced fashion".

There may or may not be justification for the scepticism of the "social dimension" critics. Whatever the case may be, however, it is abundantly clear today that the motivation for internal market completion of the kind underlying the proposed Services Directive is now stronger than ever.

Strong evidence for this can be seen in the emphasis placed by documents such as the "Kok II" Report upon "effective delivery" of the Lisbon Strategy during the forthcoming period 2005-2010 – an emphasis which has been substantially echoed in the Commission's preparatory documentation for the Spring 2005 Council Meeting.

However, it has been evident for some time that a variety of concerns, fears, and misconceptions have abounded in relation to the particular initiative for a Services Directive. In particular, there appears to have been some perception of a "social dumping" threat posed by increased mobility of workers from some of the most-recently joined Member States (following enlargement on 1 May 2004) to labour markets in "Old Europe" (with, allegedly, superior terms and conditions of work, including higher levels of pay).

Just to quote from the note prepared by the Dutch Presidency following discussion of the initiative during the European Council meeting on 25-26 November 2004 in Brussels:

> … It was generally felt that the proposed Directive needs to be further clarified in order to better communicate what it does and does not mean. The Directive would, for example, not undermine the European social model or affect the Posting of Workers Directive.

Indeed, the first of those fears – that the proposed Directive will "undermine the European social model" – has been trumpeted particularly loudly, and calls for considered comment.

By contrast, however, the second concern – that the proposed Directive will (presumably, in some "negative" sense) "affect the Posting of Workers Directive" – appears remarkably ill-founded, given the way in which the proposed Directive has been constructed and drafted, precisely so as to support and achieve consistency with the regime established by the 1996 Posting of Workers Directive.

As regards the former concern, it is as well to recall how the Barcelona European Council, in March 2002, sought to define that elusive creature "the European social model". In their terms, it was declared that, "The European social model is based on good economic performance, a high level of social protection and education and social dialogue."

While the endorsement of "good economic performance" reflects, to a great extent, the "Lisbon mantra" itself, and the aspirations to "a high level of education and social dialogue" have been central to the qualitative dimension of the European Employment Strategy since its inception in 1997, it is, of course, the issue of maintaining "a high level of social protection" which lies at the heart of concern about the impact of a measure such as the draft Services Directive.

In particular, what is often described as "social dumping" – the competitive advantage potentially to be derived from the provision of relatively lower levels of employment protection, health and safety provision, environmental protection, and a variety of related matters – has constituted a cause for concern throughout the quarter of a century since the "chill wind" of the "Chicago School" of economics began to blow across Europe from the shores of Lake Michigan.

5. A EUROPEAN "MODEL" TO ADDRESS THE PARTICULAR PROBLEMS OF LABOUR IN THE CONTEXT OF THE PROVISION OF SERVICES?

Yet, when one looks at developments since the beginning of the 1980s, what strikes the dispassionate observer is that the European Union has managed, by and large, to come up with a "model" in relation to implementation of the "social dimension" which successfully addresses many of the key threats posed by "social dumping" in the labour market.

Indeed, stimulated by a number of specific practices and strategic issues highlighted before the European Court of Justice in the 1989 case of *Rush Portuguesa Lda v. Office national d'immigration (National Immigration Office)*,[189] the most evident manifestation of that "anti-social dumping model" is to be seen in the 1996 Posting of Workers Directive.

To use the Commission's own description of the purpose underlying that 1996 Directive, it is said to have been adopted in order "to abolish the obstacles and uncertainties that impede implementation of the freedom to supply services, by improving legal certainty and facilitating identification of the employment conditions that apply to workers temporarily employed in a Member State other than the Member State whose legislation governs the employment relationship. It endeavours to strike a balance between the economic freedoms bestowed by the EC Treaty and employees' rights during their period of posting."

The approach adopted by the Posted Workers Directive has been to place emphasis upon the situation and circumstances pertaining in the location where the work is carried out. In this context, Article 3(1) of the Posted Workers Directive, which is entitled "Terms and conditions of employment", is the key to the "anti-social dumping model", where it provides that:

---

189 *Supra.*

> Member States shall ensure that, whatever the law applicable to the employment relationship, the [relevant] undertakings … guarantee workers posted to their territory the terms and conditions of employment covering the following matters which, in the Member State where the work is carried out, are laid down:
>
> – by law, regulation or administrative provision, and/or
>
> – by collective agreements or arbitration awards which have been declared universally applicable …

The Article then proceeds to list the relevant matters as being:

(a)   maximum work periods and minimum rest periods;
(b)   minimum paid annual holidays;
(c)   the minimum rates of pay, including overtime rates; this point does not apply to supplementary occupational retirement pension schemes;
(d)   the conditions of hiring-out of workers, in particular the supply of workers by temporary employment undertakings;
(e)   health, safety and hygiene at work;
(f)   protective measures with regard to the terms and conditions of employment of pregnant women or women who have recently given birth, of children and of young people;
(g)   equality of treatment between men and women and other provisions on non-discrimination.

These provisions, which are unequivocally of a "social dimension" nature, are complemented by rules relating to the requirements for, and provision of, relevant information.

This, as has already been indicated, is the response at the level of the European Union to the "mischief" highlighted in the *Rush Portuguesa* case, where the damage which was taken to be inflicted upon the collectively bargained regime in the country of utilisation was considered a key problem. Indeed, the circumstances underlying that 1989 litigation were precisely of the kind to which a number of MEPs have been referring of late (exploitation of differential wage levels, undermining of collectively agreed terms and conditions of work, etc.).[190]

That "Posting of Workers Directive model" approach has been mirrored in subsequent decisions of the European Court of Justice, and one now commonly sees the formulation of an expression insisting upon "the protection of temporary

---

190   Including the Rapporteurs to the European Parliament committees most closely involved with the legislative progress of the draft Services Directive – respectively, the Committee on the Internal Market and Consumer Protection (Evelyne Gebhardt), and the Committee on Employment and Social Affairs (Anne Van Lancker). See footnote 153 *supra*.

workers, the requirements of health and safety at work, and the need to ensure that the labour market functions properly, and abuses are prevented".

This model, as has already been pointed out, endeavours to ensure that the "social policy dimension" is effectively infused – maintaining a measure of "employment protection" by guaranteeing terms and conditions, and seeking to avoid any undermining of the stability of national industrial relations and/or collective bargaining arrangements, in the country of posting.

Nor has there been any major problem identified in the course of implementing the Posting of Workers Directive. Indeed, when, in mid-2003, the European Commission completed its review of experience, the broad conclusion was that "None of the Member States has encountered any particular legal difficulties in transposing the Directive..."

In the light of these developments, and given that there has been no suggestion that the Posted Workers Directive has failed to address the particular form of "social dumping" highlighted by the *Rush Portuguesa* case, one would have thought that the appropriate "anti-social dumping model" for the proposed Services Directive should be to replicate the "model" adopted by the 1996 Posted Workers Directive itself. And, indeed, that is precisely what the drafters of the proposed Services Directive have done! The position adopted in the proposed Directive is precisely to reflect the stance adopted by the Posted Workers Directive.

This is achieved by providing for derogations from the so-called "country of origin principle" in any situation where this would conflict with the arrangements established by the Posted Workers Directive. Thus, from a technical perspective, Articles 17 and 24 of the proposed Services Directive give effect to a general derogation from the "country of origin principle" spelled out in Article 16, and express cross-reference is made to the Posted Workers Directive both in the Preamble and in the body of the text. Such an approach, therefore, seeks to address both the "internal market dimension", and, at the same time, to ensure that the "social policy dimension" is effectively safeguarded.

While there may be room for argument that the range of associated matters, as currently drafted, remains too narrow – for example, requiring extension to cover matters such as health, safety & hygiene at work, or vocational and professional training – the "anti-social dumping model" appears in its full glory, with no "back door" left open to the kinds of practices witnessed in the *Rush Portuguesa* situation a decade and a half ago.

In short, despite the torrent of abuse which has been directed towards the draft proposal for the Services Directive, it may turn out to be the case that:

1.   The "model" established by the Posted Workers Directive (of wages, and other terms and conditions, being established through the mechanisms – including collective bargaining structures – in the country of posting) could be the appropriate "model" for dealing both with "social dumping" concerns and for ensuring that no disruption is caused to established industrial relations,

collective bargaining, and social dialogue arrangements at the level of the Member State in the country of posting; and

2.   The proposed Services Directive serves to reinforce that "model", by bringing (*inter alia*) temporary work placement activities within the scope of the measure, but derogating from the "country of origin principle" so far as concerns matters falling within the list set out by Article 3 of the Posted Workers Directive.

6. "SOCIAL DUMPING": THE "REAL" THREAT?

This being the case so far as the immediate proposal for a Services Directive is concerned, it is, nevertheless, still open to argument that the underlying threat of "social dumping" remains very much alive and well in the European Union of 25 Member States", but for reasons which have little or nothing to do with the arrangements set out in the proposal for a Services Directive.

Perhaps the most important reason for this, it may be suggested, lies in an Achilles' heel of European Union social policy instruments which, to the mind of this commentator, as well as to many other observers, has for too long served to undermine generally the effectiveness of social protection measures agreed and implemented at the European level.

The problem lies in the failure at the level of the Union adequately to define who is, and who is not, within the scope of protection of those social protection measures – and, in particular, where the scope of protection is stated to be extended to "workers", the failure of the Union legislator and the Court of Justice to develop a European-level definition of "worker" for this purpose.

For the real threat of "social dumping", in the sense in which the public and media debate has been proceeding in relation to the proposed Services Directive, is not in practices of the kind highlighted by the *Rush Portuguesa* litigation. It does not flow from anything in the proposed Services Directive itself, or from shortcomings in the operation of the Posted Workers Directive. Instead, it is particularly manifest in the emergence of large numbers of individuals (variously designated as "self-employed", "false self-employed", or the like), who simply fail to come within the current scope of European Union social policy protections, by virtue of evading the relevant national Member State definition (or application) of the notion of "worker" or "employee". As a consequence, there are significant *lacunae* in relation to the whole social protection *acquis* – whether we are speaking of collective dismissals, transfers of undertakings, health and safety under the umbrella of the 1989 Framework Directive, or more recent measures on part-time, fixed-term, or other specified groups of "workers".

Furthermore, this state of affairs will continue until such time as we see a move away from the received wisdom that, for example:

> "employee" shall mean any person who, in the Member State concerned, is protected as an employee under national employment law;[191]

or that

> this agreement applies to all workers, men and women, who have an employment contract or employment relationship as defined by the law, collective agreements or practices in force in each Member State.[192]

Nor does it really assist matters – and this observation may appear strange coming from the lips of a university professor! – for the European Commission to promote theoretical and highly esoteric analyses of narrow national labour market practices in this area, or to encourage the introduction of yet more Euro-babble such as "para-subordination" or the like.[193] For this is a fundamental issue of huge practical significance. If something positive is to be done about the threat of "social dumping" in relation to labour market practices across the European Union, this question of defining, on a consistent and European-wide basis, who are the addressees of social policy regulation, constitutes an essential first step. There, it might be suggested, is a truly worthy focus for domestic public debate about the true impact of the European Union, and for the headline-writers of the mass media to turn their attention.

So far as the proposed Services Directive is concerned, let us embrace it for what it is – an element in the completion of the Single Market, which utilises the "anti-social dumping model" of the 1996 Posted Workers Directive to ensure that precisely the kinds of practices which were highlighted in the *Rush Portuguesa* case are not permitted to return "through the back door". Indeed, there is an added significance to this particular initiative, since, given the reticence in the Commission's most recent communication on the *Social Agenda 2006-2010* to commit to any large-scale programme of legislation in the social field at European level, it is probably the case that the proposed Services Directive offers the only significant focus for regulatory change and/or innovation for the immediate future.

Taken in that light – and freed from so many of the misrepresentations of those who would seek to pursue a less "Europe-friendly" agenda for their own domestic political benefit – the Frankenstein's monster-like image of the proposed "Bolkestein

---

191   Article 2 of the 2001 Transfers Directive.
192   Clause 1(2) of the Annex to the 1996 Parental Leave Directive.
193   See, for example, the interesting analysis provided by Professor Adelberto Perulli, in his report for the European Commission, *Economically dependent / quasi-subordinate (parasubordinate) employment: legal, social and economic aspects*, presented to a Public Hearing organised jointly by the Committee on Employment and Social Affairs of the European Parliament and DG Employment and Social Affairs, on 19 June, 2003. It may be noted, however, that the experience from which the generalised conclusions of this report are drawn derive almost entirely from practices specific to the German and Italian national regulatory situations.

Directive"[194] will cease to alarm, and, with the dawning of enlightenment, will simply disappear as a tangible harbinger of "social dumping" to undermine the "European social model". Perhaps, in future, we shall discover that, for all the alarm currently being generated, to quote the words of Mary W. Shelley, the author of *Frankenstein*,

> You will rejoice to hear that no disaster has accompanied the commencement of an enterprise which you have regarded with such evil forebodings.[195]

---

194 As the measure has come to be dubbed – by reference to the name of the Commissioner responsible for internal market affairs at the time of the launching of the initiative (EU Commissioner Frits Bolkestein).

195 Mary W. Shelley, *Frankenstein* (1818).

5. THE IMPLEMENTATION OF THE PROPOSED DIRECTIVE ON SERVICES IN THE INTERNAL MARKET – A FRENCH PERSPECTIVE

Jacques Rojot

It is difficult to gauge the impact of any single event on the outcome of the vote of the French electorate on 29 May 2005, rejecting the proposed Treaty on the Constitution of Europe. Strange political coalitions, on both sides advocated the vote yes as well as the no vote, cutting deeply across traditional political parties lines. However, the proposal of the Services Directive in the internal market played a not insignificant role during the campaign. Rather than the text of the proposed Directive, which few bothered to read, it was the shadows cast by the impact of "globalisation", under the guise of a geographically extended European Union, and of the possible end of the so-called "French model", whatever that may be in practice, that the debate centred on.

It should be recalled at the outset that the proposal, when discussed and drafted within the European institutions, received the full approval of the relevant French Government representatives.

However, as the prospect of the practical consequences of the proposed Directive, were it to be enacted, came closer, it became embroiled with the political campaign on the referendum on the Treaty on the proposed Constitution, and the authorities began to have second thoughts.

The Government requested from the Conseil d'Etat, the highest French administrative authority, an opinion on the impact on the French legal order of some of the provisions of the proposed Services Directive in the internal market.

The advice of the Conseil d'Etat, published in 2005 as part of the yearly report on the activities of the Conseil d'Etat, is worth considering in depth. Most of this paper summarises and discusses its main features.

The Government had asked four specific questions. However, before answering them, the Conseil d'Etat, in an introduction, noted several points, which are recalled in the later discussion of the questions raised.

It first noted that the proposed Directive addressed the freedom of establishment as well as the free provision of services between the Member States. Then it was noted that, in Chapter 1, the notion of services included any economic activity normally provided for consideration, without requiring that this consideration be paid by the beneficiaries and independently of the mode of paying for the economic counterpart, which is itself the object of the consideration. Therefore, services performed by the

State in the performance of its mission in the social, cultural, education and judiciary fields (section 50 of the Treaty) are considered excluded. Moreover, section 2 of the proposed Directive specifically excluded several sectors. Also, section 3 provides that the application of the proposed Directive does not exclude the application of the provisions of other EC legislation concerning services.

Chapter II, section 1, in relation to the freedom of establishment, aims to ease the procedures applicable to the access and exercise of a service activity, notably with the institution of a single point of contact and the use of electronic procedures. Section 2 covers cases in which authorisation is required and section 3 lists prohibited requirements and a procedure for the evaluation of requirements.

Chapter III concerns the free movement of services. Section 1 sets out the country of origin principle. Chapter IV is devoted to the quality of the services. Chapter V to the supervision of the activities and the providers and Chapter VI is devoted to the creation of codes of conduct at Community level.

Within that overall framework, the Council raises several points worthy of interest, some of which – but by far not all – have been alleviated by modifications in the proposed Directive.

The proposed Directive introduces a profound change in method, for it abandons the former procedure of harmonisation of the Law and regulations of the Member States, by providing for generalised application of the principle of the country of origin, under which providers are subject only to its requirements. Thus, the Law applicable to the provision of services would no longer be the one of the state within which they are provided. Thus several national laws will be simultaneously applied, in competition with one another, on a single national territory. This raises difficult questions concerning several French constitutional principles regarding national sovereignty, equality before the law and lawfulness of crimes and penalties which may be breached.

Although the country of origin principle has already been put in practice, that has occurred in limited sectors, whereas under the proposed Directive it would be extended to activities which are heterogeneous in nature.

The apparent simplicity of the principle raises concerns as to legal certainty and how it may be interpreted. It cannot mask the large number of uncertainties for providers and consumers, as well as uncertainties about the nature and the extent of powers devoted to Member States, and therefore carries the risk of significant litigation, at least until strong case law is established, which would be counterproductive to the very goal of the completion of the internal market. Besides, its economic logic is contrary to, for instance, the law of the consumer, which privileges the law of the country of the beneficiary of the provision of services.

Also, it would be necessary to identify more clearly the services excluded from the scope of the proposed Directive by section 45 of the Treaty concerning activities, even occasional in nature, which relate to the exercise of public authority. Some public officers and ministerial officers, appointed by the Minister of Justice cannot be included.

Also, third country undertakings established within the Community, which, unlike subsidiaries are not subject to host state national law should be excluded.

It is necessary to harmonise the proposal with section 50 of the Treaty, regarding temporary activities carried out by citizens of another Member State, under conditions that are imposed on nationals of the host state.

Legal certainty is further undermined when the proposed Directive is seen alongside the *acquis communautaire*, mentioned in Article 3(2), superimposing additional regulations, notably in the case of activities already operating the principle of mutual recognition.

A question is raised regarding the regulation, by the French Civil Code, of the protection of safety, public health and public order, given the extensive definition in the proposed Directive of the "coordinated domain" and of the "requirements" (by the Member States). Section 3 of the Civil Code provides for the territorial application of such regulations, breach of which constitutes a criminal offence. The proposed Directive does not seem to allow clearly for the application of these provisions, notwithstanding exceptional situations provided for in Articles 17, 19 and 37. A clarification is necessary to know whether the application of national supervisory regulations is impacted by the origin of the provider of services, which cannot be left to later court decisions.

More generally, given the huge scope of the field covered by the Directive, one should underline the risks of the concurrent application by each Member State of the civil and commercial law of all other Member States, depending on country of origin, with the foreseeable divergences in application of the rule of the law. This would breach the principle of the lawfulness of crimes and penalties.

Further questions are raised by the fact that criminal law is not excluded. An extreme case would see a national court applying the substantive, not procedural, criminal law of another country on its own territory.

For all these reasons, questions as to the breach of national sovereignty by the proposed Directive remain.

Additionally, the application of competing substantive criminal laws in one national territory would also breach the principle of equality before the law.

Further, the free provision of specially regulated services (for instance health services) also weakens the role played in their regulation in France by national associations of providers, given that the role of such associations has not been harmonised.

Finally, the prohibition in Article 14(5) on applying, case-by-case, an economic test in circumstances where authorisation for the establishment of a provider of services is required, would exclude the present French policy of harmonising the establishment of super- and hypermarkets across the national territory.

In conclusion, a note from the Commission of Foreign Affairs of the National Assembly of March 2005, taking into account some of the results of the negotiations which occurred following the opinion of the Conseil d'Etat – notably derogations from the principle of the country of origin regarding minimum wage, working time, safety; hygiene and qualifications – nevertheless maintains notable reservations.

These reservations concern:

–   The will of the Member States to exert real and thorough inspections and the complexity of that process;
–   The absence at the present time of cooperation between Member States, upon which rests the successful operation of the provisions of the Directive;
–   Finally and most importantly, the adoption of the main objection of principle given by the Conseil d'Etat, coupled with the acknowledgement of the risks of "social dumping". It regrets the substitution of a logic of competition of national regulations (resulting from the generalisation of the principle of country of origin) which could lead to alignment with the lowest national standards in place of the traditional method of harmonisation of national law.

6. THE IMPLICATIONS OF THE SERVICES DIRECTIVE ON LABOUR LAW – A GERMAN PERSPECTIVE

Manfred Weiss

1. INTRODUCTION

It evidently is the purpose of the envisaged Services Directive to promote the freedom of services as embedded in the Treaty from its very beginning. There is no doubt that this freedom is an important pillar of the common market and, therefore, deserves to be made efficient. However, as the reactions on the draft of 2004 and the debate initiated by these reactions show, this attempt is met by serious doubts on the impact such a Directive might have. These doubts mainly refer to the still existing gap of working conditions in the different Member States. The fear of "social dumping" by facilitating the possibility to provide services throughout the Community has become a phenomenon which no longer can be ignored. In high wage countries with high labour standards, this fear has become a core subject of the public debate. This issue may even have a significant effect on the referenda to be conducted in the process of ratification of the Constitutional Treaty as the French example shows. In Germany, the debate is closely linked with the discussion on social impacts of EU enlargement, in particular whether further enlargement (Romania, Bulgaria) should be continued, renegotiated or stopped. In short, and to make the point: the (rational or perhaps irrational) fears caused by the project of the Services Directive have already significantly poisoned the climate at least in high wage countries. This cannot be ignored.

The indicated debate in the meantime has already had significant effects and led to hectic activities on European level in reconstructing the original concept of the Commission's draft. According to the latest stage of affairs it seems to be clear that "in the absence of a minimal level of harmonisation at EU level or, at least, of mutual recognition on the comparable rules within the Member States, the country of origin principle cannot be the basic principle governing temporary cross-border provision of services".[196] The most important implication of the new approach seems to be that labour law should not be affected by the Directive but

---

196 European Parliament – Committee on Employment and Social Affairs, 26 April 2005, Provisional 2004/0001(COD), 4

left to the rules in the Treaty and in secondary European Community law. What is meant is best specified by the Amendment 36 proposed by European Parliament's Committee on Employment and Social Affairs which reads as follows:[197]

> The country of origin principle should not apply to terms and conditions of employment which, pursuant to Directive 96/71/EC, apply to workers posted to provide a service in the territory of another Member State. This should not only concern terms and conditions of employment which are laid down by law but also laid down in collective agreements or arbitration awards that are officially declared or de facto universally applicable within the meaning of Directive 96/71/EC. Moreover, this Directive should not prevent Member States from applying terms and conditions of employment on matters other than those listed in Directive 96/71/EC in the case of public policy provisions. … Finally, this derogation also should include the right for the Member States where the service is provided to determine the existence of an employment relationship and the distinction between self-employed persons and employed persons, including "false self-employed persons".

This is definitely important progress compared to the original proposal for the Directive. In order to be able to evaluate whether it will lead to a socially satisfactory solution it seems to be appropriate to have a closer look at the experiences so far. Since such an analysis is only possible on the basis of familiarity with the real conditions I take the experiences in Germany as an example in order to develop an empirical platform from which it might be safer to speculate on the implications of the envisaged Directive for working conditions and labour law.

2.   THE GERMAN EXPERIENCE

2.1. The Period before Directive 96/71/EC

Freedom of services led to dramatic effects in the German building industry in the late 1980s. Construction companies from Member States with significantly lower levels of working conditions and labour standards provided their services in Germany. Due to the lower labour costs they were able to offer their services much cheaper than German companies. This led to a substitution effect: German companies had less work, many of them went into insolvency and many workers in the German construction industry lost their jobs. Up to 1996 this development became more and more dramatic: in 1996 the number of workers of foreign service-providing companies in the construction industry amounted to 150,000. At the same time

---

197   *Ibid.*, 24

180,000 workers in the German construction industry had lost their jobs.[198] This situation quickly led to strong political pressure on the Government. At first, the German Government joined the efforts to get an EC instrument which was supposed to make sure that the posted workers abide by the German minimum conditions, in particular regarding wages. However, it turned out that the first proposal for such a Directive as presented by the Commission in 1991 did not get the necessary support in the Council.

Frustrated by this failure, Germany – as well as Austria, Belgium and France which faced similars – passed a statute on their own,[199] ignoring the question whether in view of the guarantee of freedom of services in the EC Treaty they were entitled to do so. The statute was supposed to impose the essential minimum working conditions, including wages, to the posted workers.

Different from the other Member States, however, Germany – mainly for historical reasons – does not have a statutory minimum wage. Minimum wages are regularly fixed by collective agreements, concluded for certain activities, be it for the territory of Germany as a whole or be it – in most caes – for a specific region.[200] But even where the collective agreement is supposed to cover the whole territory of Germany, differences still exist between the territories of former West and East Germany. The problem, however, is the limited scope of application with such collective agreements. They only cover employment relationships between members of the parties to the collective agreement, employers' associations and trade unions. Such collective agreements evidently could not be imposed on posted workers since not even the non-organised workers and employers in Germany were covered by them. Therefore, the statute referred to collective agreements declared universally binding. Such a mechanism of extension exists, but it has to meet quite a few substantial and procedural requirements. The most important substantial requirement in this context is the fact that the employers already covered by the collective agreement must employ at least 50% of the workers in the particular branch of activity and region for which the collective agreement is concluded. As far as procedure is concerned, the Federal Minister for Economy and Labour is only entitled to pass such a universally binding decree on application of either one or both parties to the collective agreement. More important, however, is the fact that he needs the prior consent of a committee of six persons, three representatives of industry, coming from the Confederation of Trade Unions and from the Confederation of Employers' Associations. Since the members of this committee are not representing a particular branch of activity they tend to focus on the workers' and employers' interests in the German economy as a whole. This has led to difficulties. When the statute was passed the social partners in the building industry not only concluded a collective agreement on a minimum wage but also applied for a universally binding

---

198   M. Kittner, B. Zwanziger (eds), *Arbeitsrecht – Handbuch für die Praxis* (2nd edn, 2001) 2142
199   Arbeitnehmer-Entsendegesetz vom 26. Februar 1996, BGBl. I, 2033
200   For this structure and the developments see the background information in M. Weiss and M. Schmidt, *Labour Law and Industrial Relations in Germany* (3rd edn, 2000) 149 et seq.

decree. The Minister was eager to meet this request. However, he did not get the consent of the committee since its members from the employers' side considered the negotiated minimum wage to be far too high. Therefore, renegotiation was necessary. Finally, the social partners in the building industry agreed on a much lower minimum wage and paved the way to the universally binding decree which finally was declared by the Minister.

2.2. The Implementation of Directive 96/71/EC

When Directive 96/71/EC had to be transposed in Germany the main concern was to make sure that such a disaster could not happen again. Therefore, in amending the original statute in the end of 1998 (in force since 1 January 1999),[201] the procedure for getting a decree of universal application was facilitated. The consent of the above mentioned committee is no longer necessary: it is now exclusively up to the Federal Minister of Economy and Labour to decide on the request coming from both or one of the social partners in the building industry. This innovation met resistance in the employers' camp and was considered to be unconstitutional, violating the constitutional guarantee of negative freedom of association. The Federal Constitutional Court, however, rejected this assumption and declared the new structure to be compatible with the Constitution. It remains controversial[202] whether the requirement that the respective employers' association employs at least 50% of the workers in the branch of activity and region for which the collective agreement is concluded, will be met within this new structure. However, in the building industry this precondition is not a problem anyway. Therefore, this controversy so far has had no practical consequences. On the basis of the new statutory provisions, in the meantime, collective agreements in the building industry on minimum wage were declared to be universally binding without any problem, regularly adapting the level to changing conditions. This level still differs between the territories of former West and former East Germany.

In implementing the Directive the German legislator went beyond the building industry and made sure that in all branches of activity the legal provisions on essential minimum working conditions are also applied ti workers performing work in Germany who are employed by an employer abroad. Collective agreements which are declared to be universally applicable are also binding for these employment relationships with the exception of clauses on annual holiday or on minimum wage. This means that in reference to wages, the German minimum conditions laid down in a universally binding collective agreement can only be imposed on

---

201   Neuregelung vom 19. Dezember 1998, BGBl. I, 3843
202   See on the one hand W. Daeubler, *Kommentar zum Tarifvertragsgesetz*, 2003, 1550 and M. Loewisch and V. Rieble, *Muenchner Handbuch Arbeitsrecht*, 2nd edn, Vol. 3, "Kollektives Arbeitsrecht", 415 and on the other hand T. Blanke, "Die Neufassung des Arbeitnehmer-Entsendegesetzes", *Arbeit und Recht*, 1999, 417 (426)

posted workers in the construction industry. In all other matters there is no way to reach such an agreement.

Even if on the regulatory level the situation at least for the construction industry looks satisfactory, this unfortunately is not reflected in practice. There is a significant deficit during implementation. The supervising authorities neither have the resources nor the personnel to efficiently monitor the respective rules. Apparently all kinds of strategies were invented to circumvent the respective obligations. Wages, working time, etc., as listed in documents often do not correspond to reality. In short, and to make the point: there is a big gap between law on paper and law in action. Therefore, it sounds strange, at least from a German perspective, if in reviewing the Directive the Commission in 2003 came to the conclusion that "none of the Member States has encountered any particular legal difficulties in transposing the Directive". Such a statement can only be explained by the fact that the evaluation of transposition of Directives by the Commission (as I know from own experiences in which I was formerly involved) strictly remains on the normative level and does not take into account the difficulties of factual implementation.

2.3. The Actual Situation

In Germany, the formal requirements of most trades to provide services were traditionally very high. In order to facilitate the possibility to offer such services, these standards in the end of 2003 were significantly lowered by the legislator. After the EU enlargement in 2004 this led to serious problems in Germany which now play a big role and which have already provoked legislative attempts to cope with the situation.

In some of these trades, in the meantime, large numbers of contractual workers from the new Central and Eastern European Member States have taken over jobs either by being posted workers of a company in the new Member States – which in many cases is merely a fictitious letter-box company – or by offering their services as a self-employed worker, in both cases for much less money than German service providers would take. This again has led to an increase of unemployment in certain trades. This subject has become an important issue in the media, not least due to the fact that the unemployment rate in Germany is rising dramatically, officially already amounting to about 5 million. In this climate, politicians do everything they can to prevent xenophobic reactions. This has led to a debate on the question as to whether Germany should also have a statutory minimum wage as most of the other Member States. Ideas in this direction, however, met strong resistance, mainly from the employers' side. Critics argued that a statutory minimum wage would be counter-productive for the development of the German economy. In the end it turned out that majority support for a statutory minimum wage could not be achieved. Therefore, the Government at the end of April 2004 opted for a different solution, presenting a bill for an amendment to the statute on posted workers. Thereby, the rules already applying to the construction industry are supposed to be extended to other trades and should no longer be limited to posted workers but also include self-employed persons. In the meantime, this bill has met strong resistance, mainly from the German Confederation of Employers' Associations. This extension is fought using more or less the same arguments as already used in the debate on a statutory minimum wage. A general extension to all trades is not only likely to have a similar counter-productive economic effect as a statutory minimum wage but is also in question for reasons of constitutionality. Therefore, in its present version, the bill stands no chance: it would be blocked at the latest in the second chamber of the legislative machinery where the conservative parties, strongly resisting this proposal, have a clear majority. In the end it might be possible to perhaps reach a compromise: extension of the present statute on posted workers only on those trades in which clear empirical evidence shows that intervention is urgently necessary.

However, even if such an extension might come: it would not help very much. In the respective trades the unions are extremely weak and the employers' associations – on the assumption that the requirement of at least 50% of workers employed by the employers are already covered by the collective agreement – in most cases would not even meet the requirement to apply for a decree of universal application. And of course, the problem of factual implementation would be the same as the situation in the construction industry already.

2.4. The Problem of Self-Employment

The most serious problem, however, – which again plays a big role already in the construction industry – would be the fact that such a provision would be meaning-less to the self-employed. There is neither a statutory wage nor are there sufficient structural preconditions for collective agreements on minimum payments for services. Even if, according to law, economically dependent self-employed persons (so-called "employee-like" persons) can be covered by collective agreements, this is purely theoretical. Neither are these "employee-like persons" organised, nor is there any established trade union which would make any effort to include them in collective agreements. And the "employee-like persons" are not integrated into the social security system. There is no indication whatsoever that this situation might change. In short, the self-employed would remain a group that would undermine the strategy of the envisaged amendment.

It is here where the real problem starts: German companies in different trades (including the construction industry) now conclude contracts with big numbers of seemingly self-employed workers from the new Member States. The sheer number makes it impossible for the monitoring authorities to cope with the problem. In a way the situation just has to be tolerated. However, one might think that these monitoring activities could perhaps be made more efficient. This would be true if it were relatively easy to draw the demarcation line between employment and self-employment.

This seems to be the underlying assumption in the latest proposal of the European Parliament's Committee on Employment and Social Affairs. It not only clarifies in the already quoted proposal for the amendment 36 that it is up to the Member States where the service is provided to determine the existence of an employment relationship and the distinction between self-employed persons and employed persons, including "false self-employed persons" but stresses again this principle in the justification to the proposed amendment 13a: "it should be the country on whose territory the work is being done that should determine who is to be regarded as a worker". Otherwise the country of origin could facilitate the possibility of escaping an employment relationship strictly speaking and thereby undermine any attempt to impose minimum payments to those who provide services abroad as "false self-employed persons" under the rules determining the status in the country where the service is provided. The question, however, arises in how far this reasonably sound principle would be really helpful in practice. In my view it ignores the fact that it has become extremely difficult to draw a demarcation line between employment and self-employment. Again the German example may illustrate this difficulty.

Germany does not have any statutory definition of the notion of employee as regards labour law. There is only a statutory definition of the self-employed in a specific section of the Commercial Code. This Section reads: "He who essentially is free in organising his work and in determining his working time is presumed to be self-employed". Thus, personal freedom is the main characteristic of being self-employed. This is why the traditional definition of employee implies just the opposite of personal freedom, i.e. personal subordination. According to this still prevailing definition, an employee is a person who is obliged to work for somebody else on the basis of a private contract in a relationship of personal subordination. The key element of this formula has become personal subordination.

For a considerable time, the notion of "personal subordination" was accepted as a helpful and valid criterion to define an employment relationship.[203] Personal subordination has always been understood to differ from mere economic dependency on the employer. Therefore, the question whether or not a person is an employee has nothing to do with the salary the individual is earning. This difference between mere personal subordination and economic dependence is still valid, but meanwhile the problem is that nobody knows exactly what personal subordination really means. The traditional view of an individual simply obeying his employer's orders in determining the organisation of his work, or his working time, does not correspond with many features of today's working reality where autonomy and creativity have become characteristic signs. Therefore, the inadequacy of this traditional notion of several decades has already become a big issue. The debate on the notion of

---

203   For a more detailed assessment of this development see Weiss and Schmidt, *supra* footnote 200, 43 et seq.

an employment relationship in essence is a debate on the scope of application of labour law as such.

In this debate, the notion of dependent employment has been changed significantly by the jurisdiction of the Federal Labour Court. First of all, the Federal Labour Court made perfectly clear that it is not up to the parties to the individual contract to define the legal character of the relationship. Whether or not labour law is applicable depends on the actual content of a relationship. In other words: there is no possibility of escaping the constraints of labour law just by mutual agreement on the labelling of the contract. This view evidently implies that the real content of such a relationship is evaluated. And here is the core of the development: the Federal Labour Court no longer simply relies on the notion of "personal subordination" as a criterion to distinguish an employee relationship from a self-employed relationship, but tries to adapt its content to the changed conditions in working life by additional criteria and indicators.

This attempt, however, has not facilitated the identification of an employment relationship but has made it much more sophisticated and thereby more and more unclear. The Federal Labour Court has turned the notion of personal subordination into a very complex structure consisting of a wide range of elements, which have to be combined and evaluated as an entity. Thus, it is always up to the courts to determine whether or not in a particular case the combination of factors indicating the status of an "employee" is sufficient or not. It is still far from being clear or transparent. Just to illustrate this complexity some factors of this approach to identify an employment relationship may be mentioned: the enterprise expects the individual to always be ready to accept new tasks, the individual is not free to refuse tasks offered by the enterprise, the individual is to a certain extent integrated in the organisational structure of the enterprise, the time required by the individual for performing the tasks for an enterprise is rather long, etc. There is not a single element which could be considered as the decisive one. It always needs a broader perspective in each individual case. The underlying question leading all these different factors is the following: to what extent can the situation of the respective individual be compared to those who undoubtedly are subordinated employees? More important, however, is the fact that the notion of "personal subordination" is not abolished as the decisive criterion, it is merely adapted to ever changing new circumstances. In addition, the new formula will alwys have to be interpreted by the courts, which is not very helpful in promoting legal certainty.

It has to be remembered that the traditional model of an employment relationship was the factory where employees cooperated in a coherent organisational structure. This is exactly the perspective which also led the Federal Labour Court to the conclusion that the integration into the organisational structure is one of the relevant factors to indicate the existence of an employment relationship. The problem, however, is that this traditional model is rapidly eroding. There is an increasing externalisation of functions by way of outsourcing. Secondly, new information and communication technologies allow to an increasing extent a relocation of work-performance. The "virtual factory" and the "virtual office" are becoming characteristic features of today's and especially tomorrow's reality.

The pressure of cost reduction has become a decisive element in today's management strategies. In order to remain competitive, enterprises look for ways to get rid of the constraints of labour law and social security law. Therefore – to just take some examples for illustration – in the building industry more and more bricklayers, electricians, floor-tilers and even crane drivers are considered to be self-employed, at least it has become very questionable which status they have. The same is true in the transport industry where truck drivers to an ever increasing extent offer their services as independent contractors. In the case of the crane driver, the crane, and in the case of the truck driver, the truck, is quite often leased to, or even owned by these individuals. Hotels and restaurants to an increasing extent are relying on self-employed persons for all kind of services. The number of one-person self-employed activities (in Germany they are labelled "Me Stock Company") is rapidly increasing. In short: the contractual patterns stepping out of the traditional employment relationship have become a mass phenomenon. It is no longer a problem of merely a few cases. And of course, it is not only a problem of those coming from another country of origin to offer services.

The advantage to the partners of such independent contractors are particularly evident in Germany. As already mentioned, the social security system is linked to the employment relationship in a traditional sense. Those who are classified as employees automatically are integrated into the compulsory social security system, covering health insurance, invalidity insurance, retirement insurance and unemployment insurance. This implies that employer and employee have to pay contributions to the social security system, with each side paying half the total amount. These contributions, in the meantime, have climbed up to more than 40 per cent of the gross wage. Economically speaking, these contributions are increasing the wage costs for the employer and at the same time lowering the net income of the employee significantly. This link between employment relationship and social security system is commonly understood to be the biggest incentive for employers as well as for employees to transform employment relationships into patterns of independent contractual work. In a short term perspective this looks for both sides like a win-win situation, even if, of course, the independent contractual workers are then forced to take care of themselves for protection in case of sickness, unemployment or retirement, which in reality they often neglect. The price for them is high. But often they have no choice but to accept such an independent contractual relationship. The effect for the social security system in any case is extremely negative: the system loses necessary financial resources.

Whether all those people who are contracting as self-employed really *are* self-employed in a legal sense, is of course very doubtful. There is a widespread assumption that most of them are, in reality, employees. Therefore, the notion of "false self-employed" has been invented to illustrate the phenomenon. It is evident that the updated version of subordination as elaborated by the Federal Labour Court is not very helpful in coping with this challenge. And the examples show that it may well be doubtful whether it makes sense at all to determine the level of protection by recourse to the old-fashioned category of subordination.

This insight has led to the search for a new approach. Since autonomy, creativity, working time flexibility, as well as the freedom to decide on the work performance as such, become more and more important features of the modern working reality, in a controversial scholarly debate an alternative solution is suggested, not fully replacing but at least amending the traditional category of "subordination". The key notion in this context has become "entrepreneurial risk". The decisive perspective is the fair balance between entrepreneurial risks and chances. If an individual is in a contractual relationship which puts on him or her entrepreneurial risks but which due to "subordination" does not allow him or her to make use of entrepreneurial chances, according to this opinion, he or she is considered to be an "employee". If, however, the individual is only subordinated to an extent, which allows him or her to act as an entrepreneur on the market and to make use of his or her own chances, he or she is considered to be "self-employed". Again it is of course difficult to determine which of the two alternatives is given in a specific case. Therefore, again, indicators are offered. Factors indicating an employee's status are the following: the individual has no entrepreneurial organisational structure on his or her own, the individual has no collaborators (family members not included) but works on his or her own, the individual does not dispose on business rooms of his or her own, the individual has no business capital on his or her own, the individual has only one contractual partner for whom he or she works, the individual does not act on the market on his or her own, the individual is not free to choose the location of work, the individual is rather restricted in his or her disposition on working time, the individual does not have clients of his or her own and finally the individual is not free in determining the price for goods or services. By contrast, the lack of these factors would indicate self-employment. For some it is also an indication of self-employment if the entrepreneurial risks were taken voluntarily. This, however, is a very doubtful category in view of high unemployment where – as already indicated above – many people do not have a choice to opt for alternatives.

This new approach as suggested in the scholarly debate in Germany would be no less complex than the redefined category of "subordination" as sketched above. Again, no single factor will be the decisive one: in each individual case an overall evaluation would be necessary. Therefore, it is very doubtful whether it might be a helpful tool in actual practice.

The implication of this very sketchy analysis for the present debate on the Services Directive is far-reaching: due to the complexities, the uncertainties and the ever changing realities of working life it would be a naïve illusion to believe that a clear demarcation line can easily be drawn. Therefore, it would also be naïve to think that administrative authorities might be in a position to efficiently monitor the respective status of being employed or self-employed. In actual practice – at least in Germany – doubtful cases, if they are questioned at all, may lead to long-lasting law suits which are not helpful at all to resolve the problems implied by this mass phenomenon. Therefore, the authors of the Services Directive should not hold out too much hope in the principle which gives the host Member State power to determine and to monitor the respective status. Reality – as the German example shows – is much more complex.

3. CONCLUSION

In reflecting what the lesson of the experiences made in Germany may be for the project of a Services Directive it is of utmost importance to understand that a mere reference to the so-called *acquis communautaire* or to the legal framework of the Directive on posted workers cannot solve the problems which arise in actual reality. Even now, without the Services Directive it shows at least in Germany that the available mechanisms do not work mainly for three reasons: (1) the minimum wage linked to collective agreements and a decree on universal application is too complicated to be handled efficiently and will not work in quite a few areas where it would be needed; (2) monitoring of factual implementation has turned out to be inefficient, deviation in actual practice has become a wide spread phenomenon; (3) self-employment is a way out of all the constraints which exist at the moment for all the reasons explained above. These problems would become much more dramatic once the Services Directive facilitates the mobility of services even further.

Theoretically one might think of at least successfully coping with the problem of self-employment by developing Community-wide definitions of employment and self-employment to be implemented in all Member States equally. This attempt, however, would ignore the impact of the scholarly debates on this issue during the last few years. It has turned out that the complexity of today's reality cannot be mastered simply by way of general definitions: there will always be exceptions.

Theoretically, it might also be a possible solution enforceable by way of European Community law for each Member State to introduce a statutory minimum wage not only for employment relationships but also for self-employed persons who are economically dependent, even if it may be doubted whether, for the self-employed, this might be a feasible instrument in practice. However, the Community does not even have a legislative power to impose such a structure. The legislative competence for pay is still excluded. Even if there were such a legislative power: the strategies of deviation as observed, for example in the German construction industry, could not be prevented. And of course, thereby the possibilities of efficient monitoring would not be improved.

This leads us to the basic question as to whether it is possible at all on Community level to develop a regulatory pattern which would guarantee that the extension of cross-nationally provided services will not lead to socially unacceptable and therefore politically dangerous situations, dangerous not only for the respective Member States but also for the future of the Community as a whole. I do have serious doubts. As long as the gaps in reference to essential working conditions, in particular to wages, are as big as they are presently, any attempt in this direction will be counteracted by all kinds of strategies which can only be monitored to a very limited extent. Therefore, it may well be doubted whether a project like the Services Directive in the context of this reality is a good idea. However, the debate on the Services Directive – instead of being technocratic and focusing on details – should be used as an example to discuss the much broader, and for the Community's survival, crucial issue on how to reconstruct the framework of the Treaty (including the Treaty on the Constitution) in order to finally organise a fair balance between economic and social goals. The problem is that the so-called basic freedoms embedded in the Treaty since 1957 with a focus on optimising the allocation of economic resources are still interpreted as if there has not been a change of perspective in the meantime. For decades, however, we attempted to generate a balance between the economic and the social dimension, stepping away from the philosophy of the original Treaty of the European Economic Community. This development so far has its most significant symbol in the chapter on "Solidarity" in the Charter of Fundamental Rights of the EU.[204] However, in spite of this development, and in spite of some lip service to the contrary, the agenda of the Community still treats the social dimension as a mere annex to the economic project which is still considered to be the core of the matter. Occasional attempts of the ECJ to better reconcile (particularly in Albany!)[205] the two dimensions have unfortunately not yet led to a real debate on how to reconstruct the Treaty in this direction.[206] This, however, urgently has to change.

In this context it has to be remembered that it was (and in my view still should be) very controversial whether Article 57 para. 2 in connection with Article 66 of the EC Treaty really were empowering the Community to pass the Directive on posted workers. Again the ECJ jurisdiction attempted to find a balance in trying to reconcile economic and social considerations. The function of this jurisdiction is questionable: instead of openly address the still existing imbalance and the one-sided perspective of the EC Treaty, it somehow hides the problem by offering an acceptable result in spite of the Treaty. In my view, it would have been much better if the ECJ would have used this opportunity to demonstrate the imbalance of the two dimensions in the Treaty and thereby forced the political actors on Community level to finally rethink the concept as a whole. Maybe then, the disaster of the French referendum could have been prevented. Let us hope that it is not yet too late.

In a redesigned Treaty it should be made perfectly clear that cheap labour should not be a competitive tool within the Community. This is the evident implication of Article 31 of the Charter of Fundamental Rights of the EU which reads: "Every

---

204   See for the development and function of these fundamental social rights M. Weiss, "The Politics of the EU Charter of Fundamental Rights", in B. Hepple (ed.), *Social and Labour Rights in a Global Context* (2002) 73 et seq.

205   ECJ of 21 September 1999, C-67/96 (Albany International), ECR 1999, I-5751; see in this context the brilliant essay by S. Sciarra, "Market Freedom and Fundamental Social Rights", in B. Hepple, *ibid.*, 95 et seq.

206   For such a debate see C. Joerges, "What is Left of the European Economic Constitution?", European University Institute, Department of Law, Florence, *EUI Working Papers*, Law 2004, 13

worker has the right to working conditions which respect his or her health, safety and dignity". This is the core of the so-called "European Social Model" supposed to distinguish this region of the world from others. A redesigned Treaty has to make sure that this requirement does not remain a dead letter. In such a context the discussion of promoting cross-national mobility of services might then become a more sophisticated one.

7. PROBLEMS OF SURVEILLANCE AND CONTROL OF LABOUR STANDARDS – LESSONS FROM THE EUROPEAN SOCIAL CHARTER

Andrzej M. Swiatkowski

The object of this paper is to outline the enforcement mechanism established by the Council of Europe which is designed to enforce Community health and safety standards established by the European Social Charter. Directive 91/383 and the other directives examined by the European Parliament under the European forum on freedom of services and labour law and social security: the posted workers Directive 96/71, the insolvency protection Directive 80/987 as well as Regulation 1408/71 on the application of social security schemes to employed person, to self-employed and to members of their families moving within the Community – these instruments were all invoked to give impetus to negative views of the country of origin principle introduced by the draft Services Directive in the internal market.[207] The proposed Services Directive assumes that surveillance and control of rules of labour law is carried out by the country in which services are provided and work is performed.

Community labour law directives do not provide any specific rules concerning procedures and sanctions according to which substantive rules of the directives are to be enforced. Instead, domestic rules are applied.[208] The revolutionary concept introduced by the proposed Services Directive restricts the application of host country labour law provisions and introduces the country of origin principle. This new concept is based on the assumption that a unitary system of legal remedies exists in the various Member States of the European Union. If such a system of legal sanctions exists, the effective enforcement of labour regulations by administrative institutions of the country of origin ought not to be problematic. But without labour regulation by the host state, major difficulties will arise in maintaining throughout the Community the same labour standards in the provision of services, work performed and implementation of supervisory measures.

---

207 N. Bruun, Employment Issues, memorandum. European Parliament Public Hearing on the Proposal for Directive on Services in the Internal Market, Brussels 2004.
208 J. Malmberg (ed.), *Effective Enforcement of EC Labour Law* (The Hague/London/New York: Kluwer Law International, 2003) 5.

According to the proposed Services Directive, national remedies and procedures ought to be able to provide effective enforcement, regardless of the substantive right guaranteed either by the country of origin or the host country. In my opinion, the country of origin principle introduced by the proposed Services Directive decreases legal complexity and increases transparency in the process of effective enforcement of EC labour law. It entrusts the basic obligation of effective enforcement of EC labour regulations to the country concerned with labour law issues which is the country of origin. The success of this innovation relies on the assumption that there is a unitary system of legal remedies and procedure in all Member States. Therefore, the key issue relating to the effective enforcement of EC labour law is the system of supervision.

In this paper, I describe the system of supervision of social rights established by the Council of Europe. The supervision of the European Social Charter relies upon national reports presented by the Member States and collective complaints submitted by NGOs. Reports are examined and complaints adjudicated by an independent and impartial body whose task is to determine whether the legislation and practice of the Member States conform to international standards proclaimed by the international treaties. The European Committee of Social Rights plays an important role as the guardian of social rights guaranteed by the European Social Charter. In my opinion, the system of supervision of labour standards established by the Council of Europe could serve as the pattern for implementation of legal obligations imposed upon the Member States, which take responsibility for effective implementation of EC labour regulations by their own nationals regardless of the place they conduct their respective businesses: whether in the country of origin or in the territory of the host country.

The European Social Charter (both under its basic version of 1961 and the revised version of 1996) imposes on the authorities of the Member States of the Council of Europe the duty of ensuring the right to safe and healthy working conditions for workers (Article 3).[209] With a view to ensuring effective exercise of that right, the authorities of the Member States, together with their social partners (representatives of both the workers and the employers) are obliged to determine, implement and periodically review a coherent national social policy on occupational health and safety, and the protection of workers' health. The primary aim of the policy in the Council of Europe Member States is to improve occupational health and safety and to prevent accidents and injury to health arising out of, in connection with, or occurring in the course of work, particularly by minimising the causes of hazards inherent in the working environment (Article 3, subparagraph 1). For those purposes, the authorities of the Council of Europe Member States are obliged to issue health and safety regulations (Article 3, subparagraph 2) and to provide for the enforcement of such regulations by supervisory measures (Article 3, subparagraph 3). The Council

---

209 *European Social Charter, Collected Texts* (5th edn, Strasbourg: Council of Europe Publishing, 2005).

of Europe Member States have also undertaken to promote the progressive develop-ment of occupational health services for all workers with essentially preventive and advisory functions (Article 3, subparagraph 4). Within the confines of the study on administrative supervision of labour law, I am going to concentrate exclusively on the perception of the enforcement by measures of supervision of issuing health and safety regulations (Article 3, subparagraph 2 of the Revised European Social Charter) by the European Committee of Social Rights (the former Committee of Independent Experts). First of all, the provision of Article 3 subparagraph 2 of the Charter overlaps to some extent with the provision of Article 20 subparagraph 5 of the (Basic) European Social Charter as well as with Article A, subparagraph 4 of the Revised Social Charter. Each of those two provisions is identical in content and obliges the authorities of the Member States of the Council of Europe, which ratified either the European Social Charter of 1961 or the Revised Social Charter of 1996 or both the above-mentioned international treaties, to maintain a system of labour inspection appropriate in national conditions. Those provisions contain a clearly defined obligation and are not subject to the technical supervision of the Committee of Social Rights of the Council of Europe. Only in the context of supervision of compliance by Member States with the ratified resolutions of the European Social Charter is the nature of requirements put forward by the Committee of Social Rights to the authorities of the Member States – to maintain a system of labour inspection appropriate in national conditions – revealed. Such an inspection system serves as the basic (and, in some cases, as the only) administrative means of supervising compliance with national labour law.

Given that it is necessary to create an effective system of labour inspection in the Member States of the Council of Europe, legal analysis is required. The European Committee of Social Rights claims that national labour inspectors may supervise compliance with labour law at the national level in Member States which have ratified the European Social Charter. The scope of competence is determined by Article 3 subparagraph 1 of the Charter.[210] According to the European Committee of Social Rights, the above-mentioned standard may be applied universally. It covers all sectors of the economy and public administration. It applies to all workers employed in particular departments regardless of the legal basis of the employment relationship.[211] It also applies to those running their own business – the "self-employed".[212]

---

210 L. Samuel, *Fundamental Social Rights. Case Law of the European Social Charter* (2nd edn, Strasbourg: Council of Europe Publishing, 2002) 67 et seq. D. Harris, J. Darcy, *The European Social Charter* (2nd edn, New York: Transnational Publishers, inc. Ardsley, 2001) 70 et seq.

211 *European Social Charter. Committee of Independent Experts. Conclusions I, 1969-1970* (Stras-bourg: Council of Europe Press, 1995) 22; *European Social Charter. Committee of Independent Experts. Conclusions II, 1971* (Strasbourg: Council of Europe Press, 1995) 12 et seq.

212 *European Social Charter. Committee of Independent Experts. Conclusions XIII-3* (Strasbourg: Council of Europe Publishing, 1996) 205 (Italy).

Administrative supervision of labour law must be effective. According to the European Community of Social Rights, this requires imposing penal and mixed penal and administrative sanctions on those who fail to apply the mandatory occupational health and safety regulations.[213] Moreover, claims which may be lodged by those who benefit from the duty imposed by Article 3 of the Charter (the employees and the self-employed) must be regulated. Such persons may submit their claims to the persons or bodies responsible for ensuring occupational safety.

Article 3 of the European Social Charter amounts to a rule that a coherent national policy on occupational safety, occupational health and the working environment must be formulated, implemented and periodically reviewed (subparagraph 1) and in each respect those obligations must be supported by guarantees. Those guarantees are set out in the provisions obliging the authorities of the Member States to issue health and safety regulations (subparagraph 2), to enforce such regulations by supervision (subparagraph 3) and to promote, for the benefit of all workers, the progressive development of occupational health services of an essentially preventive and advisory nature (subparagraph 4). For a labour lawyer attempting to ensure administrative supervision of the law, the clearest of the Charter regulations is given in Article 3, subparagraph 2. A precise definition of what constitutes an undertaking must be given. Secondly, a system of administrative supervision over the above-mentioned duties is to be established and maintained. According to the concept followed by the European Social Charter, the system of administrative supervision should be implemented by the national labour inspectorate. In establishing standards of compliance with Article 3 subparagraph 2 of the European Social Charter, the European Committee of Social Rights took the stand that a failure to perform the duty determined in Article 3, subparagraph 1 of the European Social Charter is automatically viewed as a breach by the Member State of Article 3 subparagraph 3. That position was taken on the basis of a literal interpretation of Article 3, subparagraph 3 of the Charter. Under Article 3, subparagraph 3 of the Charter, the Member States of the Council of Europe were obliged (in both official languages of the Council of Europe – English and French) to ensure the application of "such regulations" (*ces règlements*). The European Committee of Social Rights, during the first 13 cycles of supervision of compliance with the regulations of the European Social Charter, understood "such regulations" as meaning any legal regulations issued by Member States' authorities in order to fulfil the duties formulated in Article 3, subparagraph 1 and 2 of the Charter.[214] The Committee of Social Rights revised its opinion on the matter in its conclusion given in the 14th cycle of supervision of 1998. It did not give reasons for such a radical change of opinion, but simply stated in one sentence that there was no systematic connection between conclusions made on the grounds of Article 3, subparagraphs 1 and 2 of the European Social Charter, since each of

---

213   *Conclusions I, op. cit.*, p. 23.
214   *European Social Charter. Committee of Independent Experts. Conclusions XII-1, 1988-1989* (Strasbourg: Council of Europe Press, 1992) 83; *Conclusions XIII-3, op. cit.*, p. 209 (Greece), p. 212 (The Netherlands).

the aforementioned regulations contains specific requirements on enforcing the right to safe and healthy working conditions.[215] Each of the requirements presented above is subject to evaluation.

The Committee of Social Rights is right to an extent. Article 3, subparagraph 1 of the Charter is focused on social policy whereas Article 3, subparagraph 2 concerns occupational health and safety regulations. Issuing regulations ensuring safe and healthy working conditions stems from a specific social policy primarily oriented towards the improvement of occupational health and safety and prevention of accidents and health hazards. A failure to issue health and safety regulations by any of the Member States shall constitute a breach of the provisions of Article 3 subparagraph 2 of the Charter. Should the breach result from a specific national policy on health and safety regulations, the state may be in breach of subparagraph 1 of Article 3. However, some countries may implement a coherent national policy thus meeting the requirements of Article 3, subparagraph 1 of the European Social Charter while refraining from issuing any health and safety regulations which, in turn, shall be considered a breach of Article 3, subparagraph 2 of the Charter. In some circumstances, a breach of Article 3, subparagraph 2 of the European Social Charter may be tantamount to a breach of Article 3, subparagraph 1 of the Charter. However, this is not always the case.

In the course of the fourteenth supervision cycle, the Committee of Social Rights developed criteria for evaluating the effectiveness of labour law supervision carried out by the National Labour Inspectorate. Further to the conclusion presented during the 8th supervision cycle,[216] the Committee of Social Rights adopted as a criterion of effective application of Article 3, the relation between accidents or occupational diseases and the number of all workplaces and the workplaces inspected in a year. Other criteria include: the number of National Labour Inspectors authorised to perform the inspection and types of sanctions imposed by the labour inspectors on employers in breach of workers' rights to safe and healthy working conditions. However, the Committee of Social Rights – aware that the number of accidents and stated cases of occupational disease established formally cannot serve as a sufficient indicator of effective administrative supervision of labour regulations, as early as in the conclusions to the thirteenth supervision cycle – obliged the Member States' authorities to include information on the number of supervisions carried out in workplaces supervised by national labour inspectors in their national reports. The information also has to contain: the number and percentage of employees of workplaces supervised by labour inspectors, the number of labour inspectors employed by the National Labour Inspectorate and information on the professional competence of the inspectors.[217] The Committee of Social Rights stated that an

---

215 *European Social Charter. Committee of Independent Experts. Conclusions XIV-2*, vol. 2 (Strasbourg: Council of Europe Press, 1998) 43 (General Introduction).

216 *European Social Charter. Committee of Independent Experts. Conclusions VIII, 1984* (Strasbourg: Council of Europe Press, 1995) 54-55.

217 *Conclusions XIII-1, op. cit.*, pp. 92-93.

effective system of adjustment of the Member States to the regulations and standards developed by the Committee on the basis of those regulations of the European Social Charter required that a National Labour Inspection Unit is set up and maintained in accordance with specific standards. Therefore, effective national supervision of labour regulations is a prerequisite for abiding by the European Social Charter Regulations. In order to assess whether each of the Member States managed to create an effective supervision system the Committee imposed an obligation on the Member States of the Council of Europe to supply it with regular information on their National Labour Inspection units. The information must include: the number of inspectors, their competence and the legal measures they are entitled to employ when dealing with undertakings in breach of the economic and social rights of the employed and the self-employed.

The decisions relating to supervision of application of the European Social Charter regulations and on the European Labour Law standards as devised by the European Committee of Social Rights lead to two conclusions:

1)   According to the Committee, administrative supervision of labour regulations correspond to the supervision carried out by the National Labour Inspectorate. The National Labour Inspectorate is a specialised public authority equipped with relevant competences and authorised to apply coercive measures;

2)   When assessing the efficiency of measures of national supervision to ensure states' compliance with the European Social Charter, regulations in assessing the data presented by Member States' authorities, the Committee employs some auxiliary criteria devised by international organisations other than the Council of Europe.

The most complete regulation on the status and competences of labour inspectors is derived from International labour law devised by the International Labour Organisation. As early as 1919, during the first session of the ILO, a recommendation concerning labour inspection (of health services) was adopted. During the 30th session of the ILO in 1947, Convention 81 regarding Labour Inspection in Industry and Commerce[218] was adopted, together with recommendation 81 on Labour Inspection.[219] During the 53rd session of the ILO, Convention 129 on Labour Inspection in Agriculture[220] was adopted. In 1995, a Protocol was annexed to Convention 81. The Protocol extended the range of labour inspectors' competence to "non-

---

218   *Konwencje i zalecenia Międzynarodowej Organizacji Pracy* (ILO Conventions and Recommendations) 1919-1994, vol. I (Warsaw: Wydawnictwo Naukowe PWN, 1996) 341 et seq.

219   *Ibid.*, p. 349.

220   *Konwencje i zalecenia Międzynarodowej Organizacji Pracy* (ILO Conventions and Recommendations) 1919-1994, vol. II (Warsaw: Wydawnictwo Naukowe PWN, 1996) 751 et seq.

commercial services", thus public administration was included in supervision by National Labour Inspectorates.[221]

ILO Convention 81 was implemented on 7 April 1950 and ratified by 128 countries,[222] including 33 Member States of the Council of Europe. The aforementioned ILO conventions and recommendations on labour inspection were supplemented by ILO Convention 150 on the role, tasks and the organisation of labour, adopted during ILO session 64 in 1978[223]. In the course of the same session a recommendation on the role, tasks and the organisation of labour administration was adopted.[224] Other ILO conventions and recommendations regulate the technical standards of the functioning of labour inspectors in various economic sectors including: the construction industry (recommendation 54 of 1937), agriculture (recommendation 133 of 1969), and dock handling (recommendation 160 of 1979). Moreover, working conditions of persons employed in some branches of the economy as well as those under special protection are regulated by a number of international regulations. Compliance of the ILO Member States with those regulations is supervised by national labour inspectorates. Of the aforementioned regulations, ILO Convention 81 is particularly important as it specifies the tasks of the national labour inspectors. The labour inspectors are obliged to supervise the application of labour law regulations in matters concerning the protection of fair conditions of work such as reasonable working hours, safe and healthy working conditions, the employment of children and young persons. The inspectors are also obliged to carry out supervision in other cases in which they have to ensure compliance with labour law regulations.

According to ILO Convention 81, they also have to supply technical information and advice to employers and workers on the most effective means of complying with the legal provisions. The convention in question states that one function of the system of labour inspection is to bring to the notice of the competent authority any defects in or abuses of both work safety and hygiene of workers not specifically covered by existing legal provisions (Article 3, subparagraph 1). Any further professional duties which may be entrusted to labour inspectors shall not be such as to interfere with the effective discharge of their primary duties or to prejudice in any way the authority and impartiality which inspectors require in their relations with employers and workers (Article 3, subparagraph 2). The inspection staff shall be composed of public officials whose status and conditions of service are such that they are assured of stability of employment and are independent of changes of government and of improper external influences (Article 6). Labour inspectors provided with proper credentials shall be empowered to enter freely and without

---

221   W. Von Richthofen, *Labour Inspection: A Guide to the Profession* (Geneva: International Labour Office, 2002) 79 et seq.
222   Lists of Ratifications by Convention and by Country (Geneva: International Labour Office, 2003) 93-94.
223   Konwencje (ILO Conventions), *op. cit.* v.II, p. 993 et seq.
224   *Ibid.*, p. 997 et seq.

previous notice, at any hour of the day or night, any workplace liable to inspection, to enter by day, any premises which they have reasonable cause to believe to be liable to inspection, to carry out any examination, test or inquiry which they may consider necessary in order to satisfy themselves that the legal provisions are being strictly observed. In particular the labour inspectors are be empowered:

– to interrogate alone, or in the presence of witnesses, the employer or the staff of the undertaking on any matters concerning the application of legal provisions;
– to require the production of any books, registers or other documents, the keeping of which is prescribed by national laws or regulations relating to conditions of work, in order to see that they are in conformity with the legal provisions, and to copy such documents or make extracts from them;
– to enforce the posting of notices required by the legal provisions;
– to take or remove, for purposes of analysis, samples of materials and substances used or handled, subject to the employer or his representative being notified of any samples or substances taken or removed for such purpose (Article 12, subparagraph 1).

ILO Convention 81 gives labour inspectors the powers to take steps with a view to remedying defects observed in plant, labour or working methods which they have reasonable cause to believe constitute a threat to the health or safety of the workers. In order to enable inspectors to take such steps they are empowered, subject to any right of appeal to a judicial or administrative authority which may be provided by law, to make or to have made orders requiring such alterations to the installation or plant, to be carried out within a specified time limit, as may be necessary to secure compliance with the legal provisions relating to the health and safety of the workers or measures with immediate executory force in the event of imminent danger to the health and safety of the workers (Article 13, subparagraph 2). ILO Convention 81 states that workplaces shall be inspected as often and as thoroughly as is necessary to ensure the effective application of the relevant legal provisions (Article 16).

The European Union Member States were bound by the Framework Directive No. 391 of 12 June 1989 on the introduction of measures to encourage improvements in the health and safety of workers at work (89/39/EEC).[225] Of the 45 Member States of the Council of Europe, the 25 European Union Member States are bound to take every action during all the stages of work at the workplace in order to prevent or reduce occupational risks. Directive 89/391/EEC contains general principles concerning the prevention of occupational risks, the protection of health and safety, the elimination of risk and accident factors, informing, consultation, and balanced participation in accordance with national laws and/or practices and training of workers

---

225   OJ L 183/1.

and of their representatives, as well as general guidelines for the implementation of those principles (Article 1, subparagraph 2).[226] In general, the employer shall have a duty to ensure the health and safety of workers in every aspect related to the work (Article 5, subparagraph 1), employers should enlist competent external services or persons to carry out activities related to protection and prevention of occupational risks. This shall not discharge them from their responsibilities in this area. Being confined by this duty, employers shall implement the measures on the basis of the following general principles of prevention: evaluating the risks which cannot be avoided; combating risks at source; adapting the work to the individual; adapting to technical progress; replacing the dangerous by the non-dangerous or the less dangerous; developing a coherent overall prevention policy; giving appropriate instructions to the workers. Framework Directive 89/391/EEC requires that employers allow workers and their representatives to participate in all actions carried out within the workplace in order to ensure the safety and protection of the lives and health of the workers. Administrative supervision of compliance with duties regulated by the Framework Directive and other detailed directives is carried out by National Labour Inspection units and individual European Union Member States.

International organisations such as the Council of Europe, the International Labour Organisation, and the European Union would all like the Member States to achieve the desired results. In matters concerning occupational health and safety and protection of the workers' health; in all aspects of labour, the international organisations request that the Member States' authorities protect the lives and health of workers from any hazards which may arise in the process of performing work and from working conditions. The international organisations leave it to the authorities of the Member States to choose the methods to achieve that result. Their protection techniques are effective. Owing to cultural differences in Europe, the Council of Europe advises each signatory state to "maintain a system of labour inspection appropriate to national conditions" (Article A, subparagraph 4 of the Revised European Social Charter).

The Member States of the Council of Europe are given two options as far as basic protection techniques are concerned: they can introduce either preventive measures or sanctions. Guaranteeing safe and hygienic working conditions for workers – as well as protecting their lives and health – can be achieved by providing employers with information and advice as to what measures they should use, or by imposing penalties on those employers in breach of their obligations. ILO Convention 81 not only permits but recommends that each Member State should organise its national labour inspection system using these two types of measures. These measures are not contradictory. There is no state in Europe whose authorities prohibit labour inspectors from advising employers on protection from occupational risks. Some

---

226   A.M. Swiatkowski, *Bezpieczeństwo i higiena pracy* (Health and Safety) (Krakow: Universitas, 2003) 164 et seq.

countries such as the Netherlands try to discourage labour inspectors from advising large companies. The Dutch authorities believe that employers who need advice on the organisation of work in accordance with occupational health and safety regulations, and on guaranteeing protection of health to workers, should employ professional consultants from consulting companies. That approach is confirmed by Framework Directive 89/391/EEC which obliges employers to ensure that the workplace is professionally equipped with occupational health and safety services. The duty of the National Labour Inspectorate is to carry out administrative supervision of occupational health and safety services in workplaces.[227]

In Sweden, the state authorities advise labour inspectors to refrain from applying coercive measures at least during the first stage of supervision of compliance with labour law regulations. The labour inspectors are even advised to negotiate with the workers the conditions under which regulations are applied. They are to administer penalties only in the event that employers do not comply with the agreements made. That approach is based on the Scandinavian labour law model. The model, in turn, is based on agreements made by social partners.[228] The agreements were extended to organisational units created in order to carry out administrative supervision of labour regulations in Sweden. In some states (e.g. France, Greece and the countries of Latin America) national labour inspectors participate in collective labour agreements independently of social partners. In some instances, these are the national collective labour regulations that impose on labour inspectors legal duties of managing affairs prior to the existence of collective labour agreements.[229] The authorities of the majority of European countries leave it to the labour inspectors to decide which of the two aforementioned measures they should apply in supervising compliance with labour regulations. In most cases, national labour inspectors advise employers on what measures of occupational protection to apply and administer penalties in the event that employers do not comply with the advice given.[230]

Emphasis on a specific technique employed by national labour supervision by a core (and, in many countries, a sole) supervising body is dependent on the scope of competences entrusted to the labour inspector.[231] In some European countries (Belgium, Bulgaria, France, Spain), the competence of the National Labour Inspectorate is very broad. It includes supervision of compliance with all individual and collective labour regulations and also with social insurance regulations. In other European countries (The Netherlands, Germany, Sweden and Great Britain) the competence assigned to labour law inspectors includes: occupational health and

---

227   A.T.J.M. Jacobs, *Labour and Social Security in the Netherlands. An Introduction* (Den Bosch: BookWorld Publications, 1997) 59; W. Von Richthofen, *op. cit.*, pp. 101-102.

228   N. Bruun, B. Flodgren, M. Halvorsen, H. Hydén, R. Nielsen, *The Nordic Labour Relations Model. Labour Law and Trade Unions in Nordic Countries – Today and Tomorrow* (Aldershot: Dartmouth Publishing Company, 1992) 144 et seq.; R. Fahlbeck, *Labour and Employment Law in Sweden* (Lund: Juristförlager, 1997) 38 I et seq, pp. 71-72.

229   W. Von Richthofen, *op. cit.*, p. 32.

230   W. Von Richthofen, *op. cit.*, p. 101.

231   J. Malmberg *et al.*, *op. cit.*, pp. 113-114; W. Von Richthofen, *op. cit.*, p. 29.

safety, protection of the employment of women, protection of young employees and working hours.[232] In Poland, the Act of 6 March 1981 on National Labour Inspection (*Panstwowa Inspekcja Pracy*)[233] authorises the labour inspectors to carry out supervision of compliance with labour regulations (in particular the occupational health and safety rules and regulations – Article 1). The already wide competence of the labour inspectors was further broadened by the powers enumerated in Article 8 of the Act. The inspectors still carry out administrative supervision of employers' compliance with the labour regulations (in particular with occupational health and safety regulations). They supervise compliance with regulations concerning employment relationships, remuneration and other provisions related to employment relationships, working hours, the rights of workers with family responsibilities, the employment of children and young persons and the disabled, and provisions regarding the starting up of farms for individual farmers (Article 8, subparagraph 1, point 1). Article 9, subparagraph 1 of the National Labour Inspection Act, mentions areas in which labour inspectors are obliged to supervise compliance with labour regulations. A vital competence of labour inspection is the supervision of compliance by all undertakings with the occupational health and safety rules and regulations. The Constitution of the Republic of Poland of 2 April 1997[234] guarantees the right to safe and healthy working conditions, not only to workers but to all people.(Article 66, subparagraph 1).[235] The Polish professional labour inspectors have been given wide competences, which include supervision of compliance with all labour regulations.[236] In Poland, the National Labour Inspectorate is, together with judicial bodies, one of the vital institutions which guarantee compliance with labour regulations.[237]

In evaluating the practice of the European Committee of Social Rights concerning supervision of labour regulations by national labour inspection bodies, its preference for objective indicators of labour inspection deserves some criticism. During the fourteenth cycle of supervision of Member States' compliance with the European Social Charter, it was stated that Portugal did not comply with Article 3, subparagraph 2 of the Charter because in 1996, labour inspectors had supervised workplaces, where only 6 per cent of workers were employed.[238] The opinions and

---

232 J. Malmberg *et al.*, *op. cit.*, pp. 113-114.
233 Uniform text: Journal of Law, 2001, No, 124, item 1362 as amended
234 Dz.U. No. 78, item 483.
235 T. Nycz, *Konstytucyjne gwarancje bezpiecznych i higienicznych warunków pracy* (Constitutional guarantees of healthy and safe conditions of work) (Tarnobrzeg: Wydawnictwo TARbonus, 2000).
236 A. M. Swiatkowski, *Polskie prawo pracy* (Polish Labour Law) (Warsaw: LexisNexis, 2003) 392. Organisational unit having no employees shall be excluded from the administrative supervision of labour law by the labour supervision bodies. (Resolution of the Supreme Court of 8 II 1989 r., III AZP 18/88, OSNCP 1990, file1, item 10).
237 A. Świątkowski, *Zasady prawa pracy* (Principles of Labour Law) (Warszawa, 1997) 300 et seq.; T. Strek, *Państwowa inspekcja pracy* (Labour Inspection) (Krakow: 1998).
238 *Conclusions XIV-2*, *op. cit.*, pp. 641-642.

decisions of the European Committee of Social Rights on administrative supervision of labour regulations in Member States are based almost exclusively on statistical data on the number of inspections, supervised workplaces, workers employed in the supervised workplaces and the number of accidents at work.[239] As far as Member States' compliance with the European Social Charter regulations on the rights of children and young persons to protection (Article 7), the European Committee of Social Rights calls our attention to the frequency with which employers are fined and of the financial severity of the punishments levied.[240]

As the Committee focuses its attention almost exclusively on statistics, some extreme cases of breaches of the European Social Charter can be identified. The Charter's regulations oblige the Council of Europe Member States to ensure some proper measures, including a system of labour inspections and supervision, and guaranteeing the right to safe and healthy working conditions to both workers and the self-employed. Development and maintenance of this system of administrative supervision of labour regulations requires an investigation into the degree of importance to the national authorities of prevention practices. Placing emphasis on the role of prevention in the administrative supervision of labour regulations requires expanding the competence of the labour inspectors in those Member States in which the range of the inspectorate's activity was narrowed down to occupational health and safety. The authorities of all Member States are obliged to introduce a new national labour inspection system which would cooperate with social partners. First of all, labour inspectors should act as advisors to social partners on compliance with regulations on worker protection and social security regulations. The system of administrative supervision of labour regulations which has been the dominant one in Europe should be replaced by separate systems implemented in each workplace. Such systems should be based on informing workers about the range of social and workers' rights they have.

These rights have been established either in the course of social partners' normative agreements or by the state and consist in the employers' having to consult with workers and their representatives in decision making. Effective administrative supervision of labour regulations requires a range of information, and the extension of dialogue and cooperation of social partners with supervisory bodies. Only such cooperation can ensure protection of occupational health and safety in the workplace. The cooperation of social partners with National Labour Inspectorates is to help employers and state authorities take proper action and preventive measures. The European Committee of Social Rights should extend the checklist on which national reports on the types of preventive activities and measures applied, in order to ensure effective protection of the social rights guaranteed in the European Social Charter.

---

239 L. Samuel, *op. cit.*, p. 70.
240 See: "Form of the Reports Submitted in Pursuance of the Revised European Social Charter", in *European Social Charter. Collected Texts, op. cit.*, p. 323 et seq.

With an improved checklist, the methods of carrying out supervision should also improve. Participation of the National Labour Inspectorate in the altered system of social law protection permits further supervision of labour regulations.

The proposed Services Directive strengthens the legal responsibility of the country of origin for effective enforcement of EC labour law within the Member States. It corresponds with existing pillars of the private enforcement model of EC law: direct effect, indirect effect and Member State liability.[241] What is needed as a prerequisite for the effective enforcement of EC labour law by the Member States in which service providers are registered, is an impartial body directly connected with the Commission which is able to provide required information on any case of non-compliance by any Member State with a unitary system of sanctions and procedure within the European Union. The rest ought to be considered technical issues – such as how the Member States organise their respective administrations to control activities performed beyond their own borders according to the country of origin principle.

---

241   J. Malmberg, *op. cit.*, p. 38 et seq.

8. MONITORING OF LABOUR STANDARDS IN CASE OF POSTING: SOME TROUBLESOME ISSUES UNDER THE PROPOSED SERVICES DIRECTIVE

Frank Hendrickx

1. INTRODUCTION

It is not news to say that Europe is not a state, let alone a federal state, in the classic sense of the word. This is due to the relative differences and divergence of systems to be found among EU Member States. But even in a further developed federal context, Member States would not be the same, and full convergence would not necessarily be reached. However, whatever the phase of (European) integration, conditions should be met to effectively respond to business and labour in a globalised environment.

There are various options to be dealt with in the economic market, the market of services and the market of labour. Given the variety of Member State approaches, and given the absence of a minimum level of harmonisation at European level, the EU can probably only proceed with second-best solutions.

In a better Europe, it can be argued, territorial coincidence would not matter. Regardless of the territory of the state, individuals and companies would be subject to the same – or equivalent – standards. It would bring non-discrimination and free movement closer to reality. There would not be an environment based on competition between states. Possibly, higher levels of mutual trust would be reached.

Although it may also – in a rather controversial way given the current time frame – be argued that the four freedoms (persons, goods, capital, services) of the EC Treaty lead to harmonising national systems of social protection, the actual construct is strongly different: country territory matters; legal conditions for business are quite different; labour protection is strongly dependent on national law; welfare systems are far from harmonised.

One of the intrinsic problems of the EU is that it has strong competences to de-regulate markets, but remains rather weak in re-regulating them, certainly as far as the labour market is concerned.

The European Commission's proposed draft Services Directive (or "Proposal")[242] is central to the outlook of this European legal framework. It brings up notions of further removal of barriers, a country of origin principle and mutual recognition.

But it is precisely in the absence of a minimum level of harmonisation at EU level, that a system of mutual recognition and the introduction of a country of origin principle may be a dangerous exercise. It creates tensions between the respective systems of different Member States. In the area of social policy, it even has the potential to break into classical national approaches. This is, quite likely, why the Proposal has been criticised so much.

Nevertheless, the motivation for the Proposal is not so wrong *per se*. It is to be "part of the process of economic reform launched by the Lisbon European Council with a view to making the EU the most competitive and dynamic knowledge-based economy in the world by 2010. Achieving this goal means that the establishment of a genuine internal market in services is indispensable. It has not hitherto been possible to exploit the considerable potential for economic growth and job creation afforded by the services sector because of the many obstacles hampering the development of service activities in the internal market".[243]

The attention of the Proposal is wide but still to the point. It concentrates on freeing the services market, and while it touches upon labour market issues, such as posting of workers, it does so only from a relatively narrow point of view. The Proposal therefore seems to presuppose what is currently lacking in the field of labour law and social policy: a sufficient minimum harmonisation and mutual trust and confidence among the Member States in the area of social policy.

This can be illustrated with the core question of this paper: is the competent Member State authority (in whose territory the service is provided) best placed to ensure the effectiveness and the continuity of supervision and to provide for protection of recipients? And in case of trans-border services involving cross-border employment, are adequate means available for institutions looking after the application of their own labour laws?

2. STATE CONTROL AS A BASIS FOR COMPLIANCE

Already a long time ago, the ILO has recognised that the monitoring and enforcement of labour law is a precondition for decent social protection. This idea constitutes the main aim of a set of ILO Conventions and Recommendations.

---

242   These terms are used to identify document COM(2004)2 final/3, 5 March 2004, p. 83.
243   COM(2004)2 final/3, 3.

2.1. The ILO Concept

The Labour Inspection Convention, 1947 (No. 81) [and its Protocol of 1995] and the Labour Inspection (Agriculture) Convention, 1969 (No. 129) both oblige the maintenance of a system of labour inspection in industrial, commercial and agricultural workplaces. Such systems must operate to the standards set in these instruments. The Protocol extends the scope of Convention No. 81 to the non-commercial service sector. Convention No. 81 covers industrial undertakings and may, at the time of ratification, be extended to cover commercial workplaces. Convention No. 129 covers only agricultural workplaces. The provisions of the Conventions are virtually identical.

The following obligations, arising from the Conventions, can be brought under the attention:

– labour inspection under the control of a central authority;
– effective coordination between inspection services, other government services and public and private institutions engaged in similar activities;
– strength of labour inspection services sufficient to secure effective discharge of duties;
– authority for inspectors to enter workplaces;
– regular workplace inspection;
– adequate penalties for violations of laws and regulations;

Conventions Nos. 81 and 129 are supplemented by Recommendations Nos. 81 and 133 respectively. The 1995 Protocol to Convention No. 81 obliges the ratifying States to apply the provisions of the Convention to the non-commercial service sector, as defined in the Protocol.

The model behind this can be understood in the following straightforward and summarised terms:

– *central entity*: a state makes labour laws; it monitors its own labour laws; it enforces compliance with its own labour laws;
– *adequacy*: effective coordination, authority and penalties.

Leaving aside that the introduction of labour inspection services is only one way of reaching labour law compliance, the ILO concept has been well responded to in the Member States of the EU, although it might be problematic when applied to in an increased global or European internal market (e.g. of services and workers) context.

In the EU:

– Twenty-five Member States make their own (national) labour laws, the European level remaining at a distance. This is obviously linked with desires of national sovereignty in the area of social policy;

–   European-wide, one has to deal with at least 25 central entities (even more,
     taking into account some Member States' federal structures) designed to
     look after the application of their own labour laws;
–   Those labour laws have to be applied (and enforced) in national courts.

Further developments in European law have shown how well-established the classical view on labour law monitoring and enforcement by one country (the country
of employment) is. The exercise by a worker of his right to free movement will
make him subject to another Member State's labour law. It is well-known that the
principle used in the Rome Convention of 19 June 1980 on the law applicable to
contractual obligations, allows for other laws to be made (or to remain) applicable
than the law of the country of employment. However, there are strong reservations
with regard to mandatory provisions of labour law of the work state.[244] Furthermore,
even when legitimate choices are made, a often heard criticism is that national courts
are often rely too readily on the *lex fori*. Even stronger criticism may be found in
this respect with regard to the application of the EEX – EVEX Treaties.[245]

     The applicable labour law is, however, determined differently in case of temporary
assignments abroad, such as in the case of trans-border posting of workers.

     It is within this context that the Posting Directive has been adopted, precisely
to preserve the model mentioned above, whereby national states control their own
content of, and freedom in, monitoring of labour laws.

2.2. The Posting Directive

In the cases of *Rush Portuguesa*[246] and *VanderElst*[247] the European Court of Justice
stated that Community law does not preclude Member States from extending their
legislation, or collective labour agreements, to any person who is employed, even
temporarily, within their territory, no matter in which country the employer is
established. In other words, the Court accepted the principle that Member States
hold control over the application of labour law in their territories, albeit within
the scope of private international law. As indicated above, however, the private
international law provisions have to be significantly nuanced due to the provisions
of Articles 6 and 7 of the Rome Convention, which intend to protect the worker
from the "freedom of choice" principle, and set to protect territorial law. For

---

244   Articles 6 and 7, Rome Convention 1980.
245   Convention on the Jurisdiction and Enforcement of Judgements in Civil and Commercial Matters
      (EEX) and the Lugano Convention on jurisdiction and the enforcement of judgements in civil
      and commercial matters (EVEX).
246   Case C-113/89 [1990] ECR I-1425.
247   Case C-43/93 [1994] ECR I-4221.

example, rules of a special mandatory character will apply even if a worker is only temporarily employed in a country.[248]

2.3. Responsible Authority

The Posting Directive[249] affirms these principles, as the Preamble shows:

> Whereas Community law does not preclude Member States from applying their legislation, or collective agreements entered into by employers and labour, to any person who is employed, even temporarily, within their territory, although his employer is established in another Member State; whereas Community law does not forbid Member States to guarantee the observance of those rules by the appropriate means.[250]

Furthermore, the Posting Directive defines the "hard core" subjects of employment law that are to be applied in the country where the work is performed, regardless of the law applicable to the employment situation.

From a monitoring perspective, it is the host state that is responsible for the application of the mandatory labour laws governing a posting situation in its own territory. In its evaluation report, the Commission has indicated two types of measures that are used by Member States to ensure compliance with the provisions of the Directive:[251]

– measures to *monitor* the legality of postings; and
– measures to *penalise* possible irregularities ascertained.

2.4. Adequate Monitoring

In the framework of the Posting Directive, it is also important to refer to effective and adequate monitoring of applicable labour laws. The Commission's report indicates that, besides the usual inspections of undertakings or workplaces, certain States have adopted two other types of methods to facilitate monitoring of compliance with the transposition rules:[252]

– the keeping of records at the place where the services are provided, and

---

248 Cf. Article 7, Rome Convention 1980.
249 Directive 96/71/EC of 16 December 1996 (OJ 1997 L 18/1) concerning the posting of workers in the framework of the provision of services.
250 Preamble 12.
251 COM(2003)458 final, 10.
252 COM(2003)458 final, 10.

–   the declaration of the provision of services to the national authorities.

The European Commission has furthermore rightly pointed out – and it was well seen by the Posting Directive – that (foreign) interested parties in posting assignments need to have advance information about the terms and conditions of employment applicable in the host country in order for them to be able to perform the services required and comply with the mandatory provisions applicable to employees during their period of posting.[253] Also, Houwerzijl's paper points out the Court's view that accessible and transparent information is a condition *sine qua non* for an effective application of the Posting Directive.[254] But in the idea of the Posting Directive, the burden of information, i.e. the burden associated with dealing with differences in national labour legislation, is put on the foreign interested parties. It is also clear that, in return, the host state's obligation laid down in Article 4(3) of the Posting Directive, should be taken seriously. It imposes on Member States acting as a host country an obligation to give information to the general public about the working conditions applicable to posted workers.

Article 4 of Directive 96/71/EC also obliges Member States to designate one or more liaison offices or national bodies and to notify the other Member States of this. Article 4 furthermore provides for cooperation between the public authorities responsible for monitoring the terms and conditions of employment referred to in Article 3 of the Directive. In its assessment report, the Commission indicated that, in order to *facilitate access to information* on the applicable terms and conditions of employment, a good few Member States have produced brochures or *vademecums*, which are also available on their websites.[255]

3.   PRE-CONDITIONS OR A ROAD OF TRUST: PROPOSED SERVICES DIRECTIVE

At first sight, the Proposed Services Directive maintains the traditional view on monitoring of compliance with labour law: the host state is responsible for monitoring and can take compliance measures. However, looking further into the text, the Proposal provides for significant and express derogations from the principles of the Posting Directive. It seems to suppose preconditions that cannot be met in the current state of play.

---

253   COM(2003)458 final, 9.
254   This was stated by the ECJ in Cf. Joined cases C-369/96 and C-376/96 [1999], ECR I-8453.
255   COM(2003)458 final, 10.

3.1. Principles with regard to Monitoring of Labour Law

In principle, the Proposal retains the classic viewpoint:

–   The host state carries out the *monitoring*:
        Article 24, paragraph 1 provides: "Where a provider posts a worker to another
        Member State in order to provide a service, the Member State of posting
        shall carry out in its territory the checks, inspections and investigations
        necessary to ensure compliance with the employment and working conditions
        applicable under Directive 96/71/EC"
–   The host state can take *compliance measures*:
        Article 24, paragraph 1 provides that the Member State of posting "shall
        take, in accordance with Community law, measures in respect of a service
        provider who fails to comply with those conditions".

3.2. Exceptions

However, the host state is limited in the further text of Article 24, as regards matters
governed by the Posting Directive.

   According to Article 24, the Member State of posting may not make the provider
or the posted worker subject to any of the following obligations, as regards the
matters covered by Directive 96/71/EC (referred to in point (5) of Article 17 of
the Proposal).

–   to obtain *authorisation* from, or to be registered with, its own competent
        authorities, or to satisfy any other equivalent requirement;
–   to make a *declaration*, other than declarations relating to an activity referred
        to in the Annex to Directive 96/71/EC which may be maintained until 31
        December 2008;
–   to have a *representative* in its territory;
–   to hold and keep employment *documents* in its territory or in accordance
        with the conditions applicable in its territory.

3.3. Comments

At this point, the Proposal can be criticised, not only in respect of the introduction of the country of origin principle, but also from the perspective of adequate
monitoring for compliance.

   It can be concluded in line with Bruun's analysis that the proposed Services
Directive seems to turn to a reverse idea of equal treatment used in traditional free
movement concepts: "employees of service providers moving to another Member
State are *not* entitled to equal treatment, but are subject to the principle that they

are governed by the rules of their country of origin."[256] The question is, however, whether *adverse treatment* is being pursued here. More likely, the reasoning of equal treatment in the Proposal might be more noble in that "unlike cases should not be treated alike", in order to put services of posting on a "competitive equal level" compared to home based (host state) services.

The idea, nevertheless, seems to break with the traditional view that the (host) state regulates, and is responsible for compliance with, its own labour laws. Indeed, following the Posting Directive, service providers at least have to comply with the "hard core" provisions of the state of posting, but are curtailed in monitoring compliance. Furthermore, some elements of national labour market policy (e.g. prior authorisation, …) are deregulated in favour of freedom of service.

In this regard, it may be argued that the Proposal seems to overestimate the present European social policy "level playing field". The assumptions underlying the Proposal do not appear to be realistic. The Proposal actually supposes a certain level of harmonisation of legal systems and a fair amount of mutual trust among Member States. This, apparently, does not exist.

The presuppositions are confirmed by the Proposal itself.

> With a view to establishing the mutual trust between Member States necessary for eliminating these obstacles, the proposal provides for:
>
> – *harmonisation* of legislation in order to guarantee equivalent protection of the general interest on vital questions, such as consumer protection, particularly as regards the service provider's obligations concerning information, professional insurance, multidisciplinary activities, settlement of disputes, and exchange of information on the quality of the service provider;
>
> – *stronger mutual assistance between national authorities* with a view to effective supervision of service activities on the basis of a clear distribution of roles between the Member States and obligations to cooperate.[257]

In its Proposal, the Commission also explains that *derogations to the country of origin principle* have been determined, according to two types of consideration:[258]

(1)   The Community *acquis*. Certain derogations are provided for in order to take into account the fact that *existing Community instruments* apply the rule according to which cross-border service provision may be subject to the legislation of the country of destination. Concerning a rule contrary to Article 16 of the Directive, derogations are necessary in order to ensure

---

256   N. Bruun, *EP Public Hearing, 11 November 2004. Employment Issues. Memorandum*, 10.
257   COM(2004)2 final/3, 4.
258   COM(2004)2 final/3, 5 March 2004, 25.

coherence with this *acquis*. Such derogations concern Directive 96/71/EC (posting of workers) and Regulation (EEC) No. 1408/71 (social security).

(2)   The level of disparity between national regimes. For certain activities or matters, *too wide a divergence in national approaches* or an insufficient level of Community integration may exist and prevent the application of the country of origin principle. As far as possible, the Directive harmonises, or provides for strengthened administrative cooperation, in order to establish the *mutual confidence* necessary for the application of the country of origin principle.

The Commission argues that, in certain cases or policy areas, it is not possible at this stage to achieve such harmonisation in this Directive or to establish such cooperation and it is therefore necessary to allow for a derogation from the country of origin principle. But it does not refer to social policy here and therefore, the country of origin is, to the extent mentioned above, kept in this respect. In this sense, the Commission denies the underlying *reality of the very widely divergent systems* and national approaches with regard to labour market policy and compliance monitoring.

With regard to monitoring, the Proposal also seems to fall short of introducing adequate measures. It de-regulates (prohibiting certain compliance measures such as documents, authorisation, declaration, representatives) but keeps the re-regulation quite underdeveloped. According to Article 24, paragraph 2 of the Proposal, the Member State of origin shall ensure that the provider takes all measures necessary to be able to *communicate* the *information*, both to its competent authorities and to those of the Member State of posting, within two years of the end of the posting, such as: information on the identity of the posted worker; his position and the nature of the tasks attributed to him; the contact details of the recipient; the place of posting the start and end dates for the posting; the employment and working conditions applied to the posted worker.

The Member State of origin shall *assist the Member State of posting* to ensure compliance with the employment and working conditions applicable under Directive 96/71/EC and shall, on its own initiative, communicate to the Member State of posting the specified information where the Member State of origin is aware of specific facts which indicate possible irregularities on the part of the provider in relation to employment and working conditions.

This considerably turns away from the traditionally used road of compliance monitoring. As the Proposal is based on vague assumptions of trust and cooperation, not on concrete tools of policy, and by denying the Member States sufficient tools of monitoring, it also seems to bring those countries further away from the applicable ILO requirements regarding effective means and procedures in monitoring of labour law through inspection, such as those mentioned in the applicable Conventions (strength of labour inspection services sufficient to secure effective discharge of duties; authority for inspectors to enter workplaces; regular workplace inspection; adequate penalties for violations of laws and regulations). In this respect, the

Proposal does not seem to be well-considered. Either the preconditions have to be dealt with, or the opportunity of the country of origin-principle in the discussed context has to be revisited.

9. SURVEILLANCE AND CONTROL OF LABOUR STANDARDS AT EU LEVEL

Michele Colucci

1. INTRODUCTION

Social Europe is the product of a slow evolution. Right from the start of the Community project and in the spirit of the founding fathers, there has been the conviction, on the one hand, that competence in social matters remains with Member States and, on the other hand, that social progress will very logically follow from the economic one brought about by the Common Market.

Therefore improving working conditions in the European Union depend to a large extent on agreement-based relations or national legislation. However, the Commission has adopted several acts setting up minimum standards at European level in order to improve labour standards and to guarantee workers' rights.

In this perspective, three Directives based on Article 94 EC between 1970 and 1980 on collective redundancies,[259] transfers of undertakings,[260] and insolvency of employers[261] provided more protection to the workers. The same is true for the Directive on the protection of pregnant women,[262] the protection of young people at work,[263] the posting of workers in the framework of the provision of services,[264] and

---

259 Council Directive 75/129/EEC of 17 February 1975, as last amended by Council Directive 98/59/EC of 20 July 1998 on the approximation of the laws of the Member States relating to collective redundancies, OJ L 225, 12.8.1998, pp. 16-21.

260 Council Directive 77/187/EEC of 14 February 1977 on the approximation of the laws of the Member States relating to the safeguarding of employees' rights in the event of transfers of undertakings, businesses or parts of businesses. OJ L 61, 5.3.1977, pp. 26-28. Act as last amended by Council Directive 98/50/EC of 29 June 1998.

261 Council Directive 80/987/EEC of 20 October 1980 on the approximation of the laws of the Member States relating to the protection of employees in the event of the insolvency of their employer. OJ L 283, 28/10/1980, pp. 23-27. Act as last amended by Directive 2002/74/EC of the European Parliament and of the Council of 23 September 2002.

262 Council Directive 92/85/EEC of 19 October 1992 on the introduction of measures to encourage improvements in the health and safety at work of pregnant workers and workers who have recently given birth or are breastfeeding (tenth individual Directive within the meaning of Article 16 (1) of Directive 89/391/EEC) OJ L 348, 28.11.1992, pp. 1-8.

263 Council Directive 94/33/EC of 22 June 1994 on the protection of young people at work OJ L 216, 20.8.1994, pp. 12-20.

264 Directive 96/71/EC of the European Parliament and of the Council of 16 December 1996 concerning the posting of workers in the framework of the provision of services. OJ L 18, 21/01/1997 pp.

the Directive laying down a general framework for the information and consultation of workers in the European Community.[265]

Finally several measures have been taken subsequent to Framework Directive 89/391/EEC,[266] which contains a number of basic provisions concerning the organisation of health and safety measures at work and the responsibilities of employers and workers; such measures include several separate Directives concerning specific groups of workers, workplaces or substances.

All the above mentioned acts contain provisions aiming at both to ensure comparable protection for workers' rights in the different Member States and to harmonise the cost that such rules entail for the concerned parties. At the same time they only lay down a minimum provision and do not preclude Member States from introducing laws, regulations or administrative instruments more favourable to workers.

They also make reference to national administrative authorities in ensuring the respect of EU legislation and the labour standards.

With regard to labour standards, the Proposal for a Services Directive[267] (hereafter "the Proposal") basically codifies existing Community legislation in the field of services taking in due account the relevant case law of the Court of Justice.[268]

This paper will focus on some key points of the Proposal, its scope, and its relationship with existing EU legislation in the services sector, in order to better understand the mechanisms provided at EU level for the surveillance and control of labour standards.

2. THE PROPOSAL FOR A SERVICES DIRECTIVE: THE COUNTRY OF ORIGIN PRINCIPLE AND SOME KEY POINTS

In order to eliminate the obstacles to the free movement of services, the Proposal provides for the application of the *country of origin principle*, according to which a service provider is subject only to the law of the country in which it is established

---

1-6.

265   Directive 2002/14/EC of the European Parliament and of the Council of 11 March 2002 establishing a general framework for informing and consulting employees in the European Community – Joint declaration of the European Parliament, the Council and the Commission on employee representation. OJ L 80, 23.3.2002, pp. 29-34.

266   Council Directive 89/391/EEC of 12 June 1989 on the introduction of measures to encourage improvements in the safety and health of workers at work. OJ L 183, 29.6.1989, pp. 1-8.

267   Proposal for a Directive of the European Parliament and of the Council on services in the internal market, COM(2004) 2 final/3, Brussels, 5.3.2004, available on http://europa.eu.int/eur-lex/en/com/pdf/2004/com2004_0002en03.pdf

268   Judgements of 26 April 1988, *Bond van Adverteerders*, Case 352/85, point 16; 27 September 1988, *Humbel*, 263/86, point 17; 11 April 2000, Deliège, C-51/96 and C-191/97, point 56; 12 July 2001, *Smits and Peerbooms*, Case C-157/99, point 57.

and Member States may not restrict services from a provider established in another Member State (Article 16).

This principle is accompanied by derogations that are either general, or temporary, or applicable on a case-by-case basis.

It recognises the *right of recipients to use services* from other Member States without being hindered by restrictive measures imposed by their country or by discriminatory behaviour on the part of public authorities or private operators.

It sets up a *mechanism to provide assistance to recipients* who use a service provided by an operator established in another Member State.

In the case of *posting of workers* it allocates tasks between the Member State of origin and the Member State of destination and provides for the necessary supervision procedures.

It provides for harmonisation of legislation in order to guarantee equivalent protection of the general interest on vital questions, such as consumer protection, particularly as regards the service provider's obligations concerning information, professional insurance, multidisciplinary activities, settlement of disputes, and exchange of information on the quality of the service provider.

Finally it requires *stronger mutual assistance between national authorities* with a view to effective supervision of service activities on the basis of a clear distribution of roles between the Member States and obligations to cooperate.

3. SCOPE OF THE PROPOSAL

It is important to distinguish between services excluded from the scope of the Directive, services that are covered by all provisions of the Directive except by the country of origin principle, and services covered by the country of origin principle. In particular, there are many sectors excluded from the scope of the proposed Directive: general sectors such as services of general interest (e.g. police and justice), services covered by Article 45 of the EU Treaty (e.g. notaries, bailiffs, etc.), financial services, transport services, and electronic communication services.

Furthermore, there is a long list of derogations from the country of origin principle. It is important to understand the scope of these exclusions, which have been introduced to tackle potential confusion. There are 23 derogations in the proposed Directive, plus some transitional derogation, to be applied up to 2010, and derogations in some individual cases under specific conditions.[269]

Many service sectors are excluded from the principle because the existing legislation is based on a different approach, for example: postal services, distribution of electricity, distribution of gas, distribution of water, legal services (lawyers and

---

269   For a more detailed analysis of the country of origin principle please refer to all explanatory documents prepared by DG Internal Market of the European Commission available at http://europa. eu.int/comm/internal_market/services/index_en.htm

barristers), services regulated by the Directive on professional qualifications, i.e. all professional services that require a specific qualification. Given the combined economic importance of these services sectors, the coverage of the Proposal as regards the free movement of services is further reduced.

Finally, cross-border provision of services under the country of origin principle apply directly to all business-to-business relations in the following sectors: business services,[270] distribution services,[271] construction services,[272] tourism and catering services,[273] vehicle renting services, household support services and private healthcare services, audiovisual services,[274] leisure services,[275] personal care services.

This means that approximately 50% of EU GDP is covered by the Proposal while the remaining part is regulated by existing EU legislation.

4. THE FEARED RISKS LINKED TO THE DIRECTIVE

The fact that providers would be only subject to the national standards in their Member State of origin could lead to a "race to the bottom" in quality standards, and to a "social" as well as a "legal dumping", since Member States might be induced to attract service providers by lowering their standards: in fact service providers may decide to establish themselves in countries with the lowest standards in terms of social, environmental and public health regulations as well as the lowest tax burdens.

4.1. Social Dumping

After the latest EU enlargement in 2004, some Member States and trade union organisations fear that service providers from those EU countries with lower labour costs and social standards would be able to provide cheaper services because they would not comply with core working conditions and labour law rules of the host country.[276]

---

270   These are for example advisory and management consulting, legal or fiscal advisory services, certification services, engineering consulting, IT management consulting, advertising, new agencies, marketing services, design services, trade fairs services, after-sales services and other maintenance services; security services, cleaning industry, facilities management services, real estate services, recruitment services temporary agencies.

271   For example wholesale services, services of commercial agents, retail distribution services (butchers, bakers, grocery trade, etc).

272   Masons, painters, plumbers, etc.

273   Tourism agencies, tourist guides, Catering services, etc.

274   TV, music, film creation and production, etc.

275   Sports centres and amusement park services, gardening services.

276   This is the position of the ETUC (European Trade Union Confederation) available at <www.etuc.org>.

In that regard it is important to stress that since the 1996 Posting of Workers Directive is applicable to workers performing their job outside their country work for a limited period of time.

This Directive protects posted workers against "social dumping" by obliging Member States to ensure that, whatever the law applicable to the employment relationship, companies posting workers in a host country guarantee to those posted workers the terms and conditions of employment laid down in the host Member State's legislation.

The Directive covers matters such as maximum work periods and minimum rest periods, minimum paid annual holidays, minimum rates of pay, conditions for hiring-out of workers, in particular by temporary employment agencies; health and safety at work, equality of treatment between men and women and other provisions on non-discrimination.

The Proposal only lays down minimum provisions, Member States may always do better and decide to impose stricter rules. They can also extend the list of issues to which the host country law applies, to meet public policy provisions.

A general derogation from the country of origin principle is foreseen for all matters covered by the Posting of Workers Directive (Article 17). Furthermore the host country is in charge of controlling compliance with the Posting of Workers Directive on its territory.

Finally, companies cannot use this Proposal to establish letter-box firms in Member States with lower wages and social security contributions and provide services from there into other Member States. The Proposal will allow more effective control of the real place of establishment of companies that will not be determined on the basis of formal criteria, such as the location of the registered office, but on the basis of where a company's effective seat is.

4.2. Legal Dumping

The Proposal does not forbid the judicial authorities from applying the local criminal law to a foreign service provider: national criminal laws always prevail, except for the penal aspects related to a fraudulent breach of contract.

There are also criticisms on the potential conflict with other existing laws governing contractual and non-contractual obligations that would undermine legal certainty to the detriment of providers and users.[277]

First of all, the Directive does not prevent the choice of law in the contract between the parties and, in addition, excludes from the country of origin principle all service contracts concluded by consumers unless they are governed by EU harmonisation law.

---

277 In that regard please see UNICE position paper on the Directive of 4 October 2004 (<www. unice.org>).

The freedom of the parties to choose the applicable law does not apply to the regulations and supervision of the country of destination regarding issues of public health, safety and security.

The question is which law applies in cases where there is no contract and no choice has been expressed or it is unclear.

Following the Proposal, the country of origin principle applies and therefore it is the law of the country of origin of the service provider which applies from the moment of the conclusion of the contract. Clarifications might however be necessary so as to determine which legislation is applicable to labour contracts that are not covered by the Posting of Workers Directive. Further analysis might be necessary as to ensure that there is no risk of contradiction between application of the country of origin principle by default (i.e. in case of no clear choice of law by the parties) and the provisions of the International Convention on the law applicable to contractual obligations (also known as "Rome I").[278]

Particularly important in that regard is the provision contained in Article 6 of the Convention with regard to individual employment contracts:

> in a contract of employment a choice of law made by the parties shall not have the result of depriving the employee of the protection afforded to him by the mandatory rules of the law which would be applicable hereafter in the absence of choice.

> A contract of employment shall, in the absence of choice in accordance with Article 3, be governed:

> (a) by the law of the country in which the employee habitually carries out his work in performance of the contract, even if he is temporarily employed in another country; or

> (b) if the employee does not habitually carry out his work in any one country, by the law of the country in which the place of business through which he was engaged is situated; unless it appears from the circumstances as a whole that the contract is more closely connected with another country, in which case the contract shall be governed by the law of that country.

Taking into due account such a provision, the country of origin principle ensures that service providers who want to provide their services across borders on a temporary basis only have to comply with the law of their country of establishment without having to adapt to the laws of 25 different countries. It thus provides for the necessary legal certainty, especially for SMEs that would not otherwise engage in cross-border service supply.

---

278 Convention on the law applicable to contractual obligations opened for signature in Rome on 19 June 1980 (80/934/EEC) OJ L 266, 9.10.1980, pp. 1-19.

Nevertheless the risk remains that service providers would choose as a permanent basis of establishment the EU Member State where the rule applied in case of conflict would be the most favourable for the provider.

4.3. Race to the Bottom?

According to some authors in a liberalised service market EU Member States would compete to attract service providers to their territory and would therefore bring their legislation down to a lower level of protection for consumers.

The risk of a "race to the bottom" is also avoided since the proposed Directive provides, in derogations from the country of origin principle, for a range of safeguards regarding public order, public safety or public health whereby Member States can draw up national rules covering those fields that foreign service providers must also comply with.

The Proposal will not force Member States to liberalise or privatise "public services" or open them up to competition. The Directive is merely intended to facilitate and simplify the development of service activities at EU level in those areas which are already open to competition. In addition, it will still be up to each Member State to decide the areas which would or would not be open to competition.

Besides the Proposal excludes the regulated professions, covered by the soon-to-be-adopted Directive on the Recognition of Professional Qualifications, from implementation of the country of origin principle.[279] These are namely professions in the healthcare sector (doctors, nurses, dentists, midwifes, pharmacists and all the healthcare professions that are regulated at national level (specific diploma, specific authorisation process, etc.) but also professions such as architects, engineers, accountants, etc.

The main purpose of the Directive on professional qualifications is to consolidate and simplify some 15 existing directives, some of which date as far back as 1977. The new Directive should ensure that all EU Member States have mutually recognised the various national systems, and that professionals provide all necessary documents to the relevant authority of the host country when delivering cross-border services.

The Proposal will leave these arrangements absolutely unchanged.

---

279   Proposal for a Directive of the European Parliament and of the Council on the recognition of professional qualifications, COM(2002)119 final, available at http://europa.eu.int/eur-lex/en/com/pdf/2002/en_502PC0119.pdf

5.   A COMBINATION OF TECHNIQUES TO GUARANTEE SUPERVISION

The Proposal is based on a combination of techniques for regulating service activities and their control demanding a control "at source" and an high degree of cooperation among the national administrative authorities

5.1. Supervision "at Source"

The country of origin principle not only enables operators to provide services in one or more other Member States without being subject to those Member States' rules, but it also means that the Member State of origin is responsible for the effective supervision of service providers established on its territory even if they provide services into other Member States.

In fact according to the Commission, the competent authorities of the country of origin are best placed to ensure the effectiveness and continuity of supervision of the provider and to provide protection for recipients not only in their own Member State but also elsewhere in the Community.[280]

Nevertheless such obligation does not mean that Member States have to carry out factual checks and controls in the territories of other Member States. According to the administrative cooperation obligations provided for in the Proposal, such checks and controls can be carried out by the authorities of the country where the service provider is temporarily operating but in a non-discriminatory way.

Nevertheless the risk of inadequate supervision, as it has been already with other directives, still remains. Therefore national governments will have to provide supervision in close liaison with one another, and national inspectorates will have to work together.

For these purposes Member States shall designate one or more points of contact, the contact details of which shall be communicated to the other Member States and the Commission (Article 34).

They should also set up a "well functioning electronic information system" in order to allow competent authorities to easily identify their relevant interlocutors in other Member States and to communicate in an efficient way (Article 34).

The question remains whether governments will be ready to allocate the necessary funds to set up this electronic system and whether a national administrative authority will be able to communicate in a foreign language with the colleagues from another country.

---

280   Determination of judicial jurisdiction does not fall within the scope of this Directive but within that of Council Regulation (EC) No. 44/2001 of 22 December 2000 on jurisdiction and the recognition and enforcement of judgements in civil and commercial matters18, or other Community instruments such as Directive 96/71/EC of the European Parliament and of the Council of 16 December 1996 concerning the posting of workers in the framework of the provision of services.

5.2. Mutual Assistance between National Authorities

In order to ensure that supervision is effective, the Proposal asks for mutual assistance and requires administrative cooperation between authorities by organising the allocation of supervisory tasks and exchange of information.

In effect, administrative cooperation is essential to make the Internal Market for services function properly. Lack of cooperation between Member States results in multiplication of rules applicable to service providers or duplication of controls for cross-border activities and can also be used by rogue traders to avoid supervision or to circumvent applicable national rules on services. It is, therefore, essential to provide for clear legally binding obligations for Member States to cooperate effectively.

The Member State of origin shall supply information on providers established in its territory when requested to do so by another Member State and in particular confirmation that a service provider is established in its territory and exercising his activities in a lawful manner. In particular they shall ensure that registers in which providers have been entered, and which may be consulted by the competent authorities in their territory, may also be consulted, in accordance with the same conditions, by the equivalent competent authorities of the other Member States (Article 35).

Then, upon becoming aware of any unlawful conduct by a provider, or of specific acts, that are likely to cause serious damage in a Member State, Member States shall inform the Member State of origin, within the shortest possible period of time.

The Member State of origin shall undertake the checks, inspections and investigations requested by another Member State and shall inform the latter of the results and, as the case may be, of the measures taken. In the event of difficulty in meeting a request for information, the Member State in question shall rapidly inform the requesting Member State with a view to finding a solution.

6. THE SERVICES PROPOSAL AND THE EXISTING COMMUNITY RULES ON POSTING OF WORKERS

The cross-border provision of services often means that the service provider has to move his employees temporarily to the Member State where the service is provided. However, a number of administrative and legal obstacles hamper such posting of workers which render cross-border services provision more costly and very complicated in particular for SMEs.

The Proposal, therefore, seeks to reduce administrative burdens for companies, while at the same time strengthening control through reinforced cooperation between Member States. In particular Article 36 states that where a provider moves temporarily to another Member State in order to provide a service without being established there, the competent authorities of that Member State shall participate in the supervision of the provider.

At the request of the Member State of origin, the competent authorities shall carry out any checks, inspections and investigations necessary for ensuring effective supervision by the Member State of origin. In so doing, the competent authorities shall act to the extent permitted by the powers vested in them in their Member State.

The Proposal aims to reinforce the application of the Posting of Workers Directive according to which minimum working conditions of the country where a worker is posted have to be respected. In comparison with the Posting of Workers Directive, there are three new elements:

Firstly, the Proposal imposes a clear legal obligation on the host Member State to ensure not only that its working conditions – including minimum wages – are applied to all workers posted to its territory, but also to carry out effective supervision (including checks and controls on the spot if necessary).

Secondly, the Proposal would oblige the Member State of establishment of the service provider to assist the authorities of the host Member State in the supervision of the service provider when it operates temporarily in the host Member State.

These obligations to cooperate between Member States would make supervision more efficient and ensure that violations of the host Member State's laws can be dealt with more effectively.

At the request of the host Member State, the authorities in the country of establishment will have to carry out checks and controls or impose sanctions on companies who do not cooperate with the authorities of the host Member State. This is needed because the authorities in the host Member State often cannot check facts and circumstances at the place of establishment of the company or they are not capable of verifying whether a company is really and legally established in another Member State (or whether it just maintains a letter-box firm there). Therefore, they need the assistance of the authorities in the Member State where the company is established. This is particularly important in cases where the posting has come to an end but investigations have not been completed.

Thirdly, the Directive abolishes a limited number of administrative requirements which are especially burdensome and disproportionate, particularly for SMEs, i.e. prior authorisations and declarations to the host Member State, the obligation to ship all labour documents normally held at the place of the company to the place of posting and keep them there, and the obligation to designate a permanent representative established in the host Member State.

6.1. Labour Standards under Directive 96/71/EC

Existing Community legislation, namely the Posting of Workers Directive 96/71/EC, continues to apply in full, providing that posted workers, including temporary workers, are subject to the working conditions of the Member State where the worker is posted i.e. the host Member State.

These working conditions cover minimum wages, working time and minimum rest periods, minimum paid leave, the protection of temporary workers, health, hygiene and safety standards, protection of young people and pregnant women, equality of treatment between men and women and other provisions on non-discrimination including with respect to disabled people. All these matters covered by the Posting of Workers Directive are excluded from the country of origin principle.

This means that a company cannot pay wages to posted workers lower than the minimum wages in the host Member State (thus an Italian company posting workers to Belgium would need to pay Belgian minimum wages).

It also means that companies from another Member State must abide by the health and safety rules in the host country, e.g. regarding the way the workplace must be organised, requirements as to protective gear for workers, and so on. This concerns not only minimum working conditions laid down by law but also those laid down by collective agreements.

6.2. Control on Labour Standards

The Proposal provides that the host Member State is responsible for ensuring the application of its working conditions to posted workers. The host Member State has every right to carry out controls on the spot, for example on construction sites, to demand information from the company which has posted workers and to enforce its laws regarding working conditions.

Although the Proposal aims at eliminating some administrative requirements (i.e. prior authorisation, designation of a permanent representative in the host MS etc.), such administrative requirements are not the most efficient means to exercise control and only some Member States actually have those requirements.

There are many other effective enforcement and control possibilities, such as controls on the spot, for instance, on building sites, enforcement prompted by complaints by workers or competitors, or easy access to justice for posted workers (including arbitration or mediation procedures). Moreover, the proposed Directive establishes a system of mutual assistance between the authorities of the country of origin and the host country. The authorities in the host country can ask for the assistance of the country of origin if they have any problems in getting information and relevant documents from companies even after the termination of the posting. This will strengthen control and supervision.

7. ENFORCEMENT AND CONTROL OF PROTECTION OF TEMPORARY WORKERS

The protection of temporary workers is equally covered by the Posting of Workers Directive, which provides that the host Member State's legislation regarding the conditions of hiring out of workers, in particular the supply of workers by temporary employment undertakings, applies.

Temporary workers who are hired out by a temporary employment agency in one Member State to a user company in another Member State thus are protected by the legislation of the host Member State. If in a host Member State there are restrictions on the use of temporary workers or particular conditions, for instance, regarding the maximum length of employment of a temporary worker, those rules continue to apply.

As is the case for posted workers in general, enforcement and control of protection of temporary workers can be ensured by many means. These include on-the-spot controls, enforcement prompted by complaints by interim workers or competitors, allowing interim workers to complain directly to the host Member State's labour authorities, or easy access to justice for interim workers. In addition, the Member State of origin will be responsible for ensuring that employment agencies established on its territory fully cooperate with the host Member State's authorities and provide them with all necessary information.

8. CONCLUSION

Labour standards are important but their enforcement through adequate and effective monitoring measures is equally important.

Misconceptions and unfounded criticisms have been generated during the debate on the Proposal.

In fact it does not repeal existing EU legislation that already harmonises many aspects of European citizens' and companies' activities in the service sector, such as the existing directives on safety, security, working time, etc. The specific legislation has priority over general legislation such as this Proposal and the basis of the Proposal is to set up rules to be applied by default if nothing else is yet harmonised at EU level.

In order to remove legal and administrative barriers to the development of a free market for services in the EU, the Proposal deals with cooperation procedures between Member States. This is a necessary step in order to ensure that national administrations and the various regulatory authorities will progressively understand the various regimes of their neighbouring countries and that these regulations will progressively be simplified for the benefit of all providers and the differences will be narrowed.

It is worrying that Member States would have very limited possibilities to supervise service providers active on their territory, and questionable whether Member States of origin would be motivated to provide such supervision by allocating new human and financial resources.

10. THE POINT OF VIEW OF THE FEDERATION OF BELGIAN ENTERPRISES ON THE SERVICES DIRECTIVE

Arnout De Koster

1. THE BENEFITS OF THE SERVICES DIRECTIVE

The advantages of the proposed Directive and the need for a genuine internal market for services in the EU in order to attain the growth and competitiveness objectives of the Lisbon Agenda are clear.

1.1. Creation of a Genuine Internal Market in Services

Free movement of services is an essential element that is still missing in the completion of the internal market in Europe. People, goods and capital can now cross borders without facing unjust restrictions. Businesses, workers and consumers can benefit greatly from the increased size of the internal market in goods, capital and over 450 million consumers. The EU economy has built up tremendous strength from allowing economic players to take advantage of the scale of the market.

But barriers still exist in the area of free movement of services. In fact, one can state that the single market in services, although enshrined in the text of the Treaty from its conception, does not exist in practice. There are some sectoral exceptions where progress has been made, e.g. financial services, but this was because of the necessity to put into place the free movement of capital.

The reality is that we operate in an "internal" market, with 28 different sets of legislation for a wide range of service sectors.[281] The large majority of other services suppliers who want to widen their horizons in other EU countries have to comply with these different sets of obligations in each country. In practice, many of them do not even get as far as starting on a "foreign" adventure. All these rules and permits are holding back the entire European services economy, which represents 70% of the EU GDP. For the goods sectors, companies have integrated the notion

---

281 With the Agreement on the European Economic Area, the EU Internal Market was in 1994 extended to include the three EFTA countries, Norway, Iceland and Liechtenstein, thus the Internal Market now consists of 28 countries.

of the EU market. In the service sectors, outside their own domestic market, any activity is still considered as providing a service in a "foreign country", not within the European Union entity. For a European service provider, there is no difference between establishing itself or selling its service in the EU or in any other country in the world that has opened its market in the framework of the GATS negotiations, as most of the OECD countries and many others have done in a large number of service sectors in the framework of the WTO negotiations.

The European Court of Justice (ECJ) has repeatedly confirmed the rights of service providers to practise their freedom of establishment and freedom of movement of their services in other EU Member States. But, the impacts of the judgements are limited to the parties and to other plaintiffs who take advantage of the case law. Notwithstanding the fact that Europe does not want to be ruled by a "government of judges", ECJ case law is clearly not sufficient to achieve the completion of the internal market in services.

1.2. Reinvigorating the European Economy

The European Union has as one of its highest priorities in fulfilling the Lisbon Agenda stated that Europe must become the most competitive knowledge-based economy in the world. Many studies have established that Europe must give high priority to completion of the internal market in order to achieve that objective. The service sector plays a crucial role in this regard.

If Europe wants to be the most innovative economy in the world, there must be more competition in the service sectors. Competition leads to innovation and higher productivity as well as creation of new jobs. To encourage businesses to invest in research, innovation and development in new services, they need to be able to take advantage of the full scale of the EU market so as to be sure that the investments costs can be recouped. According to experts, around 50% of the services that we will consume in 2050 have not yet been invented. We must ensure that Europe invents a large proportion of them.

The proposed Directive will be instrumental in fulfilling the employment goals of the Lisbon Agenda. Roughly 96% of total net job creation in the EU between 1997 and 2002 came from the service sectors. This shows the high employment-generating potential of the service sectors – a potential that needs to be released further if we want to prevent the ongoing evolution from a manufacturing-based to a service-based economy from resulting in net job losses.

Empirical evidence shows that full implementation of the Directive will lead to increased trade and cross-border investment in services. This will generate higher income, which in turn increases the demand for services and employment in these sectors. Last year, the Netherlands Bureau for Economic Policy Analysis (CPB) calculated that the removal of barriers to trade and establishment as foreseen by the Directive would in time produce 15 to 35% growth in both intra-EU services trade and the stock of direct investment in services.[282]

According to a recent report carried out by Copenhagen Economics[283] for the European Commission, full implementation of the proposed Directive in the services sectors covered would bring about the following:

1. Creation of 600,000 additional jobs in the EU;
2. Reduction of existing barriers to service provision by more than 50%;
3. Reduction of the prices of the services concerned by the Directive which will benefit both consumers and firms using these services as inputs;
4. Benefits for European consumers, businesses and governments from enhanced productivity, higher employment and increased wages;
5. A rise by 0.4 per cent of wages in the EU while the price of services in the EU would fall – by an average of 7.2 per cent in the regulated professions.

1.3. Concrete Benefits for all European Economic Players

In addition to the benefits and the macro-economic figures mentioned above, the proposed Directive is expected to bring about concrete benefits for all interested parties, namely service providers, consumers, employees and governments. It has to be stated, however, that, in order to realise the full potential of the Directive, some clarifications would have to be introduced to the current text. The normal legislative process in the EU institutions and a constant dialogue with interested stakeholders should be used for that purpose.

1.3.1. Benefits for the Service Providers

1.3.1.1. Accelerate the Authorisation Process for EU Companies

One of the main objectives of the Directive is to facilitate the establishment of a business in another Member State, *inter alia* through creation of a one-stop shop in each Member State to which businesses from other European Union countries can turn with all their administrative questions. This will reduce the costly and lengthy administrative burden and allow a quicker authorisation process, with wider use of e-government. Thus, companies that were hesitating to set up an office (subsidiary or branch) in another country (and in particular in a neighbouring country), due

---

282 CPB Netherlands Bureau for Economic Policy Analysis, A quantitative assessment of the EU proposals for the Internal Market for Services, September 2004.

283 "Economic Assessment of the Barriers to the Internal Market for Services", January 2005 available at: http://europa.eu.int/comm/internal_market/services/docs/strategy/2004-propdir/2005-01-cph-study_en.pdf5.

to the complex procedure involving many different administrations (regulatory authority and/or the professional body of the sector, social administration, fiscal administration, trade register, etc.) will have to deal with just one a "Single Point of Contact", where all formalities will be completed.

The Directive aims to simplify the procedures by asking the governments to accept any documents from another Member State which serve an equivalent purpose to what they ask for in their own internal process. It is the additional cost faced by providers due to different regulatory requirements, as confirmed by the recent CPB study (see above) which deters service companies from establishing and providing cross-border services. By the end of 2008, it should be possible to fulfil all these procedures electronically. This should further speed up and reduce the costs of authorisation. Authorisations should be handled within a short pre-determined period of time and absence of reply after the deadline would imply a positive response. Currently, a representative of the applicant company must often visit the authorities many times and wait for replies. Certified originals of documents from the home Member State's authority are often required. This extends the process even more and further discourages potential applicants.

Example:

Economic need tests for opening a new commercial presence are often burdensome and costly:

1.   A Swedish company indicated that the costs of the study plus external consultant and use of internal coordinating staff ranged from EUR 165,000 to EUR 475,000 per test. The total for 22 applications in the EU amounted to EUR 5.9 million.

2.   According to another company, the direct and indirect costs of gaining the requisite advise on legal and regulatory requirements in order to establish a presence in a single EU Member State stood at between EUR 80,000 and EUR 160,000.

1.3.1.2. An opportunity to test a market without the establishment burden

Another important purpose of the Directive is to facilitate cross-border service provision, *inter alia* through introduction of the country of origin principle: the legislation of the country where the business has its head office is applicable in the commercial transaction. As indicated above, most small and medium services companies (SMEs) do not even attempt to set up abroad because of the complexity of obtaining the authorisation. Similarly, the large majority of SMEs currently do not attempt to export their services to other EU Member States. Indeed, for many service sectors, the providers have to know the legislation of the recipient countries, and therefore adapt the product to the different legislations of the countries in which they want to operate in. This is a major brake to the development of the services economy. By allowing the provider to offer its service across EU borders under the national conditions applicable in his own Member State, these disincentive obstacles will be lifted and should provide an opportunity to companies, particularly SMEs, to go to a neighbouring market and test whether they might find new consumers for their service.

The proposed Directive not only facilitates the provision of services between EU countries by establishing the country of origin principle but it also ensures that the service provider will benefit from simplified administrative procedures.

Examples of companies that could have benefited from the Directive:

1. A French firm commissioned to install an electrical appliance in Luxembourg found it would have taken twice as long to satisfy the Luxembourg notification requirements as to carry out the installation – so it dropped out of the contract.
2. A Belgian firm found it had to notify the French authorities just to be entitled to measure a kitchen with a view to a contract there – so it decided it was not worth it.
3. German companies meeting German and EU standards for installing fire protection being obliged to satisfy Dutch ability tests.
4. A Dutch service provider being required to obtain a Belgian VAT number just to participate in a Belgian exhibition.

1.3.2. Benefits for the consumers

The proposed Directive also aims to improve rights, information and quality of services for those who use the services. For instance, the country of the customer may not impose restrictive measures so as to forbid or to discourage him from purchasing services provided by a company from another EU Member State (prior declaration, limit of fiscal deductions, etc.).

All categories of users of services will benefit from the Directive: private (individual) consumers and companies acting as consumers of services.

a) Private (individual) consumers:

The introduction of new service providers in the national EU markets will allow consumers
– to have larger choice of services, discover new services that might have not been introduced into their market due to lack of competition;
– to enhance quality of service and better information on service providers;
– to buy services in the local market at a lower price, due to increased competition between providers and a reduction in providers' costs because of higher potential economies of scale.

b) Companies acting as consumers:

This category of consumers would also benefit greatly from the completion of the internal market in services. Manufacturing companies that are used to the concept of the "EU Internal Market" know that there are likely opportunities to find better service providers coming from other EU Member States (newly established in the host country, or providing a service temporarily from their home country, particularly in the border regions).

The proposed Directive will set up an assistance process for the recipients of services. Member States will have to ensure that users can obtain, in their Member State of residence, all the necessary information they might need on the legislation of the country of the provider, e.g. consumer protection, legal dispute settlements, etc.

The Directive also puts a strong emphasis on the quality of services, aiming to ensure consumers' rights. In particular, EU governments are asked to ensure that proper information on providers and their services is available to consumers, as in the case of a national provider (name, address, registration number, supervisory authority, contractual clause on the law applicable, etc., professional insurance and guarantees when necessary, after-sales guarantee).

Finally, for EU consumers of non-hospital healthcare services in another EU country, the Directive ensures that the assumption of related costs is the same as that assumed by the social security system of the country of residence of the consumer.

1.3.3. Benefits for employment

It is also argued that the introduction of further competition in the service sector and the potential entry of new companies from other EU Member States might result in the destruction of existing jobs. It has been repeatedly proven that the market in the service sector will continue to grow and that there will be a large reservoir of new opportunities for the services market in Europe. This would lead to higher employment and creation of new and more innovative services through a more efficient and competitive organisation of services.

This conclusion has been shown in multiple studies, and further illustrated by the experience from the liberalisation of some service sectors in recent years, for example in the telecommunications sector, where analysts agree that innovation has been accelerated by the introduction of competition in the EU market, and that it has been accompanied by the creation of jobs. A large body of empirical and theoretical OECD research relating to different service sectors shows that reducing the level of regulation, as targeted by the proposed Directive, generally leads to significant employment gains in the sectors concerned.

1.3.4. Benefits for Governments

In all sections of the proposed Directive, EU governments are asked to strengthen their cooperation. The governments will thus build up mutual trust between themselves, in particular through harmonisation of legal provisions, cooperation on supervising services and promotion of codes of conduct at EU level. The obligations on Member States to exchange information on the various laws in place and to examine the compatibility of their legal system and authorisation processes in the various service sectors with the Directive's requirements would improve the efficiency of internal procedures in public administration. This in turn should create a better mutual understanding of the legal processes which should lead to a regulatory convergence, which would strengthen the notion of a European Internal Market for Services.

2. REMARKS

2.1. Specific Remarks on the Directive Bolkestein – Provisions

2.1.1. Scope

Given the specific nature of the healthcare sector, the FEB proposes adding this sector to the list of sectors excluded from the Directive's scope of application.

The FEB is indeed concerned about the consequences of including healthcare in the Directive's scope of application.

Firstly, this could potentially damage the autonomy of the Member States in terms of the organisation and financing of their healthcare systems (cf. Article 15: possible prohibition of the mechanisms allowing spending on health insurance to be controlled, after an evaluation has been undertaken).

Secondly, as regards the mobility of patients in Europe (cf. Article 23), the FEB is concerned about the possible net cost which will have to be borne by the social security system in the host country and about the legal insecurity resulting from the inconsistencies between this proposal for a Directive and Regulation 1408/71. The FEB would prefer to see discussions continued within the framework of the open method of coordination.

2.1.2. Definitions of the Notion Establishment

The FEB believes that a better and more precise definition of the concept of establishment is necessary to enable it to refer to both companies which are governed by the law within one Member State and conduct all their business activities in another Member State, and companies which conduct the majority of their activities in that other Member State.

The concept of "establishment" as set out in the Directive does not in any way enable fictitious companies to be excluded from the market. In fact, the definition of the concept of establishment and the absence of a definition of a "fixed establishment" gives rise to a large amount of legal uncertainty in determining applicable law.

Moreover, the Schnitzer ruling handed down by the European Court of Justice (C-215/01 of 11 December 2003) does not provide enough clarity in the event that the activity has been "pursued … on a virtually continuous basis and under a whole series of contracts". According to this ruling, it falls to the competent court to determine at what point in time the situation must be regarded as "establishment". However, the Court of Justice seems to prefer to support theory of the Constitution (cf. case C-212/97 of Centros Ltd. of 9 March 1999). As a result, measures of a given Member State would apply not only to the providers that originate from this Member State, but also to other providers that decide to establish a company in accordance with the law of this Member State in order to bypass the more stringent measures prevailing in their own country of origin, whilst all their activities – or the majority of them – are exclusively conducted in their country of origin. This is unacceptable.

2.2. Freedom of Establishment for Service Providers – Authorisations

2.2.1. Authorisation Schemes

The FEB is calling for the introduction of an explicit derogation with the intention of excluding the temporary agency and construction sectors from all Articles (among others Articles 9, 16.3 and 20) that aim, within the framework of freedom of establishment or free movement of services, to prohibit systems of prior authorisation or approval, professional access schemes and schemes for registering contractors. Ideally, this should be stipulated in the Directive itself or at least in a recital which, for example, would highlight the fact that the systems of authorisation and approval established in these two sectors of activity pursue an overriding reason relating to the public interest, namely, the protection of workers.

In the absence of equivalent measures at European level pertaining to conditions of access to and provision of the services in question, the FEB is calling for Belgian systems of authorisation or approval supported by the social partners in the sectors involved (mainly the temporary agency and construction sectors), to be maintained. It is concerned about the possibility of abolishing these schemes when their aim is to protect both companies using these services from unreliable, or even "malafide" service providers, and workers whose protection is justified by an overriding reason relating to the public interest.

The FEB believes that currently in the targeted sectors, there is no true "level playing field" for the conditions of service access and provision or for monitoring these conditions.

Moreover, we are likely to see competition distorted since there would be no obligation to approve foreign providers while these authorisations would still be maintained for Belgian companies, as they request.

It is also suggested that it is necessary to flesh out the definition of "overriding reason relating to the public interest". This proposal is based on recital 24a of the consolidated document circulated on 10 January 2005 (Doc. 5161/05) by the Luxembourg Presidency, which stipulated that, in accordance with case law of the Court of Justice of the European Communities, this concept covered the following reasons: "public policy, public security, public health, the protection of consumers, recipients of services, workers, the environment including the urban environment, the health of animals, intellectual property, the conservation of the national historic and artistic heritage or social policy objectives and cultural policy objectives".

The following reasons are also included in the concept: the protection of citizens – including the protection of physical integrity, health and safety – and the guarantee of reliability of the service provider; the absence of such a guarantee leads to the criminal co-liability of the user.

It is indeed fundamentally important for the Member States to be able to refer to sufficiently broad criteria so they can prove their systems of authorisation and approval are well founded and hence ensure they are maintained.

In fact, In the absence of equivalent measures at European level pertaining to conditions of access to and provision of the services in question, the FEB is calling for Belgian systems of authorisation or approval, supported by the social partners in the sectors involved (mainly the temporary agency and construction sectors), to be maintained. It is concerned about the possibility of abolishing these schemes when their aim is to protect both companies using these services from unreliable, or indeed dishonest, service providers, and workers whose protection is justified by an overriding reason relating to the public interest.

The Belgian employers believe that currently in the targeted sectors, there is no true "level playing field" for the conditions of service access and provision or for monitoring these conditions.

Moreover, we are likely to see competition distorted since there would be no obligation to approve foreign providers while these authorisations would still be maintained for Belgian companies, as they request.

2.2.2. Conditions for the Granting of Authorisation and the Duration of Authorisation

Article 10 should be completed so that the granting of authorisation may be made dependent on the need to take account of the specific circumstances of each local situation.

The FEB believes that the pure fact that a service provider is granted authorisation to set up their activities in a defined place on a territory cannot be taken to mean that this provider automatically has the right to conduct their activities throughout the whole territory. It must be possible to take the specific circumstances of each local situation into account (cf. mainly local, regional or national provisions relating to commercial establishments).

It is also necessary to complete the list of derogations regarding the unlimited character of the granted authorisations.

2.3. Free Movement of Services

2.3.1. Country of Origin Principle and Derogations

The FEB is calling for an exemption from the prohibition in question to be included in this subparagraph in the form of a new paragraph, which states that:

> an authorisation scheme may however be maintained if the following conditions – set out in Article 9.1 – are satisfied:
>
> – the authorisation scheme does not discriminate against the provider in question;
>
> – the need for an authorisation scheme is objectively justified by an overriding reason relating to the public interest;
>
> – the objective pursued cannot be obtained by means of a less restrictive measure, in particular because an *a posteriori* inspection would take place too late to be genuinely effective.

The FEB believes that the criteria set out within the framework of freedom to establishment which enables systems of authorisation to be maintained under certain conditions, must also apply within the framework of free movement of services.

In fact, In the absence of equivalent measures at European level pertaining to conditions of access to and provision of the services in question, the FEB is calling for Belgian systems of authorisation or approval supported by the social partners in the sectors involved (mainly the temporary agency and construction sectors), to be maintained. It is concerned about the possibility of abolishing these schemes when their aim is to protect both companies using these services from unreliable, or indeed dishonest, service providers, and workers whose protection is justified by an overriding reason relating to the public interest.

The FEB believes that currently in the targeted sectors, there is no true "level playing field" for the conditions of service access and provision or for monitoring these conditions.

Moreover, we are likely to see competition distorted since there would be no obligation to approve foreign providers while these authorisations would still be maintained for Belgian companies, as they request.

Finally, in view of the current situation (lack of genuine cooperation between national administrations), the FEB is expressing doubts about the feasibility of the measures planned in recitals 37 and 38 of the consolidated document circulated on 10 January 2005 by the Luxembourg Presidency (Doc. 5161/05) which stipulated that the country of origin principle "should be supplemented by an assistance mechanism enabling the recipient, in particular, to be informed about the laws of the other Member States …".

The FEB suggests making this subparagraph more specific and reformulating it as follows: "Directive 96/71/EC and the ways this Directive has been implemented in national legislation".

The FEB believes that it is important for all means of control held by the Member States for transposing Directive 96/71/EC on the positing of workers to be excluded from the scope of application of the country of origin principle.

Moreover, the FEB is insisting that the responsibility for monitoring compliance with this Directive remains in the hands of the Member State where the service is provided (and that the latter is guaranteed the effective support by the authorities in the country of origin).

2.3.2. Rights of Recipients of Services

2.3.2.1. Prohibited Restrictions

The FEB suggests supplementing this subparagraph as follows: "without prejudice to the derogations set out in Article 17.5".

The FEB is against any measure aiming at removing means of control held by the Member State where the service is provided within the framework of the positing of workers.

2.3.2.2. Assumption of Healthcare Costs

Assuming that the healthcare sector has not been excluded from the Directive's scope of application, the FEB is calling for this Article to be better defined under the conditions stipulated by the European Commission in its "Explanatory note from the Commission Services on the provisions of the proposed Directive on services in the Internal Market relating to the assumption of healthcare costs incurred in another Member State with a particular emphasis on the relationship with Regulation No. 1408/71" which was circulated on 16 July 2004 (Docs 11570/04 COMPET 128, ETS 47, SOC 363, JUSTCIV 112, CODEC 920).

The FEB wants to avoid a potential residual cost which will be borne by the Belgian social security system, if a European patient is treated in Belgium.

Therefore, the FEB would like to draw attention to the above-mentioned note and, in particular, to the following conclusions:

1. The definition of hospital care in Article 4(10) could be reworded on the basis of discussions with Member States. In particular, it could be made clearer that the Member State of affiliation of the patient is to determine what is considered as hospital care regardless of whether this treatment is hospital care in the Member State where the treatment is obtained. It could also be made clearer, by moving the definition now appearing under Article 4(10) to Article 23, that the definition has no meaning other than allowing a proper application of the distinction made in Article 23 between hospital and non-hospital care.
2. It could be specified that Regulation 1408/71 will apply in cases where an authorisation is either necessary or asked for by patients. It could be made clearer that the Proposed Directive incorporates the conditions laid down by Regulation 1408/71 under which an authorisation cannot be refused. A cross-reference to this Regulation could be made in Article 23(2).
3. It could be made clearer in Article 23 (3) that a patient cannot make a profit when receiving treatment abroad and that his right to assumption of costs is always limited by the actual costs incurred.
4. It could be specified that Article 23 does not require Member States to reimburse travel and accommodation costs and that this issue is dealt with at national level.
5. The level of assumption of healthcare costs incurred in another Member State without authorisation could be further clarified, in particular.
6. It could be explained that the extent of the sickness cover is entirely determined by the Member State of affiliation of the patient as regards the limits of the costs assumed, the medical treatments covered and the conditions for granting those medical treatments including the need to consult a generalist or a specialist prior to certain types of tests or treatments.
7. It could be explained that Member States which do not operate a reimbursement system but a system of benefits-in-kind may establish reimbursement tariffs i.e. they may calculate the nominal cost of the treatment which they would normally assume for a certain treatment provided in kind and, on the basis of this, fix thresholds for reimbursement of costs for that treatment in another Member State.

2.3.3. Posting of workers

The FEB suggests the deletion of this section.

The FEB stresses a major contradiction between the Commission's concern to safeguard the measures in Directive 96/71 on the posting of workers (cf. derogation set out in Article 17.5) and its intention to significantly restrict the scope of the controls and obligations imposed by the Member State where the service is provided. The FEB thinks that implementing these restrictions would result in the elimination of instruments set out in the law of 5 March 2002 allowing the working conditions, which the foreign provider is obliged to apply in Belgium, to be controlled. In practice, this would make the controls in our country obsolete.

As a result, the FEB is against any measure in the proposal for a Directive which aims to remove means of control held by the Member State where the service is provided within the framework of the posting of workers. That is until the moment that a true "level playing field" is created within an enlarged internal market.

Moreover, the FEB regrets that this Article gives preference to *a posteriori* controls conducted by the authorities of the country of origin.

The FEB believes that the proof of compliance with the legal conditions for residence and employment of workers accompanying the foreign service provider – the only requirement set out by the Directive – must be provided to the Belgian authorities and the companies concerned "*ex ante*" and not "in the shortest possible time".

In the event of abuse and illegal employment, the responsibility will ultimately be borne by the customer company in Belgium.

2.4. Quality of Services

2.4.1. Professional Insurance and Guarantees

The FEB is against introducing the obligation that the providers mentioned in this subparagraph be covered by professional indemnity insurance. It believes that, on the contrary, precedence should be given to the free development of innovative insurance solutions geared to meet specific needs and tailored to the profile of those providers wishing to conduct their activities on a cross-border basis.

In fact, the compulsory professional indemnity insurance scheme introduced in Article 27.1 does not take account of the major differences between the situations in various Member States regarding such matters as insurance markets for civil liability insurance, exposure to risks, the applicable legislation, case law and so forth. Hence it is extremely difficult for an insurer to evaluate precisely the risk represented by a service provider conducting activities in different Member States. Many insurers are unable to offer insurance products on a cross-border basis.

Moreover, Article 27 does not provide details of the activities of the services in question, in other words, the activities which "present a direct and particular risk to the health or safety of the recipient or a third person, or to the financial security of the recipient".

In fact, Article 27.5 only allows for the Commission, with the help of a Committee, to draw up a list of services with the characteristics mentioned in Article 27.1, including those regarding the nature and the extent of the risk. However, the number of compulsory insurances available and the manner in which national courts treat civil liability cases make the situations in the various Member States so different that any attempt at harmonisation would be impossible.

The FEB believes that Article 27.1 will end up making certain activities uninsurable and preventing the service providers in question from operating in other European Member States. Assuming that cover was available, the cost would be extremely high and would have to be passed on in the prices of the services provided. This would have a very negative impact on the providers in question and could end up detrimentally affecting their competitiveness.

The subparagraph should be deleted. The same for the subparagraph relating to supplying information on the existence or otherwise of an after-sales guarantee and on its content in any document relating to the provision of the service.

The FEB believes that this demand gives rise to a disproportionate obligation which is accentuated by the fact that all communication media are targeted. Moreover, the FEB stresses a contradiction between Article 28.1, which stipulates that the aforementioned information must be supplied at the "request" of the recipient, and Article 28.2, which extends the obligation to supply the aforementioned information in any information documents supplied by providers, setting out a detailed description of the services offered. In this respect, the FEB would like to point out that Directive 1999/44, on certain aspects of the sale of consumer goods and associated guarantees, states that it is only *on request by the consumer* that the guarantee shall be made available in writing or feature in another durable medium available and accessible to him.

11. THE POINT OF VIEW OF THE ETUC[284]

Catelene Passchier

The European Trade Union Confederation is very concerned about some key provisions in the European Commission's draft Services Directive in the Internal Market. It warns that they could speed up deregulation, seriously erode workers rights and protection and damage the supply of essential services to European citizens.

The ETUC acknowledges a certain potential for job creation in many service sectors across Europe. It recognises efforts in the Commission's draft Directive to improve the efficiency of the internal market through reducing administrative costs and setting up single points of contact for service providers.

However, the draft as it stands is seriously flawed, as it threatens to undermine existing collective agreements, national labour codes, and the success of the European social model. For these reasons, the ETUC cannot support it.

1. GENERAL (NON-EXHAUSTIVE) REMARKS

1.1. The Broader Framework of the Lisbon Agenda: A Balance between Economic, Social and Environmental Interests

The Lisbon strategy is based on three pillars, linking economic reform with promoting sustainable economic growth, better quality jobs and social cohesion. The social dimension, and an impact assessment of social and employment effects is missing.

The impact assessment, made by the Commission, shows many discrepancies and a lack of clarity. On the one hand, it recognises that it is very difficult, if not impossible, to provide a reliable global estimate of the effect of barriers to services on the EU economy. On the other, it states that millions of jobs will be created. We are still waiting for a comprehensive analysis, focused on the problem of creating of jobs and better quality jobs within the EU. It is important that the potential benefits of the Directive are not exaggerated.

---

284 This is the text of the contribution by Mrs C.E. Passchier, representing the ETUC on the occasion of the public hearing of the European Parliament, Committee on the internal market and consumer protection in association with the Committee on Employment and Social Affairs, on the proposal for a Directive on Services in the Internal Market, on 11 November 2004.

In fact, trade union research shows that previous liberalisations have led to the destruction of existing jobs and the erosion of social cohesion. The Commission must, therefore, prepare a more indepth assessment of its impact in these areas.

Also, a more detailed analysis is needed, which specifies the kind of services that are supposed to suffer from barriers, or benefit in terms of employment growth from the removal of barriers.

For instance, with regard to health services, it is highly questionable if the Directive would bring any benefits. In the "Employment in Europe 2004" report published by DG Employment in September, a comparison was made between employment structures in the US and Europe, and it was shown that health and social services are one area where between 1998 and 2003, "employment growth rates in a majority of EU Member States out-performed those observed for the US". This section of the report concludes:

> ... the key to increasing employment in services is in the creation of jobs in the comparatively high-paying, high-productivity services, such as business services, education and health and social services. To achieve this, the spill-over effects on employment in services from product demand in industry need to be better exploited and further increases in final demand for services are necessary. The latter will follow on from further increases in the labour market participation of women and older people, from more and more efficient investment in human capital and lifelong learning, sharing the related costs and responsibilities between public authorities, companies and individuals, and from the support of public spending in areas such as education and health and social services.

This basically means:

–   that health services as currently organised are already successful in creating employment, and in many cases skilled and high-paying jobs. (So if this is already happening, why risk undermining this by introducing a measure that could create a race to the bottom?)
–   that this success could be built on, not by increasing competition but by investing in training and increasing support from public spending.

1.2. Services of General Interest, Health Services and Social Services should not be Covered

1.2.1. A Positive Legal Framework on SGI Is Needed

The Commission has to keep its promise to consult widely with civil society on the freedom of social services, i.e. social protection systems, healthcare services, social housing, long-term care, education, social assistance. This consultation must to take place *before* the Commission and the Council propose other measures affecting their operation. A positive legal framework on SGI is needed first.

The draft Services Directive may force Member States to remove regulations, and may prevent them from planning the future of these services. This may have the effect of a liberalisation of these services. The ETUC considers that the challenge that the EU faces regarding healthcare or care of the elderly are too important to leave to the market. Public authorities must be able to exercise control and may have laws promoting services of general economic interest.

All services have an economic aspect. SGEIs which are not remunerated will not be affected by EU law on free movement of services and, therefore, not by the proposed Directive. There is an argument for excluding all SGEIs from the Services Directive until the relevant European law is enacted under the new Constitution specifying the principles and conditions on which they are to operate to enable them to fulfil their missions.

Regarding health services, healthcare provision in all Member States is intrinsically linked to social security, which remains the sole responsibility of national authorities. These services belong to a public health policy which is defined by Member States and they cannot be assimilated to a mere freedom to provide services.

As regard the various problems with healthcare services and the reimbursement of healthcare costs incurred abroad: these issues are so much intrinsically linked to the public policy on healthcare, that they need to be regulated within the framework of Regulation 1408/71, also to prevent the persistence of contradictory regulations between this Regulation and the draft Services Directive.

1.3. The Country of Origin Principle Causes a Race to the Bottom, and Will Lead to "Less Europe" Instead of More

Application of the country of origin principle to cross border service providers is an open invitation for abuse and manipulation. Instead of promoting fair competition on the basis of "level playing fields" (which is the major reason for harmonisation), the application of the country of origin principle can lead to very negative effects on those areas that are not Europe-wide harmonised. These types of measures would encourage service providers to establish themselves (officially, or only via letter-box companies) in the EU Member States with the lowest tax rates, environmental requirements and protection of workers rights. On the other hand, countries with higher standards of protection will feel obliged to lower them, in order to stay competitive.

Also, the country of origin principle, far from achieving a clear, transparent, and coherent situation for companies with regard to the applicable regulatory framework, will create new confusion and legal complexities. It would allow various national regimes to co-exist in the same host country and could lead to the juxtaposition of possibly 25 national regulations. This would make law enforcement practically impossible. It would openly invite Member States to enter into "regime competition", with workers, consumers and the environment being the big losers.

The ETUC believes that it is possible to improve the internal market for services without the detrimental introduction of the country of origin principle.

As the Kok II Report states: "no services market at the expense of social dumping".

2. ON LABOUR LAW

2.1. Labour Law and the Country of Origin Principle: An Impossible Combination

According to the Commission, the draft Services Directive "does not aim to address issues of labour law as such". The Commission's civil servants have also have put great efforts in to show that trade unions have unjustified fears and objections regarding the effects of the Draft Directive on labour law.

However, they have not convinced the ETUC.

On the contrary, after studying carefully all the proposed texts and explanations on the table, we are convinced that the Directive interferes with labour law issues in a far-reaching and totally unacceptable way.

Questions arise already at the start of the Directive, when the term "coordinated field" is introduced.

The definition tells us that this means "any requirement applicable to access or the exercise of service activities". In point 23 of the preamble, it is stressed that it does not matter to which legal field they belong under national law.

In Article 16 of the Directive, it is further explained what kind of provisions fall within the meaning of the coordinated field. The text is rather vague, and includes a general reference to "contracts" but one could imagine, that only the commercial activities of the service provider are somehow addressed.

But what should one think, when in Article 17 under the derogations one finds the following references:

Exclusion of:

–   matters covered by the Posting Directive;
–   the provisions of 1408/71 with regard to applicable law;
–   the freedom of parties to choose the law applicable to their contract; and
–   contracts for the provision of services concluded by consumers to the extent that the provisions governing them are not completely harmonised at Community level.

In the explanatory note, preceding the draft text, the issue of private international law is addressed.

Where the Commission makes a reference to the Rome II Convention, a specific derogation to ensure coherence with the draft Services Directive is envisaged.

With regard to the Rome I convention (about the law applicable to contractual relations), a general remark is made that the conversion of this Convention to a new Community instrument, according to the Commission's green paper on this issue "must leave intact Internal Market principles contained in the Treaty or in secondary law".

And the text continues, by saying that both conventions play an important role, especially with regard to the derogations of the country of origin principle, notably the derogation for contracts concluded by consumers, and the derogation relating to the non-contractual liability of the provider in case of an accident.

However, the text is revealing in what it does *not* say: no word about the specific regulations in the Rome I Convention (in Articles 6 and 7) about the law applicable to employment contracts?

It is important to mention, that the derogation for consumer-contracts is of the same nature as the derogation for employment contracts: the free choice of law is limited for reasons of protection of the consumer / worker, and the imbalance of power between the contracting parties.

The combined effect of Article 16 (country of origin principle) and Article 17 (exclusion of Posting Directive and the freedom of parties to choose the law applicable to their contract) could be, that in all situations of cross border provision of services in which workers are implied (most situations!), and the Posting Directive would not apply (see examples in annex) either the law of the country of origin would apply, or the law chosen by the parties.

No possibility for correction on the basis of the Rome I Convention!

This would lead to an outrageous infringement in the labour law and collective bargaining systems of the Member States of the EU.

Even public labour law, like working time legislation and health and safety regulations, which in most Member States have a territorial effect, could be questionable.

The effects are such, that the ETUC wants to ring alarm bells.

Maybe the Commission did not have this effect in mind, when drafting the text of the Directive.

But why not then make it explicit from the outset, in the scope of the Directive, that labour law, and the law applicable to employment contracts, was not covered, and not part of the coordinated field?

Or why not refer in Article 17,20 to all the relevant aspects of the Rome I Convention?

Or is this really the dream of some people within the Commission, to find an indirect way to tackle labour law and collective bargaining arrangements, as barriers to the free market of services?

2.2. Exclusion of the Posting Directive: Not Clear, and Not Enough

It is important to stress, that the Posting Directive cannot be understood without putting it against the broader framework of the Rome I Convention.

The Posting Directive deals with situations, as described in the Rome I Convention, in which the habitual place of work is *not* the host country and the worker only temporarily performs work in another country (in which situation the law that "objectively" applies, according to the Rome Convention, is the law of the country where the worker normally works). In these situations, however, according to Article 7 of the Rome Convention, certain mandatory rules of the country where the work is performed apply.

The Posting Directive provides for a clear framework, indicating which minimum rules of the country of work always have to apply, and also how to deal with minimum regulations in collective agreements.

If one would take away the broader framework of the Rome Convention, and only provide for simplistic derogation of the Posting Directive on the one hand, while allowing for a free choice of law in all other cases, the effects would – again – be unacceptable (see examples in Annex).

Aspects that urgently need clarification are therefore: what if a Member State applies more mandatory rules to posted workers, than the minimum provided for in this Directive. Do they still apply, as long as they stay within the area of the Posting Directive? How do you interpret in this regard the formula "matters covered by the Posting Directive"?

The Posting Directive is not clear at all about when there is a situation of "temporary" posting, and when the posting is not temporary anymore. In the current situation, even though there is a lot of uncertainty about this issue, at least from the perspective of worker protection there would be the fall back situation of the Rome I Convention.

But if the draft Services Directive would indeed interfere with Articles 6 and 7 of the Rome Convention, the issue becomes of great importance: as soon as a worker is no longer a "temporary" posted worker, the country of origin principle (or free choice of law) would apply, and all protection of mandatory rules of the host state would disappear.

A final issue to clarify (linked to the next point about enforcement) is the issue of temporary agency work, as dealt with in the Posting Directive. In Article 3 of this Directive, one of the minimum regulations regarded as a mandatory rule that always has to apply, is "the conditions of hiring out workers, in particular the supply of workers by temporary employment undertakings".

How to interpret this provision? In many countries, these "conditions" include a lot of supervisory, licensing and other mechanisms. In the view of the ETUC, these have to be seen as "matters covered by the Posting Directive". But in that case this would contradict with the provisions of Article 24 (see below).

2.3. Labour Law Can Only Be Effectively Enforced at the Workplace and in the Country where the Work is Performed

The draft Services Directive, in its eagerness to abolish all barriers to services, comes up with proposals (in Article 24) that make enforcement more complex and less effective.

The good news is the part of Article 24 that demands more support of the Member State of posting with regard to monitoring and enforcement.

However, in the name of mutual confidence and recognition, the Member State of posting, while notably being the one that is responsible for the enforcement of its own legislation, is seriously hindered by the prohibitions as listed in Article 24.

Authorisation, licenses and registration could be a very efficient and convenient way to prevent abuse and fraud, for instance with regard to temporary agency work.

Even a country like the Netherlands, which six years ago abolished the licensing system, because it was thought the temporary agency sector was mature enough to ensure normal business practices, has recently reversed this decision, because of the explosive growth of malafide intermediaries, employing an increasing number of undocumented migrant workers, making enormous profits, and escaping every public control.

Taking such a measure is seen as an instrument, in the interest of the bonafide service providers!

What if the Netherlands applied the new rules equally and without discrimination on foreign temporary agencies? Would the draft Services Directive then say, that, yes, it may be allowed under community law to have these measures installed on the national level vis-à-vis national service providers, but *not* vis-à-vis foreign service providers?

Would that not create very unfair competition, be an invitation for fraud and manipulation, and in the end destroy the possibilities of Member States taking efficient and reasonable action to protect their labour markets, workers and service providers alike?

The same could be said about the specific prohibition to check the legal status of a third country national by the host Member State (Article 25).

It should be possible for Member States to take appropriate measures to prevent the exploitation of irregular migrant labour by cross-border service providers and national service providers alike.

2.4. Temporary Agency Work Deserves Its Own Directive

The ETUC is convinced that the draft Services Directive is not the right document to deal with Temporary Agency Work, and in particular not with the special aspects of monitoring, supervision and enforcement that continue to be necessary in a sector that is so vulnerable to possible abuses and fraud.

The Draft Directive on Temporary Agency Work should deal with this issue in a balanced way, also taking into account ILO Convention 181 (which was adopted by the ILO Conference in 1997 with an overwhelming majority and the support of all "old" EU Member States), which explicitly allows for systems of licensing and supervision, to allow Member States to protect their labour markets, and promote good quality temporary agency work.

2.5. Collective Bargaining: A Fundamental Right

In its first report on the state of the internal market (2002) the Commission expressed the view that collective bargaining would be an obstacle to the further development of the internal market for services. The fact that this view was then expressed is already very worrying in itself!

Although the Draft Directive does not explicitly tackle collective bargaining arrangements, the ETUC is very worried about several aspects in the text, that could put industrial relations systems and collective bargaining and Member States in danger, and could interfere with fundamental rights like the freedom of association and collective bargaining, and the right to take industrial action.

Some specific issues need to be raised here.

The definition of a "requirement", as given in Article 4 of the Draft, seems to cover collectively agreed measures. In several Member States it is the social partners that develop ways and means to deal with, for instance, the conditions for hiring out workers in collective agreements. In some Member States, it has been a deliberate policy to move away from public interference, and leave the issue fully or partly for regulation by the social partners.

If these measures as such are allowed under current Community law, it should not be possible to interfere with them on the basis of the Services Directive.

According to Draft Article 24, it is prohibited to demand from a service provider that he has a representative on his own territory. This prohibition directly interferes with the system of industrial relations and collective bargaining in Sweden and Denmark (see also example), and can therefore not be accepted.

3. CONCLUSION

The ETUC is of the opinion, that the draft Services Directive as it currently stands is an open invitation to abuse and manipulation, and a threat to the European social model. Instead of harmonising upwards, it causes regime competition between Member States, and a race to the bottom, to the detriment of workers, consumers, and the environment.

Maybe the goal is good, but this vehicle is not the right one.

4. EXAMPLES

NB: The Posting Directive is only applicable in cases of workers that *temporarily* perform work outside the country where they *normally* work.

4.1. Long-term Provision of Cross-border Services

Company established in UK sends its UK – workers for a longer period (longer than 12 months) to work in France

= not posting

–   means according to Rome I Convention (Article 3): free to choose law applicable to employment relationship, e.g. UK or French law. If they do not make an explicit choice, the law of the country where the worker habitually carries out his work, i.e. France, will apply (unless there is a closer connection with another country);
–   but (Article 6,1 Rome Convention), in case there is a choice to be made, this choice cannot deprive the worker from the protection (key provisions/mandatory rules) he would get from the law that would apply to him, if the parties would not have explicitly made a choice of law (i.e. the most logical law to apply to a labour contract, also called the law that "objectively" applies to the employment contract); in this case, "the law of the country in which he habitually carries out his work" (probably France, in some cases maybe the UK);
–   and/or (Article 7 Rome Convention), if a choice is made, this choice cannot prevent the mandatory rules applying from the country with which the situation has a close connection (in this case: France).

Situation on basis of draft Services Directive:

–   country of origin applies;
–   unless parties have made a different choice of law (Article 17,20);
–   could mean that a UK company that sends UK workers for a long term to France would not even have to apply French mandatory rules (for instance on working time; and instead could make use of the UK opt-out).

4.2. Foreign Service Providers Hiring Local Workers

Company established in UK hires French workers to work in France (regardless of period for which they are hired)

= not posting (because in this case the worker is not sent to a country other than the country in which he normally works)

–   means according to Rome I Convention: free to choose applicable law (UK or France);
–   but: mandatory rules of France will apply.

Situation on basis of draft Services Directive:

–   country of origin applies;
–   unless parties have made a different choice of law;
–   could mean that a UK company that hires French workers to work in France would not have to apply even French mandatory rules (for instance on working time; and instead could make use of the UK opt-out).

4.3. Letter-box Companies

Company based in Belgium, using a Polish letter-box company to send Ukrainian workers to Belgium:

If they are sent out short term ("temporarily")

= posting

–   choice of law allows choice of Polish law;
–   mandatory rules of Belgium apply, including collective agreements;
–   rules on licensing apply on equal footing with Belgian companies.

Changes on basis of draft Services Directive

–   questionable if extensive implementation of Posting Directive in Belgium will be interpreted fully as "matters covered by the Posting Directive" are exempt from the country of origin principle;
–   no longer allowed to license, etc.;
–   if the service is a temporary agency, the question is, if the regulations on licensing will be interpreted as "the conditions of hiring out of workers", and, as such, covered by the Posting Directive (and therefore exempt from the draft Services Directive);
–   not allowed to demand documents about legal status of the workers
–   not allowed to demand proof that the worker has an employment history in Poland (important for social security).

If they are sent out long term:

= not posting

–   choice of law allows for choice of Polish (or even Ukrainian) law
–   however, Rome I would correct this, and provide for protection of mandatory rules of place of habitual work (Belgium)
–   at least " international" mandatory rules of Belgium would apply

Changes on basis of draft Services Directive

–   country of origin would apply (Poland)
–   unless parties have made a different choice of law (Ukraine??)
–   no corrections possible for mandatory rules of Belgium

4.4. Limited Protection with regard to Collective Bargaining

Company established in UK sending UK workers to work temporarily (short term) in Sweden:

= posting

–   mandatory rules, Sweden would apply (for instance, working time regulations), but that is a limited set of rules, not including minimum wages; also, the act to implement the Posting Directive has not made use of the possibility of extending the scope of the Directive to collective agreements;
–   application of minimum wages and other collectively agreed regulations depend on the possibility of enforcing collective bargaining on the service provider. To be able to do this, the service provider would need to have a representative on Swedish soil, that could sign a collective agreement and against whom industrial action could be taken if he is unwilling to sign;
–   enforcement is also organised by social partners.

Situation on basis of draft Services Directive:

–   it cannot be requested that a representative is based in Sweden;
–   therefore the minimum collectively agreed regulations cannot be negotiated nor enforced;
–   if industrial action is taken towards the service provider, demanding that he does provide a representative in Sweden, this could be interpreted as unlawful industrial action.

12. EURO-CIETT POSITION PAPER ON REQUIRED AMENDMENTS TO THE DIRECTIVE ON SERVICES IN THE INTERNAL MARKET

CIETT

1. GENERAL COMMENTS

Euro-CIETT welcomes the proposal for a Services Directive in the Internal Market and its objective to create a real internal market in services.

Euro-CIETT believes the Services Directive should be examined within the framework of the European Employment Strategy and in particular the Lisbon employment creation and worker integration targets. The development of a strong services sector and the establishment of a well functioning internal market for services is essential if the EU is to achieve the Lisbon objectives of increase of growth, employment and labour market integration.

Euro-CIETT proposes in this position paper, a limited number of amendments to the original Commission proposal. Euro-CIETT has furthermore taken account of the Draft Internal Market and Consumer Protection Committee Report on the Services Directive (Gebhardt Report) and the Draft Opinion of the Employment and Social Affairs Committee. Euro-CIETT strongly disagrees with most of the amendments proposed by these committees, as expressed in the related Euro-CIETT position papers.[285]

In order for the Services Directive to achieve its stated objective, it should apply to all services with very few exceptions. Agency work is a service sector and as such should remain within the scope of the Directive. Excluding such an important number of service providers (private employment agencies have more than 15,000 branches in the EU) would significantly weaken the proposed Directive and would not lead to the creation of an effectively functioning single market in services, thus deterring the EU from reaching the Lisbon objectives.

---

285 Euro-CIETT: Euro-CIETT Position Paper on the EP's internal market committee draft report presented by Ms. Gebhardt on the Proposal for a Directive on Services in the Internal Market; Euro-CIETT: Euro-CIETT Position Paper on the draft opinion of Anne Van Lancker, MEP, on the Proposal for a Directive on Services in the Internal Market.

Agency work is a key element of the services sector in all Member States, which already contributes to achieving the Lisbon objectives, with currently over 7 million workers employed by the agency work industry. The sector's contribution could be further increased given the appropriate regulatory framework, notably the review and lifting of unjustified obstacles to agency work.

In line with the objective of job creation and labour market integration, Euro-CIETT fully supports the provision contained in Articles 14 and 15 of the Commission's proposal to review regulations that act as a restriction on agency work, with a view to lifting these where they are not justified on the grounds of worker protection.

Simplification, which in no way should undermine the existence of authorisation schemes in Member States that are objective, proportionate, clear and non-discriminatory, can be one of the essential premises for the development of a high-quality agency work industry.

Euro-CIETT fully supports the country of origin principle and the approach to exclude matters covered by Directive 96/71/EC on posting of workers from application of the country of origin principle as already foreseen under Article 24 of the proposed Directive.

However, certain changes are necessary with regard to the application of this principle as well as with regard to the posting of workers.

2. COUNTRY OF ORIGIN PRINCIPLE

Euro-CIETT believes that the provisions of the proposed Directive would benefit from the introduction of a clearer system of reciprocal acknowledgement of authorisation schemes between Member States where such schemes already exist. To introduce this level of reciprocal acknowledgment between Member States, Euro-CIETT proposes the following modification to Article 10.3:

> **Amendment to Article 10.3**: The conditions for granting authorisation for a new establishment shall not duplicate requirements and controls which are equivalent or essentially comparable as regards their purpose, to which the provider is already subject in another Member State or in the same Member State. The contact points referred to in Article 35 and the provider shall assist the competent authority by providing any necessary information on those requirements. The purpose of this information being the mutual recognition of equivalent or essentially comparable authorisation schemes or other requirements between the Member States, so as to enable the free movement of services.

3. POSTING OF WORKERS

With respect to the posting of workers, cooperation between the country of origin and the country of posting (host country in the terminology of Directive 96/71/EC) on exchange of information on the details of the posting is essential, as well as carrying out the necessary checks to ensure compliance with the employment and working conditions applicable under the Directive. Authorities in the country of posting should, as such, have full rights to enforce the Posting of Workers Directive and authorities in the country of origin have the duty to inform them of the posting.

Therefore, Euro-CIETT proposes to maintain the Commission's Article 24 and amend it in such a way that it sufficiently guarantees an appropriate exchange of information on the details of the posting between authorities of the country of posting. To ensure this, Article 24 should be amended to ensure effective controls in the country of posting. This should take place from the start of the posting, and not within two years as originally proposed by the Commission.

> **Amendment to Article 24.2**: "In the circumstances referred to in paragraph 1, the Member State of origin shall ensure that the provider takes all measures necessary to be able to communicate the following information, both to its competent authorities and to those of the Member State of posting from the start of posting, both to its competent authorities and to those of the Member States of posting.

> **Amendment to Article 24, new paragraph 3**: "The country of destination shall have the full right to exercise controls of the workers posted on its territory, in order to verify the implementation of the essential working conditions as laid down by the Posting of Workers Directive."

4. FINAL ASSESSMENT

Furthermore, Euro-CIETT would like to emphasise that the proposed Services Directive has no bearing on social security coverage for posted workers, given that social security matters are covered by the existing EU Regulation 1408/71 on the application of social security schemes to employed persons and their families moving within the Community. The existence of illegal activities or the abusive use of social security premiums between Member States, to gain an unfair competitive advantage in the service sector marketplace, must be pursued and eliminated.

The agency work sector is a high quality industry, which provides for the necessary flexibility in today's highly demanding market, while fully guaranteeing employee rights and effectively fighting illegal and abusive employment services activities.

Euro-CIETT calls for a fast examination of the proposed Directive by the Council of Ministers and the European Parliament so that restrictions to the freedom of establishment for service providers and the free movement of services between Member States are eliminated and the internal market for services completed.

5. ABOUT EURO-CIETT

Euro-CIETT is the European organisation of CIETT, the International Confederation of Private Employment Agencies. Euro-CIETT is the authoritative voice representing the interests of agency work businesses in Europe. It is recognised as such by European organisations (including EU, UNI-Europa, UNICE, Dublin Foundation) as well as national governments.

Euro-CIETT brings together 21 national federations of private employment agencies and six of the largest staffing companies worldwide (Adecco, Kelly Services, Manpower, Randstad, USG, Vedior).

The Euro-CIETT mission is to seek greater recognition for the contribution that private employment agencies make to labour markets, especially in relation to three key aspects: employment creation; access to and integration in the labour market of diversified categories of workers (disabled, first-time entrants, long-term unemployed); economic growth and financial contribution.

13. THE SERVICES DIRECTIVE NEEDS TO BE "SOCIALLY" ADJUSTED – A POLITICAL VIEW FROM THE EUROPEAN PARLIAMENT

Anne Van Lancker

1. INTRODUCTION

Launched by the Commission in January 2004, the proposal for a Directive on Services in the Internal Market[286] sets out a general legal framework to reduce barriers to cross-border provision of services within the European Union. As draftswoman in charge of this Directive for the Committee on Employment and Social Affairs, I share the view that the elimination of obstacles to the provision of services between Member States is an important element in achieving the goal set by the Lisbon European Council of making the European Union the most competitive and dynamic knowledge-based economy in the world capable of sustainable economic growth with more and better jobs and greater social cohesion. The services sector is a very important economic sector, representing about 70% of turnover and employment in certain countries in Europe, "[b]ut its growth potential is seriously hampered by various obstacles", states the European Commission. However, the way in which the Directive seeks to solve this problem is highly controversial and dangerous. The elimination of these "obstacles" as proposed in this Directive would not only remove redundant red tape and bureaucratic rules, but also affect rules and legislation providing quality guarantees, protection of consumers, the environment or workers. The balance between economic, social and environmental interests of the Lisbon Agenda is clearly missing. At the same time, I share the opinion of many experts and MEPs that many concerns need to be addressed before this Directive can enter into force.

The draft opinion I presented to the committee is based on the findings of the public hearing,[287] on the impact study[288] as well as on the contributions from

---

286 Hereafter: "the proposal".
287 Public Hearing on the Proposal for a Directive on Services in the Internal Market, organised by IMCO and EMPL, 11 November 2004. Directorate-General for Internal Policies, Notice to Members IV/2004 – PE 350.059v01-00.
288 Towards a European Directive on Services in the Internal Market: Analysing the Legal Repercussions of the Draft Services Directive and its Impact on National Services Regulations, Wouter Gekiere, Institute for European Law, KU Leuven, 24 September 2004.

various organisations and expert groups. In my working document,[289] I set out the orientations for amendment and identified the following controversial issues: the legal basis and scope of the proposal, the implications of requirements relating to establishment, the introduction of the country of origin principle and the relationship with other Community instruments. The opinion that was voted on 12 July in committee,[290] therefore seeks to address the following major concerns about the Services Directive.

2. SCOPE OF THE PROPOSAL

The proposal reflects a horizontal approach; it covers a wide variety of services ranging from purely commercial services to healthcare and social services. As many experts have pointed out, this proposal fails to take into account that the services covered have heterogeneous features and raise a wide variety of public policy considerations. It is highly questionable if such a heterogeneous range of sectors can be governed adequately by one framework Directive. It would have been preferable to continue with a sectoral approach, combining the establishment of a genuine internal market for a more homogeneous set of services with the necessary conditions with regard to the protection of quality standards, environmental and social protection, etc. The horizontal approach can only work if sensitive sectors are excluded and if major changes are made to the provisions on establishment and temporary provision of services. Therefore, it is essential that professions and activities which are permanently or temporarily connected with the exercise of official authority in a Member State, services provided by temporary employment agencies and services provided by security agencies be excluded from the scope of the proposal.

In any event, services of general interest should be excluded from the scope of the Directive. Even though this notion is not clearly defined at EU level, there is a consensus that these services are not purely commercial, but serve to guarantee basic rights of citizens in areas such as health, welfare, housing, transport, energy, employment, etc. National, regional or local authorities should therefore be able to organise, finance and/or guarantee these services. The discussion about the role of the EU in defining these services and the way they are organised and financed is the object of an ongoing process that should lead to a European framework Services Directive of general interest.

---

289   Working Document on the Draft Services Directive, 11 January 2005, Committee on Employment and Social Affairs, draftswoman Anne Van Lancker, PE 353.364v01-00.

290   Opinion of the Committee on Employment and Social Affairs for the Committee on the Internal Market and Consumer Protection on the proposal for a Directive of the European Parliament and of the Council on Services in the Internal Market, 19 July 2005, drafted by Anne Van Lancker, PE 357.591v03-00.

In order not to affect the freedom of Member States – on the basis of the principle of subsidiarity – to define what they consider to be services of general economic interest as referred to in Articles 16 and 86(2) of the Treaty and not to anticipate a framework Services Directive of general interest, the proposal should not apply to services which the Member States and/or the Community subject to specific universal or public service obligations, by virtue of a general interest criterion. For reasons of legal certainty and consistency with sectoral internal market Directives, specific network services, transport services and audiovisual services should also be excluded from the scope of this proposal.

Finally, it is essential to ensure that the Services Directive does not deal with the fields of labour law or social security law. It may not affect labour relations between workers and employers and the said fields should be excluded from its scope. The notion of labour law includes collective agreements as well as industrial action. This means that collective agreements at company level (such as in Germany) as well as collective agreements that are not declared universally applicable (such as in Sweden) should not be affected by the provisions of this proposal.

3. ESTABLISHMENT

As regards requirements relating to establishment, the current proposal will narrow down Member States' national regulatory powers to translate their duties in the social sphere into national/regional authorisation schemes. The screening operation to which Member States have to submit their national authorisation schemes could substantially enhance the European Commission's right to systematically monitor future national regulations and thus constitute a disproportionate interference with national regulatory competences. It is important to make sure that Member States wishing to take measures relating to a provider who is established in another Member State and who wishes to establish on their territory can rely upon the "rule of reason" grounds, as developed progressively by the Court of Justice, including the following grounds in the social field: social policy objectives, protection of workers, including their social protection, preservation of the financial balance of the social security system, maintaining a balanced medical and hospital service open to all and patient safety. Including a number of clarifications and amendments in the opinion is justified by reasons of subsidiarity, proportionality, legal certainty as well as consistency with EC Treaty rules and the case law of the European Court of Justice.

4. COUNTRY OF ORIGIN PRINCIPLE

As regards the provision of services on a temporary basis, Article 16 of the proposal provides that service providers will only have to comply with the provisions of the country in which the service provider is established. The proposal does not give a clear definition of what is meant by the temporary nature of a service activity, which leaves room for abuse. The definition of "establishment" included in Article 4(5) refers to the pursuit of an economic activity through a fixed establishment of the provider for an indefinite period. On the basis of these criteria, the dividing line between activities constituting an establishment and activities constituting a temporary service activity is not clear. Nor does the current definition prevent service providers from setting up special constructions (e.g. letter-box companies) in a Member State with lower taxation, environmental, consumer and/or social requirements. Under the Treaty this would qualify as a form of establishment. Consequently, the Member State under whose laws the letter-box company is incorporated, will, for the purposes of the proposal, be the country of origin. In order to avoid abuse, the definition of establishment needs to be sharpened.

The coordinated field to which the scope of the country of origin principle is linked covers any requirement applicable to, access to, and the exercise of, a service activity, in particular requirements governing the behaviour of the provider, the quality of content, advertising, contracts and the provider's liability. However, regarding this "coordinated field", the proposal only contains a series of information duties which service providers have to comply with and provisions on professional insurance and guarantees and information of recipients on the existence of after-sales guarantees.[291] This lack of balance is an open invitation to perform services while complying with the regulations of the Member State with the lowest standards.

The country of origin principle can only work if there is a minimum level of harmonisation at EU level or if there are at least comparable rules within the Member States: minimum harmonisation should relate to quality norms, the protection of public order, minimum vocational training, professional qualification requirements and supervisory mechanisms. Standards relating to quality of services, protection of consumers, employees and environment should also be safeguarded. Such a harmonisation process is only realistic if criteria and conditions are designed for each specific category of services. The Services Directive clearly breaks with the "Delors method" in the establishment of an internal market, since no such harmonisation or mutual recognition on the basis of comparable rules is foreseen.

This lack of harmonisation could launch a competition to the bottom between rules of the different Member States, since service providers could easily establish in the Member State where requirements concerning quality or content of the services or conditions of service provision are the lowest. It is also clear that supervision of the provider and his services by the country of origin can never work.

In the absence of a minimum level of harmonisation at EU level or, at least, of mutual recognition on the basis of comparable rules within the Member States, the country of origin principle cannot be the basic principle governing temporary cross-border service provision in the European Union. My opinion clearly links the

---

291   Proposal, Articles 26-28.

country of origin principle with the fields coordinated by this Directive (information on service providers, professional insurance and guarantees, information on after-sales guarantees and settlement of disputes) and other Community instruments. If there is no coordination/harmonisation at EU level, Member States should remain entitled to determine the access to, and exercise of, service activities by providers established in another Member State, in accordance with the provisions of the EC Treaty and the case law of the Court of Justice.

Furthermore, the competent authorities of the Member State in which the service is provided are best placed to ensure the effectiveness and the continuity of supervision and to provide protection for recipients. Even though this supervision should be complemented by an effective system of administrative cooperation between Member States, it is unacceptable that the principle, according to which the Member State of origin carries the responsibility for the supervision of the service, replaces the supervision by the Member State where the service is provided.

5. POSTING OF WORKERS

There is a lack of coordination between the Draft and other Community instruments. Many experts have raised concerns on the conflict between the COOP and existing labour law provisions included in the Posting Directive and Rome I[292] and Rome II.

As regards the posting of workers, Article 17(5) of the proposal provides that the country of origin principle does not apply to "matters covered by the Posting Directive". This exclusion does not provide for legal clarity. It is not enough to prevent disruptive interference with important aspects of individual and collective labour law. The term "matters covered by the Posting Directive" would need further clarification and probably adaptation to exempt all matters related to cross border posting of workers that are dealt with in the Posting Directive. Hence my suggestion to exclude this topic from the scope. The exemption should not only refer to the set of minimum requirements, and the minimum regulations provided for in the Posting Directive, but to all forms of extension and implementation that are allowed by the Posting Directive (e.g. possibility for Member States to impose compliance with other matters than listed in Article 1, possibility to base the implementation of the Posting Directive on generally binding collective agreements or specific collective bargaining systems, reference to all regulations dealing with temporary agency work, etc.).

The Posting Directive only deals with situations where the worker performs work on a temporary basis in another Member State than the Member State in which he

---

292   See European Parliament, Public Hearing on the proposal for a Directive on Services in the Internal Market, Thursday, 11 November 2004, Brussels: Professor Niklas Bruun, Employment Issues, Memorandum; Catelene Passchier, Contribution on behalf of the ETUC.

habitually works (for the service provider). It needs to be situated in the broader context of Rome I. According to Rome I, the law applicable to his employment contract is the law of the country where he normally works (Article 6) but, in these circumstances, certain mandatory rules of the country where the work is performed apply (Article 7). The Posting Directive contains minimum rules on employment and working conditions of the country where the work is performed. Excluding the matters covered by the Posting Directive does not eliminate the conflict between the Draft and Rome I in the situation in which the worker is not a temporary posted worker within the meaning of the Posting Directive.[293] Under the proposal, the country of origin principle (or the free choice of law) would apply and set aside the Rome I rules, which in these cases would lead to the application of the law and/or at least the mandatory rules of the host country. Similarly, the country of origin principle would set aside Rome II according to which the mandatory rule of the host state could be applied.

At the same time, Article 24 of the proposal reduces the effectiveness of labour inspection conducted by the host Member State on the basis of the Posting Directive, because it prohibits that state from making service providers subject to obligations that are essential for the inspection services of the state in which services are provided, such as to obtain an authorisation or a registration, to make a declaration, etc. This is particularly important for those countries where implementation and enforcement depends on collective bargaining and the role of social partners. Under the current circumstances, labour law provisions can only be effectively enforced in the Member State where the work is performed; the system of administrative cooperation proposed by the Commission to facilitate enforcement between Member States lacks the necessary safeguards to be an efficient tool of labour law enforcement.

For these reasons, Article 24 was deleted and Articles 17(5) and 17(20) replaced by a clear statement that the law applicable to workers employed for the provision of services is the Posting Directive, Rome I and other relevant Community and national labour law.[294]

As regards contractual and non-contractual obligations in fields other than labour law, the proposal contains general derogations to the country of origin principle that are inspired by the rules of conflict of law included in Rome I and Rome II: freedom of choice of contract law, consumer contracts to the extent that they are not completely harmonised at EU level, non-contractual liability of service provider

---

293 This may be the case for instance: 1) if he is only hired to be posted to another Member State, and before that moment has not been employed in the country of origin by the service provider, 2) if he is a citizen from the host country, employed in the host country by a service provider which is established elsewhere, 3) if he is posted for a longer period to the host country, and therefore not anymore to be considered a "temporary" posting.

294 European Parliament, Public Hearing on the proposal for a Directive on Services in the Internal Market, Thursday, 11 November 2004, Brussels: Professor Niklas Bruun, Employment Issues, Memorandum, 22.

in case of an accident. However, the Rome I and II rules have a much wider scope. Experts demonstrated that these rules are more appropriate to safeguard a proper balance between interests involved. They also explained that the unrestricted introduction of the country of origin principle would increase legal uncertainty, among other things because service providers will be offering competing services under a different legal regime.

In conclusion, the law applicable to contractual and non-contractual obligations should be dealt with by Rome I and II[295] based on the specific and appropriate legal basis provided for in Articles 61(c) and 65 EC.

6. CONCLUSION

A lot of criticism and many reasons for concern have been formulated with regard to the proposal for a Services Directive. The objective – establishing an internal market for services – may be praiseworthy, but the chosen strategy is not. The benefits of the Directive (administrative simplification, single points of contact, better cooperation between Member States) are completely outweighed by the threats it contains. It would have been appropriate for the Commission to withdraw the proposal and come up with new proposals taking into account the critical assessments. However, since the Commission was not prepared to do that, the European Parliament will have to amend this proposal very substantially in order to make it acceptable. The positive outcome of the vote, in my opinion, in the Committee on Employment and Social Affairs is a first reassuring step in what will be a long and difficult process.

---

295 European Parliament, Public Hearing on the proposal for a Directive on Services in the Internal Market, Thursday, 11 November 2004, Brussels: Position Paper by Paul Beaumont, Professor of European Union and Private International Law, University of Aberdeen.

PART II. APPLICABLE LAW

14. THE ROME CONVENTION ON THE LAW APPLICABLE TO CONTRACTUAL OBLIGATIONS AND LABOUR LAW (1980)

Willy van Eeckhoutte[296]

It is often pretended the project of the so-called Bolkestein Directive, when it ever comes into force, will have as a consequence that employers will be entitled to employ workers of Member States of the European Union under the employment and labour law rules of the state of origin. This is simply not true. The Directive project simply says nothing like that.

The law applicable on a contract of employment is determined by the Convention on the law applicable to contractual obligations, signed in Rome on 19 June 1980,[297] hereafter called the Convention on Contractual Obligations or CCO.

The Convention on Contractual Obligations applies when a choice must be made between the laws of different countries.[298] A uni-national employment contract with no involvement with another country thus does not bring along the application of the Convention on Contractual Obligations.

The Convention on Contractual Obligations is universal in character, and not restricted to countries of the European Union. Consequently the rules contained in the Convention can lead to the application of the law of a state that is not a Member State.[299]

1. CHOICE OF LAW

The Convention on Contractual Obligations accords great importance to the choice of law made by the parties.

Indeed, the principle is that the law that the parties have chosen governs the employment contract.[300]

---

296 I am greatly indebted to my former collaborator Henri Storme and my present collaborator Sammy Bouzoumita, for permitting me to rely on their article "Arbeidsovereenkomsten in internationaal privaatrecht. Recente evolutie" [Contracts of employment in private international law. Recent evolutions], *Nieuw Juridisch Weekblad*, 2005, 290-314.

297 The consolidated version was published in the *Official Journal* C 027, 26/01/1998 pp. 0034-0046.

298 Article 1 CCO.

299 Article 2 CCO.

300 Article 179 CCO.

The choice of the law to be applied can take place *at any time*. There is nothing to prevent the law being chosen during the performance of the contract. Additionally, the parties can alter this choice.[301] Thus, for example, during (temporary) secondment, it may be agreed that the law of the country of work shall apply during the temporary posting, after which the parties may opt to resume the application of another law when the employee returns.

The parties are *completely free* in their choice of law. It is not necessary for them to choose the law of a state that has signed the Convention on Contractual Obligations. Given the universal aspirations of the Convention,[302] this is no surprise. They may even declare different laws to be applicable (a practice also known as *dépeçage*) to different parts of the employment contract. It is, however, required that it remains a consistent whole, otherwise one must fall back on the law applicable in the absence of a choice of law.

The choice of the applicable law may be *implicit or explicit*. A classic example of an implicit choice for the law of a certain country is the reference to the law on employment contracts of that country. Thus, the judge may not, as was the case before the Convention on Contractual Obligations,[303] go looking for the "law chosen by the parties" when the intention to make a choice of law is not sufficiently clear from the agreement.

The principle of freedom of choice of the law that will govern the contract is also applicable to employment contracts. But the Convention on Contractual Obligations contains important derogation mechanisms. They are inspired by the concern to apply the law that is closest to the contract and the will to protect the weaker party, the employee. The consequence is that the chosen law will have to recede frequently in favour of the law of another country.

2. OBJECTIVE CONFLICTS RULE

The law that governs an employment contract if the parties have made no choice of law is not determined by Article 4 of the Convention on Contractual Obligations, but by a special regulation under Article 6, paragraph 2 of the Convention.

In accordance with the second paragraph of Article 6, an individual employment contract is governed in the absence of a choice of jurisdiction by:

–   the law of the country in which the employee habitually carries out his work in performance of the contract (the country of employment), even if he is temporarily employed in another country, or

---

301   Article 3. 2 CCO.
302   Article 2 CCO.
303   M. Fallon, "Autonomie de la volonté et rattachement du contrat international de travail au droit belge", *Journal des tribunaux du travail*, 1984, 265-271.

–   if the employee does not habitually carry out his work in any one country, by the law of the country in which the place of business through which he was engaged is situated.

In order to be able to apply the specific rules on employment contract it has to be fixed that the parties are tied by an employment contract. The Convention on Contractual Obligations does not contain a general definition of the notion "contract of employment".

If there is a contract of employment, this has to be in accordance with the law that is indicated by the choice-of-law rules applying to the employment contract, i.e. Article 6 of the Convention on Contractual Obligations. The noteworthy consequence is that the conflict rules with regard to the employment contract are applied, while the law thus indicated can perhaps conclude that a contract other than an employment contract is presented. In either case, a qualification through the *lex fori* must be avoided. If not, it is dependent on the judge who has been appointed to settle the dispute, which can lead to "court shopping" and inevitable legal uncertainty.

2.1. The Law of the Country of Employment

If the employee *habitually* carries out his work in one country, the law of that country will be applicable. Temporary performance of the employment contract does not detract from this. By this rule, the Convention on Contractual Obligation wants to create legal security in case of a temporary secondment abroad and avoid manipulation.

But what is *habitual* and what is *temporary*? There is no definition of those terms in the Convention on Contractual Obligations, hence the legal uncertainty.

Various solutions are proposed.

a) A first solution could be to fix a *time limit*. With that approach the concept of "temporary" relates to a specific period. In the event of a time-limited posting, the law of the country of employment where the employee is habitually employed remains applicable.

But the question remains about when employment is no longer temporary. Various terms are advanced. Reference to the Regulation No. 1971/1408, which refers to a period of 12 months, could give something to go on.[304] But that would remain an arbitrary definition. One can ask the question whether it is appropriate to change the applicable law in the case of an employee who has already been

---

304   F. Pennings, "Arbeidsrechtelijke aspecten van detachering van werknemers in/uit België en Nederland", in F. Pennings (ed.), *Tewerkstelling over de grenzen*, Deventer, Kluwer, 1996, 10

in service with an undertaking for 20 years but who is posted for five years to a foreign undertaking.

b) Another solution could be to look at the *importance of the activities*. In that matter habitual work is contrasted with occasional activities. Thus, an occasional trip abroad has no influence on the law applicable. That approach requires the employment in a given country to be the main activity. This solution can bring the Convention on Contractual Obligations and the Convention on the Jurisdiction and Enforcement of Judgements in Civil and Commercial Matters (EEX) and the parallel Lugano Convention on jurisdiction and the enforcement of judgements in civil and commercial matters (EVEX)[305] into line. The Court of Justice has indicated that the term "work habitually carried out" in the sense of Article 5,1 EEX/EVEX must be understood as "the place where or from which the employee (...) actually fulfils the most important part of his obligations towards his employer". For most cases it seems improbable that a judge would deem himself competent because the work is habitually in his country, in the sense of Article 5 EEX/EVEX (or Article 2, a) of the Brussels I Regulation),[306] whereas he should consider that the law of that country is not applicable since it is not the country where the work habitually takes place.

Nonetheless, this cannot be assumed *a priori*, given that international procedure law and private international law have different objectives. Since 1 August 2004 the Court of Justice has also been empowered to interpret the Convention on Contractual Obligations. As a consequence it should become clear in the not too distant future whether the Court of Justice will interpret both concepts in a similar way.

c) A final solution is to put *temporary* versus *definitive*. In the case of temporary employment abroad, it is known in advance that the employee will return to the original employer at a given time. Consequently the *intentions of the parties* must be considered. These intentions can be discerned, *inter alia*, from the employment contract and the parties' instructions. In the Green Paper the question is asked whether it is desirable to change the notion "temporary employment in another country".[307] The Max Planck Institute for private foreign law and private international law is opposed to laying down a fixed term because it is too arbitrary. It prefers to

---

305 Signed on 18 September 1988, which "exports" the application of the European Execution Treaty to the Member States of the European Free Trade Association (AFTA): Sweden, Norway, Iceland, Finland and Switzerland.

306 Council Regulation (EC) on Jurisdiction and the Recognition and Enforcement of Judgements in Civil and Commercial Matters, which came into force between the Member States (except Denmark) since 1 March 2002.

307 Green Paper on the conversion of the Rome Convention of 1980 on the law applicable to contractual obligations into a Community instrument and its modernisation, COM(2002) 654, January 2003.

consider the will of parties.[308] Just as in the former solution, the choice is thus for an *ex ante* appraisal on the basis of the practical circumstances. For the sake of legal certainty, this interpretation of the concept "temporary employment" seems to be preferable to the others.

2.2. The Law of the Country in which the Place of Business, through which the Worker was Engaged, is Situated

When the employee does not habitually carry out his work in the same country, the law of the country in which the place of business through which he was engaged governs the employment contract. This alternative can play a role in the absence of a habitual place of employment. For example, this may be the case for an employee in the international transport sector or for a racing cyclist taking part in races in different countries or in the case of a salary split.[309]

It is necessary that the place of business is a real establishment and the worker is employed really by a certain branch, and it is not just the place of conclusion of the employment contract.

2.3. Seeking the Closest Connection

Article 6,2 *in fine* of the Convention on Contractual Obligations stipulates that when it appears from the circumstances as a whole that the contract is more closely connected with another country, the law of that country should apply. This rule is an exception and therefore has to be applied strictly.

Its purpose is to avoid the risk that the employer deliberately establishes his business in a country with less favourable employment legislation with the intention of applying the laws of that country.

According to the jurisprudence and the literature, the following starting points can indicate a closer connexion: language of the contract, incorporation in the contract of certain legal concepts, currency of payment, duration of the employment, registration in the staff register, nationality of the parties, their normal place of residence, place where the authority of the employer is exercised and place where the employment contract was concluded. Considered on their own, each of these elements is insufficient to allow a closer connexion with another country than the

---

308 Max Planck Institute for Foreign Private and Private International Law, "Comments on the European Commission's Green paper on the conversion of the Rome Convention of 1980 on the law applicable to contractual obligations into a Community instrument and its modernization", *RabelsZ* 2004, 61.

309 O. Debray and D. Ectors, "La mobilité internationale: problématique de la loi applicable aux contrats de travail", in O. Debray and D. Ectors et al., *Le contrat de travail et la nouvelle economie* (Brussels: Editions du Jeune Barreau de Bruxelles, 2001) 17.

country of employment or the country in which the place of business through which he was engaged is situated. Do not forget this is exceptional. Some people will fall back all too easily on that exception in order to apply the *lex fori*. A possible case where the exception could be applied is the situation of a frontier worker whose place of residence is in the country where his employer is established.

3.   RESTRICTIONS ON FREE CHOICE OF LAW – PREVENTION OF EVASION OF LAW

Article 3, paragraph 3 of the Convention on Contractual Obligations provides for a first correction on the principle of free choice. It stipulates that if all the elements except the choice of law have a close connection with one given country, the choice made may not prevent the application of the mandatory rules of that country.

In that case the chosen law is the only international element.

This article is of little practical significance for employment contracts, given that the application of Article 6 of the Convention on Contractual Obligations leads to the same result.

3.1. Minimal Protection from the Mandatory Rules of the Objectively Applicable Law

The rules of contract of employment law imply a protection of the rights of the weaker party, i.e. the employee. Freedom of choice of the applicable law could damage this protective objective. In order to prevent this, the Convention on Contractual Obligations provides important limitations to that freedom of choice. The choice of the law applicable therefore has only a very limited influence in the field of employment law.

As a matter of fact Article 6, paragraph 1 of the Convention on Contractual Obligations prescribes that the mandatory rules of the law, objectively applicable in accordance with the rules mentioned above, may not be avoided by opting for the law of another country. The employee thus retains the protection of the objectively appropriate mandatory rules in any event.

The majority of authors accept that this protection must be cumulatively applied to the employee's advantage.[310] The mandatory rules count as a minimum standard. The choice of law remains important in this case as *its provisions which are favour-*

---

310   *Report on the Convention on the Law applicable to Contractual Obligations* by Mario Giuliano Professor, University of Milan (who contributed the introduction and the comments on Articles 1, 3-8, 10, 12, and 13) and Paul Lagarde Professor, University of Paris I (who contributed the comments on Articles 2, 9, 11, and 14-33), OJ C 282 of 31 October 1980.

able to the employee remain applicable. The protective function of Article 6 of the Convention on Contractual Obligations appears to guide that decision.

One disadvantage of the accumulation is that it requires a thorough study of different jurisdictions.[311] For this it is important that the national labour law concerned is studied as a whole. At first glance a provision in the law of a given country can offer more protection than a similar provision in the law of another country, but when read in conjunction with other rules this is no longer the case. For example, notice periods in the law chosen may be very short, but in that country unfair dismissal might perhaps be more readily presumed than in the law of the objectively applicable country. In this case, which legal system offers the best protection against dismissal? In a decision of 8 February 1999, the labour court of Mons took an interesting approach to this and carried out a thorough comparison of dismissal for cause (compelling reasons) in Belgian and French law. It came to the decision that, when all the elements were taken into account, French law did not offer less protection.[312]

3.2. Mandatory Rules in a Third Country or of the Forum

Article 7 spoils the relatively clear picture that Articles 3 and 5 of the Convention create for conflicting law regarding employment contracts.

Article 7, para. 1 of the Convention on Contractual Obligation stipulates that when applying the law of a country, under certain conditions the judge can give effect to the mandatory rules of the law *of another country.*

These conditions are:

–   the case in question has a close connection with that country and, additionally, these mandatory rules are applicable under the law of that country regardless of the law governing the contract;
–   the judge assesses each case *in concreto* to determine whether this is necessary and proper, taking account of the nature and the purpose of the provisions, and of the consequences that might follow from application or non-application.

Summarised: Article 7,1 of the Convention on Contractual Obligations may only lead to the application of the mandatory rules of another country if *four conditions* are satisfied:

1.   the mandatory rules of the law of another country must have a close connection with the case, which excludes an indirect or weak connection;

---

311   See e.g. F. Jault, *Revue Critique de Droit International Privé* 2003, 456-462.
312   Labour Court of Appeal Mons, *Journal des tribunaux du travail* 1999, 370.

2.   the mandatory rules of another country must require international applica-
        tion;
3.   the nature and content of the mandatory rules justify international applica-
        tion;
4.   in deciding whether these mandatory rules should be given effect, account
        must be taken of the consequences of applying or failing to apply the rules.
        According to certain authors the judge may only apply the mandatory rules
        where non-application would be obviously unreasonable or unfair.[313]

This list proves it is not the intention to apply an abundance of mandatory rules
from different legal systems to the case, even on the pretext of protecting the
employee. In that case predictability and thus legal security would be totally lost.
Article 7,1 of the Convention on Contractual Obligations must therefore be used
sparingly. Some countries have made use of the right provided in Article 22,1,
a of the Convention not to apply Article 7,1. Thus German, Irish, Luxembourg,
Portuguese and Spanish and UK judges do not apply Article 7,1 of the Convention
on Contractual Obligations.

For the *lex fori* Article 7,2 Convention on Contractual Obligations contains a
special provision. The application of the rules from the law of the presiding judge by
which the case is mandatorily governed, irrespective of the agreed applicable law, is
unimpeded. It is thus a matter of applying rules of the same type as in Article 7,1 of
the Convention on Contractual Obligations, but not subject to the strict conditions
mentioned. The underlying idea is that the judge is obliged to respect the rule that
his government has enacted and that must govern the case in question, even where
it is in principle governed by a foreign law, without any discretion.[314]

Article 7 of the Convention on Contractual Obligations brings about a lot of
confusion and its real impact remains a point of discussion.[315] One of the causes is
that Article 7, like Article 3 and Article 6, speaks of "mandatory rules". The question
is whether that notion has or has not the same meaning in the three articles. If one
considers the formulation of those articles as well as their function, the answer is
negative.

Article 6 of the Convention on Contractual Obligations requires a search for the
country most closely connected to the contract, using two crucial criteria (habitual
place of work or place of recruitment) and leaves open the possibility of deciding
whether there is a closer connection with another country on the basis of other
key points. Thus Article 6 is a classic multilateral conflicts rule that indicates the
applicable law in a neutral way.

---

313   C. Deneve, *Grensoverschrijdende conflicten in het arbeidsrecht* (Antwerp: Intersentia, 2001)
      49.
314   Comp. P. Mayer, Les lois de police étrangères, *J.D.I.* 1981, 306-307.
315   See for a survey A. Junker, "Empfiehlt es sich, Art. 7 EVÜ zu revidieren oder aufgrund der
      bisherigen Erfahrungen zu präzisieren?", *IPRax* 2000, 67-69.

Article 7 works on a totally different basis. It starts from the claim made by the substantive provision itself to govern the case. The mandatory rule is applied, not because it is indicated by a conflicts rule but because the rule itself unilaterally so requires, or is so interpreted by case law.

The "mandatory rules" in Article 7 of the Convention on Contractual Obligations can therefore not be compared with the "mandatory rules" of Article 6. This last includes all the rules that must be regarded as mandatory in the national law indicated, as if it were simply a matter of internal national legal relationship (*internally mandatory rules*).[316] The "mandatory rules" in Article 7 of the Convention on Contractual Obligations are, in contrast, special provisions whereby the legislator wishes to achieve objectives which he deems so fundamental that they must be respected regardless of the applicable law.

Not all the provisions that are mandatory within the meaning of Article 6 of the Convention on Contractual Obligations are also mandatory under Article 7. This is important in relation to Article 7,2 of the Convention on Contractual Obligations in particular, because it makes the application of the *lex fori* only dependent on the above-mentioned special feature.

For the application of employment law in Belgium, ignoring this additional requirement all too often leads to the simple application of Belgian law, to the exclusion of the law indicated in the reference rule (Article 3 or 6 of the Convention on Contractual Obligations). Virtually all Belgian employment law is mandatory in nature, considered purely in internal terms. Nevertheless, that does not mean that every labour law norm also claims to apply to cases that are governed by another law, and would thus be a mandatory rule under Article 7 of the Convention on Contractual Obligations.

So one has to beware of too broad an interpretation of the concept of "mandatory rules" in the sense of Article 7 of the Convention on Contractual Obligations. In general books on the notion of the "*lois de police*", this concept is often given too broad a meaning. Thus the provisions that are intended to protect a weaker category of contractual parties, such as consumers or employees, are also labelled as *lois de police*.[317] It must nonetheless be emphasised that protective rules of this type are applied under Article 6 of the Convention on Contractual Obligations and are not automatically covered by Article 7. To fall into this last category, the rules concerned must *also have a claim to international application*.

Whether this attribute is present may be deducted firstly from the rule itself. it is possible the legislator declares that it is explicitly or (clearly) implicitly internationally applicable or expresses the intention of governing cases that in principle fall under foreign law. In this event, the rule in question has the quality of an internationally

---

316 Term employed in Max Planck, *RabelsZ* 2004, 53-59
317 S. Cascales, "L'émergence d'un concept communautaire de loi de police: analyse de la jurisprudence de la Cour de justice des Communautés européennes", in *Comment protéger les intérêts du citoyen dans l'Union Européenne d'aujourd'hui?* (Brussels: Bruylant, 2003) 264-265; S. Dion, *J.D.I.* 2004, 139; F. Jault, *Rev. Crit. Dr. Intern. Pr.* 2003, 454, R.

mandatory rule as required by Article 7 of the Convention on Contractual Obligations Requirement, regardless of the question of what its objectives are.

In most cases however there is no such description of the scope of application and one has to decide on the basis of other criteria. The *decisive criterion* is then the nature of the rule and the objective that the legislator wishes to achieve. In that case a rule will only be mandatory under Article 7 of the Convention on Contractual Obligations where it *aims to protect the political, social or economic organisation of the state or to achieve a public interest objective*.[318] It is only in this case that the rule may be deemed to govern legal relationships that are in principle governed by foreign law. The mere protection of the private interests of the weakest contracting party is thus insufficient.

The result is the following. When a Belgian judge hears a case regarding an employment contract governed by the law of country A, he not only must hold back from the application of the mandatory rules of a third country on the basis of Article 7,1 of the Convention on Contractual Obligations; he may also only allow the mandatory Belgian provisions to intervene to a limited extent. Examples are: the provisions concerning health and safety at work, the right to strike, rest on Sundays and public holidays, the employment of minors.[319] The Belgian rule that is mandatory in the sense of Article 7,2 of the Convention on Contractual Obligations, will, of course, only be applied in practice if it has a connection with the Belgian legal order which is relevant in the light of the provision concerned and its objective. Although a general rule cannot be formulated, this connection may arise, for example, through temporary employment in Belgium, the currency in which and place where wages are paid, and the place where the employer is established.

This limited interpretation of Article 7 of the Convention on Contractual Obligations fits in with the definition the European Court of Justice gave to de term "*lois de police et de sécurité*". In the *Arblade* judgement of 23 November 1999 they were defined as national provisions compliance with which is regarded as so important to the preservation of the political, social or economic organisation of the Member States concerned, that they must be observed by everyone finding themselves on the national territory of this Member State, and for every legal relationship within that country.

In the absence of publicised case law concerning the relationship between Articles 6 and 7 of the Convention on Contractual Obligations it is difficult to discover whether, in practice in Belgium, the principles set out above are respected. Some writers think not.[320] They point to the Court of Cassation's case law concerning additional compensation on termination of an employment relationship with

---

318   S. Cascales, in *Comment protéger les intérêts du citoyen dans l'Union Européenne d'aujourd'hui?*, 251-253; M. Fallon, *J.T.* 2001, 532-533; P. Mayer, *J.D.I.* 1981, 281-296; Max Planck, *RabelsZ* 2004, 55-57.

319   A. Nuyts, *Rev. Crit. Dr. Intern. Pr.* 1999, 43.

320   C. Deneve, *op. cit.*, 49-59; C. Engels, "Arbeidsovereenkomsten en toepasselijk recht", *Soc. Kron.* 2000, 165.

international aspects. The Court of Cassation has repeatedly decided that the provisions in this regard are to be seen as public order laws in the sense of Article 3, first paragraph of the Belgian Civil code. Nonetheless, it cannot be deduced with any certainty from these judgements that they are also within the meaning of Article 7 of the Convention on Contractual Obligations. In the cases in question, the breach of these provisions was not adduced. In addition, the subjects of these cases were employment contracts that were concluded before the Convention on Contractual Obligations took effect. There was then no Article 6 of the Convention on Contractual Obligations, but there was the need to offer similar protection. A broad interpretation of the concept of "public order laws" was necessary in order to achieve this. The most recent decision of the Court of Cassation concerning an international employment contract, of 3 February 2003,[321] offers no definitive answer, given that it probably relates to an employment contract from before the Convention on Contractual Obligations came into force. The seniority of the worker concerned was 35 years. The appellant adduced no breach of Article 6 or 7 of the Convention on Contractual Obligations, but criticised the finding of the judge in the lower court that Article 82 of the Belgian law on employment contracts should be applied, even though the agreement was governed by American law.

In the lower case law regarding employment contracts concluded after 1 January 1988 there can be found both judgements that appear to apply Article 7,2 of the Convention on Contractual Obligations restrictively in accordance with the principles set out above,[322] and decisions in which Article 7,2 of the Convention on Contractual Obligations is given a broad interpretation[323] or which give a solution by applying the old conflict rules, without reference to the Convention on Contractual Obligations.

In a decision of 19 November 2001 the labour court of Antwerp appears to give a broad interpretation to the idea of "special mandatory rules" within the meaning of Article 7,2 of the Convention on Contractual Obligations. For this application, the court also required that the connection between the employment contract and Belgium should be very strong, in particular through habitual employment in Belgium. That is tantamount to the application of the connecting factor of Article 6 of the Convention on Contractual Obligations in the context of Article 7 of the Convention on Contractual Obligations. Such reasoning is not logical, and runs counter to the structure of the Convention on Contractual Obligations. The decision

---

321　Cass. 3 February 2003, *R.W.* 2003-04, 499, note G. Van Limberghen, and *J.T.T.* 2003, 262, note.

322　Labour court of appeal Liège 8 November 1996, *J.T.T.* 1997, 150; Labour court Brussels 22 April 1998, *J.T.T.* 1998, 435.

323　Labour court of appeal. Brussels 16 September 2003, Tijdschrift@ipr.be 2004, No. 2, 38 (in an obiter dictum); Labour court. Huy 18 June 1999, *Soc. Kron.* 2002, 340, note M. Fallon; Labour court Liège, 19 September 1997, *Soc. Kron.* 1999, 563, note F.K.; see also Labour court. Brussels 7 October 1998, *J.T.T.* 1999, 152.

shows once more the need to keep the different techniques used in Articles 6 and 7 of Convention on Contractual Obligations strictly separate from one another.

In order to determine whether Belgian provisions under Article 7 of the Convention on Contractual Obligations are applicable to the case, the only point to be decided is what the connection the legal relationship has with the Belgian rule of law, and what Belgian rules are therefore applicable. This connection may be of various kinds, but it will usually be something other than the place of habitual employment in Belgium. In that event all Belgian mandatory rules must already be applied on the basis of Article 6 of the Convention on Contractual Obligations.

3.2.1. International Public Order

Finally, Article 16 of the Convention on Contractual Obligations stipulates the exception of international public order to the applicable law indicated by the Convention. The application of a rule of the law of any country specified by this Convention may be refused if (and only if) such application is manifestly incompatible with the public policy ("*ordre public*") of the forum. This is only possible where there is *evident incompatibility with the international public order* of the judge's country. This exception, which has appeared in all Hague Treaties since 1956, is an *ultimate remedy*, which the judge must use with great care.

According to the Court of Cassation a regulation is of "public order" when the legislator, by the provisions of this law, has intended to lay down a principle that, in his judgement, is essential for the established moral, political and economic order and that, for these reasons, inevitably excludes any application in Belgium of a contrary or different rule in foreign law, even if this is applicable in accordance with the customary rules for resolving conflicts of law. Provisions with regard to the minimum notice on termination do not relate to international public order.

As an example of a rule in labour law which conflicts with Belgian international public order, we can take the case of a contract containing absolutely no protection against (illegal) termination.

15. TOWARDS A MORE EFFECTIVE POSTING DIRECTIVE

Mijke Houwerzijl[324]

1. INTRODUCTION

Today, temporary movement of workers within the European Union is rapidly gaining popularity. Over the last twenty years, there has been a gradual increase in a particular type of temporary labour migration: cross-border posting of workers. Traditionally, only "key personnel" such as managers, professionals and specialist technicians, were posted, but since 1985 it has become more and more popular to post workers in the construction sector. More recently, the cross-border posting of workers via temporary employment agencies has been increasing. This combined growth of intra-EU posting at both the top and the bottom of the skills ladder fits into a broader international labour migration trend. As a result of globalisation, the fastest growth in the migrant workforce is seen among workers with college degrees and among workers who go abroad to fulfil seasonal and other temporary jobs.[325]

From a labour law and social policy perspective, the differences between the two groups of posted workers are significant. Whilst the employment conditions of the traditional, high skilled groups of posted workers are in general well above the statutory minimum, wages and conditions of posted workers in the construction sector and in temporary agency work are usually at lower levels. Here, competition concerning labour costs is attractive because of the sometimes huge differences in average wage rates between Member States. The gradually increasing phenomenon of posting from "low wage" Member States to "higher wage" Member States led in the mid-1990s, in particular in the construction sector, to concerns about "social dumping".[326] The Posting of Workers Directive (Directive 96/71/EC) was issued in response to these concerns and extends particular "key" employment protection provisions in force in the host country to workers posted from another Member

---

324 This contribution is partly based on the English summary of my PhD thesis (defended at the University of Tilburg, 28 January 2005). See M.S. Houwerzijl, "The Posting of Workers Directive: About the Background, Content and Implementation of Directive 96/71/EC" in *De Detacheringsrichtlijn* (Deventer: Kluwer 2005) 377-396.

325 See Philip Martin, "Merchants of Labor: Agents of the Evolving Migration Infrastructure", ILO Discussion Paper, Geneva 2005 (Web/pdf: 92-9014-752-0), p. 7.

326 See B. Köbele and J. Cremers, *European Union: Posting of Workers in the Construction Industry* (Bonn/Witterschlick: Verlag Marg. Wehle, 1994).

State.[327] The idea behind the Posting Directive is to create a balance between two potentially conflicting goals: the stimulation of the free provision of services and the protection of workers within the EU. Therefore the Posting Directive seeks to restrict competition on employment conditions through the posting of workers as far as a minimum "hard core" of employment conditions is concerned. Especially in relation to the recent enlargement of the EU with ten new Member States and the proposal for a Services Directive of the European Commission (COM 2004/0002), competition regarding labour costs is a highly sensitive political topic.

This contribution contains an overview of the content of the Posting Directive and its implementation. Some main legal and practical problems are identified and finally the need for a more effective Posting Directive is argued. But as a starting point some general observations about the history and the (former) legal framework for posted workers are made. These are necessary to put the Posting Directive in the right perspective.

2. POSTED WORKERS "SHIFTED" FROM THE FREE MOVEMENT OF WORKERS TO SERVICES

As mentioned before, posted workers are a disparate group. The Posting Directive lumps all posted workers together, irrespective of their long or short-term engagements abroad, and strong or weak labour market positions. This is, however, not in line with the original distinction between two of the four pillars of the Common Market: The free movement of workers and the free movement of services.

2.1. Posted Workers and the Free Movement of Workers

In the early 1960s when the Common Market goal of the EEC was yet to be established, the scope of the four freedoms (of workers, services, establishment and goods) had to be defined. As a broad rule it was stipulated that all workers, whether permanently or temporarily moving to another Member State, were covered by the free movement of *workers*. Although posting and temporary employment in general was not as popular at the end of the 1950s as it is today, it did take place on a small scale. In discussions about the boundaries between the four freedoms in the EEC Treaty, it was recognised that the provision of services actually involved specialised services workers. When they are needed to install a machine or to manage a new plant of a company established in another Member State, they are in fact part of the service and need to cross borders to provide the service. Hence, an exception to the main rule was created for this "very specialised, technical or

---

327   Directive 96/71/EC of 16 December 1996 (OJ 1997 L 18/1) concerning the posting of workers in the framework of the provision of services.

managerial key personnel": they could be posted to another Member State under the freedom to provide *services*.[328]

The strict limitation of this exception to key personnel can still be traced in secondary free movement of workers legislation as laid down in, for example EEC Regulations 1612/68 and 1408/71 and Directive 68/630. This legislation concerns *all* workers in the Member States, irrespective of whether they are permanent, seasonal or frontier workers *or workers who pursue their activities for the purpose of providing services*. So, posted workers who do not belong to the above mentioned "key personnel" and who are nationals of one of the Member States, used to be, exclusively, covered by the principle of the free movement of workers. Also, in secondary legislation based on the free movement of services, there used to be a standard sentence referring to the free movement of workers where the mobility of *all* workers was concerned.[329]

Why was this exception to post workers under the coverage of the freedom to provide services strictly limited to key personnel (with a strong labour market position)? Originally, the EC Treaty contains the aim of promoting "acceptable" (among highly skilled) and protecting against "unacceptable" (among the low skilled) forms of mobility of workers.[330] Under the free movement of workers (Article 39 EC) pay discrimination between nationals and non-nationals is not allowed. Migrant and domestic workers must be treated equally in their access to the labour market, wages and other working and employment conditions. This primary principle of equal treatment and non-discrimination on grounds of nationality is meant not only to entitle workers to a decent employment protection but also to prevent unfair competition (often referred to as "social dumping"). In 1974, the European Court of Justice confirmed the double intention behind the equal treatment provision in the free movement of workers legislation.[331] The Posting Directive however, is based *only* on the free movement of services. What happened between the early 1960s and 1996 that can explain this shift in legal base for posted workers legislation from a predominance for the free movement of workers to an exclusivity for that of services?

---

328 See about this discussion U. Everling, *Das Niederlassungsrecht im Gemeinsamen Markt* (Berlin: Verlag Franz Vahlen, 1963); and D. Vignes, "Le droit d'établissement et les services dans la C.E.E.", *Annuaire Français de Droit International VII*, 1961, pp. 668-725.

329 See especially the, mostly technical, Directives adopted in order of the 1961 General Programme for the abolition of restrictions on the freedom to provide services, OJ 2/32 of 15 January 1962, for example Directive 64/220/EEC (fifth recital).

330 See Robert Geyer, *Exploring European Social Policy* (Cambridge: Polity Press 2000) 62.

331 Case 167/73 [1974] ECR 360, para. 45.

2.2. Posted Workers and the Free Movement of Services

In hindsight, the reason can be deduced from case law of the European Court of Justice (ECJ). The "landmark" decision was made in the *Rush Portuguesa* case of 1990.[332] The facts in this case were as follows. On the TGV Atlantique construction site in France, work was sub contracted to Rush Portuguesa, a Portuguese firm which brought its own workers from Portugal to perform the "service". According to the French immigration authority, Rush Portuguesa broke the law because no work permits had been issued for these posted workers and they were paid well below the French wage standards. In that time, Portugal was a new member of the EU. Just like the current situation for eight of the new Member States in Central and Eastern Europe, for the first years of membership a transition period was agreed upon, in which the free movement of workers was not yet applicable to workers from Portugal (therefore they were seen as third country nationals for whom work permits were required). Meanwhile, the other freedoms, including the free movement of services, could already be invoked by firms or persons from the new Member State. So, Rush Portuguesa defended its position on the grounds of its right to the free movement of services.

The ECJ upheld this position. In contrast with the conclusion of Advocate-General Van Gerven, the ECJ rejected the argument by France that service providers could only use their freedom to provide services to post key personnel to another Member State. According to the ECJ, the principle of free movement for workers was not involved because the posted workers returned to their country of origin after the completion of their work without at any time *gaining access to the labour market of the host Member State*. For this reason, the authorities of the host Member State may not impose conditions on the supplier of services relating to the obtainment of work permits. So, "an undertaking established in one Member State providing services in the construction and public works sector in another Member State may move with its own work-force which it brings from its own Member State for the duration of the work in question." The ECJ repeated this in *Vander Elst* (1994).[333] Here, the interest of service providers to post their workers to perform services in another Member State and the interest in a right to free movement of third country nationals who permanently reside in the EC, coincided. As the right to free movement of workers in the EU is only granted to EU nationals, the ECJ's decision to "shift" posted workers to the free provision of services gives "third country workers" at least a passive right to free movement. This right only exists during the period that they are posted by their EU employers to perform a service in another Member State in the framework of the free movement of services. So, by determining that posted workers do not gain access to the labour market of the host Member State (because they are supposed to return to their country of origin

---

332   Case C-113/89 [1990] ECR I-1425.
333   Case C-43/93 [1994] ECR I-4221.

immediately after the completion of their work) the ECJ constructed a way out of the conflict between the Community goal of a border-free EU internal market and the national interests of border controls to keep immigrants out.[334]

2.3 Posted Workers and the Law of Conflicts

What did this shift from free movement of workers to services mean for the employ-ment protection of posted workers? In *Rush Portuguesa* and *VanderElst* the ECJ stated that "Community law does not preclude Member States from extending their legislation, or collective labour agreements entered into by both sides of industry, to any person who is employed, even temporarily, within their territory, no matter in which country the employer is established." Thus, host states may insist that all or part of their national employment regulations and extended collective agreements must be applied to posted workers if such regulations and collective agreements are also applicable to domestic workers. With this "employment conditions of the host state principle" the ECJ gave Member States the option (but did not oblige them!) of insisting on equal treatment between posted and domestic workers in their territory.

However, this option for Member States to insist on equal treatment between posted and domestic workers existed only within the boundaries of the law of conflicts. Because of the private law character of employment law, parties are in principle free to choose the law applicable to their employment contract. In 1980, the Member States signed the Convention on the Law Applicable to Contractual Obligations (the "Rome I Convention").[335] The Convention came into effect as of 1991. Articles 6 and 7 contain rules for international employment contracts. What mandatory statutory labour law and extended collective agreements are applicable to posted workers? Those of the host state or those of the home state – or perhaps of both? The basic rule can be found in Article 6(2)(a): the law of the country where the worker habitually carries out his work has predominance. However, Article 7 defines rules of a special mandatory character; these rules may apply even if a worker is only temporarily working in a country. Consequently, the employment contract of a posted worker may be influenced by more than one legal system: the law of the Member State where the employment contract is concluded (state of origin or home state), and the law of the Member State where performance takes place (host state) during the posting period. In practice, the existence of such complicated situations is reduced by the so-called favour principle which is contained in Article 6 and 7

---

334 Recently, the ECJ confirmed this case law in *Commission v. Luxembourg* (Judgement of 21 October 2004, Case C-445/03) by stating that the obligation in Luxembourg for service providers from another Member State to obtain work permits for posted workers with the nationality of third countries must be seen as an unjustified infringement on the freedom to provide services within the EU.

335 Convention on the Law Applicable to Contractual Obligations, OJ L 266/1 of 9 October 1980.

of the Rome I Convention. This principle aims to protect the worker against the choice of the legal system with the worst employment conditions, by stating that the most favourable conditions must prevail.

According to the Preamble of the Posting Directive (Recital 7-11), the Directive makes the optional character of Article 7 obligatory, and defines what subjects of employment law must be seen as "special mandatory". In this way the gap that Article 6(2)(a) creates for the protection of posted workers is filled in. The Posting Directive also stipulates the favour principle, although neither the Rome I Convention nor the Directive specify the method of comparison. Depending on the circumstances in a particular situation Articles 6 and 7 of the Rome I Convention play an indispensable and "residuary" role in the background for the effectiveness of the Posting Directive.

2.4   Legal Base of the Posting Directive and its Consequences

The case law of the ECJ extended the scope of the free movement of services to posted workers (in the construction sector). This paved the way for basing the Posting Directive on Article 47 (ex Article 57), paragraph 2 and Article 55 (ex Article 66) of the EC Treaty. These Articles belong to the part of the Treaty that establishes the freedom to provide services. Before the Directive was adopted, there was much criticism of this legal base. The legal base of the Posting Directive adopted was legitimised by the argument that in order to promote a true single market, a framework of rules for posted workers would have to be created in order to avoid unfair competition. From a political point of view, the undoubted merit of this legal basis is that it facilitated a qualified majority vote. Without this, the Posting Directive initiative would probably have foundered.[336]

Still, from a legal point of view, the disadvantage of the choice of (only) this legal base is that it suggests that the Posting Directive is purely intended to facilitate the cross-border provision of services. That it also serves to protect employees is by no means evident from its legal base. Moreover, basing the Posting Directive on the free movement of services, led to a shift of decision-making powers within the European Commission: nowadays, the Directorate-General (DG) Internal Market ("services and establishment" department) has the primary responsibility to initiate new proposals or clarifications on this subject. But the contents of the Posting Directive are so closely connected with the equal treatment principle enclosed in the free movement of workers that at least a shared responsibility with the DG Employment & Social Affairs would have been more logical.

---

336   For the political circumstances of the early 1990s (in which the British Conservative Government tried to veto almost everything that had to do with social policy) that influenced the political fate of the Posting Directive, see M. Biagi, "The 'Posted Workers' EU Directive", in R. Blanpain (ed.), *The Bulletin of Comparative Labour Relations in the European Union* (1998) 175.

The effect of the primary responsibility of the DG Internal Market was already visible in the evaluation of the Posting Directive in 2003.[337] Here, the focus was more on national implementation measures which might disproportionally limit the free provision of services than on legal and practical problems that effect the protection of posted workers and undermine fair competition.[338] But the proposal for a Services Directive in the internal market is definitely a more prominent example of the *Alleingang* of the DG Internal Market.[339] This proposal, initiated by the DG Internal Market, would, in its present form, create uncertainty and confusion about the legal context of the Posting Directive (especially about the role of the Rome I Convention and of communitarian and national labour law in transnational employment situations). Furthermore, the possibilities of enforcing the Posting Directive would be negatively effected by limiting the control mechanisms of host Member States in relation to posted workers.

Now that the objections to the current draft of the Services Directive are widespread, well-documented and include the above-mentioned issues related to posting,[340] it is quite obvious that this proposal needs to be improved in a more social direction before it will have a chance to be adopted. For reasons of legal certainty and consistency in Community law, it is essential that the final version of the Services Directive leaves all matters covered by the Posting Directive (including compliance) aside. Any future clarification in the field of the posting of workers should be dealt with under the existing legal framework of the Posting Directive.[341] This evokes the question as to what, if anything, should be done, either on a European or on a national level, to achieve a more effective Posting Directive?

---

337   See COM(2003) 458.

338   The EFBWW, ETUC and the European Parliament called for a better assessment of the Posting Directive. See Jan Cremers and Peter Donders, *The free movement of workers in the EU. Directive 96/71/EC on the posting of workers within the framework of the provision of services: its implementation, practical application and operation*, CLR Studies 4 (Brussels: Reed Business Information 2005).

339   See COM(2004) 0002.

340   See Niklas Bruun, *Memorandum on employment issues, for the public hearing of the European Parliament on the proposal for a directive on services in the internal market*, Brussels, 11 November 2004. Also: Wouter Gekiere, *Towards a European Directive on Services in the Internal Market: Analysing the Legal Repercussions of the Draft Services Directive and its Impact on National Services Regulations*, Research report commissioned by Anne Van Lancker, Rapporteur, Committee Employment and Social Affairs European Parliament, Leuven 24 September 2004.

341   As stated in the parliamentary Draft Opinion of 20 May 2005 of the Committee on Employment and Social Affairs (by Anne Van Lancker) for the Committee on the Internal Market and Consumer Protection on the proposal for a Directive on services in the internal market.

3   ASSESSMENT OF CONTENTS AND IMPLEMENTATION OF THE POSTING DIRECTIVE

At present, the Posting Directive is not a perfect instrument, as was admitted in the evaluations of the Directive mentioned above. In this section a (non-exhaustive) survey of the main features and problems of the Directive and its implementation is given. The focus is on subjects that are relevant for all Member States. Therefore, important provisions on optional derogations, alternatives for a system of collective agreements which have been declared universally applicable, and special provisions for (full equal treatment of) posted temporary agency workers are left aside.

The Posting Directive consists of nine provisions, which can be divided into four categories:

1)   Personal scope and definitions (Articles 1 and 2);
2)   Terms and conditions of employment for posted workers (Article 3);
3)   Measures to ensure information about and compliance with the Directive (Articles 4, 5 and 6);
4)   "Organisational" and technical details (Articles 7, 8 and 9) that need no further explanation.

3.1. Personal Scope and Definitions

3.1.1. Three Situations of Posting

Since 1990 (*Rush Portuguesa*), an employer is allowed not only to post key personnel to perform a service in another Member State but service workers in the construction and public works sector as well. However, Article 1(3) of the Posting Directive defines *three* situations of posting in the framework of the provision of services: (a) the subcontracting of workers (for example in the construction sector), (b) intra-company or intra-group secondments (the expatriation of workers, for example key personnel) and (c) the cross-border hiring out of workers by temporary employment agencies. This last situation, posting of workers via temporary agencies, was explicitly mentioned by the ECJ in *Rush Portuguesa* as not falling under the freedom of services but under the free movement of workers. Here, the ECJ drew the line where it can no longer be denied that the posted workers may indeed have access to (or at least influence) the labour market of the host country. So, in this respect the Posting Directive went beyond the settled case law of the ECJ. This third possibility further opens the door to more mobility of "cheap labour", although it is not yet clear which conditions the ECJ will accept for the free movement of posted temporary agency workers, especially for those with third country national-ity. A work permit system is not in line with EC law but the ECJ left room for an equivalent form of control (a notification system) to prevent abuse of this most eagerly awaited and therefore exploitable category of posted workers.[342]

The definitions of the three possible posting situations in Article 1(3) are not transposed precisely in many Member States. This increases the chance of confusion between national and European definitions of posting, which may lead either to withholding the protection which posted workers are entitled to on the basis of the Posting Directive or to withholding from service providers the possibilities they have under the Posting Directive. Therefore Member States should revise their national implementation legislation on this point.

3.1.2. Definition of Posting

If we consider the definition of "posted worker" in Article 2, the non-defined, open character of "posting" in Article 2(1) is noteworthy. The Directive defines a posted worker as a worker who, for a limited period, carries out his or her work in the territory of a Member State other than the state in which he or she normally works. Although this certainly promotes the use of the freedom to provide services, it is at the same time problematic in the light of the protection of workers. The temporary character of posting is only linked to the duration of the service abroad. But what if providing the service lasts more than one or two years? When does the temporary character of posting change into a more permanent type of migration? The potentially unlimited duration of the posting complicates the distinction between situations falling within the freedom of establishment and the free movement of workers on the one hand, and situations falling within the freedom to provide services on the other hand.

Therefore, it would have been better if the Posting Directive had referred – at least for the postings mentioned under (a) and (c) – to the time limit with regard to social security (in Regulation 1408/71 and – in the future – Regulation 883/2004).[343] No Member State appears to have taken the initiative to repair this explicitly at the national level. This is probably in conformity with the intention of the Posting Directive. Still, the text seems to leave some room for Member States to introduce a fixed time limit. From a legal certainty perspective, the introduction of a fixed time limit can only be done at EU level by an adjustment of the Posting Directive or by an adjustment of Article 6(2) of the Rome I Convention. The latter option would be most practical because the European Commission is already preparing a Regulation that is to replace the Rome Convention.[344]

---

342   The ECJ refers to the problem that these workers may have access to the labour market of the receiving State in para. 39 of its judgement in Case C-445/03 of 21 October 2004. The ECJ seems to suggest control mechanisms as proposed in COM(1999) 3 and COM(2000) 271, which would mean that it implicitly rejects the proposal in Article 25 (1) in the draft Services Directive.

343   Now 12 months (with the possibility of another 12 months), and in the future 24 months.

344   See Green book COM(2002) 654 of 14 January 2003.

3.1.3. Definition of a Worker

The definition of a "worker" in the Posting Directive, is determined by the legislation of the Member State to whose territory the worker is posted (Article 2(2)). This differs from the posting provisions on social security schemes in Regulation 1408/71. In 2000, the ECJ ruled that the question of whether a posted worker is an employee or "self-employed" is in fact determined by the statutory social security law of the sending Member State (the state in which the worker habitually works).[345] Sometimes a posted person may be regarded as self-employed within the framework of social security and as employee when labour conditions are concerned. In practice this may cause many misunderstandings and a lack of clarity in sectors like construction. Therefore, clear references to the definition of an employee (in this contribution referred to as "worker") and a self-employed person in the implementing legislation of the Member States are necessary. Some Member States have realised this already, others not yet.

Still, the clarification of national definitions is not enough. The only real solution for the posting of foreign "self-employed" persons (e.g. in the construction industry) whose work performance is the same as that of traditional "employees" alongside whom they work, but who have arranged their affairs (for tax or other reasons) so that they move in the shadows between employment and self-employment, lies beyond the legal framework of the Posting Directive. In fact, the possibility that self-employed persons can "post" themselves under the framework of Regulation 1408/71 (Article 14a (1)) should be reconsidered, even though this would conflict with the interests of the genuine self-employed.

3.2. Terms and Conditions of Employment

With regard to the terms and conditions of employment for posted workers, the Directive coordinates Member States' legislation in such a way as to provide a core of mandatory rules on minimum protection with which employers who post workers to the

Member State in which the service is to be provided must comply in the host country. This is laid down in Article 3. This provision is divided in ten paragraphs of which only Articles 3(1) and 3(7) will be elaborated upon in this contribution.

3.2.1. Article 3(1) – Equal treatment

Article 3(1) states that Member States are to ensure that undertakings falling within the scope of the Directive guarantee workers posted to their territory the terms and

---

345   See Case C-178/97 [2000] ECR I-2005.

conditions of employment laid down by mandatory law, including collective agreements which have been declared universally applicable insofar as they concern the
construction sector referred to in the Annex of the Directive. This equal treatment
principle regards the duration of the work, rest periods and holidays, minimum
rates of pay, health, safety and hygiene at work, the conditions of hiring-out of
workers, protective measures for pregnant women, for women who have recently
given birth, for young people and children, and equality of treatment between men
and women. Hence, the Directive determines the nature of the labour standards
which the Member States must apply but not the substance of these standards. This
key provision states the standards for the minimum protection of posted workers;
it furthers "fair competition" by guaranteeing equal treatment between posted and
domestic workers in the host country as far as the above-mentioned aspects of
employment protection are concerned. Especially the inclusion of minimum rates
of pay and paid holidays in the aspects regulated by the host country is important
to prevent unfair competition. Next to this, Article 3(1) enhances the legal certainty
of service providers by the formulation of aspects regulated minimally by the host
country and by leaving the other aspects of an employment contract to be decided
on by the contracting parties.

However, legal certainty is not served by Article 3(10). This paragraph gives the
Member States two important options: first of all, they may make more working
conditions applicable to posted workers than are stated in Article 3(1) as long as
these can be seen as public policy provisions. As explicitly stated, the application of
public policy provisions has to be carried out in compliance with the Treaty and on
the basis of equal treatment between posted and domestic workers. Member States
are limited to imposing all their mandatory law provisions on service providers
established in another Member State.[346] As a second option, Member States may
decide to apply the Posting Directive also to collective agreements in sectors other
than the construction sector. The political compromise to limit the obligatory part
of the Posting Directive to extended collective agreements in the construction
sector (see the Annex) cannot logically or legally be defended. It leads to quite
arbitrary differences in the protection of posted workers and does not enhance the
legal certainty and transparency of the applicable rules either.

For a balance between the goals of the Posting Directive (free provision of
services and protection of workers), the Member States' reliance or non-reliance
on the options mentioned in Article 3(10) is decisive. In my view, the best possible
compromise would have been non-reliance on the first option (a broader appliance
of the equal treatment principle) in exchange for full reliance on the second option
(extending the scope of the universally binding collective agreement provisions
to all sectors, not only to the construction sector). Except for the Netherlands, all
Member States that have – and frequently make use of – a system of *erga omnes*
collective agreements applied the second option. The first option is applied by seven

---

346   See Case C-164/99 [2002], ECR I-787 and Case C-165/98 [2001], ECR I-2189.

Member States, which was reason for concern in the evaluation of the European Commission. However, if we look closely at the working conditions added to the obligatory working conditions stated in Article 3(1), it seems that most of these national public policy provisions only contain rather modest national provisions meant to strengthen the compliance to the terms and conditions listed in Article 3(1).[347] Such use of the first option of Article 3(10) should not be considered a problem. However, more detailed research is needed before a final conclusion about proper or improper reliance on this option can be reached.[348]

3.2.2. Article 3(7) – The Favour Principle

The favour principle is stated in Article 3(7) of the Posting Directive as a guarantee that the "host country principle" only applies when working conditions in this country are better than in the "home country" of the posted worker. But how are we to decide which working conditions are the most favourable? Should we compare each provision on its own, or a group of rules about the same subject or all working conditions as a whole? Up to now, each Member State is allowed to develop its own method. However, no national implementation legislation specifies the method of comparison. Although in theory this complex situation may cause a lot of problems, in practice the social partners in the construction sector have developed an interesting solution for problems of comparison in states with a more or less similar socio-economic level. This solution was triggered by the judgement of the ECJ in *Guiot* and boils more or less down to application of the (ECJ) principle of mutual recognition.[349]

In the *Guiot* case, a service provider protested against charges in both the host state and the state of origin for contributions to so-called social funds in the construction sector. In *Guiot*, the ECJ ruled that the service provider only had to pay contributions in his country of origin. Social partners in the construction sector criticised this judgement because the ECJ had only considered the type of social funds, not the level of payment that workers could derive from the funds and thus not the equivalence of the schemes. Therefore, the Belgian and Dutch social partners took the initiative to repair this judgement: a comparison of their social funds led to the conclusion that workers in both countries were provided employment conditions at an equivalent level. This led to an agreement on the suspension of the application of the social fund of the host state. As a result, Belgian and Dutch service providers only had to contribute to the funds in their own countries and were no longer confronted with unjustified double charges. The German ULAK

---

347   See *Report from the Commission services on the implementation of Directive 96/71/EC*, January 2003: http://europa.eu.int/comm/employment_social/labour_law/docs/07_postingofworkers_implementationreport_en.pdf.

348   See Cremers/Donders, *op. cit.* 2005, p. 21-23.

349   Case C-272/94 [1996] ECR I-1915.

took a similar initiative, and has concluded bilateral agreements with, *inter alia*, French, Dutch, Belgian and Austrian holiday funds. These bilateral agreements are a positive development, as it is a good way of avoiding double charges without creating undue pressure on funds with high levels of protection. They could also give an incentive to collective bargaining at the European level, which would be advantageous for the social dimension of the EU.

After *Guiot* there have been four other judgements of the ECJ on conflicts in which wages and working conditions of posted workers were involved: *Arblade*, *Mazzoleni*, *Finalarte* and *Portugaia*.[350] In this "posted workers saga", the main approach starts with a comparison of protection in the host state and that in the state of origin. If protection is the same or almost the same, the social protection of the state of origin has priority. From a provision of services perspective, this makes sense, because the service provider should not be more restricted in his movement than necessary. In the first phase the case law showed a tendency to overlook relatively small differences (approx. 10%) in social protection and wage levels between Member States that are more or less on the same socio-economic level. Except for *Rush Portuguesa*, in all the judgements about the posting of workers until 2001, the parties were established in the "original" six Member States. In particular, Belgian (*VanderElst, Guiot, Arblade, Mazzoleni*), French (*Arblade*) and Luxembourg (*Guiot*) labour law regulations were involved and only superficially compared. The judgements in *Finalarte* and *Portugaia* changed this picture. Here, "high-level" German labour law was compared to its "low-level" Portuguese and English counterparts. What guideline did the Court develop in these cases, in which the gap between the wages in the host country and the wages in the home country is much wider?

The ULAK, the social fund that regulates and maintains the German paid-leave scheme in the construction sector, requires foreign service providers to pay contributions to the scheme to finance the holiday entitlements of their construction workers. It also demands them to provide information for the calculation of those contributions. In this respect, the ECJ deemed it necessary to check whether the German paid-leave scheme provides posted workers with "a genuine benefit, which significantly adds to their social protection". This should be the case not only on paper but also in practice. First, it is important to check that the worker is entitled to more holidays and a higher holiday allowance under the German rules than under the law of the home country. Secondly, it is important to check that the workers concerned are really able to assert their entitlement to holiday pay from the fund. In this light, the formalities and procedure for payment and language problems must not be too difficult for the average posted worker. Finally, the ECJ adds the condition that, given the "genuine benefit" for the posted worker, the application of the German rules must be proportionate to their public-interest objective. This means

---

350   Joined cases C-369/96 and C-376/96 [1999], ECR I-8453, Case C-165/98 [2001], ECR I-2189, joined cases C-49/98, C-50/98, C-52/98, and C68/98 to C-71/98 [2001] ECR I-7831 and Case C-164/99 [2002], ECR I-787

that the increased social protection should be balanced against the administrative and economic burdens that the rules impose on the foreign employers. Is it possible to achieve the increased protection by less restrictive rules, for example by imposing a duty on foreign employers to pay the higher holiday allowance directly to posted workers, instead of the indirect payment through the ULAK? It is up to the national judge in the Member State to decide on such important details.

3.2.3. Minimum Wage

The core of mandatory rules on minimum protection for posted workers in the host country covers, *inter alia*, the provisions relating to the minimum wage. Thus, if a Member State provides for such a wage, this will also apply to posted workers. Although the concept of a minimum wage is defined by the national legislation and practices of the host Member State, Article 3(1)(c) and the second paragraph of Article 3(7) provide some guidelines. Article 3(1)(c) gives posted workers an entitlement to the same minimum wage level and to the same payment for overtime as domestic workers. Contributions to supplementary occupational retirement schemes are explicitly kept out of this equal treatment provision on minimum wages. Next to this, Article 3(7) states that allowances specific to the posting are to be considered part of the minimum wage, unless they are paid in reimbursement of expenditure on travel, board and lodging.

In my view, this last provision is not strong enough to guarantee decent treatment of posted workers. A solution more in line with the intentions behind the Posting Directive would be to oblige service providers to pay travelling and lodging costs for their posted workers. Moreover, is it not entirely normal that every "ex-pat" working for a respectable multinational company is compensated for expenses actually incurred by reason of his posting? Why should this be less evident for posted worker with weaker labour market positions? Apparently these things are no longer as self-evident as they once used to be.

In a very recently decided case of the European Commission against Germany,[351] the ECJ even had to make clear that "it is entirely normal that, if an employer requires a worker to carry out additional work or to work under particular conditions, compensation should be provided to the worker for those additional services without its being taken into account for the purpose of calculating the minimum wage" (paragraph 40). In this case the Commission defended a method to compare the minimum wages in the host state and the country of origin that would have undermined the equal treatment between posted and domestic workers. According to the Commission, Germany failed to recognise, as constituent elements of the minimum wage, *all* of the allowances and supplements paid by foreign service supplier to their posted workers in the German construction sector, with the exception of the

---

351   Case C-341/02, Judgement of 14 April 2005.

bonus granted to workers in that industry. Indeed, not taking all these elements into account resulted in higher wage costs for foreign service providers, which made it less attractive for them to offer their services in Germany. In its judgement, the ECJ chose, in accordance with the combined goals behind the Posting Directive, a more balanced approach. The ECJ ruled that quality bonuses and bonuses for dirty, heavy or dangerous work need not be taken as component elements of the minimum wage for purposes of calculating and comparing.

Furthermore, the ECJ confirmed in this case that the comparison of wages should be made between gross minimum wage levels. This is in line with Recital 21 of the Preamble of the Posting Directive, from which it can be deduced that employment conditions on the one hand and social security on the other are, as a rule, to be handled separately. Taxation law is excluded from the Posting Directive as well. The view that gross wages should be decisive is supported by practical considerations: net earnings are essentially dependent upon the worker's personal situation. An overall comparison of the national regimes involved creates uncertainty about the outcome in each individual case.[352]

3.3. Measures to Ensure Cooperation on Information and Compliance with the Directive

3.3.1. Provisions on Information and Compliance in the Posting Directive

Accessible and transparent information is a condition *sine qua non* for an effective application of the Posting Directive.[353] Under Article 4(3), a Member State acting as a host country is obliged to give information to the general public about the working conditions applicable to posted workers. But simply stating which statutory employment legislation and extended collective agreements are applicable is by no means sufficient. Member States should translate their labour conditions, laid down in legislation and extended collective agreements, into an accessible package of conditions that corresponds with the conditions mentioned in Article 3(1). Herewith transparency and legal certainty for service providers are served and also the protection of posted workers. Whether fair competition will be furthered is more difficult to say: bona fide companies will be stimulated to provide more cross-border services with posted workers if clear information about the employment conditions in the host country is easily available. Another advantage of good information is that malafide companies can no longer hide behind the argument

---

352   This interpretation confirms that the chosen method of comparison on the level of net wages in the *Mazzoleni* case (Case C-165/98 [2001], ECR I-2189) must be seen as an exception to the main rule. Here, the distinction between posting and frontier labour was blurred.

353   This was stated by the ECJ in joined cases C-369/96 and C-376/96 [1999], ECR I-8453, referring to Article 4 of the Posting Directive and Directive 91/553/EEC (on an employer's obligation to inform employees of the conditions applicable to the contract or employment relationship).

that they were not able to find information about the host country's conditions. However, supplying reliable information will not deter companies from trying to post workers on a cheaper basis than legally possible. To combat this "unfair" and often illegal competition only measures to ensure compliance with the Posting Directive will help.

In this respect, Article 4(1) of the Posting Directive obliges the Member States to designate one or more liaison offices or one or more competent national bodies. One of the tasks of these national bodies, stated in Article 4(2), is to reply to reasoned requests from equivalent authorities in the other Member States "for information on the transnational hiring-out of workers, including manifest abuses or possible cases of unlawful transnational activities". Furthermore, Article 5 states that Member States are to take "appropriate measures in the event of failure to comply with this Directive". However, except for the jurisdiction rule in Article 6 no concrete measures are required or recommended. This is definitely a lost opportunity: At least the responsibility – or better still liability – of the service provider and the receiver of the service for the payment of wages and other employment conditions of the posted workers should have been included.

According to the ECJ, a liability clause does not run counter to the free movement of services in the EC Treaty. In the *Wolff & Müller v. Pereira Félix* case the main contractor's liability for the unpaid minimum wages of a posted worker by the subcontractor was questioned.[354] According to the main contractor, this liability clause in the German Posting Act was an infringement of the freedom to provide services, as it made necessary intensive control mechanisms with more administrative burdens for foreign subcontractors. This would make it less attractive for foreign building companies to carry out construction activities in Germany. The ECJ ruled, however, that the liability clause in the German Posting Act could be seen as an appropriate measure that Member States have to take according to Article 5 of the Posting Directive in the event of failure to comply with this Directive. This German example of an effective enforcement method shows that the main problem behind the enforcement rules in the Directive is the lack of political commitment to lay down concrete sanction mechanisms. It looks as if the Posting Directive is mainly concerned with adding to the promises which must be made to posted workers rather than with securing that the promises are actually kept.[355] Much therefore depends on the way in which the Member States implement Articles 4 and 5 of the Posting Directive: do they all (like Germany) "repair" this potential imperfect balance between the protection of workers and the obligations of the service providers when it comes to compliance measures or not?

---

354   Case C-60/03, Judgement of 12 October 2004
355   See the predictions of Paul Davies, "Posted Workers: Single Market or Protection of National Labour Law Systems?", *CMLR* (34) 1997, pp. 571-602 and W. Däubler, "Posted Workers and the Freedom to Supply Services", *ILJ* 1998, pp. 264-268.

3.3.2. Implementation in the Member States

As far as the compliance provisions in Articles 4 and 5 are concerned, the legal implementation measures taken by the Member States differ greatly. Some states implemented these by introducing special, often severe control measures, others did nothing at all. In its evaluation, the European Commission focused only on the former group, in its warning that the national control measures might be disproportionally limiting the free provision of services if administrative burdens were to turn out higher for cross-border service providers than for domestic companies.[356] The other group of states not only gives leeway to bona fide service providers but also to their malafide colleagues as they do not have to be afraid for sanctions in the host state whatsoever. That this does not serve the protection of workers and leads to distortions in competition does not seem to bother the Commission. This (again) reveals unbalanced attention for only the free provision of services goal in the Posting Directive (see section 2.4).

Apart from the strict or more *laisser faire* attitude towards compliance on paper, all Member States are confronted with more or less the same enforcement problems in practice: most liaison offices in the Member States seem to suffer understaffing and lack of adequate information. Alarmingly, these liaison offices rarely receive requests for information from service providers or workers. The mutual cooperation among liaison offices needs improvement as well, although there are some good initiatives such as mutual cooperation agreements between some Member States. One of the complications for direct communication is the language problem.[357]

The language problem occurs as well when it comes to accessible information to the general public. Most Member States do not seem to be very active in making their information available to foreign service providers and their posted workers. In its evaluation, the Commission proposes to solve the lack of easily accessible information by electronic means: an EC website is to contain links to all country information. At present, this EC website has become operational,[358] but many Member States still have no website of their own. If websites are operational they are sometimes difficult to find and the available information is not very comprehensive and/or only in the home language. Not surprisingly, the social partners in the construction sector are most active in developing information. Valuable initiatives include the establishment of direct information points in some Member States. Networks like EURES may contribute to the accessibility of information, as do networks provided by competent institutions for social security. Nevertheless, the liaison offices have the primary responsibility for delivering transparent and accessible information, not the social partners or other institutions.[359]

---

356 In this respect it cannot be a coincidence that the draft Services Directive in Article 24 tries to cut back the power of the host country to exercise its inspection tasks.
357 See for details and examples Cremers/Donders, *op. cit.* 2005, pp. 25-33 and 41-45.
358 See <www.europa.eu.int/comm/employment_social/labour_law/postingofworkers_en.htm#7>.
359 For more details see Cremers/Donders, *op. cit.* 2005, p. 23-33.

The reluctant attitude on the part of Member States when it comes to information provision, undermines the protection of posted workers as well as the bona fide performance of cross-border services. It also makes a protectionist impression, which does not serve fair competition. To serve both ends, transparent, reliable and easily accessible information is needed. How can a Member State demand fair competition from cross-border service providers if it does not act "fairly" itself in its role as a host country?

4. FINAL REMARKS

In the previous sections the historical background, content and implementation of the Posting Directive were analysed. The analysis shows problems on all three levels which, all in all, diminish the effectiveness of the Directive and let the balance between the protection of workers and the promotion of the free provision of services swing to benefit the latter. What, if anything, should be done about this?

To restore the balance and enhance the impact of the Directive in practice, the text of the Posting Directive should be modified as regards the Article 4 and 5 measures. These should be much more concrete and should oblige Member States to take the enforcement of the working conditions of posted workers on their territory more seriously. A liability clause for the user undertaking would probably be most effective, and would, at the same time, limit the costs of enforcement for the state. Next to this at least a time limit on postings should be introduced and an obligation for service providers to pay for the expenses for travelling, board and lodging of their posted workers. Finally, for reasons of consistency with the *acquis communautaire* based on the free movement of workers and for a better division of decision-making powers within the European Commission, it would be wise to broaden the legal base of the Posting Directive as well.

From a pragmatic point of view, however, priority should be given to the creation of a better balance via national implementation measures and to a better practical application and operation of the Posting Directive as it stands today. A better application in practice of the (albeit imperfect) current national and European posting rules can start immediately if only the political will is present in both sending and receiving Member States. Simultaneously, the European Commission should also be more genuinely concerned about this practical application and about reaching a balance between the goals of the Directive. This would be in contrast to its current interest, which focuses too much on removing the obstructions to the internal market and on promoting the free provision of services, regardless of whether these service activities increase through bona fide or through malafide service providers and/or temporary employment agencies.

As mentioned, a clear example of this attitude is the proposal for a EU Services Directive. In this proposal, specific provisions are included about the posting of workers, which would make the monitoring of working conditions in the host state even more difficult and would only give rather weak guarantees on the EU level in return. Of course, the European Commission is right in wanting to tackle the protectionism in too rigid administrative procedures. And the promotion of mobility and intra-state provision of services in itself is a legitimate and a desirable goal as well. However, the Commission must show at the same time that it cares about enforcement and letting control mechanisms really work, for instance, by financially supporting initiatives to make information about working conditions accessible through an EU database of collective agreement provisions. Why did it take so long, not only at the national level but at the EU level as well, to build a really informative website that links to national sites and perhaps even compares the working conditions in the various Member States both in a statutory respect and with regard to collective agreements?

The conclusion must be that policy-makers do not give priority to these things. In the long term, however, it will be in the interest of all parties involved that only bona fide mobility is promoted. Only then will European citizens in their respective roles as workers, entrepreneurs, citizens and consumers, stay or become convinced that further European integration (and a European Constitution) is in their interest.

16. IMPLEMENTATION OF THE POSTING DIRECTIVE IN BELGIUM[360]

Roger Blanpain

1. GENESIS

The Posting Directive was implemented in Belgium by an Act of Parliament of 5 March 2002.[361] The Belgian authorities thereby wanted to accomplish following goals:

- To live up to requirements of the judgement of the Court of Justice (1999) in the *Arblade* case,[362] whereby the application of certain parts of the Belgian legislation on employers of other Member States, operating in Belgium, were looked upon as contrary to principles of freedom of services;
- To provide for fair competition and respect for the rights of employees;
- To clarify the obligations, which go along with the 1980 Convention of Rome regarding applicable labour conditions to employment relations of posted workers.

2. EUROPEAN CASE LAW

In the *Arblade* case, which involved two French companies operating in Belgium on a temporary basis in the construction industry, two prosecutions were brought against Jean-Claude Arblade and Bernard Leloup in their capacity as managers for

---

360   For more detailed information on Belgian labour law, see Roger Blanpain, "Belgium", *International Encyclopaedia of Labour Law and Industrial Relations* (Kluwer Law International, 2004) 334.

361   Law of 5 March 2002 implementing Directive 96/71EC of the European Parliament and of the Council of 16 December 1996 concerning the posting of workers in the framework of the provision of services and organising a simplified system for keeping Belgian social documents. Yves Jorens and Filip Van Overmeiren, "Belgium", in Jan Cremers and Peter Donders (eds), *The Free Movement of Workers in the EU. Directive 96/71/EC on the Posting of Workers within the Framework of the Provision of Services: its Implementation, Practical Application and Operation*, CLR Studies 4 (Brussels: 2004) 69.

362   23 November 1999, C-369/96.

failure to comply with various social obligations provided for by Belgian legislation, an offence punishable by penalties under Belgian public-order legislation.[363]

The Court stated that:

> [Belgium] could require from an undertaking established in another Member State, operating in the construction sector and temporarily carrying out work in Belgium, *to pay the workers deployed by it the minimum remuneration fixed by the collective labour agreement applicable in Belgium,* provided that the provisions in question are sufficiently precise and accessible, and that they do not render it impossible or excessively difficult in practice for such an employer to determine the obligations with which he is required to comply.
>
> However, the Treaty provisions on freedom of services *preclude Belgium from requiring – even by way of public-order legislation –* an undertaking established in another Member State, operating in the construction sector and temporarily carrying out work in Belgium, to pay, in respect of each worker deployed, *employers' contributions* to schemes such as the "timbres-intempéries" and "timbres-fidélité" schemes, and to issue to each of such workers an individual record, *where the undertaking in question is already subject, in the Member State in which it is established, to obligations which are essentially comparable*, as regards their objective of safeguarding the interests of workers, and which relate to the same workers and the same periods of activity.
>
> Moreover, the Treaty provisions on freedom of services *preclude Belgium from requiring* – even by way of public-order legislation – an undertaking established in another Member State, operating in the construction sector and temporarily carrying out work in Belgium, to *draw up social or labour documents such as labour rules, a special staff register and an individual account for each worker in the form prescribed by the rules of Belgium,* where the social protection of workers which may justify those requirements is already safeguarded by the production of social and labour documents kept by the undertaking in question in accordance with the rules applying in the Member State in which it is established.
>
> That is the position where, as regards the keeping of social and labour documents, the undertaking is already subject, in the Member State in which it is established, to obligations which are comparable, as regards their objective of safeguarding the interests of workers, to those imposed

---

363   The obligations concerned the drawing-up, keeping and retention of social and labour documents, minimum remuneration in the construction industry and the systems of *"timbres-intempéries"* (bad weather stamps) and *"timbres-fidélité"* (loyalty stamps), and the monitoring of compliance with those obligations.

by the legislation of the host Member State, and which relate to the same workers and the same periods of activity.

The Treaty provisions on freedom of services *do however not preclude Belgium* from requiring an undertaking established in another Member State, operating in the construction sector and temporarily carrying out work in the first State, to keep social and labour documents available, throughout the period of activity within the territory of the first Member State, on site or in an accessible and clearly identified place within the territory of that State, *where such a measure is necessary in order to enable it effectively to monitor compliance with legislation of that State which is justified by the need to safeguard the social protection of workers.*

Finally, the Court stated:

the Treaty provisions on freedom of services *preclude Belgium from requiring – even by way of public-order legislation –* an undertaking established in another Member State, operating in the construction sector and temporarily carrying out work in the first State, *to retain, for a period of five years after the undertaking in question has ceased to employ workers in the first Member State, social documents such as a staff register and individual accounts, at the address within that Member State of a natural person who holds those documents as an agent or servant.* Such requirements cannot be justified, since the monitoring of compliance with rules concerning the social protection of workers in the construction industry can be achieved by less restrictive measures.

2.1. Adequate Protection

So, the first objective for the Belgian legislator was to see how to implement the Directive, taking into account the requirements of the European Court of Justice, without jeopardising the second goal of adequate protection of the employees involved.

The starting point is Article 3 of the Belgian Civil Code, which states that the laws of police and security have to be respected by all who live on Belgian territory. According to Belgian Court of Cassation[364] these laws concerns all matters of public interest or the interests of a given group; all mandatory laws are considered to be of such a nature.

The following are considered to be laws of police and security by Belgian case law:[365]

---

364 Cass., 25 June 1975, *Pas.*, 1975, 1, 1038.
365 *Parl. Doc.*, Chamber of Representatives, 2001-2002, 11 October 2001, Doc., 50 1441/001.

- legal minimum terms of notice;
- the competence of the judge to decide upon a reasonable term of notice;
- minimum wages;
- generally binding collective agreements;
- laws on yearly vacation and vacation pay;
- the act on working time;
- the act on the protection of the remuneration of workers;
- the act on temporary work and the putting of workers at the disposal of a user;
- the legal rules concerning dismissal for just cause;
- the legal rules concerning a clause of non-competition;
- the act concerning the legal status of the commercial traveller;
- rules concerning hygiene and safety.

The legal rules concerning arbitrary dismissal are not considered to be laws of police and security.

2.2. Starting Points

The Belgian Act of 2002, implementing the Directive on posting of workers, aims consequently at clarifying the notion of *"lois de police et de sureté"*. The Government underlined the necessity to respect the *Arblade* judgement, especially concerning following points of the judgement:

> 31. The fact that national rules are categorised as public-order legislation does not mean that they are exempt from compliance with the provisions of the Treaty; if it did, the primacy and uniform application of Community law would be undermined. The considerations underlying such national legislation can be taken into account by Community law only in terms of the exceptions to Community freedoms expressly provided for by the Treaty and, where appropriate, on the ground that they constitute overriding reasons relating to the public interest.
>
> …
>
> 33. It is settled case-law that Article 49 of the Treaty requires not only the elimination of all discrimination on grounds of nationality against providers of services who are established in another Member State but also the abolition of any restriction, even if it applies without distinction to national providers of services and to those of other Member States, which is liable to prohibit, impede or render less advantageous the activities of a provider of services established in another Member State where he lawfully provides similar services.

34. Even if there is no harmonisation in the field, the freedom to provide services, as one of the fundamental principles of the Treaty, may be restricted only by rules justified by overriding requirements relating to the public interest and applicable to all persons and undertakings operating in the territory of the State where the service is provided, in so far as that interest is not safeguarded by the rules to which the provider of such a service is subject in the Member State where he is established.

35. The application of national rules to providers of services established in other Member States must be appropriate for securing the attainment of the objective which they pursue and must not go beyond what is necessary in order to attain it.

...

38. however, overriding reasons relating to the public interest which justify the substantive provisions of a set of rules may also justify the control measures needed to ensure compliance with them.

39. It is therefore necessary to consider, in turn, whether the requirements imposed by national rules such as those at issue in the main proceedings have a restrictive effect on freedom to provide services, and, if so, whether, in the sector under consideration, such restrictions on freedom to provide services are justified by overriding reasons relating to the public interest. If they are, it is necessary, in addition, to establish whether that interest is already protected by the rules of the Member State in which the service provider is established and whether the same result can be achieved by less restrictive rules.

The Belgian legislature concluded from the *Arblade* judgement that the Posting Directive has to be implemented and interpreted in a manner consistent with the Treaty. The Court, so Belgium reasoned, accepts that every Member State is entitled, in a sovereign way in its internal order, to indicate which rules are of public order and which of these rules it considers to be applicable to posted workers. The Court, however, retains its right to see that those rules are in conformity with Articles 49 and 50 of the Treaty. The Court retains its earlier case law according to which the principle of equivalence implies that the law of the country in which the work is done has to give way when the protected interest is already covered by rules, which apply in the Member State of origin.

In other words the legal rules of the receiving country are not applicable when the country of origin provides for rights and duties which are comparable to those which apply in the receiving country. The Court will also control whether the content of the hard nucleus laid down in the Directive are in conformity with Articles 49 and 50 of the Treaty.

The Belgian act was implemented in a maximalist way.

> This wide interpretation and broadness of the Act of 5 March 2002[366] in fact has fours aspects. Firstly, the legislator chose to incorporate larger definitions in the Act than those in the Directive. Secondly, the application was not restricted to a nucleus of mandatory rules but was extended to nearly all Belgian law on terms and conditions of employment. Thirdly, as far as the application of collective agreements is regarded, this was not limited to the application of collective agreements in the construction sector, but to all sectors. And finally, the legislator made no use of the optional derogations provided by the Posting Directive.[367]

The law of 5 March 2002 is divided into 2 sections:

1)   The first section implements Directive 96/71;
2)   The second section concerns the setting up of a simplified procedure for the keeping of the Belgian social documents[368].

As far as the second section is concerned, the law of 5 March 2002 has been implemented by a regulation ("arrêté royal") of 29 March 2002.

3. IMPLEMENTATION OF DIRECTIVE 96/71

3.1. Definition of a Posted Worker

According to the Belgian 2002 Act, a worker is a person, who by virtue of a contract works for pay and under the authority of another person.

A posted worker is a person who carries out his/her work in Belgium and who either:

–   usually carries out his/her work in a country other than Belgium; or

---

366 Law of 5 March 2002 implementing Directive 96/71EC of the European Parliament and of the Council of 16 December 1996 concerning the posting of workers in the framework of the provision of services and organising a simplified system for keeping Belgian social documents

367 Yves Jorens and Filip Van Overmeiren, "Belgium", in Jan Cremers and Peter Donders (eds), *The Free Movement of Workers in the EU. Directive 96/71/EC on the Posting of Workers within the Framework of the Provision of Services: its Implementation, Practical Application and Operation*, CLR Studies 4 (Brussels: 2004) 69.

368 Guidance note regarding the Belgian law of 5 March 2002 implementing Directive 96/71EC of the European Parliament and of the Council of 16 December 1996 concerning the posting of workers in the framework of the provision of services and organising a simplified system for keeping Belgian social documents

–   was actually engaged in a country other than Belgium to directly work in Belgium.

Therefore the Belgian law applies as soon as the work is carried out in Belgium (regardless of the length of work or the type of the duties concerned).[369]

3.2. Terms and Conditions of Employment Applicable to a Worker Posted in Belgium

An employer who employs posted workers in Belgium must comply with the terms and conditions of employment, work and pay laid down in:

–   Belgian law and regulations which are subject to penal sanctions; and
–   Belgian collective agreements which are extended by royal decree and thus applicable to all employers and employees of the whole private sector, a given sector or a sub-sector. These extended agreements are subject to penal sanctions.

In this respect the Belgian Law of 5 March 2002 is broader than the European Directive as it includes:

–   all the enforceable collective agreements and not only those concerned with all building work relating to the construction as in the Directive;
–   the conditions of employment and work covered by the Directive and which are considered as public policy provisions in Belgium.

For example, the following provisions apply to a worker posted to Belgium:

–   The Law of 16 March 1971 concerning working time;
–   The Law of 4 January 1974 concerning public holidays;
–   The Law of 28 June 1971 concerning annual paid holidays;
–   The Law of 24 July 1987 concerning temporary work and the conditions of hiring-out workers;
–   The Law of 4 August 1996 concerning the well-being of workers at work;
–   The Law of 8 April 1965 concerning work rules;
–   The secondary legislation (*arrêté royal*) No. 5 of 23 October 1978 concerning the keeping of social documents;
–   The Law of 12 April 1965 concerning the protection of pay;
–   All the secondary legislation completing the above laws;

---

369   The Government can extend the application of the Act, totally or partially, to other persons who perform work under the authority of another person.

–   All enforceable collective agreements (the minimum rates of pay are usually laid down in collective agreements).

For the purposes of the Law of 5 March 2002, the pay conditions means the wages, additional benefits and allowances which have to be paid according to the extended collective agreements. The pay conditions do not include the supplementary occupational retirement pension schemes and the allowances specific to the posting which are paid by way of reimbursement of expenditure actually incurred for the reason of posting, such as expenditure travel, board and lodging.

3.3. Exemptions

The provisions concerning minimum wage and paid holidays are not applicable in the case of initial assembly and/or first installation of goods, where this is an integral part of a contract for the supply of goods and necessary for taking goods supplied into use and carried out by the skilled and/or specialist workers of the supplying undertaking, provided that the posting period does not exceed eight days.

However this exemption does not apply to activities which concern immovables and which include all building work relating to the construction, repair, upkeep, alteration or demolition of buildings and in particular the following works: excavation, earthmoving, actual building work, assembly and dismantling of prefabricated elements, fitting out or installation, alterations, renovation, repairs, dismantling, demolition, maintenance, upkeep, painting and cleaning work, and improvements.

Merchant navy undertakings and their seagoing personal are, in line with the Directive, equally exempted.

3.4. More Favourable Conditions

In accordance with the Directive, the Belgian Act does not prevent application of the home country terms and conditions of employment if they are more favourable to workers.

4. THE POSTING DECLARATION AND THE SIMPLIFIED SYSTEM FOR KEEPING BELGIAN SOCIAL DOCUMENTS

4.1. Postings of up to Six Months

An employer who posts workers to Belgium is exempted from keeping the social documents and the work rules act laid down in the Belgian Law for a period of six months provided that he/she fulfils two conditions:

1)   Before the posting he/she must send a posting declaration to the Belgian Labour Inspectorate.
2)   As far as the pay is concerned a copy of the foreign pay documents equivalent to the Belgian pay documents must be put at the Labour Inspectorate's disposal (i.e. the pay statement and the final pay statement).

The six-month period starts running from the first working day of the first worker being posted to Belgium.

Therefore the foreign employers who fulfil these two conditions will be exempted from keeping the following Belgian documents for six months:

–   The personnel register;
–   The attendance register;
–   The pay statement;
–   The final pay account (or final pay statement);
–   The work rules;
–   The student employment contract;
–   The homework employment contract;
–   The part-time employment contract;
–   The declaration of immediate employment (the employers has to inform the Belgian Office for Social Security about the starting and ending dates of employment of each member of his/her staff).

4.2. After a Period of Six Months

After six months the foreign employers are considered as employers established in Belgium and must therefore keep the social documents in conformity with the Belgian Law.

4.3. The Posting Declaration

This declaration contains information concerning the foreign employer, the worker and the working conditions. It must be sent to the Labour Inspectorate by post, fax or e-mail before the posting, using a specific form, which is available at the website of the Ministry of Employment and Labour.[370]

The Labour Inspectorate must acknowledge receipt of the declaration within five days and give the employer a registration number (by post, fax or e-mail). The posting is not allowed to take place before the employer receives the registration number.

An additional form must be sent by the employer to the Labour Inspectorate by post, fax or e-mail using the form in case of:

–   The posting of new workers;
–   The establishment of new building sites;
–   If there are changes to any of the following:
    – the employer's name or address;
    – the corporate name, the registered corporate office, the company's type of activities, the company's address;
    – the working hours and the total numbers of working hours per week;
    – the type of provision of services;
    – length of the posting and the date when the posting starts;
    – the place where the work is done;
    – the place where the equivalent documents are kept.

The additional form must mention the registration number which was previously given to the employer.

If the employer fails to inform the Labour Inspection about the posting of new workers, he will not be entitled to an exemption from keeping Belgian social documents for those new workers.

4.4. The Equivalent Pay Documents

While the worker is posted in Belgium, the following apply:

–   During the six-month period of exemption from keeping the social documents:
    – The employer must keep copies of the foreign pay documents equivalent to the Belgian pay documents at the relevant Belgian Inspectorate's

---

370   See Annex.

disposal. Those copies must be updated on a regular basis in conformity with the employer's home legislation.

- The employer can choose to keep the equivalent documents either at the work place where the worker is posted (if there are several of them, the employer needs to select one of them) or at the place of residence of the Employer's representative in Belgium. If he/she fails to comply with this obligation, the employer has to keep the Belgian pay social documents (i.e. the pay statement, "*le compte individuel*", and the final pay statement, "*le décompte de paie*").

– After the six-month period of exemption:
- The equivalent documents are kept at the above selected place at the relevant Belgian authorities' disposal (which means the employer only needs to keep them and no longer needs to update them.)
- The employer must keep the Belgian social documents laid down in the Belgian law.

4.5. When the Posting Ends

When the posting ends, the employer must notify the Labour Inspectorate administration by registered mail or leave all the social documents and a list of all the documents with the Labour Inspectorate administration.

5. FOLLOW UP: BELGIAN LIAISON OFFICE

The Liaison Office for Belgium is the Individual Labour Relations administration. It deals with queries from foreign employers concerning terms and conditions of employment applicable to their workers posted to Belgium. It also provides employers with contact details of relevant national authorities.

6. EXPERIENCE AND PRACTICE: PROBLEMS OF ABUSE AND LACK OF ADEQUATE CONTROL

According to Jorens and Van Overmeiren:[371]

> Three categories of abuse and circumvention can be distinguished: (1) legal circumvention by social engineering, e.g. the shopping for sectoral agreements holding lower social protection; (2) semi-legal circumvention in a grey zone of constructions between legality and illegality, e.g.

---

371 *Op. cit.*, 74-75.

self-employed from other countries who can be considered as workers whereby their employers circumvent the higher social protection of workers and (3) illegal circumvention/moonlighting, in some cases close to people trafficking.

Some examples:

– Supply by interim or posting agencies of German, English, Irish, Polish and other Eastern European workers to contractors at prices that do not respect minimum wage levels.

– Falsifying and uncontrollability of identity, social and labour documents.

– Combination of illegal posting and circumventing social/fiscal contributions in the state of origin.

– Ignoring social protection rules concerning working time, resting periods, safety measures.

– Aggressive infiltration of foreign posting agencies who supply low-cost workers, making it very difficult for Belgian undertakings to refuse these attracting offers.

– Fake "self-employed persons" who work for one contractor, in fact being under the authority of their "client". Those "self-employed" can freely enter the territory respecting some rules concerning residence, circumventing the Posting Directive and the Belgian mandatory rules.

– The complexity of a cascade system of contractors and subcontractors, makes goal-oriented control impossible: even the contractor at the top of the network loses sight of the situation.

– Costs for residence and food are accounted in the wage at "Hilton prices", but workers sleep in tents and get low quality food.

– Circumvention of the Belgian agency work rules in the construction sector.

– Working time on paper in accordance with the rules, but in reality posted workers work long hours from early in the morning till late in the evening or the wages respect the minimum wage levels, but the workers have to work more hours than paid for.

– Permanent presence of foreign employers by circumvention of the temporary character of posting.

– Establishment of agencies in low-cost countries (Greece, Portugal, Poland) from where workers are being posted afterwards. Certain undertakings give the opportunity to the Belgian contractors to choose a crew comprising 100%, 80% or 60% posted EU workers, the remainder coming from low-wage countries. Of course, prices differ along with percentages.

It follows that, for the correct implementation of the Directive and of national legislation:

1. Better information on prevailing labour laws and employment conditions in the various Member States, including collective agreements is needed. A European databank containing such information in the various languages is indispensable.
2. Better and more advanced collaboration is required between:
    a. The social partners across boundaries;
    b. The labour administrations and social inspectorates of the various Member States.

Only when such arrangements are provided for and are operative in practice will freedom of services go along with adequate social protection.

ANNEX I.

POSTING DECLARATION
To be sent to the
Administration of Labour Inspection
Belgian Federal Ministry of Employment and Labour
Rue Belliard 51
1000 Brussels
Phone: +32 2 233 47 57
Fax: + 32 2 233 48 27
E-mail: ils.detachement@meta.fgov.be

Section 1: Information concerning the employer who posts workers in Belgium

Surname: . . . .

First name: . . . .

Home address: . . . .

Corporate name: . . . .

Registered corporate Office: . . . .

Type of company's activities: . . . .

Company's address: . . . .

Phone: . . . .

Fax: . . . .

E-mail: . . . .

The Employer's Social Security number in his home country: . . . .

Section 2: Information concerning the employer's representative who keeps the foreign pay documents equivalent to the Belgian pay documents (i.e. the pay statement and the final pay statement)

This information is optional: the employer can choose to keep the equivalent pay documents either at the work place in Belgium or at the place of residence of the employer's representative in Belgium, see below section 6

Surname: . . . .

First name: . . . .

Corporate name: . . . .

Address: . . . .

Phone: . . . .

Fax: . . . .

E-mail: . . . .

Section 3: Information concerning each worker posted to Belgium

Surname: . . . .

First name: . . . .

Home address: . . . .

Date of birth: . . . .

Civil status: . . . .

Gender: . . . .

Nationality: . . . .

Address in Belgium: . . . .

Phone: Number and type of identity card: . . . .

Date when the contract of employment was concluded: . . . .

Date when the worker starts to be employed in Belgium: . . . .

Type of work: . . . .

Section 4: Information concerning the workings conditions applicable to the posted workers

Total number of working hours per week: . . . .

Working time schedule: . . . .

Section 5: Information concerning the posting as a whole:

Date when the posting starts: . . . .

Length of the posting: . . . .

Type of provision of services: . . . .

Place where the work is done in Belgium:. . . . .

Section 6: Information concerning the place where the equivalent documents are kept:

The employer must choose to keep the social documents either at the work place or at the place of residence of his/her representative in Belgium.

The work place of the worker posted to Belgium

(if several building sites or work places, please select one of them)

Name of the building site: . . . .

Address: . . . .

Phone number: . . . .

OR place of residence of the employer's representative who keeps the Belgian social documents

Name: . . . .

Address: . . . .

Phone: . . . .

Signature of the company's manager
(or of his/her representative in Belgium). . . . .

ANNEX II. LIAISON OFFICES IN THE EUROPEAN UNION

Coordination of liaison offices and contact person within the European Commission

Ms. Gertrud Feustel
DG Employment and Social Affairs
Telephone: 0032 2 295 22 14
Email: gertrud.feustel@cec.eu.int

Liaison office in Austria

Bundesministerium für Arbeit, Gesundheit und Soziales, Sektion III,
A – 1010 Wien,
Stubenring 1
Austria

Liaison office in Belgium

Ministère de l'Emploi et du Travail
Administration des relations individuelles du travail
Division de la Réglementation des relations individuelles du travail
Rue Belliard, 51
1040 Bruxelles
Belgium

Liaison office in Denmark

Arbejdsmarkedsstyrelsen, office 4
Att. Ms Vibeke Stærmose, Ms Gabriella Nagy, Ms Lone Rådberg
Blegdamsvej 56
Postal box 2722
DK – 2100 Copenhagen
Telephone: +45 35288100
Fax: +45 33147176
Email: ams@ams.dk

Liaison office in Finland

Social- och Hälsovårdsministeriet
PB 33, 00023 Statsrådet
Finland

Liaison offices in Germany

Liaison office for posting from Netherlands, United Kingdom and Ireland to Germany:
Landesarbeitsamt Nordrhein-Westfalen
Josef-Gockeln-Str. 7
40474 Düsseldorf

Telephone: +49 2114306 – 405 or 367
Fax: +49 2114306 – 377

Liaison office for posting from Belgium, France and Luxembourg to Germany:
Landesarbeitsamt Rheinland-Pfalz-Saarland
Eschberger Weg 68
66121 Saarbrücken
Telephone: +49 681849 – 220
Fax: + 49 681849 – 180

Liaison office for posting from Italy, Greece and Austria to Germany:
Landesarbeitsamt Bayern
Regensburger Str. 100
90478 Nürnberg
Telephone: +49 911179 -1408
Fax: +49 911179 – 42021

Liaison office for posting from Spain and Portugal to Germany:
Landesarbeitsamt Baden-Württemberg
Hölderlinstr. 36
70174 Stuttgart
Telephone: +49 711941 -2217
Fax: + 49711941 – 1640

Liaison office for posting from Denmark, Norway, Sweden and Finland to Germany
Landesarbeitsamt Nord
Projensdorfer Str. 82
24106 Kiel
Telephone: +49 4313395 – 462 … 455
Fax: +49 4323395 – 262

Liaison office in Iceland
Ministry of Social Affairs
Hafnarhúsiny v/ Tryggvagötu
IS- 150 Reykjavik
Iceland
Telephone: +3545609100
Fax: +3545524804
Email: post@fel.stjr.is

Liaison office in Ireland
The Department of Enterprise, Trade & Employment
Kildare Street, Dublin 2

Telephone: +353 1 6312121
Fax: +353 1 6312827
Email: webmaster@entemp.ie
Internet: http://www.entemp.ie

The Department's Employment Rights Information Unit may be contacted by telephone at +353 1 631 3131 or by fax at +353 1 631 3267
Details of the health and safety legislation in Ireland can be found on the website of the Health and Safety Authority at:
http://www.hsa.ie
Employment equality legislation (Maternity Protection, Adoptive Leave, Parental Leave) is included on the website of the Department of Justice, Equality and Law Reform at:
http://www.irlgov.ie/justice

Liaison office in Italy
Ministerio del Lavoro e della Previdenza Sociale
Direzione Generale per l'Impiego
Rosario Cappeleri
Via Fornovo 8
ROMA
Italia
Tel: +39 63222352
Fax: +39 6320161
E-mail: lielo@impiego.minlavoro.it
http://www.minlavoro.it

Liaison office in Liechtenstein
Amt für Volkswirtschaft
Abteilung Technik und Statistik
Gerberweg 5
FL-9490 Vaduz
Liechtenstein

Liaison office in the Netherlands
Labour Inspectorate,
P.O Box 90801,
2509 LV Den Haag
The Netherlands

Liaison office in Spain
General Social Security,
Treasury International Conventions Section,
Calle Astros, no5-7,

Madrid, Spanien Telephone: 915038060

Liaison office in Sweden
Arbetsmiljöverket
Att. Eva Karlsson
17184 Solna
Sverige
Tlf.: 0046 8 730 9072
Email: arbetsmiljoverket@av.se

Liaison office in United Kingdom
The Depart of Trade and Industry,
http://www.dti.gov.uk and http://www.homeoffice.gov.uk

17. THE IMPLEMENTATION OF THE POSTING DIRECTIVE IN ITALY

Michele Colucci

1. INTRODUCTION

The posting of workers from Italy to other EU countries is still relatively rare.[372] More frequent is the reverse practice of posting workers to Italy from other Member States.

At present, there are no figures on the number of workers posted from Italy to other EU countries. However, the practice is not particularly widespread. It mainly involves medium to high-level workers (e.g. highly specialised technicians and managers) who are in demand and usually negotiate their terms and conditions individually.

In the construction and public works sector, secondments or foreign assignments are much more frequently used than postings, whereby employees do not work for another enterprise (i.e. they are not "detached") but continue to work under the direct supervision of their employer for the entire duration of the transfer abroad. This concerns companies specialising in the construction of bridges, tunnels and other engineering work which win contracts (or more often subcontracts for specific phases of a project) and second employees for the entire duration of the work contracted. In recent years, the number of secondments by construction companies to countries like Germany and France has diminished, while those outside the EU have increased, especially to Asian countries (but also to South America). The workers seconded abroad are entirely covered by Italian law.

Employees posted to Italy from other EU Member States are usually highly specialised workers like journalists and managers in multinational companies – though no figures are available on the number of such workers. In such cases, requests for an extension of the posting (a further 12 months) are normally granted up to a maximum of five years from the start of the posting. It is growing increasingly obvious that the five-year limit on intra-EU postings is impracticable for such categories as newspaper and radio correspondents, or managers working for airlines, banks or other multinational companies, for whom the period cannot be

---

372   See in that regard L. Muratore, Posted Workers in Italy, <www.eiro.eurofound.eu.int/2003/06/tfeature/it0306307t.html>.

predetermined but depends on the need for their presence in a particular corporate setting.

As regards non-EU workers, the law permits the posting to Italy only of those with specialised skills (under Ministerial Circular No. 82/2000). This restrictive provision has curtailed the phenomenon, in that non-EU companies are subject to numerous restrictions regarding the posting of workers to Italy. Nevertheless, it is growing rapidly in some sectors, especially the construction industry, where clandestine labour is more frequent and firms consequently do not obey the law.

2. THE ITALIAN REGULATORY FRAMEWORK

Directive 96/71 has been fully transposed and enacted in Italy by Legislative decree no. 72 of 25 February 2000.[373] Previously, the posting of workers was regulated not by specific laws but by general legislation.

In accordance with the Directive, this decree ensures that the same treatment and working conditions apply to posted workers as to workers normally based in Italy. Enterprises based in an EU Member State which post workers to Italian territory under a contract for the provision of services continue to maintain an employment relationship with those workers.[374]

Unlike the EU Directive, Decree 72/2000 also applies to enterprises located outside the EU which wish to post workers to Italy. In order to regulate such cases, Ministerial Circular No. 82/2000 was issued to supplement the existing legislation, i.e. Legislative Decree No. 286/1998 (the "consolidated text of the regulations on immigration and the status of foreigners").

An Italian employer wishing to establish an employment relationship with a non-EU foreigner must apply for authorisation to the provincial labour authorities, and also provide documentation on the foreigner's accommodation.

The validity of the authorisation is limited to the duration of the work to be performed and may in no case exceed two years. The police issue a residence permit, which is not renewable. Finally, the workers concerned must have specialised qualifications (although bilateral agreements with other countries may regulate this aspect differently), and the authorisation must be submitted for approval by the trade union representatives at the company making the application and to the trade unions most representative of the sector at the provincial level.

The posting of workers from EU or non-EU countries to perform services in Italy takes place on the basis of a contract (or subcontract) which the recipient of the service (the company in Italy) concludes with the provider of the service (the posting company outside Italy).

---

373 Legislative Decree No. 72 of 25 February 2000, in *Official Journal* No. 75 of 30 March 2000.

374 M. Biagi, "La fortuna ha sorriso alla Presidenza italiana dell'Unione Europea: prime note di commento alle direttive sul distacco dei lavoratori all'estero e sui permessi parentali", DRI, 1996, 3-7.

3. THE LEGAL POSITION OF POSTED WORKERS

After the implementation of the Directive's provisions into national law, the same employment conditions (pay levels in particular) established by laws, regulations or collective agreements for resident workers also apply to posted workers performing similar services (this goes beyond the specific list of conditions to be applied to posted workers set out in the Directive).

As regards social security coverage, workers posted abroad or coming from abroad are covered by the social security system of their home country for the entire duration of the posting. This duration is fixed by bilateral agreements and varies, according to the country concerned, from a minimum of six months to a maximum of 36 (Israel and Tunisia). There is no time limit on postings to (and from) the USA, while the duration is set at 12 months (extendable) for the EU. During the posting, therefore, workers continue to pay contributions in their country of origin. However, if the posting exceeds the period established by the relevant international agreement, the workers become covered by the social security system in the country where they perform the work. This also applies to healthcare.

If workers are posted to a country with which Italy does not have a bilateral social security agreement, they are covered by contributions paid by the employer in the country of origin. If a foreign worker is posted to Italy from a country which does not have an agreement with Italy, the worker and the recipient company are subject to Italian law on social security and insurance.

As regards temporary employment agencies operating in EU Member States other than Italy, Legislative Decree No. 72/2000 allows them to post workers to companies in Italy.

In this case, the agency is subject to Law No. 196/97, and by the so-called Biagi Act, which regulates temporary agency work and guarantees equality of treatment (as regards pay, insurance and social security) between temporary agency workers and permanent workers performing similar services.

4. WORKERS IN THE CONSTRUCTION INDUSTRY

The EU Directive, although of general application, is aimed particularly at workers in the construction industry (building and public works), in which discrepancies between practice and legal standards are often observed.

The construction industry has always had the highest concentration of irregular or clandestine labour in Italy. For this reason the state, together with the social partners, has sought to apply rigid regulations on the posting of workers, especially from non-EU countries, where labour is cheap.

The national collective agreement for building workers obliges all construction companies winning contracts or subcontracts (public and private) to enrol their workers in the Special Construction Workers' Funds (*Casse Edili*) – an industry-specific insurance scheme financed by contributions from both workers and employers, providing assistance, welfare services and income support to workers in case of bad weather or lack of work.

Any employer that does not comply with this requirement is in breach of the law and may not open a building site. Moreover, the law stipulates that posted workers must be paid at the same rate as workers performing similar tasks in Italy.

In reality, in a very large number of cases, these two constraints (contractual and legislative) are not respected by firms posting non-EU workers to Italy. Whilst the basic hourly pay of an Italian construction worker is EUR 7.50, that of a posted foreign worker is EUR 3 to EUR 3.50. Moreover, these workers can reportedly be "blackmailed" by their employers, because at the first sign of protest the employer may have the worker's residence permit revoked, resulting in immediate repatriation. Although official statistics are not available, these illegal practices are spreading rapidly and are used to bring workers from Eastern Europe (especially Albania, Romania, Moldavia, the Ukraine and the former Yugoslavia) temporarily into Italy.

In recent years, the trade unions have sought to combat breaches of the law and irregular work in the construction industry through both collective bargaining and legal action in the courts.

5. ADMINISTRATION COOPERATION AND JURISDICTION

Directive 96/71 requires administrative cooperation at national level and has put in place bodies designed to ensure such cooperation.

In Italy, the competent body is the Directorate-General for Employment at the Ministry of Labour and Social Security.

Reasoned requests for information presented by the competent authorities of other Member States are handled by the provincial directorates of employment which are in charge of monitoring the market and ensuring compliance with the rules in the field.

Failure to comply with the protective rules pertaining to posted workers is not subject to specific sanctions but, rather, to the customary penalties for infringement of domestic law. In that regard the Legislative Decree sets down the competence of the Italian courts to resolve disputes arising from its application: proceedings must be brought before the Italian courts during the performance of the contract or within one year of its expiry.

6. THE ROLE OF SOCIAL PARTNERS AND COLLECTIVE BARGAINING   AGREEMENTS

Italian law requires the application of "collective agreements concluded by the organisations of employers and workers which are the most representative at national level, applicable to workers who provide similar professional services at the place at which the posted workers exercise their activity".

Italian law makes reference to agreements "applicable to workers who provide similar professional services on a subordinate basis at the place where the posted workers exercise their activity".

Collective bargaining does not deal specifically with workers posted abroad, although it does regulate temporary and provisional "work secondments" (also abroad). In the latter case, collective agreements establish the increments to normal pay (temporary transfer allowances) and the reimbursement of travel, board and lodging, as well as other expenses. The national collective agreement for building workers regulates the detachment (or secondment) of workers to another enterprise (although it does not make specific mention of secondments abroad). This practice is very similar to the leasing of workers, which is forbidden by law.

When the Directive was enacted by legislative decree, the legislator did not deem it necessary to consult the social partners because the decree established better working conditions for posted workers than those envisaged by the Directive itself. As stated, such workers are subject to the same contractual conditions as are applicable to resident workers undertaking the same work. Italian law has therefore gone further than the Directive, which ensures only a core of protective measures for posted workers (maximum work periods and minimum rest periods, minimum rates of pay, etc.).

This equality of treatment between posted workers and their Italian counterparts reassured the trade unions, which did not oppose the new rules, and satisfied the employers' associations, especially those in the construction industry, which feared unfair competition by cheaper foreign workers.

7. CONCLUSION

Posting of workers in Italy is relatively rare, and it concerns skilled workers with a medium to high position in the labour market, and therefore with strong bargaining power vis-à-vis their employers.

The situation is different in the construction sector where employers are worried about the presence of firms which use irregular or low-cost labour to engage in unfair competition. For this reason, the social partners and government have paid little attention to the posting of workers within the EU.

18. IMPLEMENTATION OF THE POSTING DIRECTIVE IN THE NETHERLANDS

Mijke Houwerzijl[375]

1. INTRODUCTION

The Posting Directive was officially implemented by means of the *Wet arbeidsvoor-waarden grensoverschrijdende arbeid* (Terms of Employment (Cross-Border Work) Act). The Act entered into force on 24 December 1999. The parliamentary history of the Act perfectly illustrates the "neutral" attitude of the Dutch Government. In brief: the Bill was sent to the House of Representatives in the spring of 1999. In the parliamentary debate, the central motto of the Government became clear: "We do not want to transpose more or less than necessary." Thus, none of the optional provisions in the Posting Directive were considered in the Bill. This neutral attitude corresponds with the general Dutch conduct concerning the implementation of EU Directives. Nevertheless, the majority of the House of Representatives were not satisfied. These politicians objected to the limitation of the collective agreement part of the Directive to the construction sector. They stated that companies in other sectors would also want equal treatment on this point. The system of universally applicable collective agreements is widespread in the Netherlands. Thus, not broadening the scope of the Bill through Article 3(10) of the Directive would mean that Dutch companies and workers outside the construction sector would not be able to compete with their foreign colleagues on an equal footing. This discussion dominated the parliamentary debate about the Bill, but did not lead to its amendment. Thus, the Bill was passed.

In the autumn of 2003, the topic was raised again. This time it was related to a debate about a transitional arrangement for the free movement of workers from Eastern European countries after their accession to the EU on 1 May 2004. At first, the Government kept defending its "neutral" position and the majority of the House of Representatives still accepted this, despite continuing attempts by supporters of "scope broadening" to put the item on the legislative agenda again. In the summer of 2004, however, the Government made a U-turn, because Dutch employers had complained about unfair competition related to the influx of cheap posted workers.

---

375 This contribution is a slightly revised version of the country report about the Dutch implementation, published in: Jan Cremers, Peter Donders (eds), *The Free Movement of Workers in the European Union*, CLR Studies 4 (Brussels: Reed Business Information) 105-114.

In the autumn of 2004, a Bill was sent to the House of Representatives with the proposal to broaden the scope of the Terms of Employment (Cross-Border Worker) Act to all universally applicable collective agreements. This Bill will probably be adopted soon.[376]

Obviously, other items were raised during the parliamentary debate about the Act. Questions were posed about the definition of "posting", about the mode of compliance of the applicable employment conditions for posted workers (Articles 4, 5, 6), about the non-use of the derogation option for postings not exceeding one month (Article 3 (3 and 4)), or "non-significant" postings (Article 3 (5) and about the application of the "favour principle" (Article 3(7)).[377] However, none of these questions led to broad discussions or to any adjustment of the Bill. Where the answers to these questions are of relevance, they are dealt with in the sections below.

2. DEFINITION OF POSTING, WORKER AND PERIOD OF WORK

In the Terms of Employment (Cross-Border Worker) Act (Article 1) the posted worker is defined as someone who works temporarily in the Netherlands and on whose employment contract foreign law is applicable. No other words are used to implement Article 1 and Article 2 of Directive 96/71.

2.1. Definition of Posting

So, the three types of posting that are distinguished in Article 1(3) of Directive 96/71 do not occur in the Act. Nevertheless, as the responsible Minister assured members of Parliament, the Act is meant to apply for all three types of posting. Explicit implementation in the Act was not deemed necessary. The problem in practice with this "implicit" method of implementation is that the posting definition of Article 1(3) does not correspond to the Dutch internal definition of posting.[378] In Dutch (legal) usage, only posting types (b) (posting in multinational companies) and (c) (posting through temporary agencies) are understood as "posting", while type (a) (temporary cross-border working in the framework of the employer's subcontract) is normally seen as something different.[379] Moreover, the definition in the Act may be confusing because it includes more workers than only temporary service workers who usually work in another Member State. It also includes workers who carry out their work in other Member States on a temporary basis. In this situation no

---

376   See Kamerstukken II, 2004/05, 29 983, No. 1.
377   See Kamerstukken II, 1998-1999, 26 524, Nos 5-6, Handelingen II, 1998-1999, No. 104, p. 5985.
378   See Kamerstukken II, 1998-1999, 26 524, No. 5, p. 3 and No. 6, p. 3.
379   A judgement of *kantonrechter* Heerlen, 24 Sept. 2003 (JAR 268/2003) shows that this confusion has already occurred in practice. See annotation M.S. Houwerzijl, AI 2004/2, pp. 39-41.

Member State can be seen as the permanent work place of a worker. Examples are international truck drivers and tour guides. Because Article 1(1) Directive 96/71 is not explicitly transposed, the Act is not limited to companies that post workers in the framework of a provision of services.

In contrast, it can be deduced from a jointly published leaflet in the construction industry that "social partners", while not mentioning the three types either, have at least limited the scope of the applicable provisions of their collective agreements to workers who "normally work for their employer in another country of the EU".[380] Article 1a (a) in the extended collective agreement for the construction sector (*Bouwcao 2003-2004*)[381] repeats the definition of the Act, but in addition stresses that a "posted worker" means in this respect every worker who *usually* works in another Member State, not being the Netherlands. This provision of the social partners is more accurate than the definition in the Act, although here the necessity of posting in the framework of a cross-border provision of services (as mentioned in Article 1 of the Posting Directive) is absent as well.

2.2. Definition of a Worker

Article 1 of the Act makes no explicit distinction between a posted worker and a (posted) self-employed worker. But parliamentary documents and the applicable legislation for posted workers under Dutch law show that only the Dutch definition of an employee is to be taken into account if a question should arise about the status of the worker.[382] In this respect no problems are expected to arise like those that led to ECJ judgements in cases like *Banks* or *Fitzwilliams* in the framework of No. 1408/71.[383] Still, the underlying practical problem is not easy to tackle: although certain branches prefer to work with self-employed workers who would surely be revealed as employees if all facts were known, in practice it is very difficult to prove this. How does one recognise a posted worker and as a result apply the Terms of Employment (Cross-Border Worker) Act? First of all these workers are difficult

---

380 See Brochure "Posting to the Dutch Construction Sector. Collective Labour Agreement for the Construction Sector, Collective Labour Agreement for Site Management, Technical and Administrative Personnel in Construction Companies", September 2003, published on behalf of the parties to these collective agreements, especially p. 2/3.

381 See the extended version of the collective agreement for the construction (*Bouwcao 2003-2004*, see AI No. 9992, e.g. Stcrt. 29.9.2003, No. 187).

382 See Article 1:1 Arbeidstijdenwet, Article 1 Arbeidsomstandighedenwet 1998 and Article 4 jo. Article 2 WMM for a definition of an employee under Dutch law. It would have been more clear if Article 610, 610 a and b BW and also 690 of book 7 BW had been mentioned in Article 1 of the Terms of Employment (Cross-Border Worker) Act. As for the last-mentioned provision, the Explanatory Memorandum makes clear that this also applies to posted temporary workers from abroad. See Kamerstukken II, 1998-99, 26 524, No. 3, p. 3.

383 See ECJ judgements in Cases C-178/97 of 30 March 2000 (*Banks*) and C-202/97 of 10 February 2000 (*Fitzwilliam*).

to find because they often work quite in isolation from the Dutch workers.[384] And if they are found, language problems and a lack of interest occur, because (most of the) posted workers have nothing to gain from a judicial procedure regarding their status.

2.3. Posted Workers from Third Countries

The scope of the Act is not limited to workers originating from one of the EU Member States. This means that posted workers from a "third country" are entitled to (at least) the same protection and their employers are obliged to comply with (at least) the same conditions as workers and employers from within the EU. Migrant law, however, makes posting from a third country different: the Foreign Nationals Employment Act requires not only a residence permit for workers from a third country but also requires employers to obtain a work permit.[385] Furthermore, the employer is obliged to treat and pay the foreign worker in conformity with all Dutch current working and employment conditions.[386]

On the level of the extended provisions of collective agreements, this full equal treatment of posted workers from third countries is stipulated as well. Article 1a(b) of the collective agreement in the construction sector states that all extended provisions are applicable to posted workers from third countries. In the last five years, a growing number of undertakings especially from (former candidate) Member States like Poland have taken place in the Dutch construction sector (and in some other industries like horticulture and cleaning). In practice, many workers from these countries work directly via Dutch temporary employment agencies. In principle, all Dutch labour law is applicable to them.

2.4. What is Temporary?

Finally, in the Terms of Employment (Cross-Border Worker) Act the "allowed" length of posting is not determined. This vagueness about the period of posting

---

384 A practical reason for this "isolation" is that working together in a team with different nationalities would lead to communication problems for the managers of the teams on a building site.

385 As yet, no difference in treatment is made between third country workers legally resident in one of the Member States and posted by an "EU employer", and third country workers who live outside the EU and who are posted by an employer established in a third country. In relation to the judgement of the ECJ in Case C-445/03 (*Commission v. Luxembourg*) from 21 October 2004, the Dutch Government announced that in the near future no work permit will be required for the first group.

386 "In conformity with Dutch current working conditions" (*marktconform*) means that not only statutory provisions but also working conditions in current collective agreements (extended and non-extended) or even more favourable company-related working conditions have to be applied.

is quite logical: it was not specified in the Directive either. It would have been a breach of the "neutral implementation attitude" to develop a Dutch policy on this point, even if we refrain from the question of whether the Directive would permit a national determination of the period of posting at all.

3. TERMS AND CONDITIONS OF EMPLOYMENT

3.1. Statutory Terms and Conditions for Posted Workers

Applicable national rules corresponding to the subject matter covered by Article 3(1) of the Posting Directive are partly identified by the Terms of Employment (Cross-Border Worker) Act. Article 1 of the Act makes sure that a couple of provisions in Book 7 (about employment contracts) of the Civil Code are applicable to posted workers in the Netherlands. Herewith (all) mandatory civil provisions about minimum paid annual holidays, equal treatment of men and women and other provisions on non-discrimination, health and safety at work (employers' liability in case of work-related accidents or disease) and one of the protective measures for pregnant women (prohibition to dismiss someone because of pregnancy) are implemented.

Although unclear when one only reads the text of the Terms of Employment (Cross-Border Worker) Act in isolation, several provisions of Dutch administrative law are applicable to posted workers as well. All special mandatory law with a "public order" character is applicable under Article 7 of the Rome Convention. This concerns provisions of the Minimum Wages Act, the Working Time Act, the Health and Safety Act, the Temporary Employment Agencies Act and the Equal Treatment Act.

3.2. Terms and Conditions Laid down in (Extended) Collective Agreements

Which collective agreements may be applied to posted workers? So far, only extended collective agreements in the construction industry are applicable to posted workers in the Netherlands (as no use is made of the second paragraph of Article 3(10) of the Posting Directive). As mentioned, this will change in the near future. The Dutch method of extension of collective agreements results in an *erga omnes* scope during the period of extension. Therefore the system fits to the definition in the first subparagraph of Article 3 (8) of the Posting Directive: "collective agreements which have been declared universally applicable" means collective agreements or arbitration awards which must be observed by all undertakings in the geographical area and in the profession or industry concerned.

The Appendix of the Posting Directive defines the construction industry more broadly than usual in the Netherlands,[387] but the Dutch Government has neverthe-less not tried to identify all the corresponding Dutch collective agreements. Some Members of Parliament insisted that the Government should do so because it would further the accessibility of the Dutch collective agreements to foreign employers and employees and it would prevent misunderstandings as well. The responsible Minister objected, saying that such an exercise would lead to more bureaucracy and, moreover, that it belonged to the competence of the social partners to decide on this issue.[388] The same answer was given about the related issue of who has the competence to decide which provisions of the collective agreement correspond to the subject matter covered by the Posting Directive.

In the Netherlands, bargaining provisions can only be made when statutory provisions leave room for derogation. In most cases derogation from a legal provision is only possible for social partners. If a bargaining provision proves to be inconsistent with (mandatory) legal provisions, this bargaining provision must be considered null and void. Article 2(6) of the Act of Extension of Provisions of Collective Agreements transposes the hard core of labour standards specified in Article 3(1) of the Posting Directive. As part of the collective bargaining process, Dutch social partners in the construction sector have labelled the applicable provi-sions in subsequent collective agreements from 1998 onwards. Between 1998 and the negotiations for the period 2002-2004 they have explored the possibilities and limitations of four collective agreements in the Dutch construction sector. These collective agreements cover most occupations and companies in the sector.

From the seven categories mentioned in Article 3 (1) of the Posting Directive, the collective agreements contain rules in six of them: (a) work and rest time, (b) holiday, (c) rates of pay, (d) workers for a temporary employment agency, (e) health and safety, and (f) protective measures (only with regard to the terms and conditions of employment for young people). In the remaining field ((g) equal treatment) the legal rules only apply (minimally) to posted workers. A special appendix stipulates which parts of the applicable provisions are meant for posted workers. The text of the applicable parts of the provisions has sometimes been rewritten to adjust it to the situation of posted workers (references to Dutch provisions and situations have been deleted). In addition, a special explanation has been given about the job-related pay system and guaranteed gross wages. Special attention has been paid to posted temporary agency workers.

Altogether, only half of the total extended agreement provisions applicable to domestic employees apply to posted workers (25 provisions out of a total of 53). Still, practically all basic working and employment conditions are included.

---

387   The exact scope can be found in the so-called NACE codes 45.10 up to and including 45.45. See appendix Regulation (EEG) No. 3037/90 of 9 October 1990 (OJ L 293 of 24.10.1990, p. 1), last change by Regulation (EG) No. 29/2002 of 19.12.2001 (OJ L 6 of 10.1.2002, p. 3).
388   See Handelingen II, 1998-1999, No. 104, pp. 5989-5990, Hand. II, 1999-2000, No. 5, p. 231 and Kamerstukken II, 1998-1999, 26 524, No. 9.

According to a spokesman from the union, the exclusion of fringe benefits and other provisions meant for "permanent workers" (such as vocational training and stipulations about the end of an employment contract), makes posted workers around 25% cheaper in labour costs than domestic workers.[389]

3.3. The Favour Principle and the Method of Comparison

Article 3(7) of the Posting Directive is not implemented explicitly in the Terms of Employment (Cross-Border Work) Act. Some Members of Parliament asked in vain for codification of the favour principle, especially because in Dutch law no legal basis for the favour principle exists. Moreover, Members of Parliament asked the Minister what method has to be followed in the Netherlands to compare the applicable labour conditions of the host country and the country of origin. Article 3(7) gives posted workers a right to the most favourable terms and conditions of employment, but no method of comparison to determine this is prescribed. Is a comparison preferable on the level of each provision, or between units of provisions covering the same subject, or is a comparison of the whole package of working and employment conditions the right starting point? According to the Minister, the Dutch legal system prescribes a comparison on the level of each provision because, in the case of posted workers only (a minimum level of) mandatory law is at stake. The mandatory character of provisions does not allow the exchange of one provision for another, depending on the arbitrary preference of an individual worker.[390]

In this regard, the Minister also mentioned the existing agreement between the Dutch and Belgian social partners in construction to acknowledge each other's collective agreements as equivalent. As a result of this agreement, the Belgian collective agreement applies to a posted worker who usually works in Belgium during the period of posting in the Netherlands and vice versa. According to the Minister, this agreement can be prolonged. But if a posted worker from Belgium appeals for more favourable Dutch provisions, the Belgium provisions have to yield as far as minimum entitlements are concerned. As long as posted workers are satisfied with the agreement, no objections against a prolongation exist.[391] This pragmatic attitude leaves enough room for collective bargaining to make the favour principle more workable in practice. The only downside to this is that it does not guarantee 100% legal certainty for employers. But when only very few or even no individual appeals are expected, this may not be considered a problem.

---

389 This estimation was made by one of the interviewed union representatives for the CLR Study. See Cremers/Donders, *op. cit.*, 2005.
390 See Handelingen II, 1998-99, No. 104, pp. 5980, 5987. This statement is confirmed in a judgement of the Hoge Raad (Supreme Court), JAR 2000/43.
391 See Handelingen II, 1998-99, No. 104, p. 5980, 5987 and Kamerstukken II, 1998-99, 26 524, No. 6, p. 4-5. See also Sengers and Donders, SR 2001/5, p. 143. They speak of "gentlemen's agreements".

4. ADMINISTRATIVE COOPERATION AND MEASURES AIMED AT COMPLIANCE

4.1. Cooperation on Information

In what way is the information on the terms and conditions of employment referred to in Article 3(1) of the Posting Directive made generally available for workers and employers from other Member States (as required in Article 4(3) of the Posting Directive)? Although it is not easily found on the website of the Ministry of Social Affairs (<www.szw.nl>), the Dutch version of the site refers to a free phone number (+31 800 9051) for individuals and companies to obtain information. Furthermore, it provides the possibility of submitting questions by e-mail. There are no plans to improve the accessibility of the information to the general public in the near future (in spite of the strong recommendation to do so in the Evaluation of the EC Commission).[392] In September 2003, social partners in the construction sector published a special leaflet in the English language, aimed at posted workers and their employers. This leaflet gives rather detailed and comprehensive information about the provisions applicable to posted workers.

4.2. Measures Aimed at Compliance

According to Article 5 of the Posting Directive the government is responsible for supervising compliance with the Terms of Employment (Cross-Border Worker) Act and the other mandatory provisions applicable. Therefore, the government is to ensure in particular that adequate procedures are available to workers and/or their representatives for the enforcement of obligations under this Directive. But because the Dutch enforcement system is mainly based on private law, the Dutch Government does not have special control mechanisms to prevent fraud and to assure the correct application of the Directive. It is left to the posted workers and the social partners involved to ensure the Directive's correct application and, if possible, to prevent fraud.

In this respect, Article 4 of the Act transposes Article 6 of the Posting Directive (on jurisdiction) in the Code of Civil Procedures. Thus, it is safeguarded that a Dutch judge has jurisdiction to decide in judicial proceedings started by a posted worker. Unions are entitled to start judicial proceedings on behalf of posted workers or on the basis of their own interest in enforcement of the Directive. This is laid down in Articles 3:305a and 305b of the Dutch Civil Code. For the statutory provisions of the Act and of the other legislation applicable, this may be especially helpful. Where collective agreement provisions are concerned, Article 3 of the Collective Labour Agreements (Declaration of Universally Binding and Non-Binding Status)

---

392   See COM(2003) 458 of 25 July 2003, p. 19/20.

Act entitles unions and employers' organisations to institute proceedings in their capacity as parties to the collective labour agreement.

Whether, for instance, the "user undertaking" of posted temporary agency workers can be held liable when the agency does not fulfil its duties to pay wages etc. to the posted worker depends on the provisions applicable to posted workers of Dutch labour and employment law. Article 7:658(4) of the Civil Code provides for such a liability of the user undertaking, namely in cases of industrial accidents or work-related disease. The user undertaking is normally not liable for the compliance of other statutory employment conditions, like minimum wages and paid holidays. In some situations, however, the user undertaking might be held liable through tort law (Article 6:162 of the Civil Code). In the construction sector, a user undertaking liability is laid down in the collective agreement.

Government intervention with regard to the Posting Directive may only come from the Labour Inspectorate, in its capacity of liaison office. The Inspectorate is allowed to check the pay slip of a posted worker. In practice this probably only happens in the course of an investigation that is targeted at illegal workers. Special attention is paid to some so-called risk sectors of which the construction industry is one. Within the Labour Inspectorate a special intervention team exists (since 2002): *BouwInterventieTeam*. This team inspects construction sites to check if illegal employment, moonlighting and other forms of fraud are taking place.

Apart from its role of enforcing the law, national and local government is the main provider of employment in the construction sector. In this role the government could be exemplary in the compliance of Dutch labour standards. When tendering, the government should contract only on condition that Dutch legal provisions of employment, of social security and fiscal character are respected by (sub)contractors. In fact, the ratified ILO Convention No. 94 obliges the Dutch Government to do so. But in practice a labour clause is not a standard condition to obtain a contract for public works. In reply to the last regular report of the Netherlands about this Convention in 2001 the Committee notes that:

> for many years the Government has been indicating that there are no major developments to be reported and consequently has not provided any information on the practical application of the Convention. ... The Committee would therefore be grateful if the Government would provide in its next report detailed and up-to-date information on the practical application of the Convention, including copies of public contracts, the model text of the labour clause currently in use, information from inspection services on the supervision and enforcement of national legislation and any other particulars bearing on the application of the Convention.[393]

---

393   This must be made available in 2007. Till then the government has time to enhance its current performance. See CEACR 2001, 72nd Session, Comments made by the Committee of Experts on the Application of Conventions and Recommendations, Labour Clauses (Public Contracts) Convention, 1949 (No. 94), Netherlands (ratification 1952), via <www.ilo.org>.

5. CONCLUSION

In short, Dutch implementation legislation and enforcement practice are not without problems. All the competent actors, not only the government, should work towards improving this situation, although the government – especially in its role as employer, when requesting tenders for public works – is well placed to do so. The social partners could also start by employing all the current possibilities of the Terms of Employment (Cross-Border Worker) Act and the Posting Directive. Broadening the scope of the Act to all extended collective agreements is a first step in the right direction.

19. IMPLEMENTATION OF THE POSTING DIRECTIVE IN POLAND

Andrzej M. Swiatkowski

The rules for employment of the European Union nationals in Poland and Polish nationals in the EU Member States are shaped in accordance with the principle of reciprocity. Articles 39 and 49, para. 1, of the Treaty establishing the European Communities apply fully solely with respect to free movement of workers and free provision of services in the framework of temporary movement of posted workers, mentioned in Article 1 of Directive 96/71/CE, between Poland and the EU Member States subject to the temporary provisions laid down in sections 2-14 of the Annex to the International Agreement signed by Poland with the EU Member States on 16 April 2004 in Athens – the Accession Treaty.[394]

Therefore, employment of Polish workers by Polish employers who, taking the opportunity created by the principle of free movement of services, start business activities in other Member States of the European Union as well as employment of nationals of other EU Member States in Poland by entrepreneurs from those Member States is subject to some restrictions. The employees posted by foreign employees do not have access to the labour market in the Member States of the EU, where their employers operate.[395] For this reason, the rules for employing nationals of EU Member States posted to perform temporary work on the territory of other EU Member States, and the rules for employing foreign employees within the framework of a free access to the "open" labour market are the same.

Mandatory legal regulations in Poland impose some restrictions with regard to employment of workers – nationals of the EU Member States – in Poland on the basis of the same rules as the rules applicable to Polish workers willing to work in other EU Member States. For this reason, there is a temporary *raison d'être* to classify workers as posted workers and workers applying directly for work on the territory of other Member States at the employers established in the EU Member States. The classification will be applied until the transitional periods introduced by the authorities of the Member States for Polish workers expire. In accordance with section 2.2 of the Annex No. XII to the Accession Treaty, the existing EU Member States may maintain some measures restricting access of Polish workers to domestic

---

394 The Journal of Laws of 2004, No. 90, item 864.
395 Not the case for Polish workers posted by Polish entrepreneurs to work in the EU Member States: L. Mitrus, *Swoboda przemieszczania się pracowników po przystąpieniu Polski do Unii Europejskiej* (Freedom of Movement of Polish Workers after Accession of Poland to the European Union) (Warsaw: Wydawnictwo Prawnicze LexisNexis, 2003) 332.

Blanpain, *Freedom of Services in the European Union*, 235–237
©2006 Kluwer Law International. Printed in the Netherlands.

labour market until five years after Poland joined the EU. At the end of the five-year period, Member States may notify the Commission that, in case of serious disruptions on their labour market or threat thereof, they will continue to apply these measures until the end of a seven-year period following the date of accession (para. 2.5 of the Annex No. XII). Germany and Austria may, after notifying the Commission, derogate from the first paragraph of Article 49 of the EC with a view to limit, in the context of the provision of services by companies established in Poland, the temporary movement of workers who are Polish nationals. The above may apply to the provision of services by undertakings having their registered seat in Poland.[396] The list of the services which may be included in this derogations applies to the following sectors specified in the Annex No. XII: construction, including related branches (Germany, Austria), industrial cleaning (Germany, Austria) and services provided by interior decorators (Germany). In the case of Austria, the limitations include horticultural service activities; cutting, shaping and finishing of stone; manufacture or metal structures and parts of structures; security activities; home nursing; social work and activities without accommodation.

Guided by the principle of reciprocity and using equivalent measures or restrictive measures arising from the procedures specified in para. 2.11 of Annex No. XII to the Accession Treaty, on 25 May 2004, the Polish Minister of Economy and Labour issued a Regulation on the scope of restrictions applicable to performance of work by foreigners in Poland.[397] The above-mentioned regulation was issued on the basis of Article 90 sec. 6 of the Act on Promoting Employment and Labour Market Institutions of 20 April 2004.[398] It came into effect on 1 June 2004. Annex No. 2 lists the scope of restrictions applicable to the performance of work by foreigners, nationals of 15 countries of the European Union and the European Economic Area listed in the Annex No. 1 to the above-mentioned Regulation: Austria, Belgium, Denmark, Finland, France, Greece, Spain, Iceland, Liechtenstein, Luxembourg, Germany, Norway, Portugal, Switzerland and Italy. Nationals of these countries intending to be employed in Poland within the framework of the free movement of workers within the European Union boundaries are required to have a valid work permit.

The work permit is issued in a legal form of an administrative decision of the *voivod* (head of province). The provisions of the Act on Promoting Employment and Labour Market Institutions constitute the legal basis for issuing a permit for performance of work in Poland. By virtue of the Act, *voivods* are obliged to assess the conditions of local labour markets before any decision on issuing a work permit to a foreigner is made. The above-mentioned obligation does not apply in case of the nationals of Denmark, the Netherlands, Norway and Italy. Similarly, it does

---

396   L. Mitrus, "Zasady zatrudniania Polaków w Unii Europejskiej w świetle traktatu akcesyjnego" (Basic rules of employment of Poles in the European Union in the light of accession treaty), *Praca i Zabezpieczenie Społeczne* (Labour and Social Security), 2004, No. 5, pp. 28-29.
397   The Journal of Laws of 2004, No. 123, item 1293.
398   The Journal of Laws of 2004, No. 99, item 1001.

not apply to the nationals of the above-listed countries for any matters with regard to the application of criteria for issuing promises and work permits introduced by the provisions of the Act as well as any circumstances justifying a refusal to issue the promise to issue a work permit or a residence permit.

It is required that the nationals of EU Member States and the states forming the European Economic Area listed in the Annex No. 1 to the Regulation of the Minister of Economy and Labour of 26 May 2004 apply for a permit to work in Poland only when they intend to be employed on the open domestic labour market. They are not required to obtain work permits in Poland if they have an employment relationship with their employers established in other EU Member States and perform activities for the benefit of their employers within the framework of their posting to Poland.

However, nationals of Austria and Germany, employed by employers conducting their business activities in any EU Member State in the sectors listed in sec. 2.2. let. a and b. of Annex No. 2 to the Regulation of 26 May 2004, posted by these employers to Poland within the framework of Article 1 of Directive 96/71/CE, enjoy a very different legal status. Posted workers, who are nationals of Austria and Germany, may work for their employers after they obtain a work permit from a competent *voivod*. In accordance with the principle of reciprocity, Polish authorities require work permits from the nationals of Austria and Germany, posted to Poland by employers established in other EU Member States operating in the same sectors and types of business activities as those mentioned in the Annex No. XII to the Accession Treaty, which met with a "ban" imposed by the authorities of Austria and German with respect to their accessibility by Polish workers.

The authorities of some EU Member States, including Austria, Germany and Poland, take special measures to protect their domestic labour markets against foreign labour force. They demand work permits from Polish nationals posted to work in Austria and Germany. By way of retaliation, the authorities of Poland introduce the identical restrictive measures in case of the nationals of Austria and Germany posted to work in Poland. In Central and Eastern Europe, it will take time for the concept of free movement of employees under the EU to become a reality.

20. POSTING AND SOCIAL SECURITY COORDINATION

Frans Pennings

1. INTRODUCTION

From its very creation in 1957, promotion of the freedom of movement of workers has been one of the European Economic Community's (EEC) pillars. Freedom of movement is seen as favourable for the economic development of the Member States as they can benefit from the effects of optimal allocation of labour.

Ensuring the freedom of movement of workers across national borders requires active measures. An important part of these measures is in the field of social security, since workers cannot be expected to work in another Member State if doing so has negative effects on their social security position. For this reason the EEC had to adopt a coordination instrument as one of its first activities. This was Regulation 3. At present Article 42 EC provides the legal basis for the coordination regulation currently in force, Regulation 1408/71.[399]

Regulation 1408/71 is not only applicable in the territory of the European Union, but also in that of the European Economic Area (EEA) and Switzerland. The EEA comprises the Member States of the European Union and those Member States of the European Free Trade Association (EFTA) which have not yet become a member of the EU, *i.e.* Norway, Liechtenstein and Iceland.

One of the problems which had to be solved in the case of migrant workers concerns the determination of the social security legislation applicable. Otherwise, it is possible, for example, that a person working in a state other than the one in which he lives, will be subject to two social security systems simultaneously, or be under no protection at all. For instance, state x may provide that people who work in its territory are insured for old-age pensions. State y may provide that people residing in its territory are insured. If a person works in state x and resides in state y, he is covered by the social security system of two countries; if he resides in state x and

---

399   Regulation 1408/71 was published for the first time in OJ 149 of 5 July 1971 and since then it has been revised several times. A consolidated version of Regulation 1408/71 was published in OJ L 28 of 30 January 1997. For the web site of the (non-official, but most recent) consolidated version, *see* http://europa.eu.int/eur-lex/en/consleg/index1.html. See, for an extensive discussion, Frans Pennings, *Introduction to European Social Security*, Antwerp, 2003.

works in state *y* he is insured in neither state. In other words, when a state applies criteria different from those of another state, conflicts of law are likely to occur.

Here exactly was the choice: to choose for the social security law of the state of employment or that of the state of origin. This choice was already made in the beginning of the 1950s. In this contribution I will describe the functioning of this law and the exceptions to it. I will identify the problems and compare them to other approaches for determining the applicable legislation.

2. THE PRINCIPLES UNDERLYING THE RULES FOR DETERMINING THE LEGISLATION APPLICABLE

The rules for determining the applicable legislation have to determine which national social security scheme is applicable. They have to prevent the possibility of no legislation being applicable due to cross border movement. They also have to avoid the situation where more than one legislation is applicable at the same time. These rules are of a compulsory nature and leave no choice for the person concerned between a "better" or "worse" scheme. As a result of these rules, it can happen that a worker is insured under a scheme with less attractive conditions than he would have been in his state of origin or state of residence.

Most rules provide that the legislation of the Member State in which a person is *employed* is applicable. The reason for the choice of the *lex loci laboris* is obvious. First of all, this implies that all persons employed by a certain employer in one state are subject to the same contribution and benefit system as that which applies to national employees. Consequently, employers are not encouraged, on improper grounds, to engage or not to engage foreign workers. The rules prevent, in other words, unfair competition, which would occur if differences in contribution rates were allowed. Competition through the paying of lower contribution rates would soon lead to a general deterioration of benefit systems. A second reason for the principle of the state of employment is that Member States usually make a connection between work and benefit rules. For instance, contribution conditions and rates, the right to benefit and the amount of benefit are usually related to wages.

More recently, some authors claimed that coordination on the basis of the state of employment principle is no longer appropriate, now that more and more social security schemes are based on residence. Eligibility is no longer restricted to employees or self-employed persons.[400] The critics of the state of employment principle argue that the reason why this principle still underlies the Regulation is that the social security

---

400   The conference "From Citizenship to Residence", held in Helsinki from 10 to 12 March 2000, was, for instance, dedicated to this topic. The Proceedings of this conference are published as R. Langer and M. Sakslin (eds.), *Coordinating Work-Based and Residence-Based Social Security* (Helsinki: 2004). See also Anna Christensen and Mattias Malmstedt, "*Lex Loci Laboris* versus *Lex Loci Domicilii* – an Inquiry into the Normative Foundations of European Social Security Law*", *European Journal of Social Security*, 2000, p. 69.

schemes of the Founding States of the EEC in 1957 were to a very large extent based on the Bismarckian model. At the time there were no residence schemes, only work-related insurances. Since then, several schemes – for instance for child care, family benefits and minimum old-age benefits – are residence-based. They conclude that the state of employment principle is no longer suitable as the general principle for the coordination of such schemes.

This approach, however, overlooks the fact that the Regulation was made in order to realise a main objective of the European Community, and later the European Union: i.e. the promotion of the free movement of workers. This must take place within the boundaries of free, but fair, competition. Free movement of workers is meant to realise an optimal allocation of labour which is assumed to be in the interest of the economies of the Member States. In order to achieve this aim, workers must be encouraged to go abroad and this means that they must not be worse off than national workers. In addition, foreign workers must not be more expensive for employers than national workers, as otherwise employers would not be expected to employ them. Nor should foreign workers be *cheaper* than national workers. Otherwise substitution of national workers for foreign workers and unemployment would be the result. It can be expected that in such a case the contribution rates will be lowered in the country of work, and, as a result, the level and conditions of benefit will deteriorate. This phenomenon, which is sometimes called "social dumping", is contrary to a main objective of the Treaty: to improve living standards.

In addition, the development of the Community and later the EU and the move-ment of workers must be seen against the background of huge differences between the Member States. For instance, workers from Italy have often gone to work in the coal mines of France or Belgium. Although since the creation of the Community the situation of the southern states has developed considerably, this phenomenon still exists; workers of the countries which recently entered the Union are also looking for work in a richer Member State.

So far, the state of employment principle has appeared to be useful to coordinate both employment and residence-based schemes. Although the Court of Justice had to solve some problems (*Kuijpers*, *Ten Holder* and *Daalmeijer* are famous examples), ultimately the schemes fit well within the coordination framework.

In 2004 a new Regulation was adopted, which still has to come into force: Regulation 883/2004. This Regulation simplifies the wording of the provisions on the conflict rules, but it maintains the main principle under lying these rules, i.e. the *lex loci laboris*.

3.   THE RULES FOR DETERMINING THE LEGISLATION APPLICABLE

The rules for determining the legislation applicable found in the Regulation have *exclusive effect*. This means that at any given time the legislation of only one Member State is applicable.

Of course, a claimant has to satisfy the conditions of the legislation which is designated as being applicable if he wishes to make a claim under that legislation. To some extent, the Regulation provides assistance in satisfying these conditions, for instance by giving rules on the aggregation of periods of insurance for specific benefits. These rules on aggregation are given in the chapters on the benefits in Title III of the Regulation.

It can happen that, even with the help of the rules for the aggregation of periods of insurance, a person may not be able to satisfy the conditions for benefit under the scheme of the competent state. If he would have qualified for benefit in the country of residence or origin, this cannot help the person concerned. The rules for determining the legislation applicable are inexorable. Differences between the national systems are not removed by the Regulation, as the objective of the Regulation is only coordination and not harmonisation of national schemes.

As a result of the rules for determining the legislation applicable, the country in which a person and his employer have to pay contributions can be decided. The rules are also relevant to decide where the person concerned has to claim benefit. This does not necessarily mean that the whole benefit is received from one country only; the Regulation gives the relevant rules for each type of benefit.

If we concentrate on the contributions, we can conclude the following. The employer and employee are subject to the social security law of one country only: in principle the state of employment. The contributions have to be paid in this country according to the rules of the country concerned.

Of course, we will not discuss all the details concerning the rules for determining the legislation applicable. Here it is relevant to mention that if a person works in two states and he lives in one of these, the rules determine the state of residence as the competent one. This means that the contributions have to be levied also on the income of the first state. The competent state thus receives all the contributions, but is also responsible for the insurance. It means that an earnings-related benefit is based on the aggregation of the two wages.

It is not difficult to imagine that employees and employers can make use of these rules. Suppose that a person living in the Netherlands accepts a job in Belgium, but prefers to (continued to) be insured in the Netherlands. In that case he may accept a job for one day a week in the Netherlands and by doing so the effect is realised. This use of the Regulation can lead to advantages for the persons concerned and their employers (e.g. Czech workers working in Austria can, by using this construction, be cheaper than national workers. The workers will in this example receive lower benefits if they make a claim.

Here it can be seen that the rules of the Regulation do not completely apply the *lex loci laboris* principles and do not prevent advantages as a result of differences in the systems which may even distort competition. In this regard it is irrelevant whether deliberate use is made of these rules or that the rules have an undesired effect.

Also in the case of a person who works in one country as an employee and in the other as a self-employed person the choice between the applicable rules have to be made. In this case the choice is made in favour of the state where the person works as an employee. This can also have implications for the persons concerned: a person working as a self-employed in a country with high contribution levels for self-employed earnings may accept, while continuing to be self-employed, a job as an employed person in another state with low or no contributions for self-employed schemes. As a result he escapes the contributions in the state where he is self-employed. The present Regulation has some provisions which prevent such manipulation of the rules for some countries, and even allow simultaneously application of two systems, but in the new Regulation these exceptions no longer exist.

It can be seen from these exceptions that also in social security sometimes another state than that determined by the *lex loci laboris* is the competent one. From situations in practice it is known that some workers and enterprises make use of the rules in order to escape higher contributions. Since these rules in practice enable such use in border areas only, the effects on the macro level are limited.

4. POSTING OF EMPLOYEES

4.1. Introduction

Another, larger exception to the *lex loci laboris* exists in the case of posting. If the legislation of the state of employment were also applicable to employees who are sent by their employer to work in another Member State for a short period only, the result would be less than ideal. For example, if a Dutch professor of social security law gives a presentation on posting of workers during a conference meeting in Brussels during one day, he would, under the rules discussed so far, be subject to the social security law of Belgium for that day. It would be awkward if he had to pay social security contributions on his Dutch wage for this day in Belgium as this would require many administrative formalities and not lead to any benefit rights. In order to prevent loss of benefit rights in the Netherlands he would ask for voluntary insurance in the latter country.

Therefore an exception is made to the main rule that the legislation of the state of employment is applicable. The exception can be found in Article 14(1) of the Regulation. The posting rules do not assign the social security system of the state of residence as such but the system under which the person was normally insured if he is sent by his employer for a temporary task in another Member State. This need not be the system of the state of residence but, of course, it often it will be the social security system of that state.

4.2. Conditions for Posting: Article 14

Article 14 of Regulation 1408/71 provides that a person employed in the territory of a Member State by an undertaking to which he is normally attached, who is posted by that undertaking to the territory of another Member State to perform work there for that undertaking, shall continue to be subject to the legislation of the first Member State, provided that the anticipated duration of that work does not exceed twelve months and that he is not sent to replace another person who has completed his term of posting.

The Regulation does not define the term "posting". From the conditions mentioned in Article 14 it follows that "posting" means a situation in which an employer sends an employee to another Member State in order to do temporary activities, while this is done for the account of this employer. In Decision 181, the Administrative Commission gives an interpretation of the term "posting" for the purposes of the Regulation.[401] This decision requires an organic link between the sending undertaking and the employed person. This is elaborated in criteria including that the sending undertaking must, among other things, be responsible for recruitment, the contract of employment, dismissal and deciding the type of activities the employee has to perform. These criteria are not exhaustive.

Secondly, it is required that the enterprise concerned is connected with the state of establishment. This means that the enterprise regularly has to perform significant activities in the state of establishment.

Decision 181 contains some rules which must enable supervision of posting. The competent authority of the sending state has to inform the borrowing employer and the employed person "suitably" on the conditions they have to satisfy. The posted employee and his employer have to inform the competent authority of the sending state of certain aspects of the posting.

It is possible that the enterprise where the employed person is posted in turn posts this employee to another employer. Decision 181 provides that the posting declarations do not apply in this case.

Posting is possible for a maximum period of twelve months. If the duration of the work to be done extends beyond the duration originally anticipated, if this is due to unforeseeable circumstances, and if posting exceeds twelve months, the legislation of the first Member State continues to apply for another maximum period of twelve months.

In the case of posting, the employer and employee have to apply for an E 101 form at the competent institutions of the sending Member State. The consent of the host state is not required for the first period of posting. For prolongation, the competent authority of the Member State in whose territory the person concerned is posted must be asked for its consent.

A question which is often raised is whether there must be a certain minimum period between two periods of posting, during which the worker must work for the enterprise by which he is later posted. Article 14 does not answer this question; although given the provisions on the limitation of the duration of posting and its prolongation requiring such a minimum period would be logical.

---

401   OJ 2001 L 329/73.

4.3. The Effects of Posting

Posting is a politically sensitive subject. This is because the result of posting is that the employee concerned continues to be subject to the legislation of the sending state, which means, in particular, subject to the rules on social security contributions of that state. This is attractive for the employee and, moreover, his employer, in particular when contributions in the sending state are lower than those of the state of employment.

The enterprise making use of the posting provisions of the Regulation has, in such a case, a competitive advantage compared to the employers who have to pay contributions in the state of employment. This advantage follows from the rules of the Regulation and is therefore legal.

One problem with posting is that some elements of posting are hard to check: is a person working on a construction site really not sent in order to replace a person who was posted before him? Is the person concerned really self-employed? Is he sent for less than 12 months?

Sometimes allegations are heard that Member States "export" their unemployed by posting as many persons abroad as possible without checking the conditions very critically.

Posting as an exception to the *lex loci laboris* principle is, however, indispensable and the effects of the correct application of the rules have to be accepted. Proposing that the host state must approve of posting in the first period of twelve months is no solution. Such a rule would be contrary to the free movement of persons as Member States might wish to restrict the number of foreign workers in order to protect their own market.

4.4. Posting by a Temporary Employment Agency

Posting may become problematic in particular in the case of temporary employment agencies. Differences in social security contributions may also in this case be the reason to make use of the posting rules. As these agencies may make use of the rules merely to benefit from the differences in contribution rates, this is a special problem. Unfair competition and social dumping are thus a potential problem.

The Court of Justice was asked therefore whether a temporary employment agency can use the posting rules, in particular in the situation where a person has never worked before in the sending state.

In the *Manpower* judgement,[402] the Court ruled that the provisions on posting apply also in the case of an employed person who has not worked in the state where the enterprise is established, but who is recruited exclusively to be sent abroad. In that situation an organic link is required between the undertaking and the employed

---

402   Case 35/70, [1970] ECR 1251.

person. It is also required that the enterprise normally performs its activities in the territory of the first Member State. If they satisfy these criteria, temporary employment agencies can use the posting system set out in Article 14.

In Decision 181 a condition was added to these criteria. In the case of an undertaking whose activity involves the temporary posting of workers to other enterprises, the requirement of the existence of an organic link means that the sending enterprise has, among other things, the responsibility for recruitment, contract of employment, dismissal and deciding the type of activities. This enumeration is not exhaustive.

A temporary employment agency can make use only of the posting rules if it normally posts employees in the territory of the sending Member State. A temporary employment agency is, therefore, not allowed to predominantly or exclusively post employees in another Member State. As a result, a business based, for instance, in the UK which wants to recruit Portuguese workers cannot open an office (a letter-box company) in Portugal, with the sole objective of employing Portuguese workers in the UK by means of this office. It cannot make use of the posting rules of Article 14 of the Regulation in order to benefit from the lower Portuguese social security contributions.

In the *Fitzwilliam* judgement,[403] the Court clarified the criterion that temporary work agencies have to perform substantial activities in the sending state in order to be able to make use of the posting rules.

> Fitzwilliam is an Irish agency for temporary work, which places temporary workers both in Ireland (in all sectors) and in the Netherlands (in agriculture). The workers are engaged under contracts of employment governed by Irish law and are subject to the Irish social security system. Fitzwilliam's turnover during the years from 1993 was higher in the Netherlands than in Ireland. Given the volume of Fitzwilliam's business in the Netherlands, the Dutch benefit administration considered that the workers sent by Fitzwilliam to the Netherlands were wrongly affiliated to the Irish social security system.

The Dutch benefit administration required a service-providing undertaking to have a certain volume of activity in the Member State in which it is established in relation to the activity in the host state in order to satisfy the condition that it has substantial activities in the state of establishment. For this purpose, activities in the same branches of the economy have to be compared, in this case the turnover in agriculture.

The Court considered that only an undertaking which habitually carries on significant activities in the Member State where it is established may be allowed to make use of the posting rules. The competent institution of that state must examine all criteria characterising the activities of that enterprise. Those criteria include the

---

403   Case 202/97, [2000] ECR I-883.

place where the undertaking has its seat administration, the number of administrative staff working in the Member State of establishment and in the other Member State, the place where the majority of contracts with clients are concluded, the law applicable to the employment contracts with the workers on the one hand, and the contracts with the clients on the other, and the turnover during a typical period in each Member State concerned. This list is not exhaustive; the choice of criteria must be adapted for each specific case. However, the nature of the work entrusted to the workers is not one of those. Consequently, in order to determine that the enterprise carries on significant activities it was not relevant that the workers in the Netherlands predominantly worked in agriculture and the workers in Ireland mainly in other areas. Nor was it required that the majority of the turnover has to be acquired in the state of establishment; the criterion is solely that the activities must be of a significant nature. In this case this criterion appeared to be satisfied.

A special rule applies for temporary employment agencies with regard to the calculation of the posting period. The posting provisions apply, in principle, for twelve months. If the employee returns for a short period to the sending state in order to work in that state and subsequently returns, it is straightforward to extend the maximum period of posting (twelve calendar months) by the period of interruption. In the case of a temporary employment agency, where there will often be periods of interruption of posting, this would lead to an extremely non-transparent and complex situation.

4.5. Posting of Self-employed Persons

Self-employed persons can also be posted. The basis for this is Article 14a(1) of the Regulation. This Article reads that a person normally self-employed in the territory of a Member State who performs work in the territory of another Member State shall continue to be subject to the legislation of the first Member State, provided that the anticipated duration of the work does not exceed twelve months. The second section of this provision gives, just as in the case of employed persons, the possibility of extending this period by a maximum of twelve months in the case of unforeseeable circumstances.

The meaning of this provision was questioned in the *Banks* judgement.[404] The dispute was between Mr Banks, a UK national and opera singer, who was engaged by the Royal Theatre in Brussels. Mr Banks resides in the United Kingdom, where he normally works and is subject to the British social security system as a self-employed person. His engagement for the Brussels opera lasted for less than three months in total. The Theatre withheld from his fees contributions due, by reason of him being subject to the general system of social security for employed persons. Mr Banks, however, produced an E 101 certificate issued by the United

---

404   Case 178/97, [2000] ECR I-2005.

Kingdom certifying that he was self-employed and that during the period he worked in Belgium he remained subject to United Kingdom social security legislation in accordance with Article 14a(1)(a). Mr Banks challenged his being made subject to the Belgian social security scheme for employed persons.

The question was whether Article 14a(1)(a) was applicable in this case: this Article refers to "work" performed in the territory of another Member State. How was this word to be interpreted? Work as an employed person or as a self-employed person? Is the system of the sending state or the host state relevant? The German, French and Netherlands Governments maintained that the term "work" refers exclusively to self-employment, given that it is for the legislation of the Member State in which the work is performed to determine its nature (i.e. Belgium, which would mean in this case that the work would be considered as work as an employed person and the posting rules could, therefore, not be applied).

The Court, however, followed the argument of Mr Banks, who argued that the word "work" ordinarily has a general meaning designating without distinction performance of work in either an employed or a self-employed capacity. This means that a self-employed person can be posted even if this is for activities as an employed person. The German and Netherlands Governments had expressed concern that such an interpretation of the word "work" would have serious consequences. It would enable any person to become affiliated to the social security scheme for self-employed persons of a Member State in which contributions are modest, with the sole purpose of going to another Member State in order to work there for a year as an employed person without paying the higher contributions in force in that latter state. The Court put this fear in perspective: the person concerned must be normally self-employed in the territory of a Member State and this obligation assumes that the person concerned habitually carries out significant activities in the territory of the Member State where he is established. Thus, such a person must already have been carrying out his activity for some time at the moment when he wishes to take advantage of the provision in question. Similarly, during the period in which he works in the territory of another Member State, that person must continue to maintain, in his state of origin, the necessary means to carry on his activity so as to be in a position to pursue it on his return. Moreover, the activities in the other Member State must constitute a work assignment, that is to say a defined task, the content and duration of which are determined in advance, and the genuineness of which must be capable of proof by production of the relevant contracts.

These criteria are laid down in Decision 181 of the Administrative Commission. This decision describes the infrastructure which the self-employed person must maintain in the sending state: the use of an office, payment of social security contributions and taxes, possession of a professional membership card, a VAT number, registration with the chamber of commerce or professional organisation (the relevance of the criteria depends on the legislation of the sending state).

According to the *Banks* judgement, self-employed persons can be posted as well as employed persons, whereas it is the sending state which has to determine to which category the person concerned belongs. It would be more logical if the sending state provides for a posting certificate only if a person undertakes activities as a self-employed person in the host state according to its own definition. The broad approach of the Court can mean that the person who starts to work as an employed person is neither insured in the scheme for the self-employed in the sending state, nor is he insured in the system of the host state.[405]

In the *Banks* case, the jobs were exceptional and the result is therefore acceptable. Posting problems also concern, however, other types of jobs, such as construction workers who are sent with posting certificates for a self-employed person to sites in other countries, where the activities are considered as employed person's work. When this type of posting is not restricted, fair competition is at risk. An alternative could be that posting is possible only for activities as self-employed for which the legislation of the sending state is decisive. The choice of the latter law fits in with the other freedom guaranteed under the Treaty: freedom of services. To the advantage of the approach of the Court, it can be said that it is a simple one: it is only relevant whether a person has worked already in the sending state before he was posted and whether the work will last for less than twelve months.

4.6. The Relevance of a Posting Certificate

Workers and self-employed persons will sometimes not take the trouble to obtain an E 101 form, the posting certificate, especially if they work abroad for a short period only. Of course, workers nowadays frequently go abroad for one or two days in order to work there. Probably in the majority of cases of posting they will not take the trouble to obtain a posting certificate.

Fortunately, the posting rules of the Regulation apply once the criteria of Article 14 or Article 14a are fulfilled. Consequently, having a posting certificate is not a constitutive condition for posting. In line with this conclusion, the Court decided that posting certificates can be awarded with retroactive effect (see, for instance, the *Banks* case).

In the *Fitzwilliam* judgement, already discussed in the previous section, the question was raised as to what meaning was to be given to the posting certificate. Is the E 101 certificate binding on the social security institutions of another Member State and for what period? Is it binding until it is withdrawn by the issuing state or can the other Member State declare that it is not binding on the grounds that it was issued on the basis of wrong facts?

The Court considered that the certificate is aimed at facilitating freedom of movement for workers and freedom to provide services. The competent institution has to carry out a proper assessment of the facts relevant to the application of the

---

405   *See* D. Pieters, "An Overview of Alternative Solutions for Overcoming the Problematic Issues of Coordination", in Ministry of Labour and Social Security and European Commission (ed), *The Free Movement of the Self-Employed within the European Union and the Coordination of National Social Security Systems* (Athens: 2001) 127 ff.

posting rules. Consequently, it has to guarantee the correctness of the information contained in an E 101 certificate. It is clear that the obligation to cooperate arising from Article 10 EC would not be fulfilled if the institutions of the host state were to consider that they were not bound by the certificate. In so far as an E 101 certificate establishes a presumption that posted workers are properly affiliated to the social security system of the Member State of establishment, such a certificate is binding on the host state. The opposite rule would undermine the principle that employees are to be covered by only one social security system, would make it difficult to know which system is applicable and would consequently impair legal certainty. As long as an E 101 certificate is not withdrawn or declared invalid, the competent institution of the host state must take account of the fact that those workers are already subject to the social security system of the state of establishment.

However, the competent institution of the Member State which issued the certificate must reconsider the grounds for its issue and, if necessary, withdraw the certificate if the competent institution of the host state expresses doubts as to the correctness of the facts on which the certificate was based – in particular, if the information does not correspond to the requirements of Article 14. Should the institutions concerned not reach agreement on this issue, it is open to them to refer the matter to the Administrative Commission. If the Administrative Commission does not succeed in reconciling the points of view of the competent institutions on the question of the legislation applicable, the Member State to which the workers concerned are posted may at least bring infringement proceedings under Article 227 EC in order to enable the Court to examine in those proceedings the question of the legislation applicable to those workers and, consequently, the correctness of the information contained in the certificate.

5. POSTING ON THE BASIS OF ARTICLE 17

Another important exception from the main rules is laid down in Article 17. This Article states that "two or more Member States, the competent authorities of these States, or the bodies designated by these authorities may by common agreement provide for exceptions to the provisions of Articles 13 to 16, in the interest of certain categories of persons or of certain persons". This provision allows agreements on, for instance, employed persons who are sent by their employer to work in another state for more than twelve months, because of their special knowledge or proficiency, or because of specific objectives of the undertaking or organisation concerned.[406] In many Member States, the competent bodies limit the duration of such agreements to a maximum period of five years.

---

406   The Administrative Commission recommends that competent bodies of the Member States make
        agreements on the basis of Article 17, *see* Recommendation 16 of 12 December 1984, OJ C 273
        of 24 October 1985.

Article 17 can be applied to any person(s) and, as a result, is not limited to employed and self-employed persons. Consequently, the exceptions to the rules for determining the legislation applicable can be applied to any person(s), regardless of whether they perform occupational activities.

Is it possible to make an Article 17 agreement to repair situations with retroactive effect? This may be necessary if the wrong legislation – or if no legislation at all – has been applied to a person and if this has to be corrected. This question was raised in the *Brusse* judgement.[407] The Court considered that Article 17 allows a deviation from the general rules of Title III and that it is up to the Member States to apply it, provided that it is in the interest of the employed person. This includes agreements that have retroactive effect. The decisive criterion is, as we can see in the judgement, whether it is in the interest of the employed person that the agreement is made.

6. REGULATION 883/2004 AND POSTING

The text of the new Regulation provides that a person who pursues an activity as an employed person in the territory of a Member State on behalf of an employer that normally carries out its activities there and who is posted by that employer to the territory of another Member State to perform work on behalf of his employer shall continue to be subject to the legislation of the first Member State, provided that the anticipated duration of that work does not succeed 24 months and that he is not sent to replace another person. This provision is more generous than the present rule and the initial Proposal which mention 12 months.

The new text differs from the present text of the Regulation (Article 14), which refers to the person "employed in the territory of a Member State by an undertaking to which *he is normally attached* who is posted by that undertaking to the territory of another Member State to perform work there for that undertaking". The new text concerns:

> a person pursuing an activity as an employed person in the territory of a Member State and who goes to the territory of another Member State to perform work on behalf of his employer who habitually employs personnel in the territory of the first Member State shall continue to be subject to the legislation of that state, provided that the anticipated duration of that work does not succeed twelve months and that he is not sent to replace another person who has completed his term of posting.

The text of Regulation 1408/71 uses the phrase "normally attached". This term is interpreted as saying that the employer in the sending country must have an "organic"

---

407   Case 101/83, [1984] ECR 1285.

link[408] with the employed person. This provision intends to preclude posting by brass-plate companies (who intend to benefit from lower contributions in the state where they are formally established). The term "normally attached" is missing in the new text and it is doubtful whether these conditions (*see* also those established in the *Fitzwilliam* judgement) still apply when the Regulation no longer uses the term. The new text requires that the employer must habitually employ personnel in the territory of the sending state.

Article 9(2) provides for the opportunity of posting as a self-employed person. This provision concerns a person normally pursuing an activity as self-employed and who goes on to perform the same activity in the territory of another Member State. The new text thus requires the same activities whereas the present text requires "work", which may be of a different type from that which was performed before. The work can also be as an employed person, as appeared from the *Banks* judgement. It is not clear whether the term "the same activity" requires that it must also be self-employed work. The text does not necessarily require so. A requirement of a minimum period of work as a self-employed person before one can invoke this rule is also advisable here.

In general it can be said that the new text does not solve the problems with posting discussed above, including how to check the conditions and interpretation questions, such as how the period must be between two periods of posting of the same employee.

7. COMPARISON WITH DIRECTIVE 96/71

In the case of posting, not only the social security rules are relevant, but also those of the Posting Directive, Directive 96/71 on the posting of workers within the framework of the provision of services. The posting provisions of social security are considerably older than this Directive. The Directive is not relevant to statutory social security provisions. It is, however, interesting to compare the approach of this Directive with that of Regulation 1408/71.

The approach of Directive 96/71 is different from that of Regulation 1408/71. The Directive is an exception to the freedom of employer and employee to chose the applicable labour law, most often the law of the state of origin. The Regulation is an exception to the *lex loci laboris*: in other words, the approach is just the opposite. Moreover, the Directive is limited to particular topics of labour law, in which the law of the hosting state has to be applied. A main example concerns the rules on the minimum wage. As a result, the Directive has no exclusive effect: a posted worker may be subject to the labour law rules of more than one Member State, namely the country of origin and the country of temporary employment. The approach of Regulation 1408/71 is different, as we have seen, as the conflict rules have exclusive effect.

---

408   *See* the *Manpower* judgement and Decision 162, discussed in section 4.4, above.

For the Regulation, the definition of the worker for the purpose of the posting rules, is determined by the statutory social security system of the sending Member State. For the Directive, a posted worker has to be connected with the provision of transnational services of an undertaking established in one Member State to another Member State by posting employed persons to that state. The question of who is a worker is defined by the receiving Member State (Article 2.2). Whereas the Regulation governs posting of both workers and self-employed persons, the Directive is confined to workers. It can be that a person is considered as self-employed for the Regulation and employed person for the Directive. This divergence of the two instruments can cause problems,[409] although the effects are hard to foresee.

Another difference between the Directive and the Regulation is that posting is limited to 12 months in the Regulation (24 months in the new Regulation), whereas there is no maximum period defined in the Directive.

As a result, in labour law the country of origin can play a larger part in labour law than in social security law; the Posting Directive serves as a basis in the labour law position of the worker. This is understandable as the labour law of the state of origin may also be more attractive than that of the host state. In social security, the situation is different: the first phase of coverage by social security means, for the most part, paying contributions and has few advantages (payment of family allowances excluded). Therefore, exclusive effect is essential in social security and the posting rules solve problems for the individual for the short term. Allowing posting for too long as regards social security will cause large problems of unfair competition and social dumping; for this reason these rules are more strict than those of the Directive.

8. SERVICES DIRECTIVE

At the beginning of 2004, a draft Services Directive in the internal market was presented,[410] which introduces *inter alia* the country of origin principle according to which service providers are subject only to the law of the country in which they are established. Member States may not restrict services provided by operators established in another Member State. It therefore enables operators to provide services in one or more other Member States without being subject to those Member States' rules. This principle also means that the Member State of origin is responsible for the effective supervision of service providers established on its territory even if they provide services to other Member States. This is laid down in Article 16. Article 17 allows for derogations from the country of origin principle, necessary in order to take account of differences in the level of protection of the general interest in certain fields, the extent of Community-level harmonisation,

---

409   J. Cremers and P. Donders, *The Free Movement of Workers in the European Union* (Brussels: 2004) 20. *See*, on the Directive, also M. Houwerzijl, *De Detacheringsrichtlijn. Over de achtergrond, inhoud en implementatie van Richtlijn 96/71/EG.* (Deventer: 2004).
410   COM(2004) 2 def.

the degree of administrative cooperation and certain Community instruments. The Directive excludes certain categories, such as the financial sector. For social security it is relevant that it is unclear whether the pension funds fall under its scope.

The Directive allows for certain derogations to the country of origin principle. On page 28 of the draft Directive it is explained that these derogations are provided for in order to take into account the fact that existing Community instruments apply the rule according to which cross-border service provision may be subject to the legislation of the country of destination. Concerning a rule contrary to Article 16 of the Directive, derogations are necessary in order to ensure coherence with this *acquis*. It has to be remarked that thus no fundamental argument is given for the difference.

Such derogations concern, *inter alia*, Directive 96/71/EC (posting of workers) and Regulation 1408/71. In respect to the Regulation, Article 17, No. 9 provides that this derogation is given "concerning the provisions determining the applicable legislation". So the Regulation is not exempted as a whole, but only in respect of the conflict rules. It is not clear yet what this formula entails. Is the role of the state of employment in respect of control and checking of the conditions reduced according to the provisions of the Directive, or are these rules maintained as otherwise the rules of the Regulation cannot be applied properly?

In addition, it has to be remarked that some issues relevant to social security are not excluded from the country of origin principle, such as reintegration obligations and dismissal law. Suppose that a worker can be allowed disability benefit only if he has done his best to find work again or to keep in work despite his illness. Employers have an obligation in this as well, and can buy insurance and make use of reintegration enterprises to fulfil their obligations. Suppose that they make use of foreign enterprises and insurances, then it may be difficult for the competent institution of social security to observe whether they have done the work well and it may be impossible in some cases to impose on the foreign companies the applicable statutory obligations of the host country, which were originally made in favour of the employees. Thus it is preferable that Regulation 1408/71 is exempted as a whole, in order to avoid misunderstandings and to include more exceptions, such as the reintegration services.

The only partial exemption of the Regulation was probably made in order to be able to give special rules on reimbursement of costs of healthcare in the Services Directive. At present the Regulation gives these rules, but their interpretation and application are seriously influenced by case law of the Court of Justice, starting with the *Kohll* and *Decker* judgements.[411] The proposal for a Directive codifies the case law of the Court of Justice.[412]

---

411   Cases 120/95 and 158/96, [1998] ECR I-1935 and I-1871.
412   See "Report on the application of internal market rules to health services: implementation by the Member States of the Court's jurisprudence", Commission Staff Working Paper, SEC(2003) 900, 28.7.2003.

If this is the sole reason for the partial exemption, it can be worded more precisely by the text of the Directive.

9. CONCLUSIONS

In the previous sections I discussed the main principle underlying the rules for determining the legislation applicable. This state of employment principle is still very relevant, as otherwise distortion of competition will be a serious threat. Posting is problematic in the light of this approach. If workers come from abroad and work for lower rates (as lower social security contributions have to be paid) there is distortion of competition. This can lead to higher unemployment of national workers. If this happens on a large scale, it is detrimental to the objectives of the Treaty, such as improvement of living conditions, promoting fair competition and the battle against unemployment.

A reasonable fear for distortion of competition exists, in the first place, in the case of posting, especially by temporary employment agencies and, to a lesser extent, in the case of self-employed persons who wish to escape the contributions for self-employed schemes by accepting a job as an employed earner in a Member State with or without much lower contributions than would be the case for self-employed activities.

With respect to the temporary employment agencies, the Regulation has to be amended in order to make sure that the agencies do not use the advantages of posting as their main weapon in competition. It is doubtful whether a rule can be made for the temporary employment agencies alone as this could be seen as infringing the freedom to provide services. A solution could be that Article 14 is amended so that posting of a worker is possible only after he has been employed by the employer for at least six months. Article 17 can still be used in particular situations if this general rule leads to unacceptable results.

21. THE PRINCIPLES OF THE FREEDOM OF MOVEMENT AND EQUAL TREATMENT IN THE CONTEXT OF THE DISCUSSION ON THE DRAFT SERVICES DIRECTIVE

Chris Engels

1. INTRODUCTION

The freedom of movement of workers in the EU is a fundamental right, alongside other fundamental rights such as the freedom to provide services.

This fundamental right of workers to move and take up employment in other Member States, implies the right of the workers concerned not to be discriminated against and thus to receive treatment equal to the treatment received by local workers of the same employer in the host Member State.

The draft Services Directive, looks at the issues of transnational provision of services and does this from a completely different perspective, namely the perspective of the service provider who wants to come and deliver services in a Member State other than the one it is established in. As a service provider it wants not to be discriminated against and wants to enter the market without any additional hurdles being imposed. The difficulties of guaranteeing equal treatment between service providers are heightened if the service provider is not just a single self-employed provider of services, but is working with its own personnel hired on the local conditions of the country in which the service provider is established. If the service provider has to fully respect all local conditions of employment and regulations in the host Member State, on top of the conditions it needs to respect in the home Member State, it will not really be able to really make use of its freedom of services.

The service provider is entitled to be able to compete in the host market under the same conditions as the nationals of that Member State, without any additional conditions (not applicable to the local players) being imposed. One fundamental question that emerges is whether the workers of the service provider using its freedom to provide services in Member States in which it is not established are entitled to receive the same treatment as the workers of the Member State in which the workers of the service provider are temporarily performing? Is this acceptable under the applicable EC Treaty provisions?

The present contribution will outline the broad principles of Article 39 of the EC Treaty and its non-discrimination principle. It will equally focus on the scope of the Article and will conclude on the applicability or non-applicability of these principles in the case in which cross-border services are provided.

2. THE FREEDOM OF MOVEMENT OF WORKERS AND THE PROHIBITION OF DISCRIMINATION ON THE BASIS OF NATIONALITY

2.1. General Principles

The EC Treaty explicitly states in its Article 39 that "Freedom of movement for workers shall be secured within the Community."[413] It further explains that this comprises the abolition of any discrimination based on nationality between the workers of the Member States as regards employment, remuneration and other conditions of work and employment.[414] This Article is a more particular expression of the general prohibition of discrimination on grounds of nationality laid down in Article 12 of the EC Treaty,[415] which will apply independently only to situations governed by Community law in respect of which there is no specific prohibition of discrimination.[416]

The European Court of Justice (ECJ) has clearly stated that:

> the provisions of the Treaty relating to the free movement of persons are thus intended to facilitate the pursuit by community citizens of occupational activities of all kinds throughout the community, and preclude national legislation which might place Community citizens at a disadvantage when they wish to extend their activities beyond the territory of a single Member State;[417]

The principle of freedom of movement and non-discrimination is reiterated in Regulation 1612/68 of 15 October 1968, on the freedom of movement of workers within the Community[418] in particular in its Article 7.

Article 7 of Regulation 1612/68 provides:

---

413   Article 39,1 EC Treaty
414   Article 39,2 EC Treaty.
415   ECJ, *Commission of the European Communities v. Republic of Austria*, Case C-465/01, 16 September 2004, No. 25.
416   ECJ, *Harald Weigel and Ingrid Weigel v. Finanzlanddesdirektion für Vorarlberg*, Case C-387/01, 29 April 2004, No. 57.
417   ECJ, *Rijksinstituut voor de sociale verzekering des zelfstandigen (RSVZ) v. Heinrich Wolf et NV Microtherm Europe and others*, Joined Cases 154 and 155/87, 7 July 1988, No.13.
418   ECJ, *Commission of the European Communities v. Republic of Austria*, Case C-465/01, 16 September 2004, No. 26.

1. A worker who is a national of a Member State may not, in the territory of another Member State, be treated differently form national workers by reason of his nationality in respect to any conditions of employment, work, in particular as regards remuneration, dismissal, and should he become unemployed, reinstatement or re-employment.

2. He shall enjoy the same social and tax advantages as national workers.

3. He shall, by virtue of the same right and under the same conditions as national workers, have access to training in vocational schools and retraining centres.[419]

The right to equal treatment between workers of the different Member States is clearly guaranteed. Article 39 of the EC Treaty and Regulation 1612/68 are directly applicable in the legal systems of the Member States and have priority over national law.[420] Both direct and indirect discrimination on the basis of nationality are prohibited.

The question still remains as to who is entitled, under the above provisions, to protection as a worker. Who is a worker according to the EU Treaty and to Regulation 1618/68? What are the conditions for their applicability, if any? The answer to these questions is self-evidently of the utmost importance within the discussion on the draft Services Directive.

2.2. Direct and Indirect Discrimination

2.2.1. Introductory Remarks

The European Court of Justice made it clear that the prohibition of discrimination on the basis of nationality is only concerned with direct or face-value discrimination on the basis of nationality:

> The rules regarding equality of treatment, both in the Treaty and in Article 7 of Regulation No. 1612/68 forbid not only overt discrimination by reason of nationality but also covert forms of discrimination which by the application of other criteria of differentiation, lead in fact to the same result.
>
> This interpretation, which is necessary to ensure the effective working of one of the fundamental principles of the Community, its explicitly recognized by the fifth recital of the preamble to Regulation 1612/68

---

419   Article 7, 1-3, Regulation 1612/68.
420   ECJ, *Commission of the European Communities v. French Republic*, Case 167-73, 4 April 1974, No. 35.

which requires that equality of treatment of workers shall be ensured "in fact and in law".[421]

In the particular case (*Sotgiu*) the ECJ defined a difference in the level of separation allowance to be paid to workers whose job was moved to another country. A difference in level and duration of payment was made on the basis of the criterion "residence at the time of taking up employment." The ECJ recognised that the use of such a criterion could in its practical effect be tantamount to discrimination on the grounds of nationality.[422]

Discrimination, so the ECJ furthermore held "can arise not only through the application of different rules to comparable situations", but also through "the application of the same rules to different situations."[423]

A thorough examination of the comparability of the situations may thus be required.

In the *Schumacker* case, the ECJ had to deal with the difference in tax treatment between residents and non-residents. The Court first stated that with respect to direct taxation, the situations of residents and non-residents are not, as a rule, comparable. Consequently, the fact that a Member State does not grant certain tax benefits to non-residents which it grants to a resident, is not, strictly, discriminatory since those two categories of taxpayers are not in a comparable position.[424] The ECJ went on to look at the particulars of the case and considered the position of the taxpayer in the case at hand extremely comparable to the situation of the resident taxpayer. Since there was no objective difference between the situation of the resident and the situation of the non-resident, there was discrimination if different rules applied.[425]

2.2.1.1. Direct Discrimination

The freedom of movement as provided for in Article 39 of the EC Treaty foresees a limited number of circumstances in which a direct distinction based on nationality would be acceptable under the Treaty, as it would not constitute prohibited discrimination. Limitations on the freedom of movement are foreseen for reasons of public policy, public security or public health.[426] Member States need to make

---

421   ECJ, *Giovanni Maria Sotgiu v. Deutsche Bundespost*, Case 152-73, 12 February 1974, No. 11.

422   *Ibid.*

423   ECJ, *Finanzamt Köln-Altstadt v. Roland Schumacker*, Case C-279/93, 14 February 1995, No. 30.

424   *Ibid.*, No. 34.

425   *Ibid.*, No. 21. See also: ECJ, G.H.E.J. *Wielockx v. Inspecteur der Directe Belastingen*, Case C-80/94, 11 August 1995.

426   Article 39,3 EC Treaty.

their assessment with respect to public policy and security issues on the basis of the individual circumstances of each case and not on the basis of general considerations.[427]

Article 39, para. 4, EC Treaty furthermore declares that it is not applicable to employment in the public sector.

The ECJ has made it clear that the concept of public sector in Article 39, para. 4 has a Community meaning and cannot be defined at the level of the Member States.[428] The concept of employment in public service does not encompass employment by a private employer, either a natural or a legal person and this regardless of the duties of the workers concerned.[429]

Since one is dealing with exceptions to the fundamental freedom of movement, these exceptions have to be construed restrictively. The interpretation is subject to control by the Community institutions. [430]

Direct discrimination cases before the ECJ have become far less numerous than a few decades ago. However, even recently some important cases have still come up.

One of the issues under discussion in the famous Bosman case [431] was the application of a rule by the football association under which in matches in the competition they organise, clubs may field only a limited number of professional players who are nationals of other Member States.[432] Since such nationality clauses restrict the chance for such players to find employment in a team in another Member State, the ECJ held the nationality clauses not to be in compliance with Article 39 of the Treaty. "Otherwise that article would be deprived of its practical effect and the fundamental right of free access to employment which the Treaty confers individually on each worker in the Community rendered nugatory".[433]

A recent Italian case in the area of direct discrimination on the basis of nationality dealt with licensing of private security firms and private security guards working in those firms.[434] The guards had to be Italian nationals. This meant that workers from other Member States were prevented from holding employment in Italy as a sworn private security guard. Self-evidently the ECJ came to the conclusion that this was contrary to Article 39 of the EC Treaty.

---

427   ECJ, *Jean Noël Royer*, Case 48-75, 8 April 1976, No. 46.
428   ECJ, *Régina v. Pierre Bouchereau*, Case 30-77, 27 October 1977, No. 33.
429   ECJ, *Commission of the European Communities v. Italian Republic*, Case C-283/99, 31 May 2001, No. 25.
430   ECJ, *Régina v. Pierre Bouchereau*, Case 30-77, 27 October 1977, No. 33.
431   ECJ, *Union royale belge des sociétés de football association ASBL v. Jean-Marc Bosman, Royal club liégeois SA v. Jean-Marc Bosman and others and Union des associations européennes de football (UEFA) v. Jean-Marc Bosman*, Case C-415/93, 15 December 1995.
432   *Ibid.*, No. 115.
433   *Ibid.*, No. 129.
434   ECJ, *Commission of the European Communities v. Italian Republic*, Case C-283/99, 31 May 2001.

An Austrian law that denied non-Austrians from running for elections in works councils and general assemblies of workers' chambers did not pass scrutiny by the ECJ in September 2004.[435] The case was another example dealing with direct discrimination on the basis of nationality.

2.2.1.2. Indirect Discrimination

As indicated above, not only direct discrimination on the basis of nationality is prohibited, but also indirect or covert discrimination. A distinguishing characteristic different from nationality may be used and may in fact lead to the same effect as the use of the prohibited criterion of nationality.

While direct discrimination is deliberate in a sense that it uses the criterion of nationality for distinguishing between workers, in cases of indirect discrimination no such criterion is used. Residence requirements or linguistic requirements have more than once been the object of the ECJ's inquiry into their permissibility.

Once a criterion is used which is not prohibited at face value, i.e. a criterion other than nationality in the context of this paper, but which puts non-nationals at a particular disadvantage, that criterion must aim at achieving a legitimate goal unrelated to any discrimination on the basis of nationality.

Furthermore the criterion that is used for making the distinction must be appropriate and necessary to achieve the legitimate goal. This means that the criterion must really lead to the aim it is supposed to achieve. It must also be necessary in as much as one will have to investigate whether the same purpose cannot be achieved by using a criterion that does not have such a disproportionate impact on non-nationals. Is there, in other words, no suitable alternative available that also reaches this legitimate aim but that has a lesser negative impact on non-nationals? In other words the criterion used needs to be proportionate.[436]

In the case of *Pilar Allué*,[437] the ECJ had to deal with legislation that restricted the employment contracts for foreign language assistants in universities in any event to one year, with the possibility of renewal. In principle, no such limits exist with regard to other teachers. It was noted, as far as the facts of the case were concerned, that only 25% of the foreign language assistants were Italian nationals and thus by definition 75% of the foreign language teachers who were not able

---

435   ECJ, *Commission of the European Communities v. Republic of Austria*, Case C-465/01, 16 September 2004.

436   See for example: ECJ, *H. Meints v. Minister van Landbouw, Natuurbeheer en Visserij*, Case C-57/96, 27 November 1997; ECJ, *Commission of the European Communities v. Hellenic Republic*, Case C-187/96, 12 March 1998, No. 19; ECJ, *Gerard Köbler v. Republic Österreich*, Case C-224/01, 30 September 2003; ECJ, *Brian Francis Collins v. Secretary of State for Work and Pensions*, Case C-138/02, 23 March 2004.

437   ECJ, *Pilar Allué and Carmel Mary Coonan and other v. Università degli studi di venezia and Università degli studi di Parma*, Joined Cases C-259/91, C-331/91 and C-332/91, 2 August 1993.

to obtain an employment contract for an unlimited duration, were non-Italians.[438] The fact that certain nationals may also be negatively impacted does not call into question a finding that a certain criterion works heavily to the detriment of non-nationals.[439] The Italian Government referred to an argument with respect to the proper management of the universities by using one-year contracts only. The ECJ clearly stated that while the Treaty does not prevent measures that are aimed at preserving the proper management of the universities, it still needed to verify whether the measures that were adopted respected the principle of proportionality.[440] When such contracts for a limited one-year period are intended to cover continuous needs, the employment contracts should be concluded for an indefinite period, just as for the other teachers.[441] It is remarkable that the ECJ, when dealing with the "less restrictive alternative", pointed out that:

> if subsequently, the number of students applying for courses in a particular foreign language drops, or if that language is no longer given the same priority in a Member State, or again if the university does not have sufficient funds to provide teaching, surplus foreign-language assistants could be dismissed in order to adjust staff numbers to the new conditions. Such a measure would be less restrictive of the freedom of movement of workers than the contested measure.[442]

The case clearly indicated that the inquiries to be made as far as proportionality is concerned are quite stringent.[443]

Quite a number of the indirect nationality discrimination cases deal with direct taxation issues related to residency requirements, even though direct taxation is an area in which the Community has no powers.[444]

---

438 ECJ, *Pilar Allué and Carmel Mary Coonan and other v. Università degli studi di venezia and Università degli studi di Parma*, Joined Cases C-259/91, C-331/91 and C-332/91, 2 August 1993, No. 12.

439 ECJ, *Kalliope Schöning-Kougebetopoulou v. Frei und Hansestadt Hamburg*, Case C-15/96, 15 January 1998, No. 23-24.

440 ECJ, *Pilar Allué and Carmel Mary Coonan and other v. Università degli studi di venezia and Università degli studi di Parma*, Joined Cases C-259/91, C-331/91 and C-332/91, 2 August 1993, No. 15.

441 *Ibid.*, No. 17.

442 *Ibid.*, No. 18.

443 See also ECJ, *Österreichischer Gewerkschaftsbund, Gewerkschaft öffentlicher Dienst v. Republik Österreich*, Case C-195/98, 30 November 2000.

444 See for example ECJ, *Klaus Biehl v. Administration des contributions du grand-duché de Luxembourg*, Case C-175/88, 8 May 1990; ECJ, *Finanzamt Köln-Altstadt v. Roland Schumacker*, Case C-279/93, 14 February 1995; ECJ, G.H.E.J. *Wielockx v. Inspecteur der Directe Belastingen*, Case c-80/94, 11 August 1995; ECJ, *P.H. Asscher v. Staatssecretaris van Financiën*, Case C-170/94, 27 June 1996; ECJ, *Florian W. Wallentin v. Riksskatteverket*, Case C-169/03, 1 July 2004.

National rules under which a distinction is drawn on the basis of *residence* are liable to operate to the detriment of nationals of other Member States, as non-residents are, in the majority of the cases, foreigners.

> A requirement that nationals of other Member States must reside in the state concerned in order to be appointed managers of undertaking exercising a trade is therefore such as to constitute indirect discrimination based on nationality, contrary to Article 48(2) [presently 39(2)] of the Treaty. It would be otherwise if the imposition of such a residence requirement were based on objective considerations independent of the nationality of the employees concerned and proportionate to a legitimate aim pursued by the national law ...[445]

The ECJ then went on to investigate whether the residence requirement was proportionate. It questioned whether it would be appropriate to achieve the aim and whether it would not go beyond what was necessary for the stated purpose of securing effective action as a manager and being in a position to be served with fines. The ECJ considered the residence requirement to be totally inappropriate. The residence requirement does not guarantee effective action as a manager. It is possible to live inside the country, but at a greater distance from the company place of business than when living just across the border. Asking for a financial guarantee was considered to be a less restrictive alternative as far as the imposition of fines is concerned. The ECJ also referred to an international convention concerning enforcement, in order to show the inappropriateness of the residence requirement.[446]

2.3. Rule of Reason – Non-discriminatory Impediments to the Freedom of Movement

The freedom of movement of workers requires an enforced principle of non-discrimination, both in law and in fact. It entails combating direct and indirect discrimination. For a certain period of time it was questioned whether impediments to the freedom of movement that are applied in a non-discriminatory fashion were equally prohibited by Article 39 of the EC Treaty.

In the *Wolf*[447] decision, the ECJ took the first step in the direction of bringing its principles with respect to the freedom of movement of workers closer to the

---

445   ECJ, *Clean Car Autoservice GesmbH v. Landeshauptmann von Wien*, Case C-350/96, No. 30-31.
446   *Ibid.*, No. 35 et seq.
447   ECJ, *Rijksinstituut voor de sociale verzekering des zelfstandigen (RSVZ) v. Heinrich Wolf et NV Microtherm Europe and others*, Joined Cases 154 and 155/87, 7 July 1988.

principles applicable with respect to the freedom of services.[448] The case dealt with the potential waiver of paying social security contributions as a self-employed worker for those already employed as a subordinate employee. It was undisputed in the case that the rules were applied irrespective of nationality of the persons concerned.[449] Nor was there any indication that the persons that were put at a disadvantage were exclusively or mainly foreign nationals. The ECJ stated that there did not seem to be a case of indirect discrimination. It held that:

> The legislation of a Member State which exempts persons whose principal occupation is employment in that Member State from the obligation to pay contributions to the scheme for the self-employed persons, but withholds such exemption from persons whose principal occupation is employment in another Member State has the effect of placing at a disadvantage the pursuit of occupational activities outside of the territory of that Member State. Articles 48 and 52 of the Treaty [presently Articles 39 and 43] therefore preclude such legislation.[450]

One was thus dealing with an unacceptable impediment to the freedom of movement of workers.

The ECJ was even more explicit in the language it used in *Ramrath*[451] and *Kraus*.[452] The former case dealt with an auditor who wanted to work as an auditor in another Member State. Whether he would take up the work as a worker or as a self-employed service provider was judged not to be important to the case.[453] The latter case dealt with the use of an academic title which was obtained abroad. The ECJ held:

> … Articles 48 and 52 preclude any national measure governing the conditions under which an academic title obtained in another Member State may be used, where that measure, even though it is applicable without discrimination on grounds of nationality, is liable to hamper or to render less attractive the exercise by Community nationals, including those of the Member State which enacted the measure, of fundamental freedoms guaranteed by the Treaty. This situation would be different only if such a measure pursued a legitimate objective compatible with the Treaty and was justified by pressing reasons of public interest … It

---

448   See K. Lenaerts and P. Van Nuffel, *Europees Recht* (European Law) (Maklu) 211, No. 192.
449   ECJ, *Rijksinstituut voor de sociale verzekering des zelfstandigen (RSVZ) v. Heinrich Wolf et NV Microtherm Europe and others*, Joined Cases 154 and 155/87, 7 July 1988, No. 9.
450   *Ibid.*, No. 14.
451   ECJ, *Claus Ramrath v. Ministre de la Justice, and l'Institut des rviseurs d'entreprise*, Case C-106/91, 20 May 1992.
452   ECJ, *Dieter Kraus v. Land Baden-Würtenberg*, Case C-19/92, 31 March 1993.
453   ECJ, *Claus Ramrath v. Ministre de la Justice, and l'Institut des rviseurs d'entreprise*, Case C-106/91, 20 May 1992, No. 24.

> would however, also be necessary in such a case for application of the
> national rules in question to be appropriate for ensuring attainment of
> the objective they pursue and not to go beyond what is necessary for
> that purpose ...[454]

This language corresponds exactly to the ECJ's language in the freedom of services cases. In the absence of discrimination on the basis of nationality it has to be determined whether there is an impediment to the freedom of movement of workers. The impediment is to be understood not only as a real hindrance to that right, but also as anything that makes the exercise of it less attractive. The impediment that is established could be acceptable. This is only the case, however, if a legitimate objective is pursued. Not just any objective, it needs to be one of pressing public interest. Even if such an interest is established it needs to be verified whether the means chosen to serve this interest can really reach that goal (appropriateness) and whether these means are not more restrictive than necessary. The last prong of the test will check for less restrictive alternatives being available.[455]

The need to protect the public from the abuse of foreign academic titles is a legitimate interest that justifies a restriction to the freedom of movement. However, not just any restriction would pass muster. The EC Treaty articles on the freedom of movement do not preclude a Member State from prohibiting one of its nationals who obtained a degree in another Member State from using that title on its territory, provided that the administrative authorisation procedure is easily accessible and does not call for the payment of excessive administrative fees. Certain appeal procedures need to be foreseen in case of refusal and the sanctions for non-compliance with the authorisation procedure should not be disproportionate to the gravity of the offence.[456]

In the *Ramrath* case a number of requirements were imposed in order to ensure compliance with the rules of professional practice. The latter was considered to be in the public interest. Requirements with respect to the existence of an infrastructure within the national territory and the auditor's actual presence appear to be justified in order to safeguard that interest. However, such requirements would

---

454   ECJ, *Dieter Kraus v. Land Baden-Würtenberg*, Case C-19/92, 31 March 1993, No. 32. See also ECJ, *Union royale belge des sociétés de football association ASBL v. Jean-Marc Bosman, Royal club liégeois SA v. Jean-Marc Bosman and others and Union des associations européennes de football (UEFA) v. Jean-Marc Bosman*, Case C-415/93, 15 December 1995, No. 92 et seq.

455   See: ECJ, *Criminal proceedings against Michel Guiot and Climatec SA, as employer liable at civil law*, Case C-272/94, 28 March 1996, No. 13.

"In the circumstances, the questions to be considered are, first, whether the requirements imposed by the Belgian legislation have a restrictive effect on the freedom to provide services; second,if so, whether overriding requirements of the public interest in that area justify such restrictions on the freedom to provide services; and third, if so, whether that interest is already protected by the rules of the State where the service provider is established and whether the same result can be achieved by less restrictive rule."

456   ECJ, *Dieter Kraus v. Land Baden-Würtenberg*, Case C-19/92, 31 March 1993, No. 42.

not be necessary if the auditor concerned is a natural or legal person authorised to practice in the country.[457]

Considerations of a purely administrative nature cannot justify the derogation from a fundamental freedom.[458] The simplification and coordination of the system of levying income tax and social security contributions or the difficulties of a technical nature that prevent other methods of collecting contributions cannot justify the imposition of higher contributions on a worker who transfers his residence to another Member State in the course of a year in order to take up employment there.[459]

It is clear that the test to be applied is the one also applied when dealing with one of the other fundamental freedoms, namely the freedom to provide services. In cases dealing with the freedom of services, the courts are clearly required to verify whether the legislation of the country of origin or the home State does not already sufficiently safeguard the interest the host State is trying to protect.[460]

In a case where an obstacle to the freedom of movement is found that is prohibited by Article 39 of the EC Treaty, it becomes "unnecessary to consider whether there is indirect discrimination on the ground of nationality, liable to be prohibited by Articles 7 and 48 of the Treaty or by Article 7(2) of Regulation No. 1612/68, or to consider the set of presumptions which might apply in that regard."[461] The focus is on whether there is an impediment or not.

---

457   ECJ, *Claus Ramrath v. Ministre de la Justice, and l'Institut des rviseurs d'entreprise*, Case C- 106/91, 20 May 1992, No. 35-36.

458   ECJ, *F.C. Terhoeve v. Inspecteurvan de Belastingsdienst Particulieren/Ondernemingen buitenland*, Case C-18/95, 26 January 1999, No. 45.

459   *Ibid.*, No. 47.

460   ECJ, *Société anonyme de droit français Seco et Société anonyme de droit français Desquenne and Giral v. Etablissement d'assurance cntre la veiliesse et l'invalidité*, Joined Cases 62 and 63/81, 3 February 1982; ECJ, *Manfred Säger v. Dennemeyer and Co. Ltd*, Case C-76/90, 25 July 1991; ECJ, *Commission of the European Communities v. French Republic*, Case C-381/93, 5 October 1994; ECJ, *Criminal proceedings against Michel Guiot and Climatec SA, as employer liable at civil law*, Case C-272/94, 28 March 1996; ECJ, *Syndesmos ton en Elladi Touristikon kai Taxidiotikon Grafeion v. Ypourgos Ergasias*, Case C-389/95, 5 June 1997; ECJ, *Criminal proceedings against Jean-Claude Arblade and Arblade and Fils SARL (C-369/96) and Jean-Bernard Leloup, Serge Leloup and Sofrage SARL (C-376/96)*, Joined Cases C-369/96 and C-376/96, 23 November 1999; ECJ, *Finalarte Sociedade de Construcao Civil Lda (C-49/98), Portugaia construcoes Lda (C-70/98) and Engil Sociedade de Construcao Civil SA (C-71/98) v. Urlaubs- und Lohnausgleichskasse der bauwirtshcaft und Urlaubs- und Lohnausgleichskasse der Bauwirtschaft v. Amilcar Oliveira Rocha (C-50/98), Tudor Stone Ltd (C-52/98), Tecnamb-Tecnoogia do Ambiante Lda (C-53/98), Turiparta Construcoes Civil Lda (C-54/98), Duarte dos Santos Sousa (C-68/98) and Santos and Kewitz Constucoes Lda (C-69/98)*, Joined Cases, C-49/98, C-50/98, C-52/98, to C-54/98 and C-68/98 to C-71/98, 25 October 2001; ECJ, *Canal Satélite Digital SL v. Administrcion General del Estado, and Distribuidora de Television Digital SA (DTS)*, Case C-390/99, 22 January 2002; ECJ, *Portugaia Construcoes Lda, Case C-164/99, 24 January 2002; Wolff and Müller GmbH and Co. KG v. José Filipe Pereira Félix*, Case C-60/03, 12 October 2004; ECJ, *Commission of the European Communities v. Grand Dutchy of Luxembourg*, Case 445/03, 21 October 2004.

461   ECJ, *F.C. Terhoeve v. Inspecteurvan de Belastingsdienst Particulieren/Ondernemingen buitenland*, Case C-18/95, 26 January 1999, 41.

3. PERSONAL SCOPE OF THE FREEDOM OF MOVEMENT

3.1. Concept of Worker

The EC Treaty itself does not define the concept of worker within the context of the freedom of movement. The concept received quite a bit of attention, however, in ECJ case law dealing with the public sector exception of Article 39(4) of the EC Treaty.[462]

In the *Lawrie Blum* case the ECJ reiterates the basic characteristics of the concept:

> Since freedom of movement for workers constitutes one of the funda-mental principles of the Community, the term "worker" in Article 48 may not be interpreted differently according to the law of each Member State but has a Community meaning. Since it defines the scope of that fundamental freedom, the Community concept of a "worker" must be interpreted broadly …
>
> That concept must be defined in accordance with objective criteria which distinguish the employment relationship by reference to the rights and duties of the persons concerned. The essential feature of an employment relationship, however, is that for a certain period of time a person performs services for and under the direction of another person in return for which he receives remuneration.[463]

The worker must be pursuing an effective and genuine performance of an economic nature, in a relationship of subordination.[464] A work relationship in which there is no subordination is excluded. A director of a company of which he is the sole shareholder was therefore not considered to be a worker.[465]

Activities of such small scale as to be regarded as purely marginal and ancillary are excluded.[466] However, the mere fact of working part-time does not exclude a person form the scope of the worker concept.[467] The same holds with respect ot the fact that the employment is of short duration.[468]

---

462 See on the equal notions of worker under Regulation 1612/68 and Article 39 EC Treaty: ECJ, *Maria Martinez Sala v. Freistaat Bayern*, Case C-85/96, No. 32.

463 ECJ, *Deborah Lawrie-Blum v. Land Baden-Württemberg*, Case 66/85, 3 July 1986, No. 16-17. See also: ECJ, *Mario Lopes de Veiga v. Staatssecretaris van Justitie*, Case 9/88, 27 September 1989, No. 13.

464 ECJ, *D.M. Levin v. Staatssecretaris van Justitie*, Case 53/81, 23 March 1982, No. 12.

465 ECJ, *P.H. Asscher v. Staatssecretaris van Financiën*, Case C-107/94, 27 June 1996.

466 ECJ, *D.M. Levin v. Staatssecretaris van Justitie*, Case 53/81, 23 March 1982, No. 12.

467 ECJ, *Claus Ramrath v. Ministre de la Justice, and l'Institut des rviseurs d'entreprise*, Case C- 106/91, 20 May 1992, No. 25.

468 ECJ, *Franca Nini-Orasche v. Bundesminister für Wissenschaft, Verkehr und Kunst*, Case C-413/01, No. 25.

Whether the worker is considered to be a blue or white collar worker under national law, or whether the worker is covered by national labour and employment law, or is a civil servant is of no interest.[469]

In order to know whether a person qualifies as a worker "all factors and circumstances characterizing the arrangement between the parties" must be looked at, "such as, for example, the sharing of the commercial risk of the business, the freedom for a person to choose his own working hours and to engage his own assistants. In any event, the sole fact that a person is paid a 'share' and that his remuneration may be calculated on a collective basis is not of such a nature as to deprive that person of his status of worker."[470] The worker can at the same time be linked to other workers by a relationship of association.[471]

Being married to the director and sole shareholder of the company does not on itself preclude a person from being a worker.[472] Factors relating to the persons conduct before or after the period of employment are not relevant in establishing worker status in the sense of Article 39 of the EC Treaty.[473]

Self-evidently a worker can take up employment in more than one place of work within the Community[474] or can take up work as a worker in one Member State combined with a self-employed status in another Member State.[475]

It should in this context be mentioned that the worker concept as used in Regulation 1612/68 does not have a consistent content in as much as it is clear that for certain provisions the worker will keep his/her worker status even after losing his/her employment, while for other provisions this will not be the case.[476]

A final observation with respect to the scope of Article 39 of the EC Treaty. It has to be mentioned that not only workers but also their employer and future employers may rely on the provision of the freedom of movement of workers. In its *Clean Car Autoservice* decision the ECJ clearly stated these principles:

---

469   ECJ, *Giovanni Maria Sotgiu v. Deutsche Bundespost*, Case 152-73, 12 February 1974, No. 5. See also: ECJ, *David Petrie and others v. Universita degli studi di Verona and Camila Bettoni*, case C-90/96, No. 36.

470   ECJ, *The Queen v. Ministry of Agriculture, Fisheries and Food*, ex parte *Agegate Ltd*, Case C-3/87, 14 December 1989; No. 36.

471   ECJ, *Merci convenzionali porto di Genova SpA v. Siderurgica Gabrielli SpA*, Case C-179/90, 10 December 1991.

472   ECJ, *C.P.M Meeusen v. Hoofddirectie van de Informatie Beheer Groep*, Case C-337/97, 8 June 1999, No. 14.

473   ECJ, *Franca Nini-Orasche v. Bundesminister für Wissenschaft, Verkehr und Kunst*, Case C-413/01, 6 November 2003, No. 28 and 32.

474   ECJ, *Claus Ramrath v. Ministre de la Justice, and l'Institut des rviseurs d'entreprise*, Case C- 106/91, 20 May 1992, No. 25.

475   ECJ, *Rijksinstituut voor de sociale verzekering des zelfstandigen (RSVZ) v. Heinrich Wolf et NV Microtherem Europe and others*, Joined cases 154 and 155/87.

476   ECJ, *Franca Nini-Orasche v. Bundesminister für Wissenschaft, Verkehr und Kunst*, Case C-413/01, 6 November 2003, No. 34 et seq. See also: ECJ, *The Queen v. Immigration Appeal Tribunal, ex parte Gustaff Desiderius Antonissen*, Case C-292/89, 26 February 1991; ECJ, *Maria Martinez Sala v. Freistaat Bayern*, Case C-85/96; ECJ, *Brian Francis Collins v. Secretary of State for Work and Pensions*, Case C-138/02, 23 March 2004.

Whilst those rights are undoubtedly enjoyed by those directly referred to – namely workers – there is nothing in the wording of Article 48 to indicate that they may not be relied upon by others, in particular employers.

It must be noted that, in order to be truly effective, the right of workers to be engaged and employed without discrimination necessarily entails as a corollary the employer's entitlement to engage them in accordance with the rules governing the freedom of movement for workers.

Those rules could easily be rendered nugatory if Member States could circumvent the prohibitions which they contain merely by imposing on employers requirements to be met by any worker whom they wish to employ, which, if imposed directly on the worker, would constitute restrictions on the exercise of the right to freedom of movement to which that worker is entitled under Article 48 of the Treaty."[477]

3.2. Situations Not Purely Internal in One Member State

It is clear that the provisions of the EC Treaty dealing with the freedom of movement of persons cannot be relied upon in purely internal situations within one Member State. The ECJ "has consistently held that the provision of the Treaty on freedom of movement cannot be applied to activities which are confined in all respects within a single Member State."[478]

Nevertheless the Treaty provisions cannot be interpreted in such a way as to exclude a given Member State's own nationals from the benefit of Community law where, by reason of their conduct they are, with regard to their Member Sate of origin, in a situation which may be regarded as equivalent to that of any other person enjoying the rights and liberties guaranteed by the Treaty.[479]

Any Community national who, irrespective of his place of residence and his nationality, has exercised the right to freedom of movement of workers and who has been employed in another Member State falls within the scope of Article 39 of the EC Treaty. The Treaty provisions can therefore be invoked against a Member

---

477   ECJ, *Clean Car Autoservice GesmbH v. Landeshauptmann von Wien*, Case C-350/96, No. 19-21.

478   For example: ECJ, *Union royale belge des sociétés de football association ASBL v. Jean-Marc Bosman, Royal club liégeois SA v. Jean-Marc Bosman and others and Union des associations européennes de football (UEFA) v. Jean-Marc Bosman*, Case C-415/93, 15 December 1995, No. 89; ECJ, *P.H. Asscher v. Staatssecretaris van Financiën*, Case C-170/94, 27 June 1996, No. 32. See also ECJ, *Klaus Höfner and Fritz Elser v. Macrotron GmbH*, Case C-41/90, 23 April 1991, No. 37.

479   ECJ, *P.H. Asscher v. Staatssecretaris van Financiën*, Case C-170/94, 27 June 1996, No. 32.

State of which he is a national where he has resided and has been employed in another Member State.[480]

4. THE GENERAL INAPPLICABILITY OF ARTICLE 39 OF THE EC TREATY TO THE SITUATIONS ENVISAGED BY THE DRAFT SERVICES DIRECTIVE

Making use or having made use of the right to free movement will entitle a worker to the same treatment as local workers, i.e. workers in service of the employer located in the Member State to which the worker has moved or will be moving. Article 39 EC Treaty guarantees that such a worker will receive the same treatment as the other workers working or applying to work for the same employer. This measure intends, the ECJ has held quite some time ago, to protect both the worker who is migrating from another Member State, and the local worker:

> According to Article 48 (2) [presently 39 (2)] it entails the abolition of any discrimination based on nationality, whatever be its nature or extent, between workers of the Member States as regards employment, remuneration and other conditions of work and employment.
>
> The absolute nature of this prohibition, moreover, has the effect of not only allowing in each State equal access to employment to the nationals of other Member States, but also … of guaranteeing to the State's own nationals that they shall not suffer the unfavourable consequences which could result from the offer or acceptance by nationals of the Member States of conditions of employment or remuneration less advantageous than those obtaining under national law, since such acceptance is prohibited.[481]

The above reflects the hypothesis underlying the entitlement to the same working conditions: no discrimination between workers of the same employer and no impediments to taking up such employment. The underlying idea is to protect both the migrating worker who is making use of his right to move and the worker in the host Member State by stating that their access to the labour market in the host state should happen under exactly the same conditions. The same labour and employment conditions apply regardless of the nationality of the worker concerned.

If an employer violates the prohibition of discrimination on the basis of nationality it will be forced to abolish such discrimination by applying the more

---

480   ECJ, *F.C. Terhoeve v. Inspecteur van de Belastingsdienst Particulieren/Ondernemingen buitenland*, Case C-18/95, 26 January 1999, No. 27-29.

481   ECJ, *Commission of the European Communities v. French Republic*, Case 167-73, 4 April 1974, No. 44-45.

favourable rules it applied to its own nationals, also to the group disadvantaged by the discriminatory treatment.[482]

While the exact nature of the relationship as a subordinate worker or a self-employed service provider may not be important in as much as the freedom to provide services and the freedom of movement of workers cover non-discrimination issues in identical terms,[483] it remains very important to make the distinction, especially when cross border services are being provided, thereby making use of the service provider's own workers.

Within the context of the freedom to provide services the focus will not necessarily be on those who eventually do the work, but primarily on the service provider as such. If the service provider works alone he/she will not work in a relationship of subordination, as required for the application of Article 39 EC Treaty. If the service provider works with staff, the workers will be in a relationship of subordination. However, they will not be subordinate to anybody in the Member State in which the services will be provided. The workers of the service provider who spend a limited period of time in another Member State will be performing in the other Member State on account of a service provider established in another Member State without gaining access to the labour market of the host state, since they will return to their home Member State afterwards. The freedom to provide services requires the provision of services of a temporary nature. This temporary nature has to be determined in light not only of the duration of the provision of the service, but also its regularity, periodical nature or continuity. The temporary nature does not preclude the service provider from equipping itself with some form of infrastructure necessary for performing the service in question.[484]

The fact of not getting access to the labour market of the host Member State really seems to make the difference in the ECJ's analysis. In its seminal *Rush Portuguesa* case the ECJ held:

> … it should be observed first of all that the freedom to provide services laid down in Article 59 of the Treaty, according to Article 60 of the Treaty, that the person providing service may, in order to do so, temporarily pursue his activity in the State where the service is provided under the same conditions as are imposed by that State in its own nationals.
>
> Articles 59 and 60 of the Treaty therefore preclude a Member State from prohibiting a person providing services established in another Member

---

482   ECJ, *Kalliope Schöning-Kougebetopoulou v. Frei und Hansestadt Hamburg*, Case C-15/96, 15 January 1998, No. 35.

483   ECJ, *B.N.O. Walrave and L.J.N. Koch v. Association Union cycliste internationale, Koninklijke Nederlandse Wielren Unie et Federacion Espanola Ciclismo*, Case 36/74, 12 December 1974, No. 7:

> "In this respect the exact nature of the legal relationship under which such services are performed is of no importance since such rule of non-discrimination covers in identiacal terms all work or services."

484   ECJ, *Bruno Schnitzer*, Case C-215/01, 11 December 2003, No. 27-28.

State from moving freely on its territory with all his staff and preclude that Member State from making the movement of staff in question subject to the restrictions such as a condition as to the engagement in situ or an obligation to obtain a work permit. To impose such conditions on a person providing services established in another Member State discriminates against that person in relation to his competitors established in the host country who are able to use their own staff without restrictions, and moreover affects his ability to provide the service.[485]

The rules on the freedom of movement of workers could not come into play in case of the freedom to provide services. If these workers seek access to the host Member State labour market, things would be different according to the ECJ. In the case of the provision of services, the workers that come along to do the work, "return to their country of origin after the completion of their work without at any time gaining access to the labour market of the host Member State."[486] Workers employed by an undertaking established in a Member State and who are deployed to another Member State for purposes of providing services there, do not purport to gain access to the labour market of the second State, as they return to their country of origin or residence after the completion of their work, so the ECJ stated.[487] In such circumstances "it follows that Article 48 [presently 39] of the Treaty does not apply."[488]

The ECJ, however, indicated that this statement might not be appropriate for all circumstances and all kinds of service. When the services involved are services such as hiring out of workers, the ECJ may consider the workers concerned to have access to the labour market and thus to some of the provisions dealing with the

485   ECJ, *Rush Portuguesa Lda v. Office National d'Immigration*, Case C-113/89, 27 March 1990, No. 11-12.

486   *Ibid.*, No. 15. See also: ECJ, *Raymond Vander Elst v. Office des Migratins Internationales*, Case C-43/93, 9 August 1994, No. 21; ECJ, *Finalarte Sociedade de Construcao Civil Lda(C-49/98), Portugaia construcoes Lda (C-70/98) and Engil Sociedade de Construcao Civil SA (C-71/98) v. Urlaubs- und Lohnausgleichskasse der bauwirtshcaft und Urlaubs- und Lohnausgleichskasse der Bauwirtschaft v. Amilcar Oliveira Rocha (C-50/98), Tudor Stone Ltd (C-52/98), Tecnamb-Tecnoogia do Ambiente Lda (C-53/98), Turiparta Construcoes Civil Lda (C-54/98), Duarte dos Santos Sousa (C-68/98) and Santos and Kewitz Constucoes Lda (C-69/98)*, Joined Cases, C-49/98, C-50/98, C-52/98,to C-54/98 and C-68/98 to C-71/98, 25 October 2001, No. 22.

487   ECJ, *Commission of the European Communities v. Grand Dutchy of Luxembourg*, Case 445/03, 21 October 2004, No. 38.

488   ECJ, *Finalarte Sociedade de Construcao Civil Lda(C-49/98), Portugaia construcoes Lda (C-70/98) and Engil Sociedade de Construcao Civil SA (C-71/98) v. Urlaubs- und Lohnausgleichskasse der bauwirtshcaft und Urlaubs- und Lohnausgleichskasse der Bauwirtschaft v. Amilcar Oliveira Rocha (C-50/98), Tudor Stone Ltd (C-52/98), Tecnamb-Tecnoogia do Ambiente Lda (C-53/98), Turiparta Construcoes Civil Lda (C-54/98), Duarte dos Santos Sousa (C-68/98) and Santos and Kewitz Constucoes Lda (C-69/98),* Joined Cases, C-49/98, C-50/98, C-52/98,to C-54/98 and C-68/98 to C-71/98, 25 October 2001, No. 23.

freedom of movement of workers.[489] The ECJ seems to consider that some of the activities are specifically intended to enable workers to gain access to the labour market of the host Member State.[490]

However, in general, it could be stated that in case of the freedom to provide services, the workers who will perform the services will not obtain access to the labour market and will therefore not qualify to benefit from the provisions of Article 39 EC Treaty.

The fact that the provision on the freedom of movement of workers of Article 39 may not apply as such, does not mean at the same time that the host Member State in which the services will actually be performed would not be able to impose any rules on the workers who come along to perform the services. Member States can indeed impose certain rules and enforce them in an appropriate way.[491] The Posting Directive clearly illustrates this by even obliging Member States to ensure that workers who are posted to their territory are guaranteed the protection of a nucleus of mandatory rules.[492]

The measures that may be imposed have to pass the "rule of reason test" as described above. The "additional" obligations imposed may clearly not go as far as those that would be required for the establishment of the business in the host Member State.[493]

Also, measures imposed by Member States in furtherance of the Posting Directive have to pass the same test. Pointing out the fact that the Member States have a wide margin of appreciation in the implementation of the Posting Directive, for example with respect to the "appropriate measures to be taken in case of non-compliance",

---

489   ECJ, *Criminal proceedings against Alfred John Webb*, Case 279/80, 17 December 1981, No. 10. See also: ECJ, *Portuguesa Lda v. Office National d'Immigration*, Case C-113/89, 27 March 1990, No. 16.

490   ECJ, *Rush Portuguesa Lda v. Office National d'Immigration*, Case C-113/89, 27 March 1990, No. 16.

491   *Ibid.*, No. 18. See also: ECJ, *Société anonyme de droit français Seco et Société anonyme de droit français Desquenne and Giral v. Etablissement d'assurance cntre la veiliesse et l'invalidité*, Joined Cases 62 and 63/81, 3 February 1982, No.14; ECJ, *Criminal proceedings against Michel Guiot and Climatec SA, as employer liable at civil law*, Case C-272/94, 28 March 1996, No. 12; ECJ, *Criminal proceedings against Jean-Claude Arblade and Arblade & Fils SARL (C-369/96) and Jean-Bernard Leloup, Serge Leloup and Sofrage SARL (C-376/96)*, Joined Cases C-369/96 and C-376/96, 23 November 1999, No. 41.

492   Directive 96/71/EC of the European Parliament and the Council of 16 December 1996 concerning the posting of workers in the framework of the provision of services, OJ L 018, 21 January 1997, 1.

493   ECJ, *Manfred Säger v. Dennemeyer and Co. Ltd*, Case C-76/90, 25 July 1991, No. 12; ECJ, *Raymond Vander Elst v. Office des Migratins Internationales*, Case C-43/93, 9 August 1994, No. 17; ECJ, *Criminal proceedings against André Mazzoleni and Inter Surveillance Assistance SARL, as the party civilly liable, third parties Eric Guillaume and Others*, Case C-165/98, 15 March 2001, No. 23; ECJ, *Portugaia Construcoes Lda, Case C-164/99, 24 January 2002; ECJ, Wolff and Müller GmbH und Co. KG v. José Filipe Pereira Félix*, Case C-60/03, 12 October 2004; ECJ, *Commission of the European Communities v. Grand Dutchy of Luxembourg*, Case 445/03, 21 October 2004, No. 17.

the EJC clearly confirmed that the Member States are hereby required to "at all times observe the fundamental freedoms guaranteed by the Treaty,"[494] including self-evidently the freedom to provide services. The Court then continued by reiterating the rule of reason test. The ECJ applies the test stringently, looking for a genuine benefit for the workers concerned, which significantly augments their social protection.[495]

5. CONCLUDING REMARKS

The freedom of movement of workers is a fundamental freedom. As a fundamental principle it received a wide interpretation by the ECJ. The same holds with respect to the other fundamental freedom to provides services. With respect to the freedom to provide services, the ECJ has diligently protected the freedom against attempts from Member States to impose all kinds of additional obligations on service providers delivering temporary services in a different Member State than the one in which they are established.

In as much as the service provider is delivering its cross-border services with its own subordinate workers who will return to their own country once the temporary services have been delivered, its workers will not gain access to the labour market of the host Member State and would not be able to invoke the principles of the freedom of movement of workers.

The ECJ has clearly stressed that the freedom to provide services cannot be restricted in an effort to protect local employment and markets. It nevertheless equally clearly indicated that upholding fair competition and ensuring worker protection are not necessarily contradictory.[496] However, Member States need to accept that worker protection does not necessarily mean the full application of the national rules to those temporarily performing in their territory.

---

494   ECJ, *Wolff and Müller GmbH und Co. KG v. José Pereira Félix*, Case C-60/03, 12 October 2004, No. 30.

495   *Ibid.*, No. 38. See also: ECJ, *Portugaia Construçoes Lda*, Case C-164/99, 24 January 2002, No. 29.

496   ECJ, *Wolff and Müller GmbH und Co. KG v. José Pereira Félix*, Case C-60/03, 12 October 2004, No. 41.

22. DIRECTIVE 96/71/EC OF THE EUROPEAN PARLIAMENT AND OF THE COUNCIL OF 16 DECEMBER 1996 CONCERNING THE POSTING OF WORKERS IN THE FRAMEWORK OF THE PROVISION OF SERVICES

THE EUROPEAN PARLIAMENT AND THE COUNCIL OF THE EUROPEAN UNION,

Having regard to the Treaty establishing the European Community, and in particular Articles 57 (2) and 66 thereof,

Having regard to the proposal from the Commission,[497]

Having regard to the opinion of the Economic and Social Committee,[498]

Acting in accordance with the procedure laid down in Article 189b of the Treaty,[499]

(1) Whereas, pursuant to Article 3 (c) of the Treaty, the abolition, as between Member States, of obstacles to the free movement of persons and services constitutes one of the objectives of the Community;

(2) Whereas, for the provision of services, any restrictions based on nationality or residence requirements are prohibited under the Treaty with effect from the end of the transitional period;

(3) Whereas the completion of the internal market offers a dynamic environment for the transnational provision of services, prompting a growing number of undertakings to post employees abroad temporarily to perform work in the territory of a Member State other than the State in which they are habitually employed;

---

497 OJ C 225, 30.8.1991, p. 6 and OJ C 187, 9.7.1993, p. 5.
498 OJ C 49, 24.2.1992, p. 41.
499 Opinion of the European Parliament of 10 February 1993 (OJ C 72, 15.3.1993, p. 78), Council common position of 3 June 1996 (OJ C 220, 29.7.1996, p. 1) and Decision of the European Parliament of 18 September 1996 (not yet published in the Official Journal). Council Decision of 24 September 1996.

(4) Whereas the provision of services may take the form either of performance of work by an undertaking on its account and under its direction, under a contract concluded between that undertaking and the party for whom the services are intended, or of the hiring-out of workers for use by an undertaking in the framework of a public or a private contract;

(5) Whereas any such promotion of the transnational provision of services requires a climate of fair competition and measures guaranteeing respect for the rights of workers;

(6) Whereas the transnationalisation of the employment relationship raises problems with regard to the legislation applicable to the employment relationship; whereas it is in the interests of the parties to lay down the terms and conditions governing the employment relationship envisaged;

(7) Whereas the Rome Convention of 19 June 1980 on the law applicable to contractual obligations,[500] signed by 12 Member States, entered into force on 1 April 1991 in the majority of Member States;

(8) Whereas Article 3 of that Convention provides, as a general rule, for the free choice of law made by the parties; whereas, in the absence of choice, the contract is to be governed, according to Article 6 (2), by the law of the country, in which the employee habitually carries out his work in performance of the contract, even if he is temporarily employed in another country, or, if the employee does not habitually carry out his work in any one country, by the law of the country in which the place of business through which he was engaged is situated, unless it appears from the circumstances as a whole that the contract is more closely connected with another country, in which case the contract is to be governed by the law of that country;

(9) Whereas, according to Article 6 (1) of the said Convention, the choice of law made by the parties is not to have the result of depriving the employee of the protection afforded to him by the mandatory rules of the law which would be applicable under paragraph 2 of that Article in the absence of choice;

(10) Whereas Article 7 of the said Convention lays down, subject to certain conditions, that effect may be given, concurrently with the law declared applicable, to the mandatory rules of the law of another country, in particular the law of the Member State within whose territory the worker is temporarily posted;

(11) Whereas, according to the principle of precedence of Community law laid down in its Article 20, the said Convention does not affect the application of provisions which, in relation to a particular matter, lay down choice-of-law rules

---

500   OJ L 266, 9.10.1980, p. 1.

relating to contractual obligations and which are or will be contained in acts of the institutions of the European Communities or in national laws harmonised in implementation of such acts;

(12) Whereas Community law does not preclude Member States from applying their legislation, or collective agreements entered into by employers and labour, to any person who is employed, even temporarily, within their territory, although his employer is established in another Member State; whereas Community law does not forbid Member States to guarantee the observance of those rules by the appropriate means;

(13) Whereas the laws of the Member States must be coordinated in order to lay down a nucleus of mandatory rules for minimum protection to be observed in the host country by employers who post workers to perform temporary work in the territory of a Member State where the services are provided; whereas such coordination can be achieved only by means of Community law;

(14) Whereas a "hard core" of clearly defined protective rules should be observed by the provider of the services notwithstanding the duration of the worker's posting;

(15) Whereas it should be laid down that, in certain clearly defined cases of assembly and/or installation of goods, the provisions on minimum rates of pay and minimum paid annual holidays do not apply;

(16) Whereas there should also be some flexibility in application of the provisions concerning minimum rates of pay and the minimum length of paid annual holidays; whereas, when the length of the posting is not more than one month, Member States may, under certain conditions, derogate from the provisions concerning minimum rates of pay or provide for the possibility of derogation by means of collective agreements; whereas, where the amount of work to be done is not significant, Member States may derogate from the provisions concerning minimum rates of pay and the minimum length of paid annual holidays;

(17) Whereas the mandatory rules for minimum protection in force in the host country must not prevent the application of terms and conditions of employment which are more favourable to workers;

(18) Whereas the principle that undertakings established outside the Community must not receive more favourable treatment than undertakings established in the territory of a Member State should be upheld;

(19) Whereas, without prejudice to other provisions of Community law, this Directive does not entail the obligation to give legal recognition to the existence of temporary employment undertakings, nor does it prejudice the application by

Member States of their laws concerning the hiring-out of workers and temporary employment undertakings to undertakings not established in their territory but operating therein in the framework of the provision of services;

(20) Whereas this Directive does not affect either the agreements concluded by the Community with third countries or the laws of Member States concerning the access to their territory of third-country providers of services; whereas this Directive is also without prejudice to national laws relating to the entry, residence and access to employment of third-country workers;

(21) Whereas Council Regulation (EEC) No. 1408/71 of 14 June 1971 on the application of social security schemes to employed persons and their families moving within the Community[501] lays down the provisions applicable with regard to social security benefits and contributions;

(22) Whereas this Directive is without prejudice to the law of the Member States concerning collective action to defend the interests of trades and professions;

(23) Whereas competent bodies in different Member States must cooperate with each other in the application of this Directive; whereas Member States must provide for appropriate remedies in the event of failure to comply with this Directive;

(24) Whereas it is necessary to guarantee proper application of this Directive and to that end to make provision for close collaboration between the Commission and the Member States;

(25) Whereas five years after adoption of this Directive at the latest the Commission must review the detailed rules for implementing this Directive with a view to proposing, where appropriate, the necessary amendments,

HAVE ADOPTED THIS DIRECTIVE:

Article 1

Scope

1. This Directive shall apply to undertakings established in a Member State which, in the framework of the transnational provision of services, post workers, in accordance with paragraph 3, to the territory of a Member State.

---

501   OJ L 149, 5.7.1971, p. 2; Special Edition 1971 (II), p. 416. Regulation as last amended by Regulation (EC) No. 3096/95 (OJ L 335, 30.12.1995, p. 10).

2. This Directive shall not apply to merchant navy undertakings as regards seagoing personnel.

3. This Directive shall apply to the extent that the undertakings referred to in paragraph 1 take one of the following transnational measures:

(a) post workers to the territory of a Member State on their account and under their direction, under a contract concluded between the undertaking making the posting and the party for whom the services are intended, operating in that Member State, provided there is an employment relationship between the undertaking making the posting and the worker during the period of posting; or

(b) post workers to an establishment or to an undertaking owned by the group in the territory of a Member State, provided there is an employment relationship between the undertaking making the posting and the worker during the period of posting; or

(c) being a temporary employment undertaking or placement agency, hire out a worker to a user undertaking established or operating in the territory of a Member State, provided there is an employment relationship between the temporary employment undertaking or placement agency and the worker during the period of posting.

4. Undertakings established in a non-Member State must not be given more favourable treatment than undertakings established in a Member State.

Article 2

Definition

1. For the purposes of this Directive, "posted worker" means a worker who, for a limited period, carries out his work in the territory of a Member State other than the State in which he normally works.

2. For the purposes of this Directive, the definition of a worker is that which applies in the law of the Member State to whose territory the worker is posted.

Article 3

Terms and conditions of employment

1. Member States shall ensure that, whatever the law applicable to the employment relationship, the undertakings referred to in Article 1 (1) guarantee workers posted to their territory the terms and conditions of employment covering the following matters which, in the Member State where the work is carried out, are laid down:

–   by law, regulation or administrative provision, and/or
–   by collective agreements or arbitration awards which have been declared universally applicable within the meaning of paragraph 8, insofar as they concern the activities referred to in the Annex:
     (a) maximum work periods and minimum rest periods;
     (b) minimum paid annual holidays;
     (c) the minimum rates of pay, including overtime rates; this point does not apply to supplementary occupational retirement pension schemes;
     (d) the conditions of hiring-out of workers, in particular the supply of workers by temporary employment undertakings;
     (e) health, safety and hygiene at work;
     (f) protective measures with regard to the terms and conditions of employment of pregnant women or women who have recently given birth, of children and of young people;
     (g) equality of treatment between men and women and other provisions on non-discrimination.

For the purposes of this Directive, the concept of minimum rates of pay referred to in paragraph 1 (c) is defined by the national law and/or practice of the Member State to whose territory the worker is posted.

2. In the case of initial assembly and/or first installation of goods where this is an integral part of a contract for the supply of goods and necessary for taking the goods supplied into use and carried out by the skilled and/or specialist workers of the supplying undertaking, the first subparagraph of paragraph 1 (b) and (c) shall not apply, if the period of posting does not exceed eight days.
     This provision shall not apply to activities in the field of building work listed in the Annex.

3. Member States may, after consulting employers and labour, in accordance with the traditions and practices of each Member State, decide not to apply the first subparagraph of paragraph 1 (c) in the cases referred to in Article 1 (3) (a) and (b) when the length of the posting does not exceed one month.

4. Member States may, in accordance with national laws and/or practices, provide that exemptions may be made from the first subparagraph of paragraph 1 (c) in the cases referred to in Article 1 (3) (a) and (b) and from a decision by a Member State within the meaning of paragraph 3 of this Article, by means of collective agreements within the meaning of paragraph 8 of this Article, concerning one or more sectors of activity, where the length of the posting does not exceed one month.

5. Member States may provide for exemptions to be granted from the first subparagraph of paragraph 1 (b) and (c) in the cases referred to in Article 1 (3) (a) and (b) on the grounds that the amount of work to be done is not significant.

Member States availing themselves of the option referred to in the first subparagraph shall lay down the criteria which the work to be performed must meet in order to be considered as "non-significant".

6. The length of the posting shall be calculated on the basis of a reference period of one year from the beginning of the posting.

For the purpose of such calculations, account shall be taken of any previous periods for which the post has been filled by a posted worker.

7. Paragraphs 1 to 6 shall not prevent application of terms and conditions of employment which are more favourable to workers.

Allowances specific to the posting shall be considered to be part of the minimum wage, unless they are paid in reimbursement of expenditure actually incurred on account of the posting, such as expenditure on travel, board and lodging.

8. "Collective agreements or arbitration awards which have been declared universally applicable" means collective agreements or arbitration awards which must be observed by all undertakings in the geographical area and in the profession or industry concerned.

In the absence of a system for declaring collective agreements or arbitration awards to be of universal application within the meaning of the first subparagraph, Member States may, if they so decide, base themselves on:

- collective agreements or arbitration awards which are generally applicable to all similar undertakings in the geographical area and in the profession or industry concerned, and/or
- collective agreements which have been concluded by the most representative employers' and labour organisations at national level and which are applied throughout national territory,

provided that their application to the undertakings referred to in Article 1 (1) ensures equality of treatment on matters listed in the first subparagraph of paragraph 1 of this Article between those undertakings and the other undertakings referred to in this subparagraph which are in a similar position.

Equality of treatment, within the meaning of this Article, shall be deemed to exist where national undertakings in a similar position:

–   are subject, in the place in question or in the sector concerned, to the same obligations as posting undertakings as regards the matters listed in the first subparagraph of paragraph 1, and
–   are required to fulfil such obligations with the same effects.

9. Member States may provide that the undertakings referred to in Article 1 (1) must guarantee workers referred to in Article 1 (3) (c) the terms and conditions which apply to temporary workers in the Member State where the work is carried out.

10. This Directive shall not preclude the application by Member States, in compliance with the Treaty, to national undertakings and to the undertakings of other States, on a basis of equality of treatment, of:

–   terms and conditions of employment on matters other than those referred to in the first subparagraph of paragraph 1 in the case of public policy provisions,
–   terms and conditions of employment laid down in the collective agreements or arbitration awards within the meaning of paragraph 8 and concerning activities other than those referred to in the Annex.

Article 4

Cooperation on information

1. For the purposes of implementing this Directive, Member States shall, in accordance with national legislation and/or practice, designate one or more liaison offices or one or more competent national bodies.

2. Member States shall make provision for cooperation between the public authorities which, in accordance with national legislation, are responsible for monitoring the terms and conditions of employment referred to in Article 3. Such cooperation shall in particular consist in replying to reasoned requests from those authorities for information on the transnational hiring-out of workers, including manifest abuses or possible cases of unlawful transnational activities.

The Commission and the public authorities referred to in the first subparagraph shall cooperate closely in order to examine any difficulties which might arise in the application of Article 3 (10).

Mutual administrative assistance shall be provided free of charge.

3. Each Member State shall take the appropriate measures to make the information on the terms and conditions of employment referred to in Article 3 generally available.

4. Each Member State shall notify the other Member States and the Commission of the liaison offices and/or competent bodies referred to in paragraph 1.

Article 5

Measures

Member States shall take appropriate measures in the event of failure to comply with this Directive.

They shall in particular ensure that adequate procedures are available to workers and/or their representatives for the enforcement of obligations under this Directive.

Article 6

Jurisdiction

In order to enforce the right to the terms and conditions of employment guaranteed in Article 3, judicial proceedings may be instituted in the Member State in whose territory the worker is or was posted, without prejudice, where applicable, to the right, under existing international conventions on jurisdiction, to institute proceedings in another State.

Article 7

Implementation

Member States shall adopt the laws, regulations and administrative provisions necessary to comply with this Directive by 16 December 1999 at the latest. They shall forthwith inform the Commission thereof.

When Member States adopt these provisions, they shall contain a reference to this Directive or shall be accompanied by such reference on the occasion of their official publication. The methods of making such reference shall be laid down by Member States.

Article 8

Commission review

By 16 December 2001 at the latest, the Commission shall review the operation of this Directive with a view to proposing the necessary amendments to the Council where appropriate.

Article 9

This Directive is addressed to the Member States.

Done at Brussels, 16 December 1996.
For the European Parliament
The President
K. HÄNSCH
For the Council
The President
I. YATES

ANNEX

The activities mentioned in Article 3 (1), second indent, include all building work relating to the construction, repair, upkeep, alteration or demolition of buildings, and in particular the following work:

1.   excavation
2.   earthmoving
3.   actual building work
4.   assembly and dismantling of prefabricated elements
5.   fitting out or installation
6.   alterations
7.   renovation
8.   repairs
9.   dismantling
10.   demolition
11.   maintenance
12.   upkeep, painting and cleaning work
13.   improvements.

23. COMMUNICATION FROM THE COMMISSION TO THE COUNCIL, THE EUROPEAN PARLIAMENT, THE ECONOMIC AND SOCIAL COMMITTEE AND THE COMMITTEE OF THE REGIONS – THE IMPLEMENTATION OF DIRECTIVE 96/71/EC IN THE MEMBER STATES

COMMISSION COMMUNICATION ON THE IMPLEMENTATION OF DIRECTIVE 96/71/EC

1. INTRODUCTION

Directive 96/71/EC of the European Parliament and of the Council concerning the posting of workers in the framework of the provision of services was adopted on 16 December 1996. It aims to abolish the obstacles and uncertainties that impede implementation of the freedom to supply services, by improving legal certainty and facilitating identification of the employment conditions that apply to workers temporarily employed in a Member State other than the Member State whose legislation governs the employment relationship. It endeavours to strike a balance between the economic freedoms bestowed by the EC Treaty and employees' rights during their period of posting.

Since the Directive is a supranational legal instrument whose transposal in one Member State directly affects employers and workers in other countries, the manner in which it is actually implemented is particularly important for all Member States. Article 8 provides that the Commission shall review the operation of the Directive with a view to proposing the necessary amendments to the Council where appropriate.

In preparation for this review, the Commission services have taken a number of steps: the first was to draft a report on the transposal of the Directive in the 15 Member States, designed to ascertain the present situation as regards national legislations and collective agreements. At the same time, the national administrations were sent a questionnaire asking them to describe the practicalities of applying the Directive and any difficulties encountered. The results of the transposal study and the replies to the questionnaire were discussed by a group of government experts.

The purpose of this Communication is to draw the conclusions from all this preparatory work concerning the transposal and practical implementation of Directive 96/71/EC in the Member States, and to define the Commission's position as to whether the 1996 Directive needs revising.

The Communication does not seek to judge the compatibility with the Directive and the Treaty of the national transposing measures mentioned herein, nor does it prejudge what position the Commission will take in its monitoring of the application of Community law.

2. DIRECTIVE 96/71/EC – ITS CONTEXT IN COMMUNITY LAW, ITS KEY CONTENT AND ITS ADDED VALUE

2.1. The Context of the Directive

With the achievement of the single market, in particular as regards freedom to supply services between Member States, a new form of worker mobility has emerged, quite distinct from the mobility of migrant workers explicitly addressed in the EC Treaty and in secondary legislation concerning the free movement of workers. The dynamic environment created by the single market, with its economic freedoms, is encouraging undertakings to develop their transnational activities and increasingly to provide transnational services. The situation of employees posted temporarily to another Member State to perform work under a service contract on behalf of their employer has raised all sorts of legal questions.

As these are transnational situations, questions often arise as to which law is applicable to the employment relationship. On this subject, the Convention of Rome of 19 June 1980 on the law applicable to contractual obligations[502] provides, as a general rule, for freedom of choice as regards the law applicable by the parties. In the absence of choice, the employment contract is governed, pursuant to Article 6(2), by the law of the country in which the employee habitually carries out his work, even if he is temporarily employed in another country. If the employee does not habitually carry out his work in any one country, the law applicable is that of the country in which the place of business through which he was engaged is situated, unless it appears from the circumstances as a whole that the contract is more closely connected with another country. According to Article 6(1) of the Convention, the choice of law made by the parties must not have the result of depriving the employee of the protection afforded to him by the mandatory rules of the law which would be applicable under paragraph 2 of that Article in the absence of choice. Article 7 provides that, under certain conditions, effect may be given,

---

502   OJ L 266 of 9.10.1980, p. 1.

concurrently with the law declared applicable, to the mandatory rules of the law of another country, in particular those of the Member State within whose territory the worker is temporarily posted.

As regards posted workers within the context of the EC Treaty, the Court of Justice has been requested on several occasions to clarify their situation in the context of the freedom to supply services as referred to in Article 49 of the Treaty. In a number of cases the Court of Justice has taken the opportunity to develop criteria, first and foremost to distinguish between freedom to supply services and freedom of movement of workers. On this point, the Court has emphasised that – unlike migrant workers – posted workers who are sent to another country to perform a service return to their country of origin after completing their mission, without at any time joining the labour market of the host Member State. Given this specific situation, the rules of primary and secondary Community law devised for migrant workers would not therefore resolve the specific problems of posting. In particular, as regards the employment conditions applicable during the period of posting, the Court has recognised that Community law does not preclude Member States from extending their legislation, or collective labour agreements entered into by both sides of industry, to any person who is employed, even temporarily, within their territory, no matter in which country the employer is established, on condition that the rules of the EC Treaty, and in particular Article 49 are complied with.[503]

In order to facilitate the free movement of services it was deemed necessary and advisable to coordinate the laws of the Member States affected by this Court of Justice case law and thus lay down, at Community level, a nucleus of mandatory minimum protection rules to be observed in the host country by employers who post workers to perform temporary work in the territory of the Member State where the services are provided. Directive 96/71/EC concerning the posting of workers, which is based on Articles 47 (ex 57), paragraph 2 and 55 (ex 66) of the EC Treaty establishes this Community catalogue of minimum rules deemed mandatory. This Directive takes account of the specific situation of posted workers and ties in with the legal context outlined above.

It should be stressed that the Directive's scope does not extend to social security; the provisions applicable with regard to benefits and social security contributions are those laid down by Council Regulation (EEC) No. 1408/71 of 14 June 1971.[504]

---

503   Judgement of 3 February 1982, *Seco and Desquenne*, point 14, 62/81 and 63/81, ECR p. 223;
      Judgement of 27 March 1990, *Rush Portuguesa*, point 18, C-113/89, ECR I-01417
504   OJ L 149 of 5.7.1971

2.2. The Key Content of the Directive

The Directive applies to undertakings which post workers to work temporarily in a Member State other than the State whose laws govern the employment relationship. It covers three transnational posting situations, namely:

–   posting under a contract concluded between the undertaking making the posting and the party for whom the services are intended,
–   posting to an establishment or an undertaking owned by the group,
–   posting by a temporary employment undertaking to a user undertaking operating in a Member State other than that of the undertaking making the posting,

with the proviso, in all three situations, that there is an employment relationship between the undertaking making the posting and the posted worker.

Undertakings established in a non-Member State must not be given more favourable treatment than undertakings established in a Member State. In this context, Recital 20 of the Directive indicates that the Directive does not affect either the agreements concluded by the Community with third countries or the laws of Member States concerning the access to their territory of third-country providers of services. The Directive is also without prejudice to national laws relating to the entry, residence and access to employment of third-country workers.

Whatever the law applicable to the employment relationship, the Directive seeks to guarantee that posted workers will enjoy the application of certain minimum protective provisions in force in the Member State to which they are posted. To this end, Article 3(1) of the Directive lays down the mandatory rules to be observed by employers during the period of posting in regard to the following issues: maximum work periods and minimum rest periods; minimum paid annual holidays; minimum rates of pay; the conditions of hiring-out of workers, in particular the supply of workers by temporary employment undertakings; health, safety and hygiene at work; and protective measures with regard to the terms and conditions of employment of pregnant women or women who have recently given birth, of children and of young people. These rules must be laid down by the legislations of the host country and/or by collective agreements or arbitration awards which have been declared universally acceptable in the case of activities in the building work sector, while Member States are left the choice of imposing such rules laid down by collective agreements in the case of activities other than building work. They may also, in compliance with the Treaty, impose the application of terms and conditions of employment on matters other than those referred to in the Directive in the case of public policy provisions.

For the purposes of implementing the Directive, Member States must designate liaison offices and make provision for administrative cooperation regarding the provision of information. The Directive also contains a jurisdiction clause which states that judicial proceedings may be instituted in the Member State in whose territory the worker is or was posted, without prejudice to the right, under existing international conventions on jurisdiction, to institute proceedings in another State.

2.3. The Added Value of the Directive

2.3.1. What Does This Directive Add as regards Private International Law?

2.3.1.1. The Rome Convention

The Rome Convention lays down the general criteria for determining the law applicable to contractual obligations. It also permits the judge – exceptionally – to set aside the law that would normally be applicable to the contract and instead apply the mandatory rules within the meaning of private international law ["règles impératives", also known in French as "lois d'application immédiate" or "lois de police"] that obtain at the place where the work is carried out (Article 7). These mandatory rules are not defined by the Rome Convention. Directive 96/71 designates at Community level mandatory rules within the meaning of Article 7 of the Rome Convention in transnational posting situations. These rules thus constitute a nucleus of minimum protection for posted workers, while respecting the principle of equality of treatment between national and non-national providers of services (Article 49 of the EC Treaty) and between national and non-national workers.

The choice-of-law rules provided for by the Rome Convention for determining the law applicable offer a general legal framework, whereas the Directive specifically concerns the situation of posted workers and is thus able to refine this legal framework.

The Directive in no way seeks to amend the law applicable to the employment contract, but it lays down a number of mandatory rules to be observed during the period of posting in the host Member State, "whatever the law applicable to the employment relationship".

2.3.1.2. Jurisdiction

Council Regulation (EC) No. 44/2001 of 22 December 2000 on jurisdiction and the recognition and enforcement of judgements in civil and commercial matters[505] establishes Community rules on jurisdiction and the recognition of judgements in civil and commercial matters. With regard to individual employment contracts, Article 19 of this Regulation provides that an employer domiciled in a Member

---

505 OJ L 012 of 16.01.2001, p. 1.

State may be sued in the courts of the Member State where he is domiciled, or in another Member State in the courts for the place where the employee habitually carries out his work or in the courts for the last place where he habitually carried out his work. This rule thus introduces, in the worker's favour, an exemption from the general principle that judicial proceedings against persons domiciled in the territory of a Member State must be instituted in that same Member State.

Article 6 of Directive 96/71/EC adds to these rules, in favour of posted workers employed temporarily in another Member State, a new specific jurisdiction clause tailored to the specific situation in which posted workers find themselves. In order to allow the right to the terms and conditions of employment guaranteed in Article 3 of the Directive to be enforced, Article 6 provides that judicial proceedings may be instituted in the Member State in whose territory the worker is or was posted.

This clause constitutes a provision governing a specific matter, as authorised by Article 67 of Regulation 44/2001, and is without prejudice to the right to institute judicial proceedings in another State pursuant to the above-mentioned provisions of the Regulation or pursuant to international conventions on the subject of jurisdiction.

2.3.1.3. What Does This Directive Add as regards the Court's Case Law?

The Court of Justice has held that Community law does not preclude Member States from extending their legislation, or collective labour agreements entered into by both sides of industry, to any person who is employed, even temporarily, within their territory, no matter in which country the employer is established. This case law thus makes it possible for Member States to extend, in compliance with the Treaty, certain rules to employees posted on their territory, whereas the Directive makes it obligatory to guarantee that certain mandatory rules concerning the terms and conditions of employment of posted workers are observed.

In addition, the case law does not specify the legislative provisions or collective labour agreements in question. The Directive therefore seeks to coordinate Member States' laws with a view to compiling a list of the mandatory rules which undertakings posting workers temporarily to another country must observe in the host country. It does not harmonise the material content of the rules categorised as "mandatory", but it identifies them and makes them binding on undertakings posting workers to a Member State other than the State in whose territory these workers habitually work.

3. THE IMPLEMENTATION OF THE DIRECTIVE IN THE MEMBER STATES

3.1. The Key Legislative Provisions (Articles 1 to 3)

Even before Directive 96/71/EC was adopted, several Member States had already established their own national legislation concerning the posting of workers in connection with the transnational provision of services. These include Germany,[506] Austria[507] and France.[508] When the Directive was finally adopted, these States adapted their legislations to bring them into line with the requirements of the Community Directive.[509]

More conventionally, other Member States, such as Spain,[510] Denmark,[511] Finland,[512] Greece,[513] Italy,[514] the Netherlands,[515] Portugal,[516] Sweden,[517] Belgium[518] and Luxembourg,[519] transposed the Directive by passing laws after the Community instrument was adopted.

All the Member States oblige undertakings established abroad and posting workers to their territory to observe their transposition legislation. The principle whereby undertakings established in a non-Member State must not be given more favourable treatment than Community undertakings is observed.

In Ireland, no specific measure transposing the Directive has been adopted, but a provision contained in the Protection of Employees (Part-Time Work) Act, transposing another Community Directive, clarifies that certain provisions of Irish law apply to posted workers in Ireland.

---

506 Law of 26 February 1996 on the posting of workers

507 *Bundesgesetzblatt I* 1995/895.

508 Law of 20 December 1993 and Implementing Decree of 11 July 1994.

509 Cf. in Germany, the Law of 19 December 1998 amending the Law of 26 February 1996 on the posting of workers; in Austria, adaptation of the AVRAG which entered into force on 1 October 1999; in France, the decrees of 4 September and 29 May 2000, amending the provisions of the French Labour Code relating to postings in connection with the international provision of services.

510 Law 45/1999 of 29 November 1999.

511 Law No. 933 of 15 December 1999, which entered into force on 17 December 1999.

512 Law 1146/1999, which entered into force on 16 December 1999, subsequently amended by Law 74/2001 of 26 January 2001 to take account of the adoption of a new law on labour agreements.

513 Presidential Decree No. 219 of 28 August 2000, which entered into force on 31 August 2000.

514 Legislative Decree No. 72 of 25 February 2000.

515 Law of 2 December 1999, which entered into force on 23 December 1999.

516 Law 9/2000 of 15 June 2000.

517 Law 1999:678, which entered into force on 16 December 1999.

518 Law of 5 March 2002 (*Moniteur belge* of 13.03.02) and Royal Decree of 29.03.2002 (*Moniteur belge* of 17.04.02)

519 Posting of workers and monitoring the implementation of labour law, Law of 20 December 2002, *Recueil de législations* A-No. 154, 31 December 2002.

In the United Kingdom, it was not deemed necessary to adopt a specific Act to transpose the Directive, since UK law applies to all employees regardless of their situation. The UK has simply amended certain more restrictive texts in order to extend their scope to posted workers.

Most Member States have defined, in their legislation, the posted worker situations covered by the Directive, and some have adopted the Directive's definitions word for word. Some legislations have also adopted the Directive's definition of "posted worker", while in other Member States the content of the concept of "posted worker" derives from the relevant legislation as a whole.

As regards determining which terms and conditions of employment established by legislative provisions apply to posted workers, the Member States fall into three categories:

–   some Member States have essentially reproduced the terms of the Directive, without indicating to which provisions of their national legislation the matters covered by the Directive correspond;

–   others have sought to identify the applicable national provisions and have inserted references to these national provisions;

–   two Member States have not adopted any specific transposition legislation concerning the national provisions applicable to posted workers; one of them has simply adopted a single provision making it clear that its labour legislation applies to workers posted on its territory.

The question of the applicability of collective agreements is particularly important, since wages are chiefly determined by collective bargaining. Most Member States' legislations provide for the application or extension of universally applicable collective agreements to posted workers. Some Member States do not have universally applicable collective agreements. Consequently, the only rules that these States apply to posted workers are those contained in the law or in other legislative texts.

As regards the exception, the derogation options and the other options provided for by the Directive, the situation can be summarised as follows:

Not all Member States have adopted the exception for assembly work – excluding activities in the field of building work – that does not exceed eight days (Article 3(2)). It should be remembered, however, that this exception does not apply to the activities in the field of building work listed in the Annex to the Directive.

Most Member States have not made use of the derogation options offered in the Directive (Article 3(3), 3(4) and 3(5)). Two Member States have combined the exception for assembly work with all the derogation options in such a way as to render their transposition legislation inapplicable to postings that do not exceed eight days.

Several Member States have made use of the option provided for in Article 3(10), first indent, of applying to the undertakings concerned terms and conditions of employment other than those referred to in Article 3 of the Directive.

Pursuant to Article 3(10), second indent, the terms and conditions of employment of the host State as laid down in universally applicable collective agreements or arbitration awards, and concerning activities other than those referred to in the Annex,[520] may be imposed on national undertakings and undertakings from other States on a basis of equality of treatment.

The following Member States have made use of this extension option: Austria, Belgium, Spain, Finland, France, Greece, Italy, Portugal and Luxembourg. In these countries, all sectors are covered.

In Germany, the extension of collectively agreed terms and conditions of employment to activities other than building work is limited to services to assist maritime navigation, as regards minimum pay, duration of paid leave, holiday pay and the additional holiday bonus. In the Netherlands, application of collectively agreed terms and conditions of employment is limited to the activities listed in the Annex to the Directive. In Denmark, the United Kingdom and Sweden, which do not have universally applicable collective agreements, this option does not apply.

3.2. The Implementation of Cooperation on Information (Article 4)

Article 4 of Directive 96/71/EC obliges Member States to designate one or more liaison offices or national bodies and to notify these to the other Member States. Article 4 also provides for cooperation between the public authorities responsible for monitoring the terms and conditions of employment referred to in Article 3 of the Directive.

Three different types of cooperation on information are mentioned in Article 4: cooperation between the public authorities responsible for monitoring the terms and conditions of employment referred to in the Directive; cooperation to examine any difficulties which might arise in the application of Article 3(10); and cooperation to ensure that the information on the terms and conditions of employment is generally available.

Interested parties need to have advance information about the terms and conditions of employment applicable in the host country in order for them to be able to perform the services required and comply with the mandatory provisions applicable to employees during their period of posting. The temporary nature of posting and the concomitant clashes between different Member States' legal systems can make it difficult to apply the provisions resulting from the transposal of the Directive and to monitor observance of these provisions. The administrative cooperation which

---

520 The Annex mentions all building work relating to the construction, repair, upkeep, alteration or demolition of buildings, and in particular the following work: excavation, earthmoving, actual building work, assembly and dismantling of prefabricated elements, fitting out or installation, alterations, renovation, repairs, dismantling, demolition, maintenance, upkeep, painting and cleaning work, improvements.

the Directive provides for between Member States in this context is therefore especially important.

All Member States have designated bodies to ensure the cooperation provided for by the Directive. These are generally the responsible departments of the relevant Ministries, the Labour Inspectorate or employment offices.

In order to facilitate access to information on the terms and conditions of employment applicable, a good few Member States have produced brochures or vademecums, which are also available on their websites.

3.3. Measures Designed to Ensure Compliance with the Directive (Articles 5 and 6)

Two types of measures are used by Member States to ensure compliance with the provisions of the Directive: measures to monitor the legality of postings and measures to penalise possible irregularities ascertained.

Besides the usual inspections of undertakings or workplaces, certain States have adopted two other types of methods to facilitate monitoring of compliance with the transposition rules: the keeping of records at the place where the services are provided and the declaration of the provision of services to the national authorities.

As regards penalties, some Member States have not introduced any new penalties to cover posting situations. In these countries, the remedies and penalties applicable are the same as those applicable under domestic law.

As required by Article 6 of the Directive, most of the Member States have made it possible to institute judicial proceedings in their territory when a worker is or has been posted there, in order to allow enforcement of the right to the terms and conditions of employment guaranteed by the Directive. This jurisdiction of the courts of the country of posting is recognised either in the legal instruments transposing the Directive or in the codes of procedure in force. Two countries have not introduced explicit provisions entitling posted workers to institute proceedings in the courts of the country of posting.

4. ASSESSMENT OF THE SITUATION

4.1. Transposition of the Directive in the Member States

According to studies by independent experts, transposition of the Directive by the Member States has, generally speaking, been satisfactory. However, the Commission would like to mention three categories of transposition problems encountered in certain Member States.

4.1.1. The Method

The Commission considers that the method used in the two countries which have not adopted a specific transposal instrument (see 3.1. above) needs to be assessed in the light of the criteria established by the Court of Justice in cases C-365/93[521] and C-144/99.[522] In these two cases the Court pointed out that it is settled law that "whilst legislative action on the part of each Member State is not necessarily required in order to implement a Directive, it is essential for national law to guarantee that the national authorities will effectively apply the Directive in full, that the legal position under national law should be sufficiently precise and clear and that individuals are made fully aware of their rights and, where appropriate, may rely on them before the national courts." The Court added that this last condition is of particular importance where the Directive in question is intended to accord rights to nationals of other Member States (*Commission v. Greece*, Case 365/93, point 9 and *Commission v. The Netherlands*, Case 144/99, point 18).

It should be pointed out that in these two countries, the posting situations covered and the rights deriving from the provisions of the Directive are not clearly defined and the jurisdiction clause contained in Article 6 of the Directive has not been implemented.

Insofar as the absence of identification of "mandatory rules" is to be interpreted as meaning that the totality of the legislation in the field of labour law applies to posting situations, it should be pointed out that the Directive in no way permits Member States to extend all their legislative provisions and/or collective agreements governing terms and conditions of employment to workers posted on their territory, and that the application of such rules must be in compliance with the EC Treaty, in particular Article 49. As regards the matters covered, the Directive lays down a catalogue of mandatory rules (listed in Article 3) applicable to posted workers, to which Member States may add only public policy provisions in the international context (see below).

4.1.2. The Nature of the Standards Applicable

According to Article 3(1) of the Directive, Member States must ensure that undertakings covered by the Directive guarantee workers posted to their territory the terms and conditions of employment established by law, regulation or administrative provision and/or by universally applicable collective agreements or arbitration awards. Thus, the Directive first determines the nature of the standards which Member States must apply, and then the content of these standards.

---

521   Judgement of 23 March 1995, *Commission/Greece*, ECR I-499, point 9
522   Judgement of 10 May 2001, *Commission/Kingdom of the Netherlands*, ECR I-3541, point 17

4.1.2.1. Collective Agreements

Not all the transposing legislation has addressed the question of determining the collective agreements applicable to posting situations. The Commission intends to look into this more closely and examine the criteria used for determining the collective agreements applicable to national undertakings on the one hand and undertakings from other countries on the other. As the Court of Justice emphasised in the Joined Cases C-49/98, C-50/98, C-52/98 to C-54/98 and C-68/98 to C-71/98,[523] these criteria may have different practical consequences in the case of "mixed" businesses, i.e. businesses which carry out activities in a variety of sectors.

Collective agreements as referred to in Article 3(1) of the Directive must, for the purposes of implementation of the Directive, be declared universally applicable within the meaning of Article 3(8). The first subparagraph of Article 3(8) of the Directive refers to erga omnes collective agreements, which must be observed by all undertakings in the geographical area and in the profession or industry concerned in order to guarantee equality of treatment between domestic undertakings and undertakings established in another Member State providing services in the territory of a Member State.

In the absence of a system for declaring collective agreements to be of universal application, the second subparagraph of Article 3(8) offers Member States options designed to guarantee equality of treatment. The group of experts which prepared the transposal of the Directive was of the opinion that if Member States, in the absence of a system for declaring collective agreements or arbitration awards to be of universal application, decide to base themselves on the two other categories of collective agreements referred to in Article 3(8), i.e. generally applicable collective agreements or collective agreements concluded by the most representative employers' and labour organisations, they must make explicit mention thereof in their legislation implementing the posted workers Directive. If their implementing legislation makes no reference to this effect, Member States may not oblige undertakings established in another Member State which post workers to their territory to observe the collective agreements referred to in the second subparagraph of Article 3(8).

Since no Member State's transposing legislation makes any mention of the options offered by the second subparagraph of Article 3(8), the Commission concludes that those Member States which do not have collective agreements declared to be universally applicable within the meaning of the first subparagraph of Article 3(8) of the Directive do not apply the terms and conditions of employment laid down in collective agreements to workers posted on their territory. In these countries, therefore, only the terms and conditions of employment laid down in legislative provisions apply to workers posted on their territory.

---

523   Judgement of 25 October 2001 *Finalarte*, points 76-83, ECR 2001, p. I-07831

4.1.2.2. The Nature of the Legislative Standards Applicable concerning Matters Other than Those Explicitly Referred to in the Directive

The first indent of the first subparagraph of Article 3(10) stipulates that the Directive shall not preclude the application by Member States, in compliance with the Treaty, to national undertakings and to the undertakings of other States, on a basis of equality of treatment, of terms and conditions of employment on matters other than those referred to in the first subparagraph of paragraph 1 in the case of public policy provisions.

As regards the meaning of public policy provisions, the Commission would point out that, at the time of adoption of the Directive, the Council and the Commission stated (Statement 10) that "the expression 'public policy provisions' should be construed as covering those mandatory rules from which there can be no derogation and which, by their nature and objective, meet the imperative requirements of the public interest. These may include, in particular, the prohibition of forced labour or the involvement of public authorities in monitoring compliance with legislation on working conditions". As explicitly stated in Article 3(10), the application of public policy provisions has to be carried out in compliance with the Treaty and on a basis of equality of treatment.

The Commission considers that the first indent of Article 3(10) has to be interpreted bearing in mind the objective of facilitating the free movement of services within the Community. Thus, the Directive lays down a nucleus of minimum rules for the protection of the rights of workers in the host State, with which undertakings posting workers must comply. Member States are not free to impose all their mandatory labour law provisions on service providers established in another Member State. They must comply with the rules of the EC Treaty, and in particular Article 49, as interpreted by the Court of Justice (c.f. the *Portugaia Construções*[524] and *Mazzoneli*[525] judgements).

The concept of public policy within the meaning of Directive 96/71/EC must be interpreted in the light of the case law of the Court, which has ruled on this concept on several occasions. The case law, while not giving a precise definition of the concept of public policy, which appears, *inter alia*, in Articles 46 and 56 of the EC Treaty, recognises that this concept may vary from one country to another and from one period to another,[526] thus leaving the national authorities an area of discretion within the limits imposed by the Treaty. However, the Court has ruled that the concept of public policy must be interpreted strictly[527] and should not be determined unilaterally by each Member State. It has ruled that recourse to the concept of public policy must be justified on overriding general interest grounds,[528]

---

524 Judgement of 24 January 2002, Case 164/99
525 Judgement of 15 March 2001, Case 165/98, ECR I-2189
526 Judgement of 27 October 1977, Case 30/77, ECR 1977, 1999
527 Judgement of 18 June 1991, Case C-260/89, ECR 1991, I-2925
528 Judgement of 14 November 1995, Case 484/93, ECR 1995, I-3955

must presuppose the existence of a genuine and sufficiently serious threat affecting one of the fundamental interests of society[529] and must be in conformity with the general principles of law, in particular fundamental rights and the general principle of freedom of expression.

As regards the classification of the national provisions at issue as public-order legislation, the Court of Justice ruled, in its judgement in the Joined Cases C-369/96 and C-376/96,[530] that "the term must be understood as applying to national provisions compliance with which has been deemed to be so crucial for the protection of the political, social or economic order in the Member State concerned as to require compliance therewith by all persons present on the national territory of that Member State and all legal relationships within that State."

To illustrate the difference between domestic public policy provisions on the one hand and public policy provisions and mandatory provisions ["*lois de police*"] in the international context on the other, we can cite the example of the rules concerning dismissal, which in some countries are domestic public order provisions. These are national mandatory rules from which the parties may not derogate by contract, and which are intended to protect a "weak" party (the worker). In these countries, any contract between an employer and employee in which the employee waived his rights to redundancy pay or agreed to shorter than normal periods of notice without compensation would be null and void in regard to national contract law. However, these same rules are not considered to be international public policy provisions or mandatory rules within the meaning of Article 7 of the Rome Convention, which would apply whatever the law applicable to the contract. Accordingly, when the employment contract is validly subject to a foreign law, the domestic public policy provisions regarding dismissal do not apply automatically.

Some of the provisions of the Rome Convention might offer Member States valuable guidance in the application of Article 3(10) of the posted workers Directive. For example, pursuant to Article 10 of the Convention the consequences of breach of a contractual obligation are governed by the law applicable to the contract by virtue of Articles 3 to 6 and Article 12 of the Convention: in posting situations this will normally be the law of the home State. This confirms that the rules of the host State concerning the consequences of breach of an employment contract (e.g. termination of the employment contract) could not be applied under Article 3(10) of the Directive.

Finally, the group of experts which prepared the transposal of the Directive considered that the concept of "public policy provisions" referred to in Article 3(10) covers provisions concerning fundamental rights and freedoms as laid down by the law of the Member State concerned and/or by international law, such as freedom of association and collective bargaining, prohibition of forced labour, the principle

---

529   Judgement of 27 October 1977, Case 30/77, ECR 1977, 1999
530   Judgement of the Court of 23 November 1999, Jean Claude Arblade/Bernard Leloup, point 30, ECR 1999, I-08453.

of non-discrimination and elimination of exploitative forms of child labour[531], data protection and the right to privacy.

Consequently, Member States whose transposing legislation obliges foreign undertakings, during the period of posting, to comply with the labour law of the host country in its totality, are clearly exceeding the framework established by the Community legislation. Other Member States which, in their transposing legislation, explicitly add to the list of mandatory rules their own domestic public policy provisions, must also revise their legislation in the light of the above.

4.2. Practical Application

4.2.1. Difficulties Encountered by the Member States' Authorities

Most of the difficulties encountered by the Member States have to do with monitoring compliance with the law. The particular nature of transnational postings, i.e. their temporary nature and the clash between different legal systems, makes such monitoring tricky and difficult.

Language barriers are the first problem. In some Member States, the inability of the monitoring services to read documents drafted in the national language of the posted workers has resulted in Member States requiring such documents to be drafted in the language of the country in which the services are provided.

Another source of difficulties is the need to compare different countries' legislations. In certain fields the competent services are not allowed simply to verify compliance with the provisions of domestic labour law but must also verify in advance whether the employer is complying with an equivalent piece of legislation in force in the country in which the undertaking is established. However, in order to compare legislations it is necessary not only to be familiar with the legislations of other Member States but also to be able to assess their equivalence to the domestic law applicable in the host country.

Particular difficulties have been encountered in trying to compare paid leave schemes for workers in the building sector. In some Member States these schemes are implemented via a system of paid leave funds under which workers' leave entitlements acquired with different employers in the course of a given year are aggregated. With a view to dividing the financial burden between the employers concerned, employers in the building sector must pay into the leave funds contributions calculated on the basis of the relevant national provisions. Insofar as employers established abroad are obliged to participate in the paid leave funds

---

531   The right to organise and collective bargaining are dealt with in ILO Conventions 87 and 98. Conventions 29 and 105 cover the prohibition of forced labour, while Convention 111 establishes the principle of non-discrimination. Convention 182 covers the worst forms of child labour.

scheme in force in the host country and must pay contributions during the workers' period of posting, two different situations may arise.

If the system of paid leave funds exists in both the countries concerned, i.e. in the country of origin of the undertaking and in the host country, the question of the equivalence of the two Member States' schemes must be decided. To address the problems involved in comparing these schemes, the paid leave funds in several Member States have set up a system of cooperation extending beyond the cooperation provided between national authorities. The aim is to ensure mutual recognition of paid leave schemes and to avoid employers being faced with having to pay double contributions when they post workers.

Comparisons are, however, more complicated if the system of paid leave funds exists in only one of the two countries concerned. It was this situation which gave rise to the judgement in the Joined Cases C-49/98, C-50/98, C-52/98 to C-54/98 and C-68/98 to C-71/98,[532] in which the Court examined the question as to whether Articles 49 and 50 (ex 59 and ex 60) of the EC Treaty preclude a Member State from imposing national rules relating to the system of paid leave funds on a business established in another Member State not possessing such a system which provides services in the first Member State and posts workers there.

The Court points out that the freedom to provide services, as one of the fundamental principles of the Treaty, may be restricted only by rules justified by overriding requirements relating to the public interest, one of which is the protection of workers, and that it is for the national court to check whether, viewed objectively, the rules in question promote the protection of posted workers. According to the Court, it is necessary to check whether those rules confer a genuine benefit on the workers concerned which significantly adds to their social protection. After considering the potential benefits of a paid leave funds scheme, the Court states that it is for the national court "to consider whether such potential benefits confer real additional protection on posted workers. That assessment must take account, first, of the protection as to paid leave that workers already enjoy under the law of the Member State where their employer is established."

The Court concludes that Articles 49 (ex 59) and 50 (ex 60) of the Treaty do not preclude a Member State from imposing national rules such as those examined in this Case on a business established in another Member State, "on the two-fold condition that: (i) the workers do not enjoy an essentially similar level of protection under the law of the Member State where their employer is established, so that the application of the national rules of the first Member State confers a genuine benefit on the workers concerned, which significantly adds to their social protection, and (ii) the application of those rules by the first Member State is proportionate to the public interest objective pursued."

It is clear that all these difficulties cannot be resolved without effective cooperation between Member States' administrations. Such cooperation should be the

---

532   Judgement of 25 October 2001 *Finalarte*

means for the monitoring services to obtain rapid information on the content of the legislation in the undertaking's country of establishment. It should also be the means for obtaining information on the situation of the service provider established in another State.

As regards monitoring compliance with the terms and conditions of employment, the Commission would also point out that the Court of Justice emphasised the importance of administrative cooperation in the context of transnational postings in the Joined Cases C-369/96 and 376/96, although these Cases did not relate to the interpretation of Directive 96/71/EC. In these two Cases the Court was called upon to consider whether Articles 49 (ex 59) and 50 (ex 60) of the Treaty must be interpreted as meaning that they preclude a Member State from requiring an undertaking established in another Member State and temporarily carrying out work in the first State to retain certain social and labour documents with an agent in the country in which the work is performed.

On the principle of keeping social and labour documents in the country of posting, the Court ruled that the imposition of this obligation on undertakings from another Member State constitutes a restriction on the freedom to provide services within the meaning of Article 59 of the Treaty, which can be justified only if it is necessary to provide effective protection for workers. The Court held that the effective protection of workers in the construction industry may require that certain documents are kept on site, or at least in an accessible and clearly identified place in the territory of the host Member State, so that they are available to the authorities of that State responsible for carrying out checks, particularly where there exists no organised system for cooperation or exchanges of information between Member States as provided for in Article 4 of Directive 96/71.

On certain arrangements for the keeping and retention of such documents, the Court also referred to the organised system for cooperation and exchanges of information between Member States, as provided for in Article 4 of Directive 96/71, will shortly render superfluous the retention of the documents in the host Member State after the employer has ceased to employ workers there.

This case law first of all invites the Member States to take all necessary measures for the setting up of an organised and effective system of cooperation in the context of the transposal of the Directive which, according to the Court of Justice, must replace certain requirements regarding the keeping and retention of social documents at the place of work. After the implementation of Directive 96/71, arguments based on differences in the form or content of the documents between those of the host country and those of the country of establishment will no longer be accepted to justify the imposition of certain obligations in this field on undertakings established in another Member State. In any assessment of the justification of these measures, it must be expected that the Court will take fully into account the cooperation provided for in Article 4 of Directive 96/71, which should enable Member States to obtain all the information necessary in connection with transnational postings.

4.2.2. *Difficulties Encountered by Service Provider Undertakings and Posted Workers*

The undertakings concerned could encounter difficulties arising from the fact that the Directive obliges them to comply with the law of a State other than the State in which they are established and the relevant provisions are often difficult to understand and sometimes also difficult to obtain. The legal instruments implementing the Directive are often complicated because they contain a multiplicity of references to other instruments. This legislative method means that the texts cannot be understood without consulting other texts to which reference is made. Furthermore, access to the applicable collective agreements may prove difficult in some Member States. Service providers also have to contend with the absence of translations of the applicable texts.

The Commission would point out in this respect that Article 4(3) of Directive 96/71/EC explicitly provides that each Member State shall take the appropriate measures to make the information on the terms and conditions of employment referred to in Article 3 generally available. The Commission is pleased that some Member States have taken measures to facilitate access to the provisions applicable to posting situations, for example by publishing information brochures or creating websites with relevant information, and encourages Member States to continue along this path.

It should also be pointed out that the Commission listed the difficulties mentioned by service providers in connection with the cross-border provision of services, notably as regards the posting of workers, in its report on the state of the internal market for services,[533] adopted on 30 July 2002.

4.3. The Acceding Countries

As regards the situation in the acceding countries, it should be remembered that these countries are obliged to transpose the provisions of the Directive prior to joining the European Union. Most of them have already adopted new provisions and/or adapted existing legislation with a view to transposing the Directive on the posting of workers.

Transposal is seemingly well under way in some countries, while in others a great deal of work remains to be done. This applies in particular to Article 3(1), whereby, as host States, they must lay down the rules to be followed by foreign undertakings providing services on their territory.

In order to get the acceding countries swiftly involved in the work of the government experts group, experts from these countries will be invited to participate in the group's meetings in 2003.

---

533   COM(2002) 441 final

5. CONCLUSION

Revision of Directive 96/71/EC

The results of the studies of the transposition of Directive 96/71/EC, as outlined above, are broadly corroborated by the Member States' answers to a questionnaire on the practical application of the provisions arising from the Directive, and by the conclusions of the group of government experts.

This group's conclusions can be summarised as follows:

–   None of the Member States has encountered any particular legal difficulties in transposing the Directive.
–   Implementing the Directive may pose practical difficulties, but most of these should disappear in the course of time thanks to better information and better administrative cooperation between public authorities (Article 4 of the Directive).
–   It seems premature to consider amending the Directive. With regard to Article 4, on which the effective implementation of the Directive primarily depends, it is clear that the information circuits and the cooperation networks will take time to build up.

These opinions and positions indicate to the Commission that it is not necessary to amend the Directive. The difficulties encountered in implementing it have so far tended to be more of a practical nature than a legal nature. Consequently, as things stand at present the Commission will not be presenting a proposal for a Directive amending the arrangements for implementing the posted workers Directive.

Identification of the Problems

The problems identified can be divided into three groups:

–   The situation in the Member States which have not deemed it necessary to adopt specific and explicit transposal measures does not conform to the criteria established by the Court's case law regarding the transposal of Community Directives. The mandatory provisions within the meaning of the Directive have not been identified and the rights and obligations arising from the Directive have not been clearly defined. The jurisdiction clause of Article 6 has not been explicitly transposed.
–   The provisions which several Member States have made applicable to posting situations under the first indent of Article 3(10) need to be reviewed in order to verify which of these provisions can be deemed to be public policy provisions within the meaning of private international law. Public policy

provisions or mandatory provisions ["lois de police"] in private international law are provisions to which a State attaches such importance that it requires them to be applied whenever there is a connection between the legal situation and its territory, whatever law is otherwise applicable to the contract or the employment relationship.

– The practical difficulties mentioned at point 4.2., namely the obstacles encountered in seeking information, in monitoring compliance with national implementing provisions and in implementing penalties are such as to limit the effectiveness of the Directive.

Proposed Solutions to the Problems

The first two groups of difficulties mentioned above are problems connected with transposing the Directive into Member State's legal systems, and as such need to be resolved at national level. There will be contacts on these matters between the Member States concerned and the Commission.

As regards the third group of difficulties, the Commission will continue to assess what it can do to help improve the dissemination of information and cooperation between Member States' administrations. At this stage, it is considering taking and encouraging the following measures:

– A group of government experts of variable composition, set up under the Commission Decision of 27 March 2002,[534] will need to meet at least twice a year in order to discuss the subjects addressed under 4.1. and 4.2. and any other practical difficulties which national administrations may have encountered. The members of the Group of Directors-General for Industrial Relations created by the aforementioned Decision are asked to nominate experts from the different competent administrations, cooperation bodies, liaison offices or Labour Inspectorates depending on the subjects to be discussed. The group will need first of all to clarify the allocation of the various cooperation tasks mentioned in Article 4 of the Directive and exchange information on the organisation and functioning of such cooperation.

– The group of experts will need to examine ways of facilitating access to information on the provisions applicable to posted workers in the host Member States, for example through clear and simple brochures, website access to information on the laws and collective agreements applicable to posting situations, and contact persons in the liaison offices, with links to the websites of the other Member States and the Commission.

---

534 Decision concerning the creation of a group of Directors-General for Industrial Relations (2002/260), OJ L 91/30

–   The Commission services will be instructed to collect all the relevant information from the Member States, make it accessible to the public on the Commission's websites and create links to the Member States' sites (laws and collective agreements, liaison offices).

–   As regards the problems of monitoring compliance with the mandatory provisions within the meaning of the Directive, the group will be asked to identify various essential items of information which must be supplied (by the undertakings concerned) to the monitoring authorities in the host country. Exchanges of information and good practice within the experts group could help to simplify and bring into closer alignment the practical arrangements so far developed by Member States, particularly as regards statements to the competent administrations. The Commission considers that this group will also be the appropriate body for seeking solutions to the language problems mentioned in this context.

–   In addition, it appears necessary not only to improve transnational cooperation via the mechanisms set up under Directive 96/71/EC, but also to evaluate the possibilities of the various forms of collaboration established outside the Directive.

–   In the context of the implementation of the Internal Market Strategy for Services decided upon at the Lisbon European Council[535], the Commission is reflecting on ways of improving the systems of administrative cooperation and will be proposing concrete measures on this matter in 2003.

–   Finally, the Commission would point out that the "Justice, Home Affairs and Civil Protection" Council of 8 May 2003 reached an agreement on a framework decision concerning the application of the principle of mutual recognition to financial penalties. In the future, therefore, a simple and effective system will facilitate the cross-border enforcement of financial penalties once the provisions of this framework decision have been implemented by the Member States.

---

535   COM(2000) 888 final of 29.12.2000

ANNEX

PROPOSAL FOR A DIRECTIVE OF THE EUROPEAN PARLIAMENT AND OF THE COUNCIL ON SERVICES IN THE INTERNAL MARKET [SEC(2004) 21]

/* COM/2004/0002 final – COD 2004/0001 */

presented by the European Commission

SUMMARY

1. This proposal for a Directive is part of the process of economic reform launched by the Lisbon European Council with a view to making the EU the most competitive and dynamic knowledge-based economy in the world by 2010. Achieving this goal means that the establishment of a genuine internal market in services is indispensable. It has not hitherto been possible to exploit the considerable potential for economic growth and job creation afforded by the services sector because of the many obstacles[536] hampering the development of service activities in the internal market. This proposal forms part of the strategy adopted by the Commission to eliminate these obstacles and follows on from the Report on the State of the Internal Market for Services,[537] which revealed their extent and significance.

2. The objective of the proposal for a Directive is to provide a legal framework that will eliminate the obstacles to the freedom of establishment for service providers and the free movement of services between the Member States, giving both the providers and recipients of services the legal certainty they need in order to exercise these two fundamental freedoms enshrined in the Treaty. The proposal covers a wide variety of economic service activities – with some exceptions, such as financial services – and applies only to service providers established in a Member State.

3. In order to eliminate the obstacles to the freedom of establishment, the proposal provides for:

---

536 "An Internal Market Strategy for Services", Communication from the Commission to the Council and the European Parliament, COM(2000) 888 final, 29.12.2000.
537 Report from the Commission to the Council and the European Parliament on "The State of the Internal Market for Services", COM(2002) 441 final, 30.7.2002.

– administrative simplification measures, particularly involving the establishment of "single points of contact", at which service providers can complete the administrative procedures relevant to their activities, and the obligation to make it possible to complete these procedures by electronic means;

– certain principles which authorisation schemes applicable to service activities must respect, in particular relating to the conditions and procedures for the granting of an authorisation;

– the prohibition of certain particularly restrictive legal requirements that may still be in force in certain Member States;

– the obligation to assess the compatibility of certain other legal requirements with the conditions laid down in the Directive, particularly as regards proportionality.

4. In order to eliminate the obstacles to the free movement of services, the proposal provides for:

– the application of the country of origin principle, according to which a service provider is subject only to the law of the country in which he is established and Member States may not restrict services from a provider established in another Member State. This principle is accompanied by derogations which are either general, or temporary or which may be applied on a case-by-case basis;

– the right of recipients to use services from other Member States without being hindered by restrictive measures imposed by their country or by discriminatory behaviour on the part of public authorities or private operators. In the case of patients, the proposal clarifies the circumstances in which a Member State may make reimbursement of the cost of healthcare provided in another Member State subject to authorisation;

– a mechanism to provide assistance to recipients who use a service provided by an operator established in another Member State;

– in the case of posting of workers in the context of the provision of services, the allocation of tasks between the Member State of origin and the Member State of destination and the supervision procedures applicable.

5. With a view to establishing the mutual trust between Member States necessary for eliminating these obstacles, the proposal provides for:

– harmonisation of legislation in order to guarantee equivalent protection of the general interest on vital questions, such as consumer protection, particularly as regards the service provider's obligations concerning information, professional insurance, multidisciplinary activities, settlement of disputes, and exchange of information on the quality of the service provider;

–   stronger mutual assistance between national authorities with a view to effective supervision of service activities on the basis of a clear distribution of roles between the Member States and obligations to cooperate;

–   measures for promoting the quality of services, such as voluntary certification of activities, quality charters or cooperation between the chambers of commerce and of crafts;

–   encouraging codes of conduct drawn up by interested parties at Community level on certain questions, including in particular commercial communications by the regulated professions.

6. With a view to taking full effect by 2010, the proposal is based on a dynamic approach involving phased implementation of some of its provisions, a commitment to additional harmonisation on certain specific matters (cash-in-transit services, gambling and judicial recovery of debts), the guarantee that it will evolve and that any need for new initiatives can be identified. Moreover, this proposal is without prejudice to any legislative or other Community initiatives in the field of consumer protection.

EXPLANATORY MEMORANDUM

1. NECESSITY AND OBJECTIVE

Services are omnipresent in today's economy, generating almost 70% of GNP and jobs and offering considerable potential for growth and job creation. Realising this potential is at the heart of the process of economic reform launched by the Lisbon European Council and aimed at making the EU the most competitive and dynamic knowledge-based economy in the world by 2010. It has not so far been possible to exploit fully the growth potential of services because of the many obstacles hampering the development of services activities between the Member States.

In its Report on "The State of the Internal Market for Services"[538] ("the report"), the Commission listed these obstacles and concluded that "a decade after the envisaged completion of the internal market, there is a huge gap between the vision of an integrated EU economy and the reality as experienced by European citizens and European service providers." These obstacles affect a wide range of services such as distributive trades, employment agencies, certification, laboratories, construction services, estate agencies, craft industries, tourism, the regulated professions etc. and SMEs, which are predominant in the services sector, are particularly hard-hit. SMEs are too often discouraged from exploiting the opportunities afforded by the internal market because they do not have the means to evaluate, and protect

---

538   COM(2002) 441 final, 30.7.2002.

themselves against, the legal risks involved in cross-border activity or to cope with the administrative complexities. The report, and the impact assessment which relates to this proposal, show the economic impact of this dysfunction, emphasising that it amounts to a considerable drag on the EU economy and its potential for growth, competitiveness and job creation.

These obstacles to the development of service activities between Member States occur in particular in two types of situation:

– when a service provider from one Member State wishes to establish himself in another Member State in order to provide his services. (For example, he may be subject to over-burdensome authorisation schemes, excessive red tape, discriminatory requirements, an economic test etc.);

– when a service provider wishes to provide a service from his Member State of origin into another Member State, particularly by moving to the other Member State on a temporary basis. (For example, he may be subject to a legal obligation to establish himself in the other Member State, need to obtain an authorisation there, or be subject to the application of its rules on the conditions for the exercise of the activity in question or to disproportionate procedures in connection with the posting of workers).

Accordingly, the aim of this proposal for a Directive is to establish a legal framework to facilitate the exercise of freedom of establishment for service providers in the Member States and the free movement of services between Member States. It aims to eliminate certain legal obstacles to the achievement of a genuine internal market in services and to guarantee service providers and recipients the legal certainty they need in order to exercise these two fundamental freedoms enshrined in the Treaty in practice.

2. BACKGROUND

This proposal for a Directive forms part of a political process launched in 2000 by the European Council:

In March 2000, the Lisbon European Council adopted a programme of economic reform aimed at making the EU the most competitive and dynamic knowledge-based economy in the world by 2010. In this context, the EU Heads of State and Government invited the Commission and the Member States to devise a strategy aimed at eliminating the obstacles to the free movement of services.[539]

---

539   Presidency Conclusions, Lisbon European Council, 24.3.2000, para. 17. The need to take action in these fields was also highlighted at the Stockholm and Barcelona Summits in 2001 and 2002.

In December 2000, in response to the call launched at the Lisbon Summit, the Commission set out "An Internal Market Strategy for Services",[540] which received the full support of the Member States,[541] the European Parliament,[542] the Economic and Social Committee[543] and the Committee of the Regions.[544] The aim of this strategy is to enable services to move across national borders within the European Union just as easily as within a single Member State. Above all it is based on a horizontal approach across all economic sectors involving services and on a two-stage process, the first involving identification of the difficulties hampering the smooth functioning of the internal market in services, and the second involving the development of appropriate solutions to the problems identified, and in particular a horizontal legal instrument.

In July 2002, the Commission presented its report on "The State of the Internal Market for Services", which marked the completion of the first phase in the strategy and provided as exhaustive a list as possible of barriers that exist in the internal market for services. This report also analyses the common features of these barriers and makes an initial evaluation of their economic impact.[545]

In November 2002, the conclusions of the Council on the Commission's report,[546] acknowledged "that a decade after the envisaged completion of the internal market, considerable work still needs to be done in order to make the internal market for services a reality" and emphasised "that very high political priority should be given to the removal of both legislative and non-legislative barriers to services in the internal market, as part of the overall goal set by the Lisbon European Council to make the European Union the most dynamic and competitive economy in the world by 2010". The Council urged the Commission to accelerate work on the initiatives foreseen in the second stage of the strategy, and in particular on the legislative instrument.

In February 2003, the European Parliament also welcomed the Commission's report, emphasising that it "insists that the Competitiveness Council reaffirm Member States' commitment to the country of origin and mutual recognition principles, as

---

540 "An Internal Market Strategy for Services" Communication from the Commission to the Council and the European Parliament. COM(2000) 888 final, 29.12.2000.

541 2336th Council meeting on the Internal Market, Consumer Affairs and Tourism of 12 March 2001, 6926/01 (Presse 103) para. 17.

542 European Parliament Resolution on the Commission Communication "An Internal Market Strategy for Services" A5-0310/2001, 4.10.2001.

543 Opinion of the Economic and Social Committee on the Commission Communication "An Internal Market Strategy for Services" (additional opinion), CES 1472/2001 final, 28.11.2001.

544 Opinion of the Committee of the Regions on the Commission Communication "An Internal Market Strategy for Services", CDR 134/2001 final, 27.06.2001.

545 This report took up, in certain respects, in the case of services, the idea provided for in the former Article 100b EC of an inventory of national measures.

546 Conclusion on obstacles to the provision of services in the internal market at the 2462nd Council meeting on Competitiveness (Internal Market, Industry, Research), Brussels, 14 November 2002, 13839/02 (Presse 344).

the essential basis for completing the internal market in goods and services"[547] and also that it "welcomes the proposals for a horizontal instrument to ensure free movement of services in the form of mutual recognition, with automatic recognition being encouraged as far as possible, administrative cooperation and, where strictly necessary, harmonisation".[548]

In March 2003, with the aim of reinforcing the economic dimension of the Lisbon strategy, the Spring European Council called for the strengthening of the horizontal role of the Competitiveness Council in order to increase competitiveness and growth in the framework of an integrated approach to competitiveness to be set out by the Commission. The establishment of a clear and balanced legal framework to facilitate the free movement of services in the internal market is one of the elements necessary for the success of the new integrated competitiveness strategy.

In May 2003, according to its "Internal Market Strategy",[549] the Commission announced that "the Commission will make a proposal for a Services Directive in the internal market before the end of 2003. This Directive will establish a clear and balanced legal framework aiming to facilitate the conditions for establishment and cross-border service provision. It will be based on a mix of mutual recognition, administrative cooperation, harmonisation where strictly necessary and encouragement of European codes of conduct/professional rules".

In October 2003, the European Council identified the internal market as a key area for improving the competitiveness of the European economy and thus creating conditions conducive to growth and employment. It "calls on the Commission to present any further proposals necessary to complete the internal market and to fully exploit its potential, to stimulate entrepreneurship and to create a true internal market in services, while having due regard to the need to safeguard the supply and trading of services of general interest".[550]

3. MAIN FEATURES OF THE DIRECTIVE

a) A Framework Directive

The Directive will establish a general legal framework applicable, subject to certain exceptions, to all economic activities involving services. This horizontal approach

---

547 European Parliament Resolution of 13 February 2003 on the Communication from the Commission to the Council, the European Parliament, the Economic and Social Committee and the Committee of the Regions: "2002 Review of the Internal Market Strategy – Delivering the promise" (COM(2002) 171 – C5-0283/2002 – 2002/2143(COS)). A5-0026/2003; point 35.
548 Point 36.
549 "Internal Market Strategy – Priorities 2003-2006" Communication from the Commission to the Council, the European Parliament, the European Economic and Social Committee and the Committee of the Regions, COM(2003) 238 of 7.5.2003.
550 Presidency Conclusions, Brussels European Council, 16-17.10.2003, para. 16.

is justified by the fact that, as explained in the report,[551] the legal obstacles to the achievement of a genuine internal market in services are often common to a large number of different activities and have many features in common.

Since the proposal is for a framework Directive, it does not aim to lay down detailed rules or to harmonise all the rules in the Member States applicable to service activities. This would have led to over-regulation and a standardisation of the specific features of the national systems for regulating services. Instead, the proposal deals exclusively with questions that are vital for the smooth functioning of the internal market in services by giving priority to targeted harmonisation of specific points, to the imposition of obligations to achieve clear results without prejudging the legal techniques by which they will be brought about, and to the clarification of the respective roles of the Member State of origin and the Member State of destination of a service. The proposal also refers to Commission implementing measures on the way that certain provisions are applied.

While establishing a general legal framework, the proposal recognises the specific characteristics of each profession or field of activity. More particularly, it recognises the specific nature of the regulated professions and the particular role of self-regulation. For example, the proposal provides (Article 17) for a number of derogations from the country of origin principle that are directly linked to the specific characteristics of certain activities; it also contains specific provisions on certain activities such as professional insurance and guarantees (Article 27), commercial communications by the regulated professions (Article 29) or multidisciplinary activities (Article 30); finally, it relies also on alternative methods of regulation specific to certain activities, such as codes of conduct for the regulated professions (Article 39).

Moreover, this proposal is without prejudice to any legislative or other Community initiatives in the field of consumer protection.

b) A Combination of Regulatory Techniques

The proposal for a Directive is based on a combination of techniques for regulating service activities, including in particular:

– the country of origin principle, according to which service providers are subject only to the law of the country in which they are established and Member States may not restrict services provided by operators established in another Member State. It therefore enables operators to provide services in one or more other Member States without being subject to those Member States' rules. This principle also means that the Member State of origin is

---

551   COM(2002) 441 *op. cit.*, part II.

responsible for the effective supervision of service providers established on its territory even if they provide services into other Member States;

– derogations from the country of origin principle, in particular in Article 17, necessary in order to take account of differences in the level of protection of the general interest in certain fields, the extent of Community-level harmonisation, the degree of administrative cooperation, or certain Community instruments. Some of these derogations will apply for a transitional period up to 2010, and are intended to allow time for additional harmonisation on certain specific questions. Finally, derogations on a case-by-case basis are possible, subject to certain substantive conditions and procedures;

– the establishment of obligations of mutual assistance between national authorities, which is vital for ensuring the high level of mutual trust between Member States on which the country of origin principle is based. In order to ensure that supervision is effective, the proposal provides for a high degree of administrative cooperation between authorities by organising the allocation of supervisory tasks, exchange of information and mutual assistance;

– targeted harmonisation to ensure protection of the general interest in certain essential fields where too wide a divergence in the level of protection, notably in the field of consumer protection, would undermine the mutual trust that is vital to the acceptance of the country of origin principle and could justify, in accordance with the case law of the Court of Justice, measures restricting freedom of movement. Harmonisation is also provided for as far as the simplification of administrative procedures and the elimination of certain types of requirement are concerned;

– alternative methods of regulation that are important for the regulation of service activities. The proposal fully recognises their role and encourages the parties concerned to draw up, at Community level, codes of conduct on particular issues.

c) Coordination of the Processes of Modernisation

The proposal for a Directive aims to coordinate, at Community level, the modernisation of national systems for regulating service activities with a view to eliminating the legal obstacles to the achievement of a genuine internal market in services. The report emphasises the resistance to modernisation of the various national legal frameworks and notes that "The fundamental principles of the Treaty, the importance attached to them by the Court, and the follow-up to the ambitious programmes of 1962 and 1985, have not always resulted in the adjustment of national legislation which might have been expected".[552]

---

552   COM(2002) 441 *op. cit.* part II, Section C 2.

Adapting legislation case by case and Member State by Member State follow-ing infringement procedures by the Commission, would be an inefficient way of responding to this need for modernisation, as it would be entirely reactive and would lack a shared political will to move towards a common objective[553]. The adjustment of legislation by all the Member States according to common principles and a common timetable will instead make it possible to benefit on a European scale from the resulting economic growth, to avoid distortions of competition between Member States that make their adjustments at different rates, and to encourage improved mobilisation around this objective, also in terms of allocation of national and Community administrative resources.

In order to transpose the Directive, Member States must:

–   simplify the administrative procedures and formalities to which service activities are subject (Sections 1 and 2 of Chapter II), particularly by means of single points of contact (Article 6), the use of electronic procedures (Article 8) and simplification of the authorisation procedures for access to and the exercise of service activities (Articles 10-13); it should be noted that the obligations to communicate information (Article 7) and to make available electronic procedures (Article 8) do not prevent Member States from maintaining other procedures and methods of communication in parallel;

–   eliminate from their legislation a number of requirements listed in the Directive that hamper access to and the exercise of service activities (Articles 14, 21, 29);

–   guarantee in their legislation the free movement of services from other Member States and consequently adapt any rules that would hamper such movement (Articles 16, 20, 23 and 25);

–   evaluate the justification and proportionality of a number of requirements listed in the Directive which, where they exist in their regulations, may significantly restrict the development of service activities (Articles 9, 15 and 30). This evaluation should lead to the elimination of unjustified requirements and will be the subject of mutual evaluation that could conclude, where appropriate, that other Community-level initiatives are necessary.

d) A Dynamic Approach

Given the scale of the obstacles identified in the report, the task of establishing a genuine area with no internal borders for services will take time. The modernisation of certain rules applied by the Member States will require fundamental changes (for example, single points of contact and the use of electronic procedures), additional harmonisation specific to certain activities, and take due account of the develop-

---

553   See impact assessment, para. 6.3.2.

ment of Community integration in other fields. In order to avoid a static approach that tackles a single problem and leaves the others unresolved, the proposal for a Directive adopts a phased approach aimed at achieving a genuine internal market for services by 2010. The proposal therefore provides for:

–   phased implementation of certain of its provisions (Articles 6-8)
–   additional harmonisation on certain specific questions, i.e. cash-in-transit services, gambling, and recovery of debts by judicial means (Article 40(1)), which are the subject of temporary derogations from the principle of country of origin (Article 18). Moreover, the need for further harmonisation could be identified, in particular in the areas of consumer protection and cross-border contracts (Article 40(2)d);
–   extension of the scope of application of the country of origin principle as rules come to be harmonised in certain fields (Articles 17 point 21 and 19(2))
–   the possibility for the Commission to take implementing measures on the way that certain provisions will be put in place (Article 42)
–   identification of the need for new initiatives, particularly through mutual evaluation (Article 40(2))

e) A Framework Facilitating Access to Services

The report emphasised that the users of services, and in particular consumers, are, together with SMEs, the main victims of the lack of a genuine internal market in services: they generally cannot benefit from a wide variety of competitively priced services and thus the better quality of life that they might expect from an area without internal borders.

By creating the conditions and legal certainty necessary for the development of service activities between Member States, and in so doing extending the range of services available, the Directive will be of direct benefit to the recipients of services. It will also guarantee better quality in the services on offer by enabling at Community level an increase in the efficiency of the supervision of service activities. The proposal also:

–   provides for the right of recipients to use the services of providers established in other Member States without being hampered or dissuaded by restrictive measures applied by their country of residence (Article 20) or discriminatory behaviour by public authorities or private operators (Article 21). For the recipients of health services, the proposal clarifies, in accordance with the case law of the Court of Justice, the circumstances in which a Member State may make assumption of the costs of healthcare provided in another Member State subject to prior authorisation;
–   guarantees specific assistance for a recipient in his own Member State, in the form of information on legislation in the other Member States, the avail-

able means of redress, and associations or organisations offering practical assistance (Article 22);

– strengthens considerably the right of recipients to information on services so as to enable them to make fully-informed choices. At present, some service activities are already subject to transparency requirements under Community rules, but many others are not because of the lack of provisions that are applicable to all service activities (Articles 26, 27, 28, 30, 31 and 32);

– strengthens the protection of recipients by providing for requirements regarding the quality of service providers – particularly the obligation to take out professional insurance in the case of services involving a particular health, safety or financial risk for the recipient (Article 27) – the provisions on multidisciplinary activities (Article 30) and the settlement of disputes (Article 32).

4. PREPARATORY WORK

This proposal is the result of numerous analyses, surveys and consultations with the Member States, the European Parliament and other stakeholders that have taken place since the launching of the Internal Market Strategy for Services in December 2000 and which are described in the impact assessment. The Economic and Social Committee and the Committee of the Regions have also made substantial contributions to the Strategy.

5. COHERENCE WITH OTHER COMMUNITY POLICIES

An internal market in services will not be established by means of a legal instrument alone but will require accompanying measures. In legal terms, the proposal is consistent with other Community instruments: where a service activity is already covered by one or more Community instruments, the Directive and these instruments will apply cumulatively, the requirements of the one applying in addition to those of the others. Where there might have been questions of compatibility in connection with a given Article, the latter provides for derogations (in Article 17, for example) or appropriate clauses describing the relationship between the Directive and the other Community instruments, in order to ensure consistency. Moreover, this proposal is without prejudice to any legislative or other Community initiatives in the field of consumer protection.

There is a range of other complementary Community initiatives under way.

– The competitiveness of business-related services. In parallel with this proposal for a Directive on services in the internal market, the Commission has presented a Communication on the competitiveness of business-related services and their contribution to the performance of European enterprises[554], in which it emphasises the importance of business services for the competitiveness of the EU and announces a series of supporting measures, including in particular the creation of a European Forum for business-related services. Whereas the Directive deals with the removal of legal and administrative barriers, the competitiveness of the services sector depends also on a number of complementary economic measures set out in the Communication on business-related services.

– Professional qualifications. This proposal for a Directive complements the proposal for a Directive on the recognition of professional qualifications[555], given that it deals with questions other than professional qualifications such as professional insurance, commercial communications and multidisciplinary activities. The two proposals are fully compatible since, where freedom of establishment is concerned, they are aimed at facilitating establishment for service providers and, where freedom of movement for services is concerned, they are based on the country of origin principle.

– Posting of workers. The employment and working conditions applicable in the event of posting of workers are set out in Directive 96/71/EC,[556] which provides for the application of certain rules of the country to whose territory a worker is posted. For the sake of consistency with that Directive, Article 17 of this proposal for a Directive contains a derogation from the country of origin principle where these rules are concerned. In order to facilitate the free movement of services and the application of Directive 96/71/EC, the proposal clarifies the allocation of tasks between the country of origin and the Member State of posting, and the administrative supervisory procedures (Article 24).

– Reimbursement of costs of healthcare. The proposal for a Directive deals with the specific question of the compatibility of prior authorisation systems for assumption of the costs of healthcare provided in another Member State with the principle of freedom of movement for services. Article 23 of the proposal incorporates the distinction between hospital and non-hospital care that has been clearly established by the consolidated case law of the Court of Justice.[557] As regards the circumstances in which such prior authorisation is justified, the proposal clarifies the specific conditions for authorisation, in accordance with the case law of the Court of Justice. Broader issues

---

554 COM(2003) 747.
555 Proposal for a Directive of the European Parliament and of the Council on the recognition of professional qualifications, COM(2002) 119 final, 7.3.2002.
556 Directive 96/71/EC of the European Parliament and of the Council of 16 December 1996 concerning the posting of workers in the framework of the provision of services.
557 See "Report on the application of internal market rules to health services: implementation by the Member States of the Court's jurisprudence", Commission Staff Working Paper, SEC(2003) 900, 28.7.2003.

have been raised in the high level reflection process on patient mobility and healthcare developments in the European Union, including patients' rights, entitlements and duties; facilitating cooperation between health systems; providing appropriate information for patients, professionals and policymakers; ensuring access and quality in cross-border care; the impact of enlargement; and in general how to improve legal certainty and reconcile national objectives with European obligations in this area. The Commission will issue a Communication in spring 2004 setting out a comprehensive strategy for addressing patient mobility and healthcare with proposals responding to the recommendations of the reflection process.

–   Safety of services. The Commission has presented a report on the safety of services for consumers,[558] which emphasises the substantial lack of data and information on the risks and safety of services. It also notes that it is impossible to identify specific gaps in Member State systems or significant differences in the level of protection, and that there is a lack of barriers to trade resulting from different national requirements that could justify harmonisation of national rules on the safety of services. The report concludes that the priority for Community action must be to improve the collection of key data in this area and set up a system for exchange of information on policy and regulatory developments. If it appears that there is a need to do so, measures establishing procedures for the definition of European standards will be adopted. The report foresees the establishment of a suitable Community framework to this effect. These analyses are, therefore, complementary to and consistent with this proposal for a Directive, which, moreover, provides for the possibility of derogations on a case-by-case basis aimed at guaranteeing the safety of services (Article 19). The Council, in its resolution of 1 December 2003 on the safety of services,[559] has warmly welcomed the Commission's report.

–   Services of general interest. The Commission has launched a broad debate on the role of the European Union in promoting the provision of high quality services of general interest on the basis of a Green Paper on services of general interest.[560] This proposal for a Directive does not go into this question as such or the question of opening up these services to competition. It covers all services that correspond to an economic activity within the meaning of the case law of the Court relating to Article 49 of the Treaty. It does not, therefore, cover non-economic services of general interest but only services of general economic interest. It should be noted that, in this proposal, certain activities that may be linked to services of general economic interest are subject, in so far as this is justified by their specific nature, to derogations from the country of origin principle. These include, in particular, postal services and electricity, gas and water distribution services. Neither does the

---

558   Report on the safety of services for consumers, COM(2003) 313 final of 6.6.2003.
559   OJ C 299, 10.12.2003, p. 1.
560   COM(2003) 270 final, 21.5.2003.

proposal cover electronic communications as far as matters covered by the legislative package adopted in 2002 are concerned nor transport services to the extent that they are regulated by other Community instruments based on Article 71 or Article 80(2) of the Treaty. Even in the fields covered by the Directive, it does not affect the freedom of the Member States to define what they consider to be services of general interest and how they should function. In particular, the Directive does not affect the freedom of the Member States to organise public service broadcasting in accordance with protocol 32 of the Treaty on public service broadcasting in the Member States.

– GATS negotiations. The proposal for a Directive is an internal market instrument and therefore concerns only service providers established in a Member State, including, as laid down in Article 48 of the Treaty, companies or firms formed in accordance with the law of a Member State and having their registered office, central administration or principal place of business within the Community. It does not cover external aspects and, in particular, does not cover:

  – the case of operators from third countries who wish to establish in a Member State (first establishment in the EU);
  – the case of operators from third countries who wish to provide services in the EU;
  – the case of branches of companies from third countries in a Member State (in the sense of Article 48 of the Treaty) who, not being companies formed in accordance with the legislation of a Member State, may not benefit from this Directive.

International trade in services is covered by international negotiations, particularly in the framework of GATS. In this connection, it should be emphasised that the EU is a very open market compared with many trading partners. The proposal does not affect these negotiations, which are aimed at facilitating trade in services and which reinforce the need for the EU swiftly to establish a genuine internal market in services to ensure the competitiveness of European businesses and strengthen Europe's negotiating position.

– eEurope: the eEurope Initiative and eEurope 2005 Action Plan aim to develop modern public services and a dynamic environment for electronic commerce in the EU. eGovernment is one of the key elements in implementation of eEurope and it also plays an important role in realising the Lisbon strategy. The proposal is thus coherent with the objective of the eGovernment initiative because it aims at simplifying administrative procedures.

– Unfair commercial practices. The proposed Directive on unfair business-to-consumer commercial practices[561] regulates those commercial practices

---

561 Proposal for a Directive of the European Parliament and of the Council concerning unfair business-to-consumer commercial practices in the Internal Market and amending Directives 84/450/EEC, 97/7/EC and 98/27/EC (the Unfair Commercial Practices Directive). COM(2003) 356 final of 18.6.2003

which cause harm to consumers' economic interests. That proposal does not cover broader regulation of economic activities such as conditions of establishment. It aims to reduce internal market barriers which arise from a fragmented approach to the regulation of traders' behaviour in relation to their consumers, such as misleading or aggressive sales tactics.

– Cooperation between national authorities responsible for the application of consumer law. The proposal of the Commission for a Regulation[562] on cooperation in the area of consumer protection establishes a network of competent authorities responsible for the protection of consumers in cross-border situations. The proposal ensures that each Member State, on request, effectively protects all EU consumers from rogue traders operating in its territory. In order to ensure effective and efficient enforcement in cross-border cases, the Regulation harmonises certain powers and procedures within the Member States. It also eliminates barriers within Member States to protecting foreign consumers. The provisions on cooperation in this Directive, which do not address the same problems, will be complemented by the Regulation in respect of consumer protection.

– Revision of the acquis in respect of consumer protection. This proposal for a Directive is coherent with the revision of the acquis in respect of consumer protection, including the move towards full harmonisation, notably in the area of contract law.

– The "notification" Directive 98/34/EC. In the case of a draft national law containing a requirement listed in Article 15(2) of this proposal for a Directive, which applies specifically to an information society service and therefore falls within the field of application of Directive 98/34/EC as amended by Directive 98/48/EC, the notification of such a draft in accordance with Directive 98/34/EC as amended by Directive 98/48/EC would also comply with Article 15(6) of this Directive. Furthermore, the Commission is currently examining the possibility of extending the field of application of Directive 98/34/EC to services other than information society services. In this case, the notification procedure provided for in that Directive would, for the services concerned, replace the notification laid down in Article 15(6) of this Directive.

– Private international law. The Commission has presented two initiatives in the area of rules on conflict of laws:

  – the proposal for a Regulation on the law applicable to non-contractual obligations[563] which aims to establish common rules on conflicts of law in order to determine the applicable law in non-contractual matters

---

562 Proposal for a Regulation of the European Parliament and of the Council on cooperation between national authorities responsible for the enforcement of consumer protection laws ("the Regulation on consumer protection cooperation") COM(2003) 443 final of 18.7.2003

563 Proposal for a European Parliament and Council Regulation on the law applicable to non-contractual obligations ("Rome II"). COM(2003) 427 final.

(the applicable law could be that of a third country). In order to ensure coherence with instruments, such as, for example, this proposal for a Directive, which are adopted in the framework of internal market policy and which apply the country of origin principle, the proposal for a Regulation provides (in Article 23(2)) for a specific derogation to ensure the application of this principle;

– the Green Paper on the conversion of the Rome Convention of 1980 on the law applicable to contractual obligations into a Community instrument.[564] The Commission states explicitly in this Green Paper "that it is clear to the Commission that such an instrument must leave intact internal market principles contained in the Treaty or in secondary law".

These instruments could, however, play an important role not only for the activities which are not covered by this Directive but also for the questions which are the object of derogations to the country of origin principle, notably the derogation in relation to contracts concluded by consumers, as well as the derogation relating to the non-contractual liability of the provider in the case of an accident occurring in the context of his activity which affects a person in a Member State which a provider visits.

Finally, it should be noted that the question of determining the jurisdiction of courts is not dealt with by this Directive, but by Regulation (EC) 44/2001 of the Council of 22 December 2000 concerning jurisdiction and the recognition and enforcement of judgements in civil and commercial matters or other Community instruments such as Directive 96/71/EC.

6. LEGAL ASPECTS

a) Legal Base and Choice of Instrument

The proposal for a Directive is based on Articles 47(2) and 55 of the Treaty[565], as well as on Articles 71 and 80(2) of the Treaty for matters concerning transport that are not regulated by other Community instruments based on the latter two Articles. This legal base is justified by both its objective and its content:

---

564 A Green Paper on the conversion of the Rome Convention of 1980 on the law applicable to contractual obligations into a Community instrument and its modernisation, COM(2002) 654 final, 14 January 2003.

565 Article 55 refers to Article 47(2), making it applicable to the free movement of services.

–   objective: Directives adopted under Article 47(2) must aim "to make it easier
     for persons to take up and pursue activities as self-employed persons", which
     is precisely the aim of this proposal;
–   content: the content of the proposal is clearly directed at effectively eliminating
     obstacles to the freedom of establishment and the free movement of services
     by means of provisions that prohibit certain requirements and guarantee the
     free movement of services. Other provisions harmonise certain questions
     in a targeted manner, or ensure administrative cooperation to the extent
     necessary for eliminating these obstacles.

As for the choice of instrument, Article 47(2) specifies the use of a Directive.

b) Subsidiarity

The proposal for a Directive is aimed at eliminating legal obstacles to the freedom
of establishment for service providers and the free movement of services. The
obstacles in question have been clearly identified on the basis of complaints,
petitions and questions from the European Parliament, consultation of interested
parties, and studies or analyses.

This aim cannot be achieved by unilateral action on the part of the Member States.
In accordance with the case law of the Court of Justice, some of these obstacles
may be justified in the absence of a Community instrument and therefore, if they
are to be eliminated, necessitate prior coordination of national schemes, including
through administrative cooperation. Other obstacles are already incompatible with
Articles 43 and 49 of the Treaty but have not yet been eliminated by the Member
States on their own initiative and would require case-by-case treatment by means
of large numbers of infringement procedures, which, as already emphasised, would
be as ineffective as it would be unmanageable.

Furthermore, the concern to keep to a minimum interference with the characteristics
of national regimes has justified certain legislative choices:

–   the proposal does not result in detailed and systematic harmonisation of all
     the national rules applicable to services; it limits itself to the essential aspects
     that must be coordinated in order to guarantee freedom of establishment and
     the free movement of services;
–   the application of the country of origin principle will make it possible to
     achieve the objective of guaranteeing the free movement of services whilst
     allowing the various national regimes to co-exist with all their distinctive
     characteristics. These regimes may not be used to restrict the provision of
     services by an operator established in another Member State;
–   the proposal avoids interference with the institutional organisation of the
     regulation of services in the Member States. For example, it merely specifies
     the functions of the single points of contact without imposing any institutional

characteristics, (type of body – administrative, chamber of commerce, professional body etc.); similarly, in its definition of "competent authority", the proposal (Article 4(8)) takes account of the fact that the competent authority for a given activity may, depending on the Member State, be a professional body, a government authority or a professional association, but does not impose one or the other.

c) **Proportionality**

The principle of proportionality referred to in Article 5 of the Treaty is the factor underlying several legislative choices in the proposal for a Directive:

–　the choice between types of regulation: harmonisation is proposed only as a last resort for matters for which neither administrative cooperation nor reliance on the adoption of codes of conduct by the interested parties at Community level are sufficient; harmonisation is proposed in areas where it is proved to be necessary, such as consumer protection;

–　the content of the harmonisation: the proposal gives as much priority as possible to the service provider's obligations as regards information so that recipients can make an informed choice;

–　the balance between the various regulatory methods: the Directive proposes a balance between, on the one hand, the scope of the country of origin principle and, on the other, the extent of harmonisation, administrative cooperation and reliance on codes of conduct, as well as the number and scope of derogations to the country of origin principle. The balance proposed represents a selective and flexible approach that takes full account of all the interests concerned;

–　the concern to provide a suitable framework for SMEs: the provisions on single points of contact, electronic procedures, information and assistance for service providers, the country of origin principle, the simplification of procedures for the posting of workers, and the voluntary measures in connection with quality policy etc. all stem directly from a wish to make it easier for SMEs to exercise the freedoms of the internal market.

All these legislative choices make it possible to propose a balanced instrument containing provisions that do not go beyond what is necessary for achieving the aim of establishing a genuine internal market in services.

7. SPECIFIC QUESTIONS

a) What Activities are Covered by the Directive (Articles 2 and 4)?

Article 2 defines the scope of the Directive ("services supplied by providers established in a Member State") and Article 4(1) defines a "service" ("any self-employed economic activity, as provided for by Article 50 of the Treaty, consisting of the provision of a service against consideration").

This definition covers a very wide range of activities including, for example, management consultancy, certification and testing, maintenance, facilities management and security, advertising services, recruitment services, including the services of temporary employment agencies, services provided by commercial agents, legal or tax consultancy, property services, such as those provided by estate agencies, construction services, architectural services, distributive trades, organisation of trade fairs and exhibitions, car-hire, security services, tourist services, including travel agencies and tourist guides, audiovisual services, sports centres and amusement parks, leisure services, health services and personal domestic services, such as assistance for old people.

The definition of "service" provided for in this proposal is based on the case law of the Court of Justice,[566] according to which "services" mean any self-employed economic activity normally performed for remuneration, which need not, however, be paid by those for whom the service is performed. The essential characteristic of remuneration lies in the fact that it constitutes consideration for the service in question, irrespective of how this consideration is financed. Consequently, a service is any activity through which a provider participates in the economy, irrespective of his legal status or aims, or the field of action concerned.

Thus the following are covered:

– services provided to consumers, to businesses or to both;
– services provided by an operator who has travelled to the Member State of the recipient, services provided at a distance (via the Internet, for example), services provided in the country of origin following travel by the recipient, or services provided in another Member State to which both the provider and the recipient have travelled (tourist guides, for example);
– services for which a fee is charged or which are free to the final recipient.

However, the definition does not cover non-economic activities, nor activities performed by the State for no consideration as part of its social, cultural, education and judicial functions where there is no element of remuneration.

---

566 Judgements of: 26 April 1988, *Bond van Adverteerders*, Case 352/85, point 16; 27 September 1988, *Humbel*, 263/86, point 17; 11 April 2000, *Deliège*, C-51/96 and C-191/97, point 56; 12 July 2001, *Smits and Peerbooms*, Case C-157/99, point 57.

b) Why Should Certain Services or Fields be Excluded from the Scope of the Directive (Article 2)?

The Directive does not apply to financial services because these activities are already covered by a comprehensive policy – the Financial Services Action Plan,[567] which is currently being implemented and is aimed, like this proposal for a Directive, at establishing a genuine internal market in services. For the same reasons, the Directive does not apply to electronic communications services and networks as far as the questions governed by the Directives in the "telecom package" adopted in 2002 are concerned (Directives 2002/19/EC, 2002/20/EC, 2002/21/CE, 2002/22/EC and 2002/58/EC of the European Parliament and of the Council). Given that transport services are already covered by a set of Community instruments dealing with specific issues in this field, it is appropriate to exclude transport services from the scope of application of this Directive to the extent that they are regulated by other Community instruments based on Articles 71 and 80(2) of the Treaty.

The Directive does not apply in the field of taxation, which has its own legal base. However, in accordance with the case law of the Court, certain tax measures that are not covered by a Community instrument may constitute restrictions contrary to Articles 43[568] (freedom of establishment) and 49[569] of the Treaty (free movement of services), particularly where they have a discriminatory effect. This is why Articles 14 (prohibited requirements in connection with freedom of establishment) and 16 (principle of country of origin in connection with free movement of services) of the proposal for a Directive apply to tax measures that are not covered by a Community instrument.

Finally, it should be noted that the Directive does not apply to activities covered by Article 45 of the Treaty. This provides expressly that the chapter on the freedom of establishment and that on services (by virtue of Article 55 of the Treaty) do not apply to those activities which are directly and specifically connected with the exercise of official authority.

c) What Are "Single Points of Contact" (Article 6)?

The concept of "single points of contact" does not involve each Member State setting up a single, physical, centralised agency for its entire territory. The point of contact is "single" only as far as the individual service provider is concerned. It means that a service provider must be able to complete all the formalities and procedures required for the exercise of service activities, particularly those relating to authorisations, through one and the same body. He must not be obliged to visit a

---

567 "Implementing the framework for financial markets: action plan", COM(1999) 232, 11.5.1999.
568 For example, Judgement of 12 March 1994, *Halliburton*, Case C-1/93.
569 For example, Judgement of 29 November 2001, *de Coster*, Case C-17/00.

number of different bodies, organisations, offices etc. but must be able to complete all the necessary formalities via a single interlocutor.

The number of single points of contact in each Member State, and their institutional nature, will vary depending on the internal organisation of the Member State and in particular the regional or local competencies or the activities concerned. Single points of contact may be the authorities that are directly competent – for issuing authorisation, for example – or bodies that merely function as intermediaries between the service providers and the directly competent authorities.

d) What Is the Difference between the Requirements to be Eliminated (Article 14) and the Requirements to be Evaluated (Article 15)?

The report lists a large number of legal obstacles resulting from requirements in the legal systems of the Member States that prevent, hamper or discourage the establishment of service providers in certain Member States. With a view to making it easier to exercise the freedom of establishment, the proposal provides for two different solutions depending on the type of requirement in question:

– on the one hand, the proposal prohibits certain requirements, listed in Article 14 ("prohibited requirements"), which, particularly in the light of the case law of the Court of Justice, are manifestly incompatible with the freedom of establishment, particularly where they have a discriminatory effect. The prohibition of these requirements will mean that, during the transposition period, each Member State will have to examine systematically whether they exist in its legal system and, if so, eliminate them;

– on the other hand, the proposal requires the Member States to examine a number of other requirements, listed in Article 15 ("requirements to be evaluated"), that have major restrictive effects on the freedom of establishment and have been reported by interested parties, but may be justified in certain cases depending on the precise content of the rules in question and the circumstances in which they apply. For this category of requirements, therefore, during the transposition period, Member States will have to conduct a "screening" of their legislation – in other words, they will have to examine whether requirements of this kind exist in their legal systems, evaluate them in the light of the conditions laid down in the Directive (objectively justifiable by an overriding reason relating to the general interest and satisfying the principle of proportionality), and eliminate them if these conditions are not met. A report on the implementation of this Article must be drawn up not later than at the end of the transposition period.

e) What Will the Mutual Evaluation Procedure Involve (Articles 9, 15, 30 and 41)?

The proposal for a Directive provides for the mutual evaluation of the application of Article 9(1), which sets out the conditions under which a service activity may be subject to an authorisation scheme,[570] Article 15, which lists a number of requirements to be evaluated, and Article 30, which specifies the conditions under which multidisciplinary activities may be limited.

The procedure consists of several phases:

– during the transposition period, Member States must first conduct a "screening" of their legislation in order to ascertain whether requirements of the kind referred to in these three Articles exist in their legal systems, evaluate them in the light of the conditions laid down in the Articles in question, and eliminate or modify them if these conditions are not met,

– by the end of the transposition period at the latest, Member States must draw up a report on the implementation of these three Articles. Each report will be submitted to the other Member States and interested parties, including national consumer associations. Member States will then have six months in which to submit their observations on each of the reports by the other Member States and during the same period the Commission will consult interested parties. This "peer review" procedure will enable exchange between Member States of best practice in the area of the modernising the regulation of services,

– by 31 December 2008 at the latest, the Commission will draw up a synthesis report, accompanied where appropriate by proposals for further initiatives.

A procedure of this kind will make it possible to keep track of the process of modernisation and reform of the regulatory schemes governing services and to identify any need for additional action at Community level.

f) How Will the Implementation of Articles 14, 15 and 16 of the Directive Relate to the Commission's Role as Guardian of the Treaty, in Particular as regards Infringement Procedures?

The list of prohibited requirements (Article 14), requirements to be evaluated (Article 15) and restrictions prohibited under Article 16 obviously do not prevent the Commission from launching, without waiting until the Directive has been

---

570   This does not concern authorisation schemes imposed or permitted by Community law (Article 9(3)), notably those in the field of the environment.

fully transposed, infringement procedures against any measures contrary to the Treaty taken by Member States that it becomes aware of, particularly following a complaint. The obligations provided for in Articles 14, 15 and 16 of the Directive and the procedures provided for in Article 226 of the Treaty have different aims. While the latter concern individual cases resulting from specific circumstances and measures in a particular Member State, the former are on the other hand aimed at ensuring, in a general and systematic fashion, that the legal systems correspond to the requirements of a genuine internal market in services in which the freedom of establishment and free movement of services are facilitated.

g) Are Requirements that are Listed Neither in Article 14 Nor in Article 15 Considered to be in Conformity with the Freedom of Establishment Provided for in Article 43 of the Treaty?

Unlike Article 16(3) of the proposal, which lays down the principle of prohibiting restrictions on the free movement of services and gives a few examples purely for illustrative purposes, Article 14 contains a list of requirements concerning freedom of establishment that must be eliminated and Article 15 contains a list of requirements relating to establishment which must be evaluated. The requirements listed are those that have been identified, particularly in the report, as having considerable restrictive effects and which must, therefore, be the subject of a systematic and general modernisation process. Articles 14 and 15 do not, therefore, concern all the types of restriction that are incompatible with Article 43 of the Treaty, and hence the absence of certain requirements from these lists does not mean that the requirements in question are presumed to be in conformity with the Treaty. Consequently, these lists in no way affect the Commission's scope for opening infringement procedures for failure to respect Article 43 of the Treaty, as the Member States are still obliged to ensure that their legislation is compatible with Community law in all respects.

h) Why Is There a Section Specifically Devoted to the Rights of Recipients of Services (Chapter III Section 2)?

The Commission receives large numbers of complaints from users, particularly consumers, who, even though they wish to benefit from cross-border services and are prepared to bear the cost of such transactions, come up against various types of obstacles. In particular, consumers are often confronted with the application of higher tariffs or with refusals to offer services simply on the grounds that they are nationals of a particular Member State or are resident in a particular country. Problems of this kind, which result not only from acts by public authorities but also from the behaviour of private operators, have been reported in several areas including, for example, participation in sporting or cultural events, access to monuments, museums and tourist sites, promotional offers, use of leisure facilities, entrance to amusement parks etc.

The persistence of discrimination of this kind restricts or eliminates the possibility of cross-border transactions and makes European citizens more acutely aware of the lack of a genuine internal market in services. This inconsistency with the idea of an area without internal borders is particularly felt by recipients now that technological developments provide the opportunity to overcome geographical distances and natural barriers by making it possible for services that had hitherto been strictly national to be provided across borders.

The principle of non-discrimination in the internal market implies that access by recipients – particularly consumers – to services offered to the public should not be denied or rendered more difficult simply because of the formal criterion of the recipient's nationality or place of residence. Consequently, the Directive lays down, to varying degrees, obligations for Member States and service providers.

For the Member States, the proposal stipulates:

–   (Article 20) that Member States may not impose restrictions on recipients on the use of services provided by operators established in a different Member State, and
–   (Article 21(1)), that neither the Member State of origin of the service provider nor the Member State of destination may apply discriminatory measures to recipients based on nationality or place of residence as such. This does not apply to cases where tariffs vary on the basis of other objective criteria such as a direct link with contributions paid by certain recipients.

For service providers, the proposal in Article 21(2) prohibits them, in their general conditions relating to access to their services, from providing for refusal of access, or subjecting access to less favourable conditions, on grounds of the nationality or place of residence of the recipient. This does not prevent service providers from refusing to provide services or applying different tariffs and conditions if they can demonstrate that this is directly justified by objective reasons, such as actual additional costs resulting from the distances involved or the technical aspects of the service.

i) Why Is the Question of the Posting of Third Country Nationals Covered (Article 25)?

The report has shown that service providers who, in the context of providing a service, post a worker who is a third country national from one Member State to another often encounter legal obstacles, including in particular the obligation for the worker in question to have a visa or work permit issued by the authorities of the Member State to which he is posted. The report has also shown that these difficulties affect a whole range of service activities, including those in high-tech sectors that are suffering from a lack of specialised workers.

If these obstacles are to be eliminated, it is vital that the Member State of posting has a number of guarantees regarding the legality of the postings and supervision by the Member State of origin. With a view to giving the Member State of origin this kind of responsibility, it will under Article 25 of the proposal be obliged, on the one hand, to ensure that service providers post workers only if they meet the residence and lawful-employment requirements laid down in their national legislation, and on the other hand to readmit the worker to their territory. In view of these guarantees, Member States of posting may not lay down requirements that conflict with the country of origin principle, such as an obligation to have an entry, exit, residence or work permit, except in the cases provided for in Article 25(2).

j) Why Does the Country of Origin Principle Not Apply to Certain Matters or Activities (Article 17)?

The derogations to the country of origin principle have been determined according to two types of consideration.

(1) The Community acquis. Certain derogations are provided for in order to take into account the fact that existing Community instruments apply the rule according to which cross-border service provision may be subject to the legislation of the country of destination. Concerning a rule contrary to Article 16 of the Directive, derogations are necessary in order to ensure coherence with this acquis. Such derogations concern Directive 96/71/EC (posting of workers), Regulation (EEC) No. 1408/71 (social security), Regulation (EEC) No. 259/93 (transport of waste) and certain instruments on the free movement of persons and the recognition of qualifications.

In other fields, the free movement of services is already the subject of a framework formed by Community instruments which adopt a specific approach compared with that taken in this Directive and which justify a derogation, in particular those dealing with protection of personal data.[571]

(2) The level of disparity between national regimes. For certain activities or matters, too wide a divergence in national approaches or an insufficient level of Community integration may exist and prevent the application of the country of origin principle. As far as possible, the Directive harmonises, or provides for strengthened

---

571 The Directive on the protection of personal data (which also applies the country of origin principle) does not use the same criterion to define the country of origin: it uses the criterion of the establishment of the "controller", while this proposal uses the establishment of the "provider". A derogation is therefore necessary to avoid any conflict which could lead to the designation of two different countries of origin according to each of the Directives.

administrative cooperation, in order to establish the mutual confidence necessary for the application of the country of origin principle. However, in certain cases, it is not possible at this stage to achieve such harmonisation in this Directive or to establish such cooperation and it is therefore necessary to allow for a derogation. These cases concern derogations relating to certain activities such as notarial acts, postal services, electricity, gas and water distribution services as well as those relating to certain questions such as intellectual property, total prohibitions justified by reasons of public policy, public security or public health, rules linked to the specific characteristics of the place where the service is provided justified by reasons of public policy, public security or the protection of public health or the environment, authorisations schemes relating to the reimbursement of the costs of hospital care, registration of vehicles leased in another Member State or derogations on contractual matters or extra-contractual liability.

PROPOSAL FOR A DIRECTIVE OF THE EUROPEAN PARLIAMENT AND OF THE COUNCIL OF [...] ON SERVICES IN THE INTERNAL MARKET [SEC(2004) 21]

/* COM/2004/0002 final – COD 2004/0001 */

(Text with EEA relevance)

THE EUROPEAN PARLIAMENT AND THE COUNCIL OF THE EUROPEAN UNION,

Having regard to the Treaty establishing the European Community, and in particular the first and third sentence of Article 47(2) and Articles 55, 71 and 80(2) thereof,

Having regard to the proposal from the Commission,[572]

Having regard to the opinion of the European Economic and Social Committee,[573]

Having regard to the opinion of the Committee of the Regions,[574]

Acting in accordance with the procedure referred to in Article 251 of the Treaty,[575]

Whereas:

(1) The European Union is seeking to forge ever closer links between the States and peoples of Europe and to ensure economic and social progress. In accordance with Article 14(2) of the Treaty, the internal market comprises an area without internal frontiers in which the free movement of services and the freedom of establishment are ensured. The elimination of obstacles to the development of service activities between Member States is essential in order to strengthen the integration of the peoples of Europe and to promote balanced and sustainable economic and social progress.

---

572 OJ C.
573 OJ C.
574 OJ C.
575 OJ C.

(2) The report from the Commission on "The State of the Internal Market for Services"[576] drew up an inventory of a large number of barriers which are preventing or slowing down the development of services between Member States, in particular those provided by small and medium-sized enterprises (SMEs), which are predominant in the field of services. The report concludes that a decade after the envisaged completion of the internal market, there is still a huge gap between the vision of an integrated European Union economy and the reality as experienced by European citizens and service providers. The barriers listed affect a wide variety of service activities across all stages of the service provider's activity and have a number of common features, including, in particular, the fact that they often arise from administrative burdens, the legal uncertainty associated with cross-border activity and the lack of mutual trust between Member States.

(3) Since services constitute the engine of economic growth and account for 70% of GDP and employment in the majority of Member States, this fragmentation of the internal market has a negative impact on the entire European economy, in particular on the competitiveness of SMEs, and prevents consumers from gaining access to a greater variety of competitively priced services. The European Parliament and the Council have emphasised that the removal of legal barriers to the establishment of a genuine internal market is a matter of priority for achieving the goal set by the Lisbon European Council of making the European Union the most competitive and dynamic knowledge-based economy in the world by 2010. Removing those barriers is essential in order to revive the European economy, particularly in terms of employment and investment.

(4) It is therefore necessary to remove barriers to the freedom of establishment for service providers in Member States and barriers to the freedom to provide services as between Member States and to guarantee providers and recipients the legal certainty necessary for the exercise in practice of those two fundamental freedoms of the Treaty. Since the barriers in the internal market for services affect operators who wish to become established in other Member States as well as those who provide a service in another Member State without being established there, it is necessary to enable service providers to develop their service activities within the internal market either by becoming established in a Member State or by making use of the freedom to provide services. Service providers should be able to choose between those two freedoms, depending on their strategy for growth in each Member State.

(5) Those barriers cannot be removed solely by relying on direct application of Articles 43 and 49 of the Treaty, since, on the one hand, addressing them on a case-by-case basis through infringement procedures against the Member States concerned would, especially following enlargement, be extremely complicated for

---

576   COM(2002) 441 final.

national and Community institutions, and, on the other hand, the lifting of many barriers requires prior coordination of national legal schemes, including the setting up of administrative cooperation. As the European Parliament and the Council have recognised, a Community legislative instrument makes it possible to achieve a genuine internal market for services.

(6) This Directive establishes a general legal framework which benefits a wide variety of services while taking into account the distinctive features of each type of activity or profession and its system of regulation. That framework is based on a dynamic and selective approach consisting in the removal, as a matter of priority, of barriers which may be dismantled quickly and, for the others, the launching of a process of evaluation, consultation and complementary harmonisation of specific issues, which will make possible the progressive and coordinated modernisation of national regulatory systems for service activities which is vital in order to achieve a genuine internal market for services by 2010. Provision should be made for a balanced mix of measures involving targeted harmonisation, administrative cooperation, the country of origin principle and encouragement of the development of codes of conduct on certain issues. That coordination of national legislative regimes should ensure a high degree of Community legal integration and a high level of protection of general interest objectives, especially of consumer protection, which is vital in order to establish mutual trust between Member States.

(7) It is necessary to recognise the importance of the roles of professional bodies and professional associations in the regulation of service activities and the development of professional rules.

(8) This Directive is consistent with other current Community initiatives concerning services, particularly those relating to the competitiveness of business-related services, the safety of services,[577] and work on patient mobility and the development of healthcare in the Community. It is also consistent with current initiatives concerning the internal market, such as the proposal for a Regulation of the European Parliament and of the Council on sales promotions in the internal market,[578] and those concerning consumer protection, such as the proposal for a Directive on unfair commercial practices[579] and the proposal for a Regulation of the European Parliament and of the Council on cooperation between national authorities responsible for the enforcement of consumer protection laws ("the Regulation on consumer protection cooperation").[580]

---

577   COM(2003) 313 final; OJ C 299, 10.12.2003, p. 1.
578   COM(2002) 585 final.
579   COM(2003) 356 final.
580   COM(2003) 443 final.

(9) Financial services should be excluded from the scope of this Directive since those activities are currently the subject of a specific action plan aimed, as is this Directive, at achieving a genuine internal market for services. Financial services are defined in Directive 2002/65/EC of the European Parliament and of the Council of 23 September 2002 concerning the distance marketing of consumer financial services and amending Council Directive 90/619/EEC and Directives 97/7/EC and 98/27/EC.[581] That Directive defines a financial service as any service of a banking, credit, insurance, personal pension, investment or payment nature.

(10) In view of the adoption in 2002 of a package of legislative instruments relating to electronic communications networks and services, as well as to associated resources and services, which has established a regulatory framework to facilitate access to those activities within the internal market, notably through the elimination of most individual authorisation schemes, it is necessary to exclude issues dealt with by those instruments from the scope of this Directive.

(11) In view of the fact that the Treaty provides specific legal bases for taxation matters and for the Community instruments already adopted in that field, it is necessary to exclude the field of taxation from the scope of this Directive, with the exception, however, of the provisions concerning prohibited requirements and the free movement of services. Harmonisation in the field of taxation has been achieved notably through Council Directive 77/388/EEC of 17 May 1977 on the harmonisation of the laws of the Member States relating to turnover taxes – Common system of value added tax: uniform basis of assessment,[582] Council Directive 90/434/EEC of 23 July 1990 on the common system of taxation applicable to mergers, divisions, transfers of assets and exchanges of shares concerning companies of different Member States,[583] Council Directive 90/435/EEC of 23 July 1990 on the common system of taxation applicable in the case of parent companies and subsidiaries of different Member States[584] and Council Directive 2003/49/EC of 3 June 2003 on a common system of taxation applicable to interest and royalty payments made between associated companies of different Member States.[585] The present Directive does not aim to introduce specific new rules or systems in the field of taxation. Its sole objective is to remove restrictions, certain of which are fiscal in nature, and in particular those which are discriminatory, on freedom of establishment and the free movement of services, in accordance with the case law of the Court of Justice of the European Communities, hereinafter "the Court of Justice", with respect to Articles 43 and 49 of the Treaty. The field of value added tax (VAT) is

---

581 OJ L 271, 9.10.2002, p. 16.
582 OJ L 145, 13.6.1977, p. 1. Directive as last amended by Directive 2003/92/EC (OJ L 260, 11.10.2003, p. 8).
583 OJ L 225, 20.8.1990, p. 1.
584 OJ L 225, 20.8.1990 p. 6.
585 OJ L 157, 26.6.2003 p. 49.

the subject of harmonisation at Community level, in accordance with which service providers carrying out cross-border activities may be subject to obligations other than those of the country in which they are established. It is nevertheless desirable to establish a system of "one-stop shops" for service providers, in order to enable all their obligations to be fulfilled by means of a single electronic portal to the tax authorities in their home Member State.

(12) Since transport services are already covered by a set of Community instruments specific to that field, they should be excluded from the scope of this Directive to the extent that they are regulated by other Community instruments adopted under Articles 71 and 80(2) of the Treaty. However, this Directive applies to services that are not regulated by specific instruments concerning transport, such as cash in transit or the transport of mortal remains.

(13) There is already a considerable body of Community law on service activities, especially the regulated professions, postal services, television broadcasting, information society services and services relating to travel, holidays and package tours. Service activities are also covered by other instruments which do not deal with a specific category of services, such as those relating to consumer protection. This Directive builds on, and thus complements, the Community acquis. Where a service activity is already covered by one or more Community instruments, this Directive and those instruments will all apply, the requirements laid down by one adding to those laid down by the others. Accordingly, appropriate provisions should be laid down, including provision for derogations, in order to prevent incompatibilities and to ensure consistency as between all those Community instruments.

(14) The concept of service covers a wide variety of ever-changing activities, including business services such as management consultancy, certification and testing; facilities management, including office maintenance and security; advertising; recruitment services, including employment agencies; and the services of commercial agents. That concept also covers services provided both to businesses and to consumers, such as legal or fiscal advice; real estate services such as estate agencies; construction, including the services of architects; transport; distributive trades; the organisation of trade fairs; car rental; travel agencies; and security services. It also covers consumer services, such as those in the field of tourism, including tour guides; audio-visual services; leisure services, sports centres and amusement parks; health and healthcare services; and household support services, such as help for the elderly. Those activities may involve services requiring the proximity of provider and recipient, services requiring travel by the recipient or the provider and services which may be provided at a distance, including via the Internet.

(15) As the Court of Justice has consistently held with regard to Articles 49 et seq of the Treaty, the concept of service covers any economic activity normally provided for remuneration, without the service having to be paid for by those benefiting from

it and regardless of the financing arrangements for the remuneration received in return, by way of consideration. Any service whereby a provider participates in the economy, irrespective of his legal status or aims, or the field of action concerned, thus constitutes a service.

(16) The characteristic of remuneration is absent in the case of activities performed, for no consideration, by the State in fulfilment of its social, cultural, educational and legal obligations. These activities are not covered by the definition in Article 50 of the Treaty and do not therefore fall within the scope of this Directive.

(17) This Directive does not concern the application of Articles 28 to 30 of the Treaty relating to the free movement of goods. The restrictions prohibited pursuant to the country of origin principle cover the requirements applicable to access to service activities or to the exercise thereof and not those applicable to goods as such.

(18) The concept of provider covers any natural person who is a national of a Member State or any legal person who is engaged in a service activity there, in exercise either of the freedom of establishment or of the freedom to provide services. The concept of provider is thus not limited solely to cross-border service provision within the framework of the freedom to provide services but also covers cases in which an operator establishes itself in a Member State in order to develop its service activities there. On the other hand, the concept of a provider does not cover the case of branches in a Member State of companies from third countries because, under Article 48 of the Treaty, the freedom of establishment and free movement of services may benefit only companies constituted in accordance with the laws of a Member State and having their registered office, central administration or principal place of business within the Community.

(19) Where an operator travels to another Member State to exercise a service activity there, a distinction should be made between situations covered by the freedom of establishment and those covered, due to the temporary nature of the activities concerned, by the free movement of services. The Court of Justice has consistently held that the temporary nature of the activities in question must be determined in the light not only of the duration of the provision of the service, but also of its regularity, periodical nature or continuity. In any case, the fact that the activity is temporary does not mean that the service provider may not equip himself with some forms of infrastructure in the host Member State, such as an office, chambers or consulting rooms, in so far as such infrastructure is necessary for the purposes of providing the service in question.

(20) The concept of authorisation scheme covers, *inter alia*, the administrative procedures for granting authorisations, licences, approvals or concessions, and also the obligation, in order to be eligible to exercise the activity, to be registered as a member of a profession or entered in a register, roll or database, to be officially

appointed to a body or to obtain a card attesting to membership of a particular profession. Authorisation may be granted not only by a formal decision but also by an implicit decision arising, for example, from the silence of the competent authority or from the fact that the interested party must await acknowledgement of receipt of a declaration in order to commence the activity in question or for the latter to become lawful.

(21) The concept of the coordinated field covers all requirements applicable to access to service activities and to the exercise thereof, in particular those laid down by the laws, regulations and administrative provisions of each Member State, whether or not they fall within an area harmonised at Community level or are general or specific in nature and regardless of the legal field to which they belong under national law.

(22) One of the fundamental difficulties faced, in particular by SMEs, in accessing service activities and exercising them is the complexity, length and legal uncertainty of administrative procedures. For this reason, following the example of certain modernising and good administrative practice initiatives undertaken at Community and national level, it is necessary to establish principles of administrative simplification, *inter alia* through the introduction, coordinated at Community level, of a system of single points of contact, limitation of the obligation of prior authorisation to cases in which it is essential and the introduction of the principle of tacit authorisation by the competent authorities after a certain period of time has elapsed. Such modernising action, while maintaining the requirements on transparency and the updating of information relating to operators, is intended to eliminate the delays, costs and dissuasive effects which arise, for example, from unnecessary or excessively complex and burdensome procedures, the duplication of procedures, the red tape involved in submitting documents, the use of discretionary powers by the competent authorities, indeterminate or excessively long periods before a response is given, the limited duration of validity of authorisations granted and disproportionate fees and penalties. Such practices have particularly significant dissuasive effects on providers wishing to develop their activities in other Member States and require coordinated modernisation within an enlarged internal market of twenty-five Member States.

(23) In order to facilitate access to service activities and the exercise thereof in the internal market, it is necessary to establish an objective, common to all Member States, of administrative simplification and to lay down provisions concerning, *inter alia*, single points of contact, the right to information, procedures by electronic means and the establishment of a framework for authorisation schemes. Other measures adopted at national level to meet that objective may involve reduction of the number of procedures and formalities applicable to service activities and the restriction of such procedures and formalities to those which are essential in

order to achieve a general interest objective and which do not duplicate each other in terms of content or purpose.

(24) With the aim of administrative simplification, general formal requirements, such as a certified translation, must not be imposed, except where objectively justified by an overriding reason relating to the public interest, such as the protection of workers. It is also necessary to ensure that an authorisation normally permits access to, or exercise of, a service activity throughout the national territory, unless a new authorisation for each establishment, for example for each new hypermarket, is objectively justified by an overriding reason relating to the public interest, such as protection of the urban environment.

(25) It is appropriate to provide for single points of contact in order to ensure that each provider has a single point at which he can complete all procedures and formalities. The number of single points of contact per Member State may vary according to regional or local competencies or according to the activities concerned. The creation of single points of contact does not interfere with the allocation of functions among competent authorities within each national system. Where several authorities at regional or local level are competent, one of them may assume the role of single point of contact and coordinator. Single points of contact may be set up not only by administrative authorities but also by chambers of commerce or crafts, or by the professional organisations or private bodies to which a Member State decides to entrust that function. Single points of contact have an important role to play in providing assistance to providers either as the authority directly competent to issue the documents necessary to access a service activity or as an intermediary between the provider and the authorities which are directly competent. In its Recommendation of 22 April 1997 on improving and simplifying the business environment for business start-ups,[586] the Commission was already encouraging Member States to introduce points of contact to simplify formalities.

(26) The setting up, in the reasonably near future, of electronic means of completing procedures and formalities will be vital for administrative simplification in the field of service activities, for the benefit of providers, recipients and competent authorities. In order to meet that obligation as to results, national laws and other rules applicable to services may need to be adapted. The fact that it must be possible to complete those procedures and formalities at a distance means in particular that Member States must ensure that they may be completed across borders. The obligation as to results does not cover procedures or formalities which by their very nature are impossible to complete at a distance.

(27) The possibility of gaining access to a service activity may be made subject to authorisation by the competent authorities only if that decision satisfies the criteria

---

586   OJ L 145, 5.6.1997, p. 29.

of non-discrimination, necessity and proportionality. That means, in particular, that authorisation schemes should be permissible only where an *a posteriori* inspection would not be effective because of the impossibility of ascertaining the defects of the services concerned *a posteriori*, due account being taken of the risks and dangers which could arise in the absence of a prior inspection. However, the provision to that effect made by this Directive cannot be relied upon in order to justify authorisation schemes which are prohibited by other Community instruments such as Directive 1999/93/EC of the European Parliament and the Council of 13 December 1999 on a Community framework for electronic signatures,[587] or Directive 2000/31/EC of the European Parliament and of the Council of 8 June 2000 on certain legal aspects of information society services, in particular electronic commerce, in the internal market ("Directive on electronic commerce").[588] The results of the process of mutual evaluation will make it possible to determine, at Community level, the types of activity for which authorisation schemes should be eliminated.

(28) In cases where the number of authorisations available for an activity is limited because of scarcity of natural resources or technical capacity, as may be the position, for example, with regard to the award of analogue radio frequencies or the exploitation of hydro-electric plant, a procedure for selection from among several potential candidates must be adopted, with the aim of developing through open competition the quality and conditions for supply of services available to users. Such a procedure must provide guarantees of transparency and impartiality and the authorisation thus granted must not have an excessive duration, or be subject to automatic renewal, or confer any advantage on the successful provider. In particular, the duration of the authorisation granted must be fixed in such as way that it does not restrict or limit free competition beyond what is necessary to enable the provider to recoup the cost of investment and to make a fair return on the capital invested. Cases where the number of authorisations is limited for reasons other than scarcity of natural resources or technical capacity remain in any case subject to the other provisions of this Directive relating to authorisation schemes.

(29) The overriding reasons relating to the public interest to which reference is made in certain harmonisation provisions of this Directive are those recognised by the Court of Justice in relation to Articles 43 and 49 of the Treaty, notably the protection of consumers, recipients of services, workers and the urban environment.

(30) In order to establish a genuine internal market for services, it is necessary to abolish any restrictions on the freedom of establishment and the free movement of services which are still enshrined in the laws of certain Member States and which are incompatible with Articles 43 and 49 of the Treaty respectively. The restrictions

---

587   OJ L 13, 19.1.2000, p. 12.
588   OJ L 178, 17.7.2000, p. 1.

to be prohibited particularly affect the internal market for services and should be systematically dismantled as soon as possible.

(31) The Court of Justice has consistently held that the freedom of establishment is predicated, in particular, upon the principle of equal treatment, which entails the prohibition not only of any discrimination on grounds of nationality but also of any indirect discrimination based on other grounds but capable of producing the same result. Thus, access to a service activity or the exercise thereof in a Member State, either as a principal or secondary activity, may not be made subject to criteria such as place of establishment, residence, domicile or principal provision of the service activity. Similarly, a Member State may not restrict the legal capacity or the right to bring legal proceedings of companies incorporated in accordance with the law of another Member State on whose territory they have their primary establishment. Moreover, a Member State may not confer any advantages on providers having a particular national or local socio-economic link; nor may it restrict, on grounds of place of establishment, the provider's freedom to acquire, exploit or dispose of rights and goods or to access different forms of credit or accommodation in so far as those choices are useful for access to his activity or for the effective exercise thereof.

(32) The prohibition of economic tests as a prerequisite for the grant of authorisation covers economic tests as such, but not requirements which are objectively justified by overriding reasons relating to the public interest, such as protection of the urban environment. That prohibition does not affect the exercise of the powers of the authorities responsible for applying competition law.

(33) In order to coordinate the modernisation of national rules and regulations in a manner consistent with the requirements of the internal market, it is necessary to evaluate certain non-discriminatory national requirements which, by their very nature, could severely restrict or even prevent access to an activity or the exercise thereof under the freedom of establishment. Member States must ensure, during the transposition period of this Directive, that such requirements are necessary and proportionate and, where appropriate, they must abolish or amend them. Moreover, those requirements must in any case be compatible with Community competition law.

(34) The restrictions to be examined include national rules which, on grounds other than those relating to professional qualifications, reserve access to activities such as games of chance to particular providers. Similarly, among the requirements to be examined are "must carry" rules applicable to cable operators which, by imposing an obligation on an intermediary service provider to give access to certain services delivered by specific service providers, affect his freedom of choice, access to programmes and the choice of the recipients.

(35) It is appropriate that the provisions of this Directive concerning freedom of establishment should apply only to the extent that the activities in question are open to competition, so that they do not oblige Member States to abolish existing monopolies, notably those of lotteries, or to privatise certain sectors.

(36) The fact that this Directive specifies a number of requirements to be abolished or evaluated by the Member States during the transposition period is without prejudice to any infringement proceedings against a Member State for failure to fulfil its obligations under Articles 43 or 49 of the Treaty.

(37) In order to secure effective implementation of the free movement of services and to ensure that recipients and providers can benefit from and supply services throughout the Community regardless of frontiers, it is necessary to establish the principle that a provider may be subject only to the law of the Member State in which he is established. That principle is essential in order to enable providers, especially SMEs, to avail themselves with full legal certainty of the opportunities offered by the internal market. By thus facilitating the free movement of services between Member States, that principle, together with harmonisation and mutual assistance measures, also enables recipients to gain access to a wider choice of high quality services from other Member States. That principle should be complemented by an assistance mechanism enabling the recipient, in particular, to be informed about the laws of the other Member States, and by the harmonisation of rules on the transparency of service activities.

(38) It is also necessary to ensure that supervision of service activities is carried out at source, that is to say, by the competent authorities of the Member State in which the provider is established. The competent authorities of the country of origin are best placed to ensure the effectiveness and continuity of supervision of the provider and to provide protection for recipients not only in their own Member State but also elsewhere in the Community. In order to establish mutual trust between Member States in the regulation of service activities, it should be clearly laid down that responsibility under Community law for supervision of the activities of providers, regardless of the place where the service is provided, lies with the Member State of origin. Determination of judicial jurisdiction does not fall within the scope of this Directive but within that of Council Regulation (EC) No. 44/2001 of 22 December 2000 on jurisdiction and the recognition and enforcement of judgements in civil and commercial matters,[589] or other Community instruments such as Directive 96/71/EC of the European Parliament and of the Council of 16 December 1996 concerning the posting of workers in the framework of the provision of services.[590]

---

589 OJ L 12, 16.1.2001, p. 1. Directive as last amended by the Act of Accession 2003.
590 OJ L 18, 21.1.1997, p. 1.

(39) As a corollary to the principle that the law of the country of origin should apply and that the country of origin should be responsible for supervision, it is necessary to lay down the principle that Member States may not restrict services coming from another Member State.

(40) It is necessary to provide that the rule that the law of the country of origin is to apply may be departed from only in the areas covered by derogations, general or transitional. Those derogations are necessary in order to take into account the level of integration of the internal market or certain Community instruments relating to services pursuant to which a provider is subject to the application of a law other than that of the Member State of origin. Moreover, by way of exception, measures against a given provider may also be adopted in certain individual cases and under certain strict procedural and substantive conditions. In order to ensure the legal certainty which is essential in order to encourage SMEs to provide their services in other Member States, those derogations should be limited to what is strictly necessary. In particular, derogation should be possible only for reasons related to the safety of services, exercise of a health profession or matters of public policy, such as the protection of minors, and to the extent that national provisions in this field have not been harmonised. In addition, any restriction of the freedom to provide services should be permitted, by way of exception, only if it is consistent with fundamental rights which, as the Court of Justice has consistently held, form an integral part of the general principles of law enshrined in the Community legal order.

(41) In cases where a provider moves temporarily to a Member State other than the Member State of origin, it is necessary to provide for mutual assistance between those two States so that the former can carry out checks, inspections and enquiries at the request of the Member State of origin or carry out such checks on its own initiative if these are merely factual checks. Moreover, it should be possible in the case of posted workers for the Member State of posting to take action against a provider established in another Member State in order to ensure compliance with the employment and working conditions applicable under Directive 96/71/EC.

(42) It is appropriate to provide for derogation from the country of origin principle in the case of services covered by a general prohibition in the Member State to which a provider has moved, if that prohibition is objectively justified by reasons relating to public policy, public security or public health. That derogation should be limited to general prohibitions and should not, for example, cover national schemes which, while not prohibiting an activity in a general manner, reserve the exercise of that activity to one or several specific operators, or which prohibit the exercise of an activity without prior authorisation. The fact that a Member State permits an activity, but reserves it to certain operators, means that the activity is not subject to a general prohibition and is not regarded as inherently contrary to public policy, public security or public health. Consequently, the exclusion of such an activity from the scope of the Directive would not be justified.

(43) The country of origin principle should not apply to specific requirements, laid down by the Member State to which a provider has moved, the rationale for which is inextricably linked to the particular characteristics of the place where the service is provided, and which must be fulfilled in order to maintain public policy, public safety, public health or the protection of the environment. Such would be the position, for example, in the case of authorisations to occupy or use the public highway, requirements relating to the organisation of public events or requirements relating to the safety of building sites.

(44) The exclusion from the country of origin principle of matters relating to the registration of vehicles leased in a Member State other than that in which they are used follows from the case law of the Court of Justice, which has accepted that a Member State may impose such an obligation, in accordance with proportionate conditions, in the case of vehicles used on its territory. That exclusion does not cover occasional or temporary rental.

(45) A number of Directives concerning contracts concluded by consumers have already been adopted at Community level. However, the approach followed by those Directives is one of minimal harmonisation. In order to limit as far as possible divergences between consumer protection rules across the Community that fragment the internal market to the detriment of consumers and enterprises, the Commission stated in its Communication on consumer policy strategy 2002-2006[591] that one of the its key priorities would be full harmonisation. Furthermore, the Commission stressed in its Action Plan on "A more coherent European contract law"[592] the need for greater coherence in European consumer law which would entail, in particular, a review of the existing law on contracts concluded with consumers in order to remedy residual inconsistencies, to fill gaps and to simplify legislation.

(46) It is appropriate to apply the country of origin principle to the field of contracts concluded by consumers for the supply of services only to the extent that Community Directives provide for full harmonisation, because in such cases the levels of consumer protection are equivalent. The derogation from the country of origin principle relating to the non-contractual liability of a provider in the case of an accident involving a person and occurring as a consequence of the service provider's activities in the Member State into which he has moved temporarily concerns physical or material damage suffered by a person in the accident.

(47) It is necessary to allow Member States the possibility, exceptionally and on a case-by-case basis, of taking measures which derogate from the country of origin principle in respect of a provider established in another Member State, for certain reasons such as the safety of services. It should be possible to take such

---

591   OJ C 137, 8.6.2002, p. 2.
592   OJ C 63, 15.3.2003, p. 1.

measures only in the absence of harmonisation at Community level. Moreover, that possibility should not permit restrictive measures to be taken in areas in which other Directives prohibit all derogation from the free movement of services, such as Directive 1999/93/EC or Directive 98/84/EC of the European Parliament and the Council of 20 November 1998 on the legal protection of services based on, or consisting of, conditional access.[593] Nor should that possibility permit the extension or limitation of derogations provided for in other Directives, such as Council Directive 89/552/EEC of 3 October 1989 on the coordination of certain provisions laid down by law, regulation or administrative action in Member States concerning the pursuit of television broadcasting activities[594] or Directive 2000/31/EC.

(48) Restrictions on the free movement of services, contrary to this Directive, may arise not only from measures applied to providers, but also from the many barriers to the use of services by recipients, especially consumers. This Directive mentions, by way of illustration, certain types of restriction applied to a recipient wishing to use a service performed by a provider established in another Member State.

(49) In accordance with the Treaty rules on the free movement of services, as interpreted by the Court of Justice, discrimination on grounds of the recipient's nationality or national or local residence is prohibited. Such discrimination could take the form of an obligation, imposed only on nationals of another Member State, to supply original documents, certified copies, a certificate of nationality or official translations of documents in order to benefit from a service or from more advantageous terms or prices. However, the prohibition of discriminatory requirements does not preclude the reservation of advantages, especially as regards tariffs, to certain recipients, if such reservation is based on legitimate, objective criteria, such as a direct link to taxes paid by those recipients.

(50) If an internal area without frontiers is to be effectively achieved, Community citizens must neither be prevented from benefiting from a service which is technically accessible on the market, nor be made subject to different conditions and tariffs, by reason of their nationality or place of residence. The persistence of such discrimination with respect to the recipients of services highlights, for the Community citizen, the absence of a genuine internal market in services and, in a more general sense, compromises the integration of the peoples of Europe. The principle of non-discrimination within the internal market means that access by a recipient, and especially by a consumer, to a service on offer to the public may not be denied or hampered by application of a criterion, included in general conditions made available to the public, relating to the recipient's nationality or place of residence. It does not follow that provision may not be made in such general conditions for

---

593   OJ L 320, 28.11.1998, p. 54.
594   OJ L 298, 17.10.1989, p. 23. Directive as amended by Directive 97/36/EC of the European Parliament and of the Council (OJ L 202, 30.1.1997, p. 60).

variable tariffs and conditions to apply to the provision of a service, where those tariffs and conditions are directly justified for objective reasons such as additional costs effectively incurred because of the distance involved or the technical characteristics of the provision of the service, or different market conditions, or extra risks linked to rules differing from those of the Member State of origin.

(51) In accordance with the principles established by the Court of Justice with regard to the freedom to provide services, and without endangering the financial balance of Member States' social security systems, greater legal certainty as regards the reimbursement of health costs should be provided for patients, who benefit as recipients from the free movement of services, and for health professionals and managers of social security systems.

(52) Council Regulation (EEC) No. 1408/71 of 14 June 1971 on the application of social security schemes to employed persons, to self-employed persons and to members of their families moving within the Community[595] and, in particular, its provisions regarding affiliation to a system of social security, fully applies to employed and self-employed workers who provide or take part in the supply of a service.

(53) Article 22 of Regulation (EEC) No. 1408/71, which concerns authorisation for assuming the costs of healthcare provided in another Member State, contributes, as the Court of Justice has emphasised, to facilitating the free movement of patients and the provision of cross-border medical services. The purpose of that provision is to ensure that insured persons possessing an authorisation have access to healthcare in another Member State under conditions which, as regards the assumption of costs, are as favourable as those applying to insured persons in that Member State. It thus confers on insured persons rights they would not otherwise have and facilitates the free movement of services. On the other hand, that provision does not seek to regulate, nor in any way to prevent, reimbursement, at the rates applicable in the Member State of affiliation, of the costs of healthcare provided in another Member State, even in the absence of a prior authorisation.

(54) In the light of the case law developed by the Court of Justice on the free movement of services, it is necessary to abolish the requirement of prior authorisation for reimbursement by the social security system of a Member State for non-hospital care provided in another Member State, and Member States must amend their legislation accordingly. In so far as the reimbursement of such care remains within the limits of the cover guaranteed by the sickness insurance scheme of the Member State of affiliation, abolition of the prior authorisation requirement is not likely seriously to disrupt the financial equilibrium of social security systems. As the Court of Justice has consistently held, the conditions under which Member States grant non-hospital

---

595   OJ L 149, 5.7.1971, p. 2. Regulation as last amended by the Act of Accession 2003.

care on their own territory remain applicable in the case of care provided in a Member State other than that of affiliation in so far as those conditions are compatible with Community law. By the same token, authorisation schemes for the assumption of costs of care in another Member State must comply with this Directive as regards the conditions for granting authorisation and the related procedures.

(55) As the Court of Justice has consistently held with regard to the free movement of services, a system of prior authorisation for the reimbursement of hospital care provided in another Member State appears justified by the need to plan the number of hospital infrastructures, their geographical distribution, the mode of their organisation, the equipment with which they are provided and even the nature of the medical services which they are able to offer. The aims of such planning are to ensure, within each Member State, sufficient permanent access to a balanced range of quality hospital care, to secure efficient cost management and, so far as is possible, to avoid wastage of financial, technical or human resources. In accordance with the case law of the Court of Justice, the concept of hospital care must be objectively defined and a system of prior authorisation must be proportionate to the general interest objective pursued.

(56) Article 22 of Council Regulation (EEC) No. 1408/71 specifies the circumstances in which the competent national institution may not refuse an authorisation sought on the basis of that provision. Member States may not refuse authorisation in cases where the hospital care in question, when provided in their territory, is covered by their social security system, and treatment which is identical or equally effective cannot be obtained in time in their territory under the conditions laid down by their social security system. The Court of Justice has consistently held that the condition relating to acceptable delay must be considered together with all the circumstances of each case, taking due account not only of the medical condition of the patient at the time when authorisation is requested, but also his medical history and the probable evolution of his illness.

(57) The assumption of costs, by the social security systems of the Member States, in respect of healthcare provided in another Member State must not be lower than that provided for by their own social security system for healthcare provided in their territory. As the Court has consistently pointed out with regard to the free movement of services, in the absence of authorisation, the reimbursement of non-hospital care in accordance with the scales of the Member State of affiliation would not have a significant effect on the financing of its social security system. In cases where authorisation has been granted, in the framework of Article 22 of Regulation (EEC) No. 1408/71, the assumption of costs is made in accordance with the rates applicable in the Member State in which the healthcare is provided. However, if the level of coverage is lower than that to which the patient would have been entitled if he had received the same care in the Member State of affiliation, the latter must assume the remaining costs up to the level which would have applied.

(58) As regards the posting of workers in the context of the provision of services in a Member State other than the Member State of origin, it is necessary to clarify the division of roles and tasks between the Member State of origin and the Member State of posting, in order to facilitate the free movement of services. The present Directive does not aim to address issues of labour law as such. The division of tasks and the specifying of the forms of cooperation between the Member State of origin and the Member State of posting facilitates the free movement of services, especially by abolishing certain disproportionate administrative procedures, while also improving the monitoring of compliance with employment and working conditions in accordance with Directive 96/71/EC.

(59) In order to avoid discriminatory or disproportionate administrative formalities, which would be a disincentive to SMEs in particular, it is necessary to preclude the Member State of posting from making postings subject to compliance with requirements such as an obligation to request authorisation from the authorities. The obligation to make a declaration to the authorities of the Member State of posting should also be prohibited. However, it should be possible to maintain such an obligation until 31 December 2008 in the field of building work in accordance with the Annex to Directive 96/71/EC. In that connection, a group of Member State experts on the application of that Directive are studying ways to improve administrative cooperation between Member States in order to facilitate supervision. Furthermore, as regards employment and working conditions other than those laid down in Directive 96/71/EC, it should not be possible for the Member State of posting to take restrictive measures against a provider established in another Member State.

(60) By virtue of the free movement of services, a service provider is entitled to post workers even if they are not Community citizens but third country nationals, provided that they are legally present and lawfully employed in the Member State of origin. It is appropriate to place the Member State of origin under an obligation to ensure that any posted worker who is a third country national fulfils the conditions for residence and lawful employment laid down in its legislation, including with regard to social security. It is also appropriate to preclude the host Member State from imposing on the worker or the provider any preventative controls, especially as regards right of entry or residence permits, except in certain cases. Nor should it be possible for the host Member State to impose any obligations such as possession of an employment contract of indefinite duration or a record of previous employment in the Member State of origin of the provider.

(61) Following the adoption of Council Regulation (EC) No. 859/2003 of 14 May 2003 extending the provisions of Regulation (EEC) No. 1408/71 and Regulation (EEC) No. 574/72 to nationals of third countries who are not already covered by

those provisions solely on the ground of their nationality,[596] third country nationals are covered by a system of cooperation on the application of social security schemes to employed persons and to members of their families moving within the Community, established by Regulation (EEC) No. 1408/71, under which the rules of the country under whose social security scheme the worker is insured are to apply.

(62) It is appropriate to provide that, as one of the means by which the provider may make the information which he is obliged to supply easily accessible to the recipient, he is to supply his electronic address, including that of his website. Furthermore, the obligation to present certain information in the provider's information documents presenting his services in detail should not cover commercial communications of a general nature, such as advertising, but rather documents giving a detailed description of the services proposed, including documents on a website.

(63) Any operator providing services involving a particular health, safety or financial risk for the recipient should be covered by appropriate professional indemnity insurance, or by another form of guarantee which is equivalent or comparable, which means, in particular, that he should have adequate insurance coverage for services provided in one or more Member States other than the Member State of origin.

(64) It is necessary to put an end to the total prohibitions of commercial communications by the regulated professions, not by removing bans on the content of a commercial communication but rather those which, in a general way and for a given profession, forbid one or more forms of commercial communication, such as a ban on all advertising in one or more given media. As regards the content and methods of commercial communication, it is necessary to encourage professionals to draw up, in accordance with Community law, codes of conduct at Community level.

(65) In order to increase transparency and promote assessments based on comparable criteria with regard to the quality of the services offered and supplied to recipients, it is important that information on the meaning of quality labels and other distinctive marks relating to these services be easily accessible. That obligation of transparency is particularly important in areas such as tourism, especially the hotel business, in which the use of a system of classification is widespread. Moreover, it is appropriate to examine the extent to which European standardisation could facilitate compatibility and quality of services. European standards are drawn up by the European standards-setting bodies, the European Committee for Standardisation (CEN), the European Committee for Electrotechnical Standardisation (CENELEC) and the European Telecommunications Standards Institute (ETSI). Where appropriate, the Commission may, in accordance with the procedures laid down in Directive 98/34/EC of the European Parliament and of the Council of 22 June 1998[597] laying

---

596   OJ L 124, 20.5.2003, p. 1.
597   OJ L 204, 21.7.1998, p. 37. Directive as last amended by the Act of Accession 2003.

down a procedure for the provision of information in the field of technical standards and regulations and of rules on Information Society services, issue a mandate for the drawing up of specific European standards.

(66) The development of a network of Member State consumer protection authorities, which is the subject of the proposal for the Regulation on consumer protection cooperation, complements the cooperation provided for in this Directive. The application of consumer protection legislation in cross-border cases, in particular with regard to new marketing and selling practices, as well as the need to remove certain specific obstacles to cooperation in this field, necessitates a higher degree of cooperation between Member States. In particular, it is necessary in this area to ensure that Member States require the cessation of illegal practices by operators in their territory who target consumers in another Member State.

(67) It is necessary to provide that the Member States, in cooperation with the Commission, are to encourage interested parties to draw up codes of conduct at Community level aimed in particular at promoting the quality of services and taking into account the specific nature of each profession. Those codes of conduct should comply with Community law, especially competition law.

(68) This Directive is without prejudice to any legislative or other initiatives in the field of consumer protection.

(69) The absence of a reaction from the Commission in the context of the mutual evaluation procedure provided for by this Directive has no effect on the compatibility with Community law of national requirements which are included in reports by Member States.

(70) Directive 98/27/EC of the European Parliament and of the Council of 19 May 1998 on injunctions for the protection of consumers' interests[598] approximates the laws, regulations and administrative provisions of the Member States relating to actions for an injunction aimed at the protection of the collective interests of consumers included in the Directives listed in the Annex to Directive 98/27/EC. In order to enable such actions to be brought in cases where the present Directive has been infringed, to the detriment of the collective interests of consumers, the Annex to Directive 98/27EC should be amended accordingly.

(71) Since the objectives of the proposed action, namely the elimination of barriers to the freedom of establishment for service providers in the Member States and to the free provision of services between Member States, cannot be sufficiently achieved by the Member States and can therefore, by reason of the scale of the

---

598   OJ L 166, 11.6.1998, p. 51. Directive as last amended by Directive 2002/65/EC of the European
      Parliament and of the Council (OJ L 271, 9.10.2002, p. 16).

action, be better achieved at Community level, the Community may adopt measures, in accordance with the principle of subsidiarity as set out in Article 5 of the Treaty. In accordance with the principle of proportionality, as set out in that Article, this Directive does not go beyond what is necessary to achieve those objectives.

(72) This Directive respects fundamental rights and observes the principles which are recognised notably in the Charter of Fundamental Rights of the European Union and, in particular, in Articles 8, 15, 21 and 47 thereof.

(73) The measures necessary for the implementation of this Directive should be adopted in accordance with Council Decision 1999/468/EC of 28 June 1999 laying down the procedures for the exercise of implementing powers conferred on the Commission,[599]

HAVE ADOPTED THIS DIRECTIVE:

Chapter I – General Provisions

Article 1 – Subject-Matter

This Directive establishes general provisions facilitating exercise of the freedom of establishment for service providers and the free movement of services.

Article 2 – Scope

1. This Directive shall apply to services supplied by providers established in a Member State.

2. This Directive shall not apply to the following activities:

(a)   financial services as defined in Article 2(b) of Directive 2002/65/EC;
(b)   electronic communications services and networks, and associated facilities and services, with respect to matters covered by Directives 2002/19/EC,[600] 2002/20/EC,[601] 2002/21/EC,[602] 2002/22/EC[603] and 2002/58/EC[604] of the European Parliament and of the Council;

---

599   OJ L 184, 17.7.1999, p. 23.
600   OJ L 108, 24.4.2002, p. 7.
601   OJ L 108, 24.4.2002, p. 21.
602   OJ L 108, 24.4.2002, p. 33.
603   OJ L 108, 24.4.2002, p. 51.
604   OJ L 201, 31.7.2002, p. 37.

(c)   transport services to the extent that they are governed by other Community instruments the legal basis of which is Article 71 or Article 80(2) of the Treaty.

3. This Directive does not apply to the field of taxation, with the exception of Articles 14 and 16 to the extent that the restrictions identified therein are not covered by a Community instrument on tax harmonisation.

Article 3 – Relationship with Other Provisions of Community Law

Member States shall apply the provisions of this Directive in compliance with the rules of the Treaty on the right of establishment and the free movement of services.

Application of this Directive shall not prevent the application of provisions of other Community instruments as regards the services governed by those provisions.

Article 4 – Definitions

For the purposes of this Directive, the following definitions shall apply:

(1)   "service" means any self-employed economic activity, as referred to in Article 50 of the Treaty, consisting in the provision of a service for consideration;

(2)   "provider" means any natural person who is a national of a Member State, or any legal person, who offers or provides a service;

(3)   "recipient" means any natural or legal person who, for professional or non-professional purposes, uses, or wishes to use, a service;

(4)   "Member State of origin" means the Member State in whose territory the provider of the service concerned is established;

(5)   "establishment" means the actual pursuit of an economic activity, as referred to in Article 43 of the Treaty, through a fixed establishment of the provider for an indefinite period;

(6)   "authorisation scheme" means any procedure under which a provider or recipient is in effect required to take steps in order to obtain from a competent authority a formal decision, or an implied decision, concerning access to a service activity or to the exercise thereof;

(7)   "requirement" means any obligation, prohibition, condition or limit provided for in the laws, regulations or administrative provisions of the Member States or in consequence of case law, administrative practice or the rules of professional bodies, or the collective rules of professional associations or other professional organisations, adopted in the exercise of their legal autonomy;

(8)   "competent authority" means any body or authority which has a supervisory or regulatory role in a Member State in relation to service activities, including, in particular, administrative authorities, professional bodies, and those professional associations or other professional organisations which, in the exercise of their legal autonomy, regulate in a collective manner access to service activities or the exercise thereof;

(9)   "coordinated field" means any requirement applicable to access to service activities or to the exercise thereof;

(10)   "hospital care" means medical care which can be provided only within a medical infrastructure and which normally requires the accommodation therein of the person receiving the care, the name, organisation and financing of that infrastructure being irrelevant for the purposes of classifying such care as hospital care;

(11)   "Member State of posting" means the Member State in whose territory a provider posts a worker in order to provide services there;

(12)   "lawful employment" means the salaried activity of a worker, performed in accordance with the national law of the Member State of origin of the provider;

(13)   "regulated profession" means a professional activity or a group of professional activities, access to which or pursuit of which, or one of the modes of pursuing which, is conditional, directly or indirectly, upon possession of specific professional qualifications, pursuant to laws, regulations or administrative provisions;

(14)   "commercial communication" means any form of communication designed to promote, directly or indirectly, the goods, services or image of an undertaking, organisation or person engaged in commercial, industrial or craft activity or practising a regulated profession. The following do not in themselves constitute commercial communications:

    (a) information enabling direct access to the activity of the undertaking, organisation or person, including in particular a domain name or an electronic-mailing address;

    (b) communications relating to the goods, services or image of the undertaking, organisation or person, compiled in an independent manner, particularly when provided for no financial consideration.

Chapter II – Freedom of Establishment for Service Providers

Section 1 – Administrative Simplification

Article 5 – Simplification of Procedures

1. Member States shall simplify the procedures and formalities applicable to access to a service activity and to the exercise thereof.

2. Where Member States require a provider or recipient to supply a certificate, attestation or any other document proving that a requirement has been satisfied, they shall accept any document from another Member State which serves an equivalent purpose or from which it is clear that the requirement in question has been satisfied. They may not require that a document from another Member State be produced in its original form, or as a certified copy or as a certified translation, save in the cases provided for in other Community instruments or where such a requirement is objectively justified by an overriding reason relating to the public interest.

3. Paragraph 2 shall not apply to the documents referred to in Article 46 of Directive ../../EC of the European Parliament and of the Council [70] or in Article 45(3) of Directive ../../EC of the European Parliament and of the Council [71].

[70] [Proposal for a Directive of the European Parliament and of the Council on the recognition of professional qualifications.]

[71] [Proposal for a Directive of the European Parliament and of the Council on the coordination of procedures for the award of public works, supply and service contracts.]

Article 6 – Single Points of Contact

Member States shall ensure that, by 31 December 2008 at the latest, it is possible for a service provider to complete the following procedures and formalities at a contact point known as a "single point of contact":

(a)   all procedures and formalities needed for access to his service activities, in particular, all necessary declarations, notifications or applications for authorisation from the competent authorities, including applications for inclusion in a register, a roll or a database, or for registration with a professional body or association;

(b)   any applications for authorisation needed to exercise his service activities.

Article 7 – Right to Information

1. Member States shall ensure that the following information is easily accessible to providers and recipients through the single points of contact:

(a)   requirements applicable to providers established in their territory, in particular those requirements concerning the procedures and formalities to be completed in order to access and to exercise service activities;
(b)   the contact details of the competent authorities enabling the latter to be contacted directly, including the particulars of those authorities responsible for matters concerning the exercise of service activities;
(c)   the means of and conditions for accessing public registers and databases on providers and services;
(d)   the means of redress available in the event of dispute between the competent authorities and the provider or the recipient, or between a provider and a recipient or between providers;
(e)   the contact details of the associations or organisations, other than the competent authorities, from which providers or recipients may obtain practical assistance.

2. Member States shall ensure that it is possible for providers and recipients to receive, at their request, assistance from the competent authorities, consisting in information on the way in which requirements referred to in point (a) of paragraph 1 are generally interpreted and applied.

3 Member States shall ensure that the information and assistance referred to in paragraphs 1 and 2 are provided in a clear and unambiguous manner, that they are easily accessible at a distance and by electronic means, and that they are kept up-to-date.

4. Member States shall ensure that the single points of contact and the competent authorities respond as quickly as possible to any request for information or assistance as referred to in paragraphs 1 and 2 and, in cases where the request is faulty or unfounded, inform the applicant accordingly without delay.

5. Member States shall implement paragraphs 1 to 4 by 31 December 2008 at the latest.

6. Member States and the Commission shall take accompanying measures in order to encourage single points of contact to make the information provided for in paragraphs 1 and 2 available in other Community languages.

Article 8 – Procedures by Electronic Means

1. Member States shall ensure that, by 31 December 2008 at the latest, all procedures and formalities relating to access to a service activity and to the exercise thereof may be easily completed, at a distance and by electronic means, at the relevant single point of contact and with the relevant competent authorities.

2. Paragraph 1 shall not apply to the inspection of premises on which the service is provided or of equipment used by the provider, or to physical examination of the capability of the provider.

3. The Commission shall, in accordance with the procedure referred to in Article 42(2), adopt detailed rules for the implementation of paragraph 1 with a view to facilitating the interoperability of information systems and use of procedures by electronic means between Member States.

Section 2 – Authorisations

Article 9 – Authorisation Schemes

1. Member States shall not make access to a service activity or the exercise thereof subject to an authorisation scheme unless the following conditions are satisfied:

(a)   the authorisation scheme does not discriminate against the provider in question;
(b)   the need for an authorisation scheme is objectively justified by an overriding reason relating to the public interest;
(c)   the objective pursued cannot be attained by means of a less restrictive measure, in particular because an *a posteriori* inspection would take place too late to be genuinely effective.

2. In the report referred to in Article 41, Member States shall identify their authorisation schemes and give reasons showing their compatibility with paragraph 1.

3. This Section shall not apply to authorisation schemes which are either imposed or permitted by other Community instruments.

Article 10 – Conditions for the Granting of Authorisation

1. Authorisation schemes shall be based on criteria which preclude the competent authorities from exercising their power of assessment in an arbitrary or discretionary manner.

2. The criteria referred to in paragraph 1 must be:

(a)   non-discriminatory;
(b)   objectively justified by an overriding reason relating to the public interest;
(c)   proportionate to that public interest objective;
(d)   precise and unambiguous;
(e)   objective;
(f)   made public in advance.

3. The conditions for granting authorisation for a new establishment shall not duplicate requirements and controls which are equivalent or essentially comparable as regards their purpose, to which the provider is already subject in another Member State or in the same Member State. The contact points referred to in Article 35 and the provider shall assist the competent authority by providing any necessary information on those requirements.

4. The authorisation shall enable the provider to have access to the service activity, or to exercise that activity, throughout the national territory, including by setting up agencies, subsidiaries, branches or offices, except where an authorisation for each individual establishment is objectively justified by an overriding reason relating to the public interest.

5. The authorisation shall be granted as soon as it has been established, in the light of an appropriate examination, that the conditions for authorisation have been met.

6. Any refusal or other response from the competent authorities, including withdrawal of an authorisation, shall be fully reasoned, in particular with regard to the provisions of this Article, and shall be open to challenge before the courts.

Article 11 – Duration of Authorisation

1. An authorisation granted to a provider shall not be for a limited period, except in cases where:

(a)   the authorisation is being automatically renewed;
(b)   the number of available authorisations is limited;
(c)   a limited authorisation period can be objectively justified by an overriding reason relating to the public interest.

2. Paragraph 1 shall not concern the maximum period during which the provider must actually commence his activity after receiving authorisation.

3. Member States shall require the provider to inform the relevant single point of contact provided for in Article 6 of any change in his situation which is likely to affect the efficiency of supervision by the competent authority, including, in particular, the creation of subsidiaries whose activities fall within the scope of the authorisation system, or which results in the conditions for authorisation no longer being met, or which affects the accuracy of information available to a recipient.

Article 12 – Selection from Among Several Candidates

1. Where the number of authorisations available for a given activity is limited because of the scarcity of available natural resources or technical capacity, Member States shall apply a selection procedure to potential candidates which provides full guarantees of impartiality and transparency, including, in particular, adequate publicity about the launch of the procedure.

2. In the cases referred to in paragraph 1, authorisation must be granted for an appropriate limited period and may not be open to automatic renewal, nor confer any other advantage on the provider whose authorisation has just expired or on any person having any particular links with that provider.

Article 13 – Authorisation Procedures

1. Authorisation procedures and formalities shall be clear, in advance and such as to provide interested parties with a guarantee that their application will be dealt with objectively and impartially.

2. Authorisation procedures and formalities shall not be dissuasive and shall not unduly complicate or delay the provision of the service. They shall be easily accessible and any charges which the relevant parties may incur from their application shall be proportionate to the cost of the authorisation procedures in question.

3. Authorisation procedures and formalities shall provide interested parties with a guarantee that their application will be processed as quickly as possible and, in any event, within a reasonable period which is fixed and published in advance.

4. Failing a response within the time period set in accordance with paragraph 3, authorisation shall be deemed to have been granted. Different arrangements may nevertheless be put in place in respect of certain specific activities, where objectively justified by overriding reasons relating to the public interest.

5. All applications for authorisation shall be acknowledged as quickly as possible. The acknowledgement must specify the following:

(a)   the period for response referred to in paragraph 3;

(b)   the available means of redress;

(c)   a statement that in the absence of a response within the period specified, the authorisation shall be deemed to have been granted.

6. In the case of an incomplete application or where an application is rejected on the grounds that it fails to comply with the required procedures or formalities, the persons having an interest in the matter must be informed as quickly as possible of the need to supply any additional documentation.

Section 3 – Requirements Prohibited or Subject to Evaluation

Article 14 – Prohibited Requirements

Member States shall not make access to or the exercise of a service activity in their territory subject to compliance with any of the following:

(1)   discriminatory requirements based directly or indirectly on nationality or, in the case of companies, the location of the registered office, including in particular:

(a) nationality requirements for the provider, his staff, persons holding the share capital or members of the provider's management or supervisory bodies;

(b) a requirement that the provider, his staff, persons holding the share capital or members of the provider's management or supervisory bodies be resident within the territory.

(2)   a prohibition on having an establishment in more than one Member State or on being entered in the registers or enrolled with professional bodies or associations of more than one Member State;

(3)   restrictions on the freedom of a provider to choose between a principal or a secondary establishment, in particular an obligation on the provider to have his principal establishment in their territory, or restrictions on the freedom to choose between establishment in the form of an agency, branch or subsidiary;

(4)   conditions of reciprocity with the Member State in which the provider already has an establishment, save in the case of conditions of reciprocity provided for in Community instruments concerning energy;

(5)   the case-by-case application of an economic test making the granting of authorisation subject to proof of the existence of an economic need or market demand, or an assessment of the potential or current economic effects of the activity, or an assessment of the appropriateness of the activity in relation to the economic planning objectives set by the competent authority;

(6)   the direct or indirect involvement of competing operators, including within consultative bodies, in the granting of authorisations or in the adoption of other decisions of the competent authorities, with the exception of professional bodies and associations or other organisations acting as the competent authority;

(7)   an obligation to provide or participate in a financial guarantee or to take out insurance from a service-provider or body established in their territory;

(8)   an obligation to have been entered, for a given period, in the registers held in their territory or to have exercised the activity for a given period in their territory.

Article 15 – Requirements to be Evaluated

1. Member States shall examine whether, under their legal system, any of the requirements listed in paragraph 2 are imposed and shall ensure that any such requirements are compatible with the conditions laid down in paragraph 3. Member States shall adapt their laws, regulations or administrative provisions so as to make them compatible with those conditions.

2. Member States shall examine whether their legal system makes access to a service activity or the exercise of it subject to compliance with any of the following non-discriminatory requirements:

(a)   quantitative or territorial restrictions, in particular in the form of limits fixed according to population, or of a minimum geographical distance between service-providers;

(b)   an obligation on a provider to take a specific legal form, in particular to be a legal person, to be a company with individual ownership, to be a non-profit making organisation or a company owned exclusively by natural persons;

(c)   requirements which relate to the shareholding of a company, in particular an obligation to hold a minimum amount of capital for certain service activities or to have a specific professional qualification in order to hold capital in or to manage certain companies;

(d)   requirements, other than those concerning professional qualifications or provided for in other Community instruments, which reserve access to the service activity in question to particular providers by virtue of the specific nature of the activity;

(e)   a ban on having more than one establishment in the territory of the same State;

(f)   requirements fixing a minimum number of employees;

(g)   fixed minimum and/or maximum tariffs with which the provider must comply;

(h)   prohibitions and obligations with regard to selling below cost and to sales;
(i)   requirements that an intermediary provider must allow access to certain specific services provided by other service-providers;
(j)   an obligation on the provider to supply other specific services jointly with his service.

3. Member States shall verify that requirements referred to in paragraph 2 satisfy the following conditions:

(a)   non-discrimination: requirements must be neither directly nor indirectly discriminatory according to nationality or, with regard to companies, according to the location of the registered office;
(b)   necessity: requirements must be objectively justified by an overriding reason relating to the public interest;
(c)   proportionality: requirements must be suitable for securing the attainment of the objective pursued; they must not go beyond what is necessary to attain that objective; and it must not be possible to replace those requirements with other, less restrictive measures which attain the same result.

4. In the mutual evaluation report provided for in Article 41, Member States shall specify the following:

(a)   the requirements that they intend to maintain and the reasons why they consider that those requirements comply with the conditions set out in paragraph 3;
(b)   the requirements which have been abolished or made less stringent.

5. From the date of entry into force of this Directive, Member States shall not introduce any new requirement of a kind listed in paragraph 2, unless that requirement satisfies the conditions laid down in paragraph 3 and the need for it arises from new circumstances.

6. Member States shall notify to the Commission any new laws, regulations or administrative provisions which set requirements as referred to in paragraph 5, together with the reasons for those requirements. The Commission shall communicate the provisions concerned to the other Member States. Such notification shall not prevent the adoption by Member States of the provisions in question.

Within a period of 3 months from the date of notification, the Commission shall examine the compatibility of any new requirements with Community law and, as the case may be, shall adopt a decision requesting the Member State in question to refrain from adopting them or to abolish them.

Chapter III – Free Movement of Services

Section 1 – Country of Origin Principle and Derogations

Article 16 – Country of Origin Principle

(1) Member States shall ensure that providers are subject only to the national provisions of their Member State of origin which fall within the coordinated field.

(2) Paragraph 1 shall cover national provisions relating to access to and the exercise of a service activity, in particular those requirements governing the behaviour of the provider, the quality or content of the service, advertising, contracts and the provider's liability.

(3) The Member State of origin shall be responsible for supervising the provider and the services provided by him, including services provided by him in another Member State.

(4) Member States may not, for reasons falling within the coordinated field, restrict the freedom to provide services in the case of a provider established in another Member State, in particular, by imposing any of the following requirements:

(a) an obligation on the provider to have an establishment in their territory;

(b) an obligation on the provider to make a declaration or notification to, or to obtain an authorisation from, their competent authorities, including entry in a register or registration with a professional body or association in their territory;

(c) an obligation on the provider to have an address or representative in their territory or to have an address for service at the address of a person authorised in that territory;

(d) a ban on the provider setting up a certain infrastructure in their territory, including an office or chambers, which the provider needs to supply the services in question;

(e) an obligation on the provider to comply with requirements, relating to the exercise of a service activity, applicable in their territory;

(f) the application of specific contractual arrangements between the provider and the recipient which prevent or restrict service provision by the self-employed;

(g) an obligation on the provider to possess an identity document issued by its competent authorities specific to the exercise of a service activity;

(h) requirements which affect the use of equipment which is an integral part of the service provided;

(i)   restrictions on the freedom to provide the services referred to in Article 20, the first subparagraph of Article 23(1) or Article 25(1).

Article 17 – General Derogations from the Country of Origin Principle

Article 16 shall not apply to the following:

(1)   postal services within the meaning of point (1) of Article 2 of Directive 97/67/EC of the European Parliament and the Council;[605]

(2)   electricity distribution services within the meaning of point (5) of Article 2 of Directive 2003/54/EC of the European Parliament and of the Council;[606]

(3)   gas distribution services within the meaning of point (5) of Article 2 of Directive 2003/55/EC of the European Parliament and of the Council;[607]

(4)   water distribution services;

(5)   matters covered by Directive 96/71/EC;

(6)   matters covered by Directive 95/46/EC of the European Parliament and of the Council[608]

(7)   matters covered by Council Directive 77/249/EEC;[609]

(8)   the provisions of Article […] of Directive ../../EC on the recognition of professional qualifications;

(9)   the provisions of Regulation (EEC) No. 1408/71 determining the applicable legislation;

(10)   the provisions of Directive …/../EC of the European Parliament and the Council [on the right of citizens of the Union and their family members to move and reside freely within the territory of the Member States, amending Regulation (EEC) 1612/68 and repealing Directives 64/221/EEC, 68/360/EEC, 72/194/EEC, 73/148/EEC, 75/34/EEC, 75/35/EEC, 90/364/EEC, 90/365/EEC and 93/96/EEC], that lay down the administrative formalities that beneficiaries must undertake before the competent authorities of the host Member States;

(11)   in the case of the posting of third country nationals, the requirement for a short stay visa imposed by the Member State of posting, subject to the conditions set out in Article 25(2);

(12)   the authorisation regime provided for in Articles 3 and 4 of Council Regulation (EEC) No. 259/93;[610]

---

605   OJ L 15, 21.1.1998, p. 14.
606   OJ L 176, 15.7.2003, p. 37.
607   OJ L 176, 15.7.2003, p. 57.
608   OJ L 281, 28.11.1995, p. 1.
609   OJ L 78, 26.3.1997, p. 17.
610   OJ L 30, 6.2.1993, p. 1.

(13) copyright, neighbouring rights, rights covered by Council Directive 87/54/EEC[611] and by Directive 96/9/EC of the European Parliament and of the Council[612] as well as industrial property rights;

(14) acts requiring by law the involvement of a notary;

(15) statutory audit;

(16) services which, in the Member State to which the provider moves temporarily in order to provide his service, are covered by a total prohibition which is justified by reasons relating to public policy, public security or public health;

(17) specific requirements of the Member State to which the provider moves, that are directly linked to the particular characteristics of the place where the service is provided and with which compliance is indispensable for reasons of public policy or public security or for the protection of public health or the environment;

(18) the authorisation system applicable to the reimbursement of hospital care;

(19) the registration of vehicles leased in another Member State;

(20) the freedom of parties to choose the law applicable to their contract;

(21) contracts for the provision of services concluded by consumers to the extent that the provisions governing them are not completely harmonised at Community level;

(22) the formal validity of contracts creating or transferring rights in immovable property, where contracts are subject, under the law of the Member State in which the property is located, to imperative formal requirements;

(23) the non-contractual liability of a provider in the case of an accident involving a person and occurring as a consequence of the service provider's activities in the Member State to which he has moved temporarily.

Article 18 – Transitional Derogations from the Country of Origin Principle

1. Article 16 shall not apply for a transitional period to the following:

(a) the way in which cash-in-transit services are exercised;

(b) gambling activities which involve wagering a stake with pecuniary value in games of chance, including lotteries and betting transactions;

(c) access to the activity of judicial recovery of debts.

2. The derogations referred to in points (a) and (c) of paragraph 1 of this Article shall not apply after the date of application of the harmonisation instruments referred to in Article 40(1) or in any case after 1 January 2010.

---

611   OJ L 24, 27.1.1987, p. 36.
612   OJ L 77, 27.3.1996, p. 20.

3. The derogation referred to in point (b) of paragraph 1 of this Article shall not apply after the date of application of the harmonisation instrument referred to in Article 40(1)(b).

Article 19 – Case-by-case Derogations from the Country of Origin Principle

1. By way of derogation from Article 16, and in exceptional circumstances only, a Member State may, in respect of a provider established in another Member State, take measures relating to any of the following:

(a)   the safety of services, including aspects related to public health;
(b)   the exercise of a health profession;
(c)   the protection of public policy, notably aspects related to the protection of minors.

2. The measures provided for in paragraph 1 may be taken only if the mutual assistance procedure laid down in Article 37 is complied with and all the following conditions are fulfilled:

(a)   the national provisions in accordance with which the measure is taken have not been subject to Community harmonisation in the fields referred to in paragraph 1;
(b)   the measures provide for a higher level of protection of the recipient than would be the case in a measure taken by the Member State of origin in accordance with its national provisions;
(c)   the Member State of origin has not taken any measures or has taken measures which are insufficient as compared with those referred to in Article 37(2);
(d)   the measures are proportionate.

3. Paragraphs 1 and 2 shall be without prejudice to provisions, laid down in Community instruments, which guarantee the freedom to provide services or which allow derogations there from.

Section 2 – Rights of Recipients of Services

Article 20 – Prohibited Restrictions

Member States may not impose on a recipient requirements which restrict the use of a service supplied by a provider established in another Member State, in particular the following requirements:

(a)   an obligation to obtain authorisation from or to make a declaration to their competent authorities;

(b)   limits on tax deductibility or on the grant of financial assistance by reason of the fact that the provider is established in another Member State or by reason of the location of the place at which the service is provided;

(c)   requirements which subject the recipient to discriminatory or disproportionate taxes on the equipment necessary to receive a service at a distance from another Member State.

Article 21 – Non-discrimination

1. Member States shall ensure that the recipient is not made subject to discriminatory requirements based on his nationality or place of residence.

2. Member States shall ensure that the general conditions of access to a service, which are made available to the public at large by the provider, do not contain discriminatory provisions relating to the nationality or place of residence of the recipient, but without precluding the possibility of providing for differences in the conditions of access where those differences are directly justified by objective criteria.

Article 22 – Assistance for Recipients

1. Member States shall ensure that recipients can obtain, in their Member State of residence, the following information:

(a)   information on the requirements applicable in other Member States relating to access to and exercise of service activities, in particular those relating to consumer protection;

(b)   information on the means of redress available in the case of a dispute between a provider and a recipient;

(c)   the contact details of associations or organisations, including Euroguichets and the contact points of the European extra-judicial network (EEJ-net), from which providers or recipients may obtain practical assistance.

2. Member States may confer responsibility for the task referred to in paragraph 1 to single points of contact or to any other body, such as Euroguichets, the contact points of the European extra-judicial network (EEJ-net), consumer associations or Euro Info Centres.

By the date specified in Article 45 at the latest, Member States shall communicate to the Commission the names and contact details of the designated bodies. The Commission shall transmit them to all Member States.

3. In order to be able to send the information referred to in paragraph 1, the relevant body approached by the recipient shall contact the relevant body for the Member State concerned. The latter shall send the information requested as soon as possible. Member States shall ensure that those bodies give each other mutual assistance and shall put in place all possible measures for effective cooperation.

4. The Commission shall, in accordance with the procedure referred to in Article 42(2), adopt measures for the implementation of paragraphs 1, 2 and 3, specifying the technical mechanisms for the exchange of information between the bodies of the various Member States and, in particular, the interoperability of information systems.

Article 23 – Assumption of Healthcare Costs

1. Member States may not make assumption of the costs of non-hospital care in another Member State subject to the granting of an authorisation, where the cost of that care, if it had been provided in their territory, would have been assumed by their social security system.

The conditions and formalities to which the receipt of non-hospital care in their territory is made subject by Member States, such as the requirement that a general practitioner be consulted prior to consultation of a specialist, or the terms and conditions relating to the assumption of the costs of certain types of dental care, may be imposed on a patient who has received non-hospital care in another Member State.

2. Member States shall ensure that authorisation for assumption by their social security system of the cost of hospital care provided in another Member State is not refused where the treatment in question is among the benefits provided for by the legislation of the Member State of affiliation and where such treatment cannot be given to the patient within a time frame which is medically acceptable in the light of the patient's current state of health and the probable course of the illness.

3. Member States shall ensure that the level of assumption by their social security system of the costs of healthcare provided in another Member State is not lower than that provided for by their social security system in respect of similar healthcare provided in their territory.

4. Member States shall ensure that their authorisation systems for the assumption of the costs of healthcare provided in another Member State are in conformity with Articles 9, 10, 11 and 13.

Section 3 – Posting of Workers

Article 24 – Specific Provisions on the Posting of Workers

1. Where a provider posts a worker to another Member State in order to provide a service, the Member State of posting shall carry out in its territory the checks, inspections and investigations necessary to ensure compliance with the employment and working conditions applicable under Directive 96/71/EC and shall take, in accordance with Community law, measures in respect of a service provider who fails to comply with those conditions.

However, the Member State of posting may not make the provider or the posted worker subject to any of the following obligations, as regards the matters referred to in point (5) of Article 17:

(a)   to obtain authorisation from, or to be registered with, its own competent authorities, or to satisfy any other equivalent requirement;

(b)   to make a declaration, other than declarations relating to an activity referred to in the Annex to Directive 96/71/EC which may be maintained until 31 December 2008;

(c)   to have a representative in its territory;

(d)   to hold and keep employment documents in its territory or in accordance with the conditions applicable in its territory.

2. In the circumstances referred to in paragraph 1, the Member State of origin shall ensure that the provider takes all measures necessary to be to communicate the following information, both to its competent authorities and to those of the Member State of posting, within two years of the end of the posting:

(a)   the identity of the posted worker;

(b)   his position and the nature of the tasks attributed to him,

(c)   the contact details of the recipient,

(d)   the place of posting,

(e)   the start and end dates for the posting,

(f)   the employment and working conditions applied to the posted worker;

In the circumstances referred to in paragraph 1, the Member State of origin shall assist the Member State of posting to ensure compliance with the employment and working conditions applicable under Directive 96/71/EC and shall, on its own initiative, communicate to the Member State of posting the information specified in the first subparagraph where the Member State of origin is aware of specific facts which indicate possible irregularities on the part of the provider in relation to employment and working conditions.

Article 25 – Posting of Third Country Nationals

1. Subject to the possibility of derogation as referred to in paragraph 2, where a provider posts a worker who is a national of a third country to the territory of another Member State in order to provide a service there, the Member State of posting may not require the provider or the worker posted by the latter to hold an entry, exit, residence or work permit, or to satisfy other equivalent conditions.

2. Paragraph 1 does not prejudice the possibility for Member States to require a short-term visa for third country nationals who are not covered by the mutual recognition regime provided for in Article 21 of the Convention implementing the Schengen Agreement.

3. In the circumstances referred to in paragraph 1, the Member State of origin shall ensure that a provider posts only a worker who is resident in its territory in accordance with its own national rules and who is lawfully employed in its territory.

The Member State of origin shall not regard a posting made in order to provide a service in another Member State as interrupting the residence or activity of the posted worker and shall not refuse to readmit the posted worker to its territory on the basis of its national rules.

The Member State of origin shall communicate to the Member State of posting, upon its request and in the shortest possible time, information and guarantees regarding compliance with the first subparagraph and shall impose the appropriate penalties in cases of non-compliance.

Chapter IV – Quality of Services

Article 26 – Information on Providers and Their Services

1. Member States shall ensure that providers make the following information available to the recipient:

(a)   the name of the service provider, the geographic address at which he is established, and the details which enable him to be contacted rapidly and communicated with directly and, as the case may be, by electronic means;
(b)   where the provider is registered in a trade or other similar public register, the name of that register and the provider's registration number, or equivalent means of identification in that register;
(c)   where the activity is subject to an authorisation scheme, the particulars of the relevant competent authority or the single point of contact;
(d)   where the provider exercises an activity which is subject to VAT, the identification number referred to in Article 22(1) of Directive 77/388/EEC;

(e)   in the case of the regulated professions, any professional body or similar institution with which the provider is registered, the professional title and the Member State in which that title has been granted; -

(f)   the general conditions and clauses, if any, used by the provider;

(g)   contractual clauses concerning the law applicable to the contract and/or the competent courts.

2. Member States shall ensure that the information referred to in paragraph 1, according to the provider's preference:

(a)   is supplied by the provider on his own initiative;

(b)   is easily accessible to the recipient at the place where the service is provided or the contract concluded;

(c)   can be easily accessed by the recipient electronically by means of an address supplied by the provider;

(d)   appears in any information documents supplied to the recipient by the provider, setting out a detailed description of the service he provides.

3. Member States shall ensure that, at the recipient's request, providers supply the following additional information:

(a)   the main features of the service;

(b)   the price of the service or, if an exact price cannot be given, the method for calculating the price so that the recipient can check it, or a sufficiently detailed estimate;

(c)   the legal status and form of the provider;

(d)   as regards the regulated professions, a reference to the professional rules applicable in the Member State of origin and how to access them.

4. Member States shall ensure that the information which a provider must supply in accordance with this Chapter is made available or communicated in a clear and unambiguous manner, and in good time before conclusion of the contract or, where there is no written contract, before the service is provided.

5. The information requirements laid down in this Chapter are in addition to requirements already provided for in Community law and do not prevent Member States from imposing additional information requirements applicable to providers established in their territory.

6. The Commission may, in accordance with the procedure referred to in Article 42(2), specify the content of the information provided for in paragraphs 1 and 3 of this Article according to the specific nature of certain activities and may specify the practical means of implementing paragraph 2.

Article 27 – Professional Insurance and Guarantees

1. Member States shall ensure that providers whose services present a particular risk to the health or safety of the recipient, or a particular financial risk to the recipient, are covered by professional indemnity insurance appropriate to the nature and extent of the risk, or by any other guarantee or compensatory provision which is equivalent or essentially comparable as regards its purpose.

2. Member States shall ensure that providers supply a recipient, at his request, with information on the insurance or guarantees referred to in paragraph 1, and in particular the contact details of the insurer or guarantor and the territorial coverage.

3. When a provider establishes himself in their territory, Member States may not require professional insurance or a financial guarantee from the provider where he is already covered by a guarantee which is equivalent, or essentially comparable as regards its purpose, in another Member State in which the provider is already established.

Where equivalence is only partial, Member States may require a supplementary guarantee to cover those aspects not already covered.

4. Paragraphs 1, 2 and 3 do not affect professional insurance or guarantee arrangements provided for in other Community instruments.

5. For the implementation of paragraph 1, the Commission may, in accordance with the procedure referred to in Article 42(2), establish a list of services which exhibit the characteristics referred to in paragraph 1 and establish common criteria for defining, for the purposes of the insurance or guarantees referred to in that paragraph, what is appropriate to the nature and scope of the risk.

Article 28 – After-sales Guarantees

1. Member States shall ensure that providers supply a recipient, at his request, with information on the existence or otherwise of an after-sales guarantee, on its content and on the essential criteria for its application, in particular, its period of validity and territorial cover.

2. Member States shall ensure that the information referred to in paragraph 1 appears in any information documents supplied by providers, setting out a detailed description of the services offered.

3. Paragraphs 1 and 2 do not affect the regulation of after-sales guarantees provided for in other Community instruments.

Article 29 – Commercial Communications by the Regulated Professions

1. Member States shall remove all total prohibitions on commercial communications by the regulated professions.

2. Member States shall ensure that commercial communications by the regulated professions comply with professional rules, in conformity with Community law, which relate, in particular, to the independence, dignity and integrity of the profession, as well as to professional secrecy, in a manner consonant with the specific nature of each profession.

Article 30 – Multidisciplinary Activities

1. Member States shall ensure that providers are not made subject to requirements which oblige them to exercise a given specific activity exclusively or which restrict the exercise jointly or in partnership of different activities.

However, the following providers may be made subject to such requirements:

(a)   the regulated professions, in so far as is justified in order to guarantee compliance with the rules governing professional ethics and conduct, which vary according to the specific nature of each profession;

(b)   providers of certification, accreditation, technical monitoring, test or trial services in so far as is justified in order to ensure their independence and impartiality.

2. Where multidisciplinary activities are authorised, Member States shall ensure the following:

(a)   that conflicts of interest and incompatibilities between certain activities are prevented;

(b)   that the independence and impartiality required for certain activities is secured;

(c)   that the rules governing professional ethics and conduct for different activities are compatible with one another, especially as regards matters of professional secrecy.

3. Member States shall ensure that providers supply the recipient, at his request, with information on their multidisciplinary activities and partnerships and on the measures taken to avoid conflicts of interest. That information shall be included in any information document in which providers give a detailed description of their services.

4. In the report referred to in Article 41, Member States shall indicate which providers are subject to the requirements laid down in paragraph 1, the content of those requirements and the reasons for which they consider them to be justified.

Article 31 – Policy on Quality of Services

1. Member States shall, in cooperation with the Commission, take accompanying measures to encourage providers to take action on a voluntary basis in order to ensure the quality of service provision, in particular through use of one of the following methods:

(a)   by having their activities certified or assessed by independent bodies;
(b)   by drawing up their own quality charter or participating in quality charters or labels drawn up by professional bodies at Community level.

2. Member States shall ensure that information on the significance of certain labels and the criteria for applying labels and other quality marks relating to services can be easily accessed by recipients and providers.

3. Member States shall, in cooperation with the Commission, take accompanying measures to encourage professional bodies, as well as chambers of commerce and craft associations, within Member States to cooperate at Community level in order to promote the quality of service provision, especially by making it easier to assess a provider's competence.

4. Member States shall, in cooperation with the Commission, take accompanying measures to encourage the development of independent assessments in relation to the quality and defects of service provision, and in particular the development at Community level of comparative trials or testing and the communication of the results.

5. Member States and the Commission shall encourage the development of voluntary European standards with the aim of facilitating compatibility between services supplied by providers in different Member States, information to the recipient and the quality of service provision.

Article 32 – Settlement of Disputes

1. Member States shall take the general measures necessary to ensure that providers supply a postal address, fax number or e-mail address to which all recipients, including those resident in another Member State, can send a complaint or a request for information on the service provided.

2. Member States shall take the general measures necessary to ensure that providers respond to the complaints referred to in paragraph 1 in the shortest possible time and make best efforts to find appropriate solutions.

3. Member States shall take the general measures necessary to ensure that providers are obliged to demonstrate compliance with the obligations laid down in this Directive as to the provision of information and to demonstrate that the information is accurate.

4. Where a financial guarantee is required for compliance with a judicial decision, Member States shall recognise equivalent guarantees lodged with a provider or body established in another Member State.

5. Member States shall take the general measures necessary to ensure that providers who are subject to a code of conduct, or are members of a trade association or professional body, which provides for recourse to a non-judicial means of dispute settlement, inform the recipient accordingly, and mention that fact in any document which presents their services in detail, specifying how to access detailed information on the characteristics of and conditions for the use of such a mechanism.

Article 33 – Information on the Good Repute of Providers

1. Member States shall, at the request of a competent authority in another Member State, supply information on criminal convictions, penalties, administrative or disciplinary measures and decisions concerning insolvency or bankruptcy involving fraud, taken by their competent authorities in respect of the provider, which are liable to bring into question either his ability to conduct his business or his professional reliability.

2. The Member State which supplies the information referred to in paragraph 1 shall at the same time specify whether a particular decision is final or whether an appeal has been lodged in respect of it, in which case the Member State in question should provide an indication of the date when the decision on appeal is expected.

Moreover, that Member State shall specify the provisions of national law pursuant to which the provider was found guilty or penalised.

3. Implementation of paragraph 1 must comply with the rights guaranteed to persons found guilty or penalised in the Member States concerned, especially as regards the protection of personal data.

Chapter V – Supervision

Article 34 – Effectiveness of Supervision

1. Member States shall ensure that the powers of monitoring and supervision provided for in national law in respect of the provider and the activities concerned are also exercised where a service is provided in another Member State.

2. Member States shall ensure that providers supply their competent authorities with all the information necessary for monitoring their activities.

Article 35 – Mutual Assistance

1. In accordance with Article 16, Member States shall give each other mutual assistance and shall put in place all possible measures for effective cooperation with one another in order to ensure the supervision of providers and the services they provide.

2. For the purposes of paragraph 1, Member States shall designate one or more points of contact, the contact details of which shall be communicated to the other Member States and the Commission.

3. Member States shall apply the information requested by other Member States or the Commission by electronic means and within the shortest possible period of time.

Becoming aware of any unlawful conduct by a provider, or of specific acts, that are likely to cause serious damage in a Member State, Member States shall inform the Member State of origin, within the shortest possible period of time.

Becoming aware of any unlawful conduct by a provider who is likely to provide services in other Member States, or of specific acts, that could cause serious damage to the health or safety of persons, Member States shall inform all other Member States and the Commission within the shortest possible period of time.

4. The Member State of origin shall supply information on providers established in its territory when requested to do so by another Member State and in particular confirmation that a service provider is established in its territory and exercising his activities in a lawful manner; undertake the checks, inspections and investigations requested by another Member State and shall inform the latter of the results and, as the case may be, of the measures taken.

5. In the event of difficulty in meeting a request for information, the Member State in question shall rapidly inform the requesting Member State with a view to finding a solution.

6. Member States shall ensure that registers in which providers have been entered, and which may be consulted by the competent authorities in their territory, may also be consulted, in accordance with the same conditions, by the equivalent competent authorities of the other Member States.

Article 36 – Mutual Assistance in the Event of the Temporary Movement of the Provider

1. In respect of the matters covered by Article 16, where a provider moves temporarily to another Member State in order to provide a service without being established there, the competent authorities of that Member State shall participate in the supervision of the provider in accordance with paragraph 2.

2. At the request of the Member State of origin, the competent authorities referred to in paragraph 1 shall carry out any checks, inspections and investigations necessary for ensuring effective supervision by the Member State of origin. In so doing, the competent authorities shall act to the extent permitted by the powers vested in them in their Member State.

On their own initiative, those competent authorities may conduct checks, inspections and investigations on the spot, provided that those checks, inspections or investigations meet the following conditions:

(a)   they consist exclusively in the establishment of facts and do not give rise to any other measure against the provider, subject to the possibility of case-by-case derogations as provided for in Article 19;

(b)   they are not discriminatory and are not motivated by the fact that the provider is established in another Member State;

(c)   they are objectively justified by an overriding reason relating to the public interest and are proportionate to the objective pursued.

Article 37 – Mutual Assistance in the Event of Case-by-case Derogations from the Country of Origin Principle

1. Where a Member State intends to take a measure pursuant to Article 19, the procedure laid down in paragraphs 2 to 6 of this Article shall apply without prejudice to proceedings before the courts.

2. The Member State referred to in paragraph 1 shall ask the Member State of origin to take measures with regard to the service provider, supplying all relevant information on the service in question and the circumstances of the case.

The Member State of origin shall check, within the shortest possible period of time, whether the provider is operating lawfully and verify the facts underlying the request. It shall inform the requesting Member State within the shortest possible period of time of the measures taken or envisaged or, as the case may be, the reasons why it has not taken any measures.

3. Following communication by the Member State of origin as provided for in the second subparagraph of paragraph 2, the requesting Member State shall notify the Commission and the Member State of origin of its intention to take measures, stating the following:

(a)   the reasons why it believes the measures taken or envisaged by the Member State of origin are inadequate;
(b)   the reasons why it believes the measures it intends to take fulfil the conditions laid down in Article 19.

4. The measures may not be taken until fifteen working days after the date of notification provided for in paragraph 3.

5. Without prejudice to the possibility for the requesting Member State to take the measures in question upon expiry of the period specified in paragraph 4, the Commission shall, within the shortest possible period of time, examine the compatibility with Community law of the measures notified.

Where the Commission concludes that the measure is incompatible with Community law, it shall adopt a decision asking the Member State concerned to refrain from taking the proposed measures or to put an end to the measures in question as a matter of urgency.

6. In the case of urgency, a Member State which intends to take a measure may derogate from paragraphs 3 and 4. In such cases, the measures shall be notified within the shortest possible period of time to the Commission and the Member State of origin, stating the reasons for which the Member State considers that there is urgency.

Article 38 – Implementing Measures

In accordance with the procedure referred to in Article 42(2), the Commission shall adopt the implementing measures necessary for the implementation of this Chapter, specifying the time-limits provided for in Articles 35 and 37 and the practical arrangements for the exchange of information by electronic means between the single points of contact, and in particular the interoperability provisions for information systems.

Chapter VI – Convergence Programme

Article 39 – Codes of Conduct at Community Level

1. Member States shall, in cooperation with the Commission, take accompanying measures to encourage the drawing up of codes of conduct at Community level, in conformity with Community law, in particular in the following areas:

(a)   the content of and detailed rules for commercial communications relating to regulated professions, as appropriate to the specific nature of each profession;

(b)   the rules of professional ethics and conduct of the regulated professions which aim in particular at ensuring, as appropriate to the specific nature of each profession, independence, impartiality and professional secrecy;

(c)   the conditions to which the activities of estate agents are subject.

2. Member States shall ensure that the codes of conduct referred to in paragraph 1 are accessible at a distance, by electronic means and transmitted to the Commission.

3. Member States shall ensure that providers indicate, at the recipient's request, or in any information documents which present their services in detail, any codes of conduct to which they are subject and the address at which these codes may be consulted by electronic means, specifying the language versions available.

4. Member States shall take accompanying measures to encourage professional bodies, organisations and associations to implement at national level the codes of conduct adopted at Community level.

Article 40 – Additional Harmonisation

1. The Commission shall assess, by [one year after the entry into force of this Directive] at the latest, the possibility of presenting proposals for harmonisation instruments on the following subjects:

(a)   the detailed rules for the exercise of cash-in-transit services;

(b)   gambling activities which involve wagering a stake with pecuniary value in games of chance, including lotteries and betting transactions, in the light of a report by the Commission and a wide consultation of interested parties;

(c)   access to the activity of judicial recovery of debts.

2. In order to ensure the proper functioning of the internal market for services, the Commission shall assess the need to take additional initiatives or to present proposals for legislative instruments, particularly in relation to the following:

(a)   matters which, having been the subject of case-by-case derogations, have indicated the need for harmonisation at Community level;

(b)   matters covered by Article 39 for which it has not been possible to finalise codes of conduct before the date of transposition or for which such codes are insufficient to ensure the proper functioning of the internal market;

(c)   matters identified through the mutual evaluation procedure laid down in Article 41;

(d)   consumer protection and cross-border contracts.

Article 41 – Mutual Evaluation

1. By the [date of transposition] at the latest, Member States shall present a report to the Commission, containing the information specified in the following provisions:

(a)   Article 9(2), on authorisation systems;

(b)   Article 15(4), on requirements to be evaluated;

(c)   Article 30(4), on multidisciplinary activities.

2. The Commission shall forward the reports provided for in paragraph 1 to the Member States, which shall submit their observations on each of the reports within six months. Within the same period, the Commission shall consult interested parties on those reports.

3. The Commission shall present the reports and the Member States' observations to the Committee referred to in Article 42(1), which may make observations.

4. In the light of the observations provided for in paragraphs 2 and 3, the Commission shall, by 31 December 2008 at the latest, present a summary report to the European Parliament and to the Council, accompanied where appropriate by proposals for additional initiatives.

Article 42 – Committee

1. The Commission shall be assisted by a Committee, consisting of representatives of the Member States and chaired by the Commission representative.

2. Where reference is made to this paragraph, Articles 3 and 7 of Decision 1999/468/EC shall apply, in accordance with the provisions of Article 8 of that Decision.

Article 43 – Committee Report

Following the summary report referred to in Article 41(4), the Commission shall, every three years, present to the European Parliament and to the Council a report on the application of this Directive, accompanied, where appropriate, by proposals for its amendment.

Article 44 – Amendment of Directive 1998/27/EC

In the Annex to Directive 1998/27/EC, the following point shall be added:

> 13. Directive../../EC of the European Parliament and of the Council of … on services in the internal market (OJ L […], […], p. […]).

Chapter VII – Final Provisions

Article 45

1. Member States shall bring into force the laws, regulations and administrative provisions necessary to comply with this Directive by [2 years after the entry into force] at the latest. They shall forthwith communicate to the Commission the text of those provisions and a correlation table between those provisions and this Directive.

When Member States adopt those provisions, they shall contain a reference to this Directive or be accompanied by such a reference on the occasion of their official publication. Member States shall determine how such reference is to be made.

2. Member States shall communicate to the Commission the text of the main provisions of national law which they adopt in the field covered by this Directive.

Article 46

This Directive shall enter into force on the day following that of its publication in the Official Journal of the European Union.

Article 47

This Directive is addressed to the Member States.

Done at Brussels, […]
For the European Parliament For the Council
The President The President […] […]

5. DESCRIPTION AND GROUNDS

5.1. Need for Community Intervention

5.1.1. Objectives Pursued

Services are everywhere in the modern economy. In the EU, services excluding public administration account for 53.6% of GDP and 67.2% of employment and offer good prospects for further growth and more jobs. However, the freedom to provide cross-border services and the freedom of establishment across borders are hampered by a large number of barriers. Realising the potential of services in the internal market, and ensuring that they deliver better quality and value to European citizens and business, is a major aim of the EU's economic reform programme.

The Commission's report on the State of the Internal Market for Services (COM(2002) 441 final), included an inventory of the barriers which hinder the development of cross-border services. These barriers affect a large variety of service activities such as distribution, employment agencies, certification, laboratories, construction, real estate agencies, craftsmen, tourism and they hit SMEs, which are predominant in the services sector (89% of SMEs are involved in services), particularly hard.

The report, and the impact assessment which accompanies the Directive on services in the internal market, examine the effects of these barriers on the EU economy and show the potential gains to be achieved by the removal of these barriers, which fragment the internal market in Services.

5.1.2. Measures Taken in Connection with Ex Ante Evaluation

(a) The ex ante evaluation on the Commission's Internal Market Strategy for Services was conducted in-house in August 2002. The Internal Market Strategy for Services consists of two stages. The first stage was concluded by the above-mentioned report on the State of the Internal Market in Services. The second stage covers the adoption of a proposal for a Directive on Services in the Internal Market as well as non-legislative measures.

(b) The ex ante evaluation explained the context of the Services Strategy, its rationale and approach and summarised the work carried out during the first stage of the Services Strategy, which focussed in particular on the wide variety of sources of evidence of barriers. It also included a preliminary outline of systems and indicators to monitor the effectiveness of the second stage of the Services Strategy.

It found that the Services Strategy had so far been well managed and provided the necessary information for the implementation of the second stage of the Services Strategy. It confirmed the need for Community action in this field and demonstrated the value added and cost-effectiveness of Community intervention.

5.2. Action Envisaged and Budget Intervention Arrangements

The Directive will address internal market barriers a combination of three inter-linked elements: the country of origin principle, harmonisation and administrative cooperation.

–   In order to facilitate cross-border establishment, there is a need for administrative simplification, a need to remove restrictions resulting from over-complex, intransparent or discriminatory authorisation procedures and a need to remove a number of other requirements which currently hamper cross-border establishment strategies of service providers.
–   The barriers affecting the freedom to provide services require mainly that Member States refrain from applying their own rules and regulations to incoming services from other Member States and from supervising and controlling them. Instead they should rely on control by the authorities in the country of origin of the service provider. However, temporary derogations from the country of origin principle will be provided – for example, for secure transport of cash and debt collection. These issues need further analysis and will be subject to external studies.
–   The application of the country of origin principle will necessitate an efficient system of administrative cooperation between Member States, establishing their respective responsibilities in the context of cross-border service provision. There might be a need for a coordinated solution in order to facilitate the exchange of information through electronic means.

The Directive will ensure a progressive approach to implementation. It will address a large number of barriers immediately while setting up a framework to resolve, within fixed time periods, the remaining barriers on the basis of mutual evaluation between Member States and further consultation with stakeholders. Therefore, the resources allocations will be extended to cover a certain period of time.

5.3. Methods of Implementation

The negotiation of the Directive in the Council and in the European Parliament will be carried out by DG MARKT staff within existing resources. The transposition of the Directive will require monitoring and assistance to the Member States. This will also be carried out by the staff of DG MARKT. Furthermore, Article 41 of the Directive specifies that Commission will be assisted by a committee consisting of Member States' representatives on certain specific issues.

…

8. FOLLOW-UP AND EVALUATION

8.1. Follow-up Arrangements

The Directive would be implemented by the Member States two years after its adoption (which is envisaged by the end of 2005), i.e. by the end of 2007. Furthermore, an additional year (until the end of 2008) is foreseen to achieve the move to the necessary system of administrative cooperation (putting in place electronic procedures, implementation of single points of contact etc.). This additional time for implementation takes account of the initial administrative investments required.

The Commission services, assisted by a committee consisting of Member States' representatives, will actively monitor and assist the 25 Member States in the transposition of the Directive. The large scope and the wide range of issues addressed in the Directive require partnership between the Commission and Member States to ensure a smooth and homogenous transposition and functioning of the Directive across the Union.

The Commission services would also monitor the expected impacts of the Directive. More specifically, with the assistance of external economic consultants (contract already concluded but will require financing in 2004) economic indicators (e.g. compliance costs of service companies, Community cross-border trade/FDI in services, involvement of SMEs in cross-border trade/FDI, price differentials) will be tracked.

8.2. Arrangements and Schedule for the Planned Evaluation

Since the real economic and social impacts will not be measurable until such time as the Directive has been fully working, it is proposed that the first ex post evaluation will feature in the report that will be presented by the Commission by 2008 and that further evaluations will feature in the reports to be presented every three years following the first report.